GOD＊STAR

THE SIRIUS MYTHOS - BOOK 1

GOD ✳ STAR

An apocalyptic vision of dark magick,
rock music and the world of UFOs

Peter J. Morris

Kinsett Publishing

2024

First Paperback Edition: 2024

Copyright: Peter J. Morris 2024

ISBN-978-1-909370-14-2

No part of this publication may be reproduced, distributed, or transmitted in any form or by any means, including photocopying, recording or other electronic or mechanical methods without the prior, written permission from the publisher, Kinsett Publishing, except in the case of brief quotations embodied in critical reviews and certain other non-commercial uses permitted by copyright law.

The publisher has used its best efforts in preparing this ebook and the information provided herein is provided 'as-is'. Neither the author nor Kinsett Publishing make any representation or warranties with respect to the accuracy or completeness of the contents of this book and disclaims any implied warranties of merchantability or fitness for any particular purpose and shall in no event be liable for any loss of profit or any other commercial damage, including, but not limited to, special, incidental, consequential, or other damages.

This book identifies product names and services known to be trademarks, registered trademarks, or service marks of their respective holders. They are used throughout this book in an editorial fashion only. Use of a term in this book should not be regarded as affecting the validity of any trademark, registered trademark, or service mark.

Kinsett Publishing is not associated with any third-party products or vendors mentioned in this book.

Cover image is courtesy of GrumpyBeere from Pixabay and all other images, except where stated, are courtesy of WikiMedia Commons.

CONTENTS

PREFACE - THE SIRIUS MYTHOS	I
A Lost World	ii
Lost in the Process	iv
Solid Foundations	v
The Importance of Sirius	vi
Establishing a Framework	viii
INTRODUCTION	**1**
Seeds of Ufology	1
Year of Years	3
Seven Savvy Scientists	4
Classifying the Impossible	6
New Era in Communications	7
Psychic Perceptions	9
A Key for Change	10
Spaced-Out	12
Talking 'Bout UFOs!	13
1. ZIGGY PLAYED GUITAR	**14**
An Alienated Landscape	17
Mad Mystical Mateus	20
Men, Minds and a Map	23
Saviour Machine	25
2. OPENING THE VORTEX	**28**
Difficult Questions	29
Regular UFO Sightings	31
Hunting UFOs	33
Ambassador for a Phenomena	35
Psychomagickal Ritual?	38

3. Beyond Good and Evil — 40

Astral Light of Mendes — 42
Strength Through Will — 45
The Era of Indigos — 48
High Noone — 50
A Coming Race — 52
Strange Days - Like These! — 54

4. Stellar Atune-ment — 59

The Great Provider — 60
Ancient Mystery Schools — 62
The Creative Word — 66
The Three Centers — 70
ETs: Sons of God? — 77

5. Songs of Revelation — 83

Music From the Ethereal Realms — 90
The Music of Sirius — 93
The Siriun Moon of Neil Peart — 100
Gojira and the Whales — 102
Blue Oyster Cult — 104
Vision From Afar — 110
Star of Sirius — 113

6. Mystical Union — 115

Beast 666 — 116
Magick, Music and Madness — 120
Engineering Success — 123
A Hidden Life — 125
Sounds of Space — 127
Where Music and Magic Meet — 130
Outlaws and Graves — 133
The Appearance of Rameses — 135
Controlling Aliens? — 136
Unmanaged Decline — 138

The Day the Music Died	140
Graham Bond Organisation	142
7. CONJURING THE DEMONIC	**144**
Demon in the Pool	147
Magick in the Cards	151
Walking Through Astral Walls	153
The Musickians	155
Ritual Robes	157
Lights of Sirius	159
Magickal Essence	161
8. BLACK STARS & WHITE ROBES	**166**
Blazing Stars	168
Lazarus	171
A Search for Meaning	175
Sign of Birth	176
Dark Saturn	179
Every Man Has a Black Star	183
9. GOLDEN PLATES	**186**
Michael Picasso	187
Elvis and the LDS	190
Cave of Secrets	191
The New Jerusalem	196
A Godlike State	198
Occult Roots?	198
The End?	201
10. TUNE IN OR BURN OUT	**204**
Radio Outages	206
Death of Ufology?	208
Close to the Edge	210
Consciousness Grid	216
Is there Life on Mars?	218
From Mars to Giza	221

8:8 - A Cosmic Gateway?	223
Apocalyptic Signs	225
School's Out!	229
11. LAST DAYS OF THE PLAN?	**231**
Church Business	233
Kolob	236
Another Star Who Fell to Earth?	243
The Sirian Gene	245
Holding Out	249
A Message in Time?	251
12. RETURN OF THE NINE	**255**
Reading the Ring	256
SPECTRA	258
Compass, Watches & Spoons	259
Mass-Landings	262
History of the Ennead	264
13. TOUCHED BY SIRIAN HANDS	**268**
Brothers from Muswell Hill	270
Deep Darkness: Into the Light	272
One Family	275
Steve Boucher and Harmony Grove	279
Johnny Sands and the Exploding Sphere	284
Official Indifference	287
The Men in Black	288
Long Gone	291
14. LORE OF THE SACRED LION	**295**
Murry Hope and the Paschats	296
Hello-Archanophus	298
The Atlanteans	299
Californian Psychobabble	301
The End of Life	303
The Lion People	305

A Royal Role	308
15. PATHWAY TO THE STAR	**312**
Lion Queen of Timbavati	314
Sacred Lion Teachings	317
Between the Paws	319
GHW and the Sacred Place of the Lion	321
The Chronotopology of Charles Muses	323
Falcon Wing Ranch	324
Esoteric Beliefs	325
Out of Africa	330
16. FROM WATERY DEPTHS	**331**
Thirst for Knowledge	332
Ogotemmeli and the Nummo	333
The True Sirius Mystery?	335
Charlie Hickson and the Amphibian Beings	338
Sirian Types	341
The Great Mask	344
Pistis Sophia	347
POSTSCRIPT: IT'S ALL IN THE EGG	**349**
The Siriun Influence	350
New Species for Old	352
Dark Well of Creative Inspiration	354
New Paradigms	355
Cosmic Hatching?	357
Three by Three	360
Musical Respect	361
A Holistic Perspective	362
Looking Ahead	364
RECOMMENDED READING	**368**
INDEX	**373**

"May the Music of Sirius be the Felicitation to the Pioneers of Earth and in Space. May a more Divine Mankind come out of your works!"

Sirius Suite, Karlheinz Stockhausen (1928-2007).

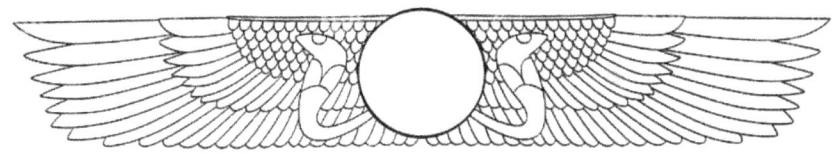

Preface - The Sirius Mythos

"Philosophy [nature] is written in that great book which ever is before our eyes —I mean the universe—but we cannot understand it if we do not first learn the language and grasp the symbols in which it is written. The book is written in mathematical language, and the symbols are triangles, circles and other geometrical figures, without whose help it is impossible to comprehend a single word of it; without which one wanders in vain through a dark labyrinth."

Galileo Galilei (1564-1642). Italian astronomer, physicist and engineer.

Throughout the ages, ancient astronomers peered skyward, observed the motion of stars and planets and then—after countless centuries of careful and systematic analysis—concluded that the cosmos is not the dark and desolate void we suppose it to be but is in fact a mystical realm; one that functions as if it were a sentient environment, 'alive' and constantly seeking to express itself in a myriad of mysterious ways. They also concluded that this vast, complex sea of eternal motion is not only observable but is, in a sense, also observing us.

Stars and planets have a profound influence upon the affairs of man. Planetary cycles and the progression of constellations each determine the rise and fall of civilisations, establish the destiny of kings and queens, and inaugurate divine revelation within all lesser mortals. It was as a result of the ancient's awareness of this effect that led them to conclude that the night-sky offers humanity an opportunity to observe a 'universal intelligence' at work. Many ancient cultures took this principle to their hearts and, prior to the onset of monotheism, the heavens were considered to be the birthing chamber for a plethora of mystical and mythological paradigms—many of which established the framework for several of today's mainstream religions.[1]

The ancient star-lore—once prevalent throughout the World—was based upon a deep, reverential, respect for the cosmos. So important was the ancient stellar wisdom to many societies that whole cities were laid out to replicate the positions and cyclic patterns of prominent stars and planets. This form of 'cosmological architecture' was very often enhanced even further via the placement and orientation of roads, temples, and other significant civic buildings. Through this process, ancient cultures projected theosophical themes and beliefs back up into the night sky where they were often immortalised by specific star groupings.[2] Even today, it is possible to study the ancient myths associated with some constellations and to read them as one might an old history book or cosmological encyclopaedia. The twelve signs of the zodiac often tells us nearly as much about the motivations of ancient societies as historical studies or archaeological excavations; for they express stories and legends that reflect the more important cultural dynamics of their era.

A Lost World

Sadly, humanity has little ability today to do anything other than just observe the messages written in the stars. Gone is our once close psychological, mythological, and spiritual relationship with the heavens and we no longer believe that the universe breathes life into and through us—thereby sustaining and enriching us psychologically and spiritually. In fact, the night sky is not even observable to several billions of people

---

[1] German philosopher Immanuel Kant (1724-1804) believed that the laws of space are known to the mind "because they are of the mind", which suggests that cosmology is a natural feature of human consciousness and that by studying the stars we also study ourselves.

[2] The way myth and legend were expressed via the constellations was generally specific to a region, culture, or society. However, many of them are remarkably similar to one another despite having been established in completely different parts of the world. This suggests that at some point in our distant past a common cosmological belief system pervaded most civilisations.

Preface - The Sirius Mythos

Above: A cosmological map of the Southern skies. (c.1660)

today due to the blanket of manmade light pollution enveloping this planet.

The ancients would have never tolerated this for one moment!

The golden age that was once replete with stellar myths and cosmic legends is now consigned to the history books. What we have lost as a result is more than a simple belief in the supernatural. The formidable, energising, and life-sustaining influence inherent within ancient mythological themes has been completely drained from our collective consciousness. Many of the psycho-mythical dynamics that once enriched and empowered humanity—giving us a broader perspective on life and what it means to be a human than that of our current technological age—have all but faded from our collective memory. Gone is that deep well of dark psychological material which at one time was widely accepted as forming a normal part of the everyday experience.

Occasionally it spontaneously reappears; but when it does, we rather dangerously suppress and condemn its influence to the darker recesses of the human 'Shadow'.[3] This is the primary reason for the deep, collective malaise that currently afflicts the whole of our World: a form of myopia that means we no longer believe in the existence of anything bigger than ourselves.

Lost in the Process

Ancient texts tells us that the astronomers of old viewed life and the heavens from a completely different perspective to that of today's astrophysicist. Way back in our early history the visible stars were not only named after gods and goddesses but were treated as if they were real forces to be reckoned with. The stars revealed deities with character; encapsulated tales of their struggles, charted their adventures, and even exposed their frailties and failings. We no longer reference ancient star-lore in our culture and any new star-cluster that are discovered by astronomers are assigned simple co-ordinates and numerical sequences by which to locate and identify them.

For over three hundred years a drive towards 'scientific rationalisation' has led to a once noble, mystical, discipline being supplanted by a world driven by astronomical classification and statistical data-collection. It is a mistaken belief which led science to conclude that everything has to be reduced to its smallest constituent parts in order to understand how it functions. This change in approach to the mystery of the cosmos emerged following the development of advanced optics and the use of powerful telescopes as a way of monitoring the Universe at work. These offered astronomers many advantages but led to their reliance upon visual (i.e. sensory observation) which eventually eradicated our former holistic perception of the heavens. Over time, science contributed to the deconstruction of a complex, multi-layered, astral gnosis. The further astronomers were able to look out into the cosmos, the more societies lost a connection to their cosmological roots. As fewer individuals practised stellar magick

---

[3] Swiss psychologist Carl Gustav Jung (1875-1961) stated that the 'Shadow' is an aspect of human consciousness in which we store repressed or unwanted psychological material.

and stellar divination—an art once deemed to be essential within the court of kings and their political advisors—the deeper our mysterious world fell into a Dark Age of ignorance and universal amnesia regarding our species true heritage . Prior to this seismic change, the *Hermetic Texts*—believed to have been written in Alexandria around 100 B.C.— described the ancient sages perspective of the heavens.

> "God arranged the Zodiac in accord with the cycles of nature (and) devised a secret engine ('viz. the system of the stars') linked in unerring and inevitable fate, to which all things in men's lives, from their birth to their final destruction, shall of necessity be brought into subjection, and all other things on earth likewise shall be controlled by the working of the engine."

Exploration of the form and nature of the "secret engine" referred to in these texts will become a dominant theme throughout this book—not within a historical context but with reference to a re-emergence within modern spiritual practices of the ancient cosmological teachings and concepts.

We may well have forgotten the ancient deities…but we are starting to understand that they never abandoned us.

Solid Foundations

The spiritual perspective I will be presenting here is, I hope, a deeply-reverential tribute to the primordial ethos that was expressed by the ancient astronomers of Alexandria. Their insights are as applicable today as they were in the past: perhaps more so. While historians insist that these spiritual principles are extensions of primeval beliefs held in their era and are of no relevance today, it is clear that the core Hermetic principle contained within the axiom "As Above…So Below" resulted in the creation of the foundations upon which modern New Age spirituality become established. Astrology, or the study of the influence of the heavens upon earthly events, is just one of several contemporary disciplines that reflect the core Hermetic principle which states that the motion of the heavens influences mundane events. Although science has, as I have previously stated, lost its cosmological perception of the solar system, it was not so long ago that science recognised and appreciated the delicate timing of the motion of the heavens. There was a popular recognition of what was described as 'The Music of the Spheres' which is a harmonious relationship between planetary cycles as expressed through sound, number and ratio.[4] This premise led to an understanding that the language of the 'Universal Intelligence' is founded upon numerical value; or, as the famous scientist and inventor Nikola Tesla (1856-1943) once put it...

> "If you want to find the secrets of this universe, think in terms of energy, frequency, and vibration."

Hermetic metaphysics reveals a vast array of cosmic influences at play throughout the heavens; including, the dominance of our Sun in illuminating our World, the gravitational pull of planets, the dynamics of the twelve constellations of our zodiac, and the subtle radiance of distant star-groups. Within this vast expanse of influences emerges one luminary that has reigned supreme in the minds of star-gazers for thousands of years. It is the star Sirius—the brightest and most iridescent of them all!

THE IMPORTANCE OF SIRIUS

From the earliest point in mankind's history, the prominence of Sirius—also commonly referred to as the Dog-Star—led to its veneration by cultures and societies all over the World. This is not just as a result of its visual dominance (it is one of the brightest stars in the night sky) but because it has a deeper, more esoteric nature which has led to it becoming associated with many strands of occult philosophy. In more recent times, it has become indelibly intertwined with elements of the UFO and extraterrestrial phenomenon.[5]

---

[4] Johannes Kepler (1571-1630) believed that these same ratios could be employed to create a "symphony of the cosmos" and asserted that "the movements of the heavens are nothing except a certain everlasting polyphony".
[5] Many night-time UFO sightings are explainable as having been mistaken for the

Preface - The Sirius Mythos

The belief that Sirius holds sway over the affairs of humanity led to its worship by all the great civilisations. For example; the ancient Egyptians, Sumerians, and Greeks, all considered Sirius immensely significant and established calendrical measurement around its motion. Their reverence for the star seems to have been based upon an even older strand of astronomical knowledge for archeologists are increasingly uncovering evidence of the adoration of Sirius stretching as far back as the Neolithic period—some twelve-thousand years ago. Subsequent analysis of many ancient sites even reveals that standing stones, dolmens, and even earth mounds, were deliberately positioned to track the motion of Sirius—particularly during its heliacal rising.[6] Examples of this have been discovered throughout Europe[7]; particularly in Turkey[8], Africa[9]; and on the Mediterranean island of Malta[10] where temple complexes were dedicated to the worship of the star.[11] The clearest example of a culture that orientated its sacred temples towards Sirius is found in ancient Egypt where the design and orientation of many predynastic remains (including the Great Pyramid of Gaza) demonstrates an acute awareness of the motion of Sirius.

Many of these ancient cultures also recognised that the star plays an important role in determining personal circumstances. Early astrologers believed that it guides the destiny of leaders: an interesting concept when you consider that Sirius has a prominent position in the astrological birth-charts of both US President George W. Bush (1946-present day) and Adolf Hitler (1889-1945).

---

shimmering appearance of Sirius.
[6] The heliacal rising of a star is an annual event marked by the point, and/or location, at which it first becomes visible on the eastern horizon immediately prior to dawn and the first rays of the rising Sun.
[7] Swagger, E A. J., *The Newgrange Sirius Mystery- Linking Passage Grave Cosmology with Dogon Symbology*, Claygate-Grosvenor House Publishing Ltd, 2012.
[8] Ananthaswamy, Anil, *World's oldest temple built to worship the dog star*, New Scientist, 2013.
[9] See Bauval, Robert, *The Egypt Code*, Disinformation Books, 2008.
[10] See Reedijk, Lenie, *Sirius, the Star of the Maltese Temples,* MaletBooks, 2018.
[11] In the 1960s, Egyptologists Alexander Badawy and Virginia Trimble suggested that the south shaft of the Great Pyramid is in direct alignment with Sirius—a theory that was further developed by Robert Bauval (1948-present day) in his seminal work *The Orion Mystery* which was written with Adrian Gilbert and published in 1994.

Establishing a Framework

Even at a very superficial level it is clear that there is a mystery at play here. Several decades spent tracing the hsitorical influence of the Dog Star —as it has been encoded within a vast swathe of arcane knowledge— has also led me to a realisation that there is a deeply occulted (hidden) mystery to this star. This enigma is so broad in its scope that a descriptive term is required to codify its multiplicity and so I call it "The Sirius Mythos"—a term I apply to describe an amalgamation of historical, mythical, mythological, metaphysical, and scientific postulations covering a period stretching from pre-history through to the 21st-century. While its many strands converge to create an immense stellar mystery, its individual components can be categorised as follows:

1. **Astrophysics:** Scientific, astronomical, and astrophysical analysis of Sirius using data gathered from observing and monitoring the star and any other stellar or planetary body it is associated with.

2. **Metaphysics:** A "meta-physical"[12] evaluation of Sirius is one based upon the study of the star using non-orthodox scientific principles. The parameters which are applied have invariably been established through the application of knowledge derived from ancient texts and drawn from an era which predates that of our current reductionist philosophies.

3. **Astrology:** The psycho-spiritual influence of Sirius using verifiable scientific data in the first instance but then applying ancient teachings to ascertain the probable impact of the star upon the personality of an individual.

4. **Esoteric:** The impact of subtle occult emanations (often referred to as "rays", "currents", or "paths") which mystics believe are directly attributable to the

---
[12] The word 'metaphysics' is derived from the Greek word 'metá', meaning 'after' and 'physiká' meaning 'physics'. It is considered one of the four main branches of philosophy with the others being epistemology, logic, and ethics.

star. This includes their impact upon the spiritual, or Soul development, of those individuals who are initiated into any of the star's convoluted esoteric mysteries.

5. **Veneration:** A study of ancient cosmological beliefs assigned to Sirius within mystical, gnostic, and religious texts. This line of research can be classified as an exoteric, or outward, expression of the Sirius Mythos.

6. **Psychomagickal:** Ritual practices forged around the energetic emanations of the star as performed by ancient and modern cults, esoteric groups, and secret societies. These are psychomagickal practices which can be classified as an esoteric, or internalised, expression of the Sirius Mythos.

7. **Denizens**: Research related to a widespread belief that sentient life-forms exist on Sirius and several of its satellites (i.e. moons and stars within its orbit). Some of these 'beings' are believed to be humanoid, others are mammalian or even hybrid in nature. This line of research also considers the possibility that one or more groups of Sirians are, from an evolutionary and technological perspective, highly-evolved and have organised themselves into complex collectives, cultures, or societies.

8. **Extraterrestrials:** The consideration of evidence that suggests some Sirian life-forms have overcome limitations of time and space and are able to travel vast distances throughout the Milky Way with relative ease. These entities are said to express 3D reality and usually require a physical vehicle (i.e., spacecraft) to reach their intended destination.

9. **Angelic:** Analysis of the belief that spiritually

advanced, ultra-dimensional intelligences based on Sirius have, throughout our past and current eras, been interacting with life on this planet in a variety of different ways. These Sirians are said to inhabit planes that reside outside of our observable 3D reality and so do not require a physical vehicle to either reach our planet or to enter our environment. Their mode of transportation may simply be consciousness itself.

10. **Starseeds:** Analysis of the belief that hybrid ET/humans, (i.e., corporeal beings comprised of m part-human and part-Sirian DNA) live within several earth-based societies. They are said to work unseen fulfilling a range of roles that includes those related to teaching, science, writing, art, healing, and New Age spiritual work where they are often referred to as 'lightworkers'.

11. **Geo-political:** Research related to a belief that over recent centuries, occult and metaphysical elements connected to the Sirius Mythos have been covertly expressed through several well-known political and scientific establishments. (This may or may not be as a result of the influence of the clandestine work by visiting Sirians as referenced in section 10).

12. **Motion:** A strand of research that acknowledges that immense Universal powers influence Sirius system and that they do so over protracted periods of time. The source of these 'aeonic permutations' are believed to originate from vastly remote regions of time and space from where they are controlled by intelligences, deities, or a demiurge which are of a form that is far beyond human comprehension.

These twelve core themes are primary components to The Sirius Mythos but within each of these categories exist further sub-divisions

Preface - the Sirius Mythos

which are not quite so clearly defined: they invariably interweave with one another to produce additional inter-connected riddles.

My choice of the term 'mythos' is quite deliberate for it is derived from the Ancient Greek term 'myth' meaning 'speech, narrative, fiction, myth, plot'.[13] In a modern context it is defined as a "pattern of basic values and attitudes of a people, characteristically transmitted through myths and the arts." [14] In the context of my research, I tend to use the word in an Aristotelian sense to define "A body of interconnected myths or stories, especially those belonging to a particular religious or cultural tradition."[15]

Strange as it might seem, the mysteries surrounding the star do have a deep cultural tradition—a somewhat odd conclusion to draw from simply observing what, on the face of it, is just a bright light in the night-sky! However, while the impact of Sirius upon and within ancient cultures can be found at many sacred sites, the existence of this Sirius Mythos is not always evident—even to archeologists and historians. For reasons that will become evident during my five-volume series of books related to the star and its mysteries, the deeper levels to this myth remained deliberately hidden and makes research into it a challenge. Decades spent uncovering it has led me to simplify its multiple complexities by focussing on five specific themes and so each book in *The Sirius Mythos* series will approach this enigma from a specific direction. Accumulatively they will contribute to a deeper understanding of an ancient Sirian starlore which was once so prevalent throughout the World, was lost, but is re-emerging in the 21st-century..

In mu opinion, The Sirius Mythos is quite possibly THE most fascinating and occulted story in the history of mankind...so hang on for the ride. We are about to enter some VERY strange worlds!

Peter J. Morris

---

[13] *Myth - Definition, History, Examples, & Facts*. Encyclopaedia Britannica.
[14] https://www.merriam-webster.com/thesaurus/mythos
[15] Oxford English Dictionary (3rd ed.). Oxford: Oxford University Press, 2003

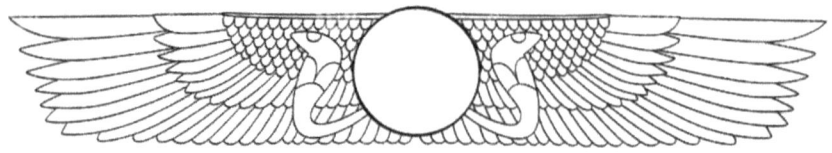

Introduction

"Two possibilities exist: either we are alone in the Universe, or we are not. Both are equally terrifying."

Science-fiction writer and TV host Arthur C. Clarke (1917-2008).

Depending on how you view the history of ufology, a majority of today's paranormal researchers conclude that the modern UFO era is fast approaching its centenary. Given that we have studied, dissected, and catalogued this beguiling mystery for so many decades you would think that humanity would have arrived at a clear idea of what the enigma is and what drives it by now. It hasn't! In fact, those who have dedicated themselves to a study of the subject for more than a couple of decades are probably no less bewildered by it than those who reported seeing strange 'airships' in our skies a hundred years ago.

The endless number of twists and turns that have taken place during its evolution—coupled with its irregular fluctuation in intensity—shows that, like so many other paranormal mysteries, the ufological timeline is far from linear. Nevertheless, when it comes to documenting the phenomenon's evolution, certain years have been more significant than others when it comes to determining its trajectory.

Seeds of Ufology

Highlights of the history of ufology includes 1947; which for many researchers establishes the commencement of the modern UFO phenomena. On June 24, American businessman Kenneth Arnold (1915-1984) was flying from Chehalis to Yakima, Washington, in his two-seater CallAir A-2 airplane when he caught sight of nine, disc-shaped objects flying in close formation near Mount Rainer. He estimated that the craft were travelling around 1,200 miles an hour (1,932 km/h). In an interview with newspaper reporters from Pendleton, Oregon, Arnold was asked to describe the objects he had seen. His response credits him with being the first person to use the term "flying saucer".

This year is marked not only by this one, pivotal UFO sighting. One month later, national America newspapers reported on what became the first officially-documented crash of a large aerial object close to the town of Roswell, New Mexico. Controversy regarding the conflicting media, military, and government accounts of what occurred still rages today but it has commonly become known as the "Roswell Crash" and proved to be a seismic cultural and societal event which has probably contributed more to the public's perception of UFOs than even Arnold's sighting.

Another significant year in the history of ufology was 1952 when, between July 13 and 29, a series of unidentified objects were seen passing over Washington, D.C. The US government were spooked by their appearance and this led to the first serious concern regarding the national security implications of the phenomena by any government.

From a more contemporary perspective, 1997 marks an important year in the annals of UFO research due to the famous "Phoenix Lights Incident"; the first major UFO sighting to capture the imaginations of millions of people all over this planet who previously showed very little interest in the subject. On this date, March 13, at least one V-shaped craft of gigantic proportions was observed by thousands of people as it flew at low altitude over the town of Phoenix, Arizona. It was the first verifiable mass-sighting of a large-sized craft and the event marked a new era in the widespread use of mobile phones and home video equipment to document unidentified aerial objects.

And finally, in 2017–twenty years after the Phoenix incident–the World experienced the closest thing yet to official UFO disclosure after two US Navy videos–titled FLIR and GIMBAL–were released by the *New York Times* purportedly showing UFOs in flight. This was the first time a government agency 'appeared' to accept the validity of the UFO phenomena; although they shied away from labelling it such and insisted on redefining Arnold's use of the term 'flying saucers' as UAPs (Unidentified Aerial Phenomenon): thereby carefully avoiding giving credence to an enigma which they had, for over 70 years, emphatically denied even existed![16]

YEAR OF YEARS

It is my contention that the significance of each of these years—and the incidents which took place in them—pales in significance when compared to a succession of other-worldly events that took place in 1972. This was a remarkable year in so many ways, but most significantly it oversaw a fundamental shift within humanity regarding its relationship with the cosmos. This sea-change in attitude towards the possibility of life in outer-space impacted all areas of society and resulted in a major reassessment by the scientific community. Some within its hallowed halls even openly considered the unimaginable possibility that intelligent beings from other worlds might be 'out there' and that they could be trying to initiate contact with us.

These sea-changes in social attitudes during 1972 were profound. Throughout the late 1960s and early 1970s—particularly in the wake of the 1969 Moon landings—the gaze of humanity had turned increasingly skywards. The worldwide broadcast of NASA's forays into outer space during the era of the Apollo space missions stimulated public interest in off-planet worlds in hitherto unprecedented ways. These were exciting times and the heightened sense of optimism felt by everybody following the Moon landings caused many to consider the prospect of establishing space-colonies both within Earth's orbit and as permanent fixtures on the surface of the Moon. It seemed that the time had come for anthropologists and sociologists to seriously consider the direction human society would take should it establish a new frontier in space.

A combination of many influences initiated a major shift in human consciousness during this year. Neil Armstrong's famous "one giant

[16] In the excitement of the moment, many researchers within the media and UFO community completely forgot the fact that covert government agencies throughout the world had, ever since the 1940s, systematically persecuted and denounced as "lunatics" those who had verifiable proof that UFOs are real.

INTRODUCTION

Above: Roswell Daily Record, July 8, 1947–the event that marks the start of the modern UFO mystery.

leap for Mankind" quote–first spoken during his initial steps onto the lunar surface in 1969–not only marked a point in our history when technology enabled us to leave this planet and, to quote Captain Kirk, to "explore new worlds" but it also indicated that humanity was now entering completely new environments–some of which might be inhabited by other beings.

SEVEN SAVVY SCIENTISTS

1972 proved to be a year which saw major changes in the collective psyche of the World. An example of this was demonstrated by The Astronomy Survey Committee of the National Academy of Sciences who publicly announced in this year that "Our civilisation is within reach of one of the greatest steps in its evolution: knowledge of the existence, nature, and activities of independent civilisations in space." The Astronomy Survey Committee comments must have raised a few eyebrows within the astronomical fraternity but they were far from being lone voices.

In December 1972, UFO Research Associates (UFOR) in

Washington published a lead article in their members monthly newsletter titled *Scientists Support ET Life Probability*.[17] Its author, Gordon I.R. Lore, Jr., reported that no less than seven prominent scientists had, in the space of just four months in the autumn of 1972, "...stated their beliefs that advanced civilizations on other planets most probably exist."

The first of these took place at the end of August 1972 when Russian scientist, Alexander Oparin—a director of the A.N. Bach Institute of Biochemistry of the U.S.S.R.'s Academy of Sciences—said that life "...has to originate not only on Earth but also on other planets." He cited the planet Mars as the most likely place for it to occur in our solar system.[18]

Secondly, on October 16, Sir Fred Hoyle, president of Britain's Royal Astronomical Society, gave a lecture at the University of Utah, in Salt Lake City where he spoke of the "... possibility of constructing electronic gear to send messages to ETs."—although he admitted that "...we may have to wait decades for replies." A news source stated that Hoyle also speculated that "...any intelligent life discovered elsewhere would undoubtedly be superior to man and would be able to tell earthlings how to solve overriding global problems."[19]

Thirdly, at a panel discussion held on the subject of "Life Beyond Earth and the Human Mind"—held at Boston University on November 18[20] and sponsored by the university and the National Aeronautics and Space Administration (NASA)—four scientists agreed that highly developed civilisations undoubtedly exist elsewhere in the universe.[21] At the event astronomers Dr. Carl Sagan and Prof. Richard Berendzen agreed that the idea of establishing contact with extraterrestrial was "...a highly commendable one." Berendzen also stated that: "The question is not so much 'if' as 'where' and 'when' -- ultimate contact seems virtually inevitable..."

[17] UFO Research Newsletter, Vol. II, No. 9. - December 1972-January 1973
[18] The Arkansas Gazette, August 26, 1972
[19] The Santa Ana Register, October 18, 1972
[20] UFO Research Newsletter, Vol. II, No. 8, p. 7
[21] The Louisville Courier Journal, November 23, 1972, and The Washington Post, November 24, 1972

On the same panel that night was biologist and Nobel Prize laureate Prof. George Wald, of Harvard University. He was also open to the idea of the existence of extraterrestrial life—albeit that he found the idea "rather terrifying" and hinted that ETs "may harm man". Although broadly in agreement with him, Anthropologist Ashley Montagu put forward a counter proposal in which he suggested that "...man would probably harm the ETs." The group consensus was that all the scientists believed that the discovery of intelligent ET life would have "awesome implications" for science, philosophy and theology.

Fourthly, at a news conference held in Rio de Janeiro, Brazil, on November 11, famed rocket scientist and the former director of NASA's Flight Operations Center Dr. Wernher Von Braun[22] stated that "...it is quite likely that one of the other planets has all the ingredients of Earth..." and he supported the idea of the existence of intelligent life in outer space.[23]

We can speculate on the reasons why so many top scientists just 'happened' to be talking openly about the existence of extraterrestrial life at the same time but at the end of the day it was the American astrophysicist Carl Sagan (1934-1996) who put it most succinctly in his 1973 book *The Cosmic Connection: An Extraterrestrial Perspective*[24] when he said:

> "Extraterrestrial life is truly an idea whose time has come."

CLASSIFYING THE IMPOSSIBLE

In what could have so easily been a direct response to Sagan's and the National Academy of Sciences comments, J. Allen Hynek (1910-1986)—a former consultant to the US Air Force's Project Blue Book UFO investigation and one of the co-founders of the Center for UFO Studies—published a ground-breaking analysis of the UFO

---

[22] Von Braun was a Nazi scientist who was brought to the United States at the end of World War II as part of their Operation Paperclip.
[23] UPI news source, November 11, 1972
[24] Sagan, Carl, *The Cosmic Connection: An Extraterrestrial Perspective*, Anchor Books/Doubleday, 1973.

Left: Pioneers in the study of UFOs - Dr. J. Allen Hynek (left) and Dr. Jacques Vallée (right).

phenomenon in his seminal 1972 work *The UFO Experience*. Hynek also held the opinion that humanity was on the brink of experiencing contact with extraterrestrials–so much so that his publication included a categorisation system which he recommended researchers applied when compiling reports of UFO/ET sightings and encounters.[25]

Almost immediately (and almost in direct response to the audacity of humans in trying to compartmentalise the UFO phenomenon) July 5, 1972 (a date that is extremely significant to the story that I shall soon unfold) saw numerous reports of what became regular sightings of triangular-shaped UFOs over Belgium. Attempts by the media to classify these strangely-shaped craft immediately rendered Hynek's system defunct and obliterated the wider UFO-community's use of such descriptive terms as 'saucers', 'globes', and 'spheres' to describe these anomalous aerial objects.[26]

New Era in Communications

The events of 1972 also saw new, computer-based technologies, starting to facilitate mankind's efforts to leave his own planet. Advances in satellite telecommunication played an increasing role in garnering support for NASA during its Apollo missions as they enabled breathtaking, high-resolution colour images to be transmitted direct into people's living rooms. This new generation of photography replaced the

---

[25] Hynek's classification system was re-assessed and expanded by Jacques Vallee in 1990 to produce the *Vallée Classification System*. It featured additional details, including consideration of the reliability of a witness to a UFO event and the possibility of a mundane explanation for a sighting.
[26] The Belgium sightings were a salient lesson in how and why we should never take the UFO mystery for granted and how it is that so many researchers feel it is a phenomenon that is continually expanding and redefining itself in a deliberate and calculating effort to stay one step ahead of we humans.

grainy, low-res, black and white TV pictures which had been broadcast throughout the early 1960s and, as a result, the astounding technicolour beauty of our cosmos could be appreciated by everyone–not just by those astrophysicists who had access to high-powered telescopes. With so many citizens of the World now party to this grand stellar revealing, 1972 finally marked the point at which our species appeared ready to accept the possibility of the existence of civilisations from other realms. On March 2, 1972, for example, NASA launched Pioneer 10: a space-probe programmed to travel to Jupiter. The craft carried a pair of gold-anodised, aluminium plaques which had been inscribed with various insignia; including an etched line-drawing of a naked male and female human-being. Designed by Carl Sagan, the information they contained was intended to convey to any alien culture who might come across them who the probe belonged to, what the species looked like that had launched the vehicle into outer space, and where in the Solar System they hailed from. The addition of these plates to Pioneer 10 surprised many at the time and led several commentators to point out the fact that their inclusion by NASA scientists was predicated on the somewhat spurious belief that extraterrestrial life DOES exist and that it would be as intelligent and inquisitive as we humans.

The Apollo Missions had raised the profile of NASA considerably by 1972 (no bad thing when you are soliciting for public funding) and they were clearly intent upon making the most of the that interest in the mission to Jupiter presented. However, while the Pioneer's somewhat comical plates was probably only a marketing gimmick, it did present the organisation a friendly light.

The press and general populace might have come to love America's space agency but behind the media screen things were not quite so cozy.[27] Accusations of corruption and obfuscation had dogged NASA ever since its founding in 1958.[28] For decades conspiracy theorists had

---
[27] Their reputation was somewhat tarnished when a shortwave radio enthusiast accidentally tuned into secret NASA radio transmissions that were not freely available to the public or the world's media. It was via this channel that the astronauts referenced seeing UFOs.
[28] Some have suggested that the word NASA is an acronym for the phrase "Never A

maintained that the organisation was or modifying photographs taken at various locations on the Moon which they suspected had originally featured UFOs. These suspicions led to the widespread theory that for over fifty years NASA have been part of a government cover-up regarding the truth about UFOs in our skies. This may or may not be true but one event that took place in 1972 certainly strengthens the theory that clandestine groups within the United States were engaged in what might vaguely be called 'non-publicised' activities.

Psychic Perceptions

While the United States, World media, and all Western governments had been outwardly ridiculing those who believed in the extraterrestrial hypothesis, it later emerged that from the beginning of the 1970s the American security services had been attempting to contact extraterrestrials using extremely non-orthodox methods. In 1972, a remote-viewing program was established by the CIA at the Stanford Research Institute at Menlo Park, California. The intention had been to create a psychic-spying program that was capable of infiltrating Soviet weapons facilities and for 'remotely-viewing' aliens. According to one of the project's founders, Ingo Swann (1933-2013), the team reported 'seeing' alien structures on the far side of the Moon in addition to a large number of extraterrestrial bases located on Earth. Rather oddly, in another clandestine 1972 programme, a secret US military group working under the code-name "Project Snowbird" was established to train military pilots in the art of test-flying recovered alien craft.[29]

While Swann and his associates were psychically scanning our Moon from afar, Edgar Mitchell (1930-2016)—one of the few men man who had actually set foot on it—made a major contribution to the field of UFO studies in 1972. In his role as pilot for the lunar module on the Apollo 14 mission, Mitchell successfully landed on the surface of the Moon on February 5, 1971. During the astronauts return trip to Earth he had a profoundly mystical experience which caused him to completely change his outlook on life. As a result, he founded the Institute of Noetic

---

Straight Answer".
[29] www.majesticdocuments.com

Sciences which he set up to research metaphysical and spiritual experiences. The organisation continues today as the Dr. Edgar Mitchell FREE Foundation and its focus is on researching individuals who claim to have had to have had contact with non-human intelligences.

The world of ufology might have been dominated by scientific achievements but, on a lighter note it was happened to be a good year for Ronald Johnson—a 16-year-old farm-boy from Kansas who won $5,000 in a competition held by the *National Enquirer*. The paper's editors offered cash prizes to any of its readers who sent them what they considered to be the best report of a UFO sighting. The top prize of $50,000 was offered to anyone who could conclusively prove to the paper's satisfaction that UFOs really do exist and that they can be shown to originate from outer space.[30] While it is not known who, if anyone, won the $50,000 it was Ronald was awarded a secondary prize after submitting a personal account of an unidentifiable object that he said landed on his family's farm on November 2, 1971.

The *National Enquirer* had, for some while, been promoting the myth of aliens and in their February 6, edition declared that the "Existence of UFOs can no longer be doubted." When a national newspaper starts to take the subject of extraterrestrials seriously then you know something is changing quite radically within public consciousness!

A Key for Change

While 1972 came to be dominated by science and technology, the seismic changes they brought to our World pale in significance when compared to a sequence of events that, had ufologists been better aware of them at the time, would have established a completely new trajectory for ufological research. These did not occur within the realms of either t

---

[30] The judges for the competition included Dr. J. Allen Hynek, Dr. Robert F. Creegan (philosophy professor at the State University of New York), Dr. R. Leo Sprinkle (psychologist, director of the University of Wyoming's division of counseling and testing). Dr. Frank Salisbury (Head of Utah State University's plant sciences department), and Dr. James Harder (professor of mechanical engineering at the University of California). (Source: *UFO Research Newsletter*, Vol. II, No. 10, January-February 1973).

Left: Cover of The National Enquirer, February 6, 1972.

technology or science, nor were they instigated at the behest of sociologists, activists, politicians, corporations, financiers, or the medical profession. Instead, the primary driving force behind social change in 1972 came from the arts and from popular music in particular: that greatest and most effectual method ever used to alter mass public consciousness.

However, while popular music is often classified as a form of mass entertainment, the essence to the exponential rise of interest in contemporary rock and pop music from the mid-1960s to early 1970s should be considered through a metaphysical lens. Energy and vibration—the twin dynamics of any musical performance had a powerful 'narcotic' effect upon its listeners and as a consequence forced open neural pathways of millions of people, fed the racial collective, and radically altered prevailing social mores.

Popular music of many genres came of age during this period; with each being natural extensions of such musical styles as the blues in the 1920s, jazz in the 1930s, doo-wop in the 1940s, rock 'n' roll in the 1950s, and commercialised pop in the 1960s. With elements that drew from each of the aforementioned musical genres, progressive rock and pop music emerged to dominate as the most popular form of entertainment. Prior to this, earlier generations of teenagers flocked to dance-halls, drove to drive-in movies, or simply created their own form of non-drug based amusement. Suddenly, they found their 'kicks' from listening to music at home on small, portable record-players, by tuning into local radio stations on their transistor radios, or by watching their favourite bands play live in a variety of venues and arenas. The spread of rock music emerged from these changing social habits and produced 'rock-gods'—larger-than-life characters who epitomised the mantra of "Get famous, get rich, get laid, drop out and stick it to the man!"

In America, the influence of members of this sub-sect of society was immense and utterly unprecedented. It was for this reason that musicians often used their elevated social status to initiate social and political change. Many famous artists used their popularity to raise awareness on a range of social issues and particularly those related to environmentalism, anti-nuclear, the Vietnam War, and race relations.

Their concerted attempts to raise awareness of social issues was not confined to attending marches, speaking at rallies, organising fund-raising concerts, or appearing on stage with political leaders. Musicians felt obligated to comment on the state of the World and invariably politicised their music by singing about World-peace, raising awareness of eco-degradation, highlighting the plight of indigenous peoples, or confronting poverty and oppression.

Oh yes, and they also sang about UFOs...well, at least some of them did!

Spaced-Out

The American and Russian space projects of the mid-1950s seeded humanity's fascination in off-world domains. It also inspired musicians to reproduce the aura of cosmic landscapes in their compositions. Space rock became a popular and accepted musical art-form in its own right. Early synthesisers and electronic keyboards opened up new musical horizons and made it possible for musicians to replicate the neurological effect of floating aimlessly through a cosmic or ethereal landscape—to create a range of ambient sounds that appeared to emulate the impression of traversing space and time.

Given the popularity of this style of music, it would be natural to assume that the worlds of rock music and ufology would make good bed-fellows but this was not the case. Even today, the level of personal interest shown towards the subject of UFOs by rock and pop musicians is played down and considered inconsequential. In the early-1970s this aspect to contemporary music was only occasionally referenced by biographers, rock commentators, and journalists—and even then only in a casual, almost condescending way. With only a few notable exceptions, the subject of musicians who have shown an interest in UFOs or who have admitted to believing in extraterrestrial life, has rarely been taken seriously by paranormal researchers.

Talking 'Bout UFOs!

The closed attitude of music journalists to the subject of UFOs has changed considerably since 1972. But back then there was a sense that this was an area of a 'rock-gods' personal life that was not open to scrutiny. Some musicians were occasionally referencing flying-saucers and extraterrestrials in their lyrics but none of them spoke openly to the news media about their interest or involvement in any aspect of the UFO phenomena to the press.

Until the Beatles trip to India in 1968, it was not common for musicians to talk about their spiritual/religious beliefs either and talking candidly in press interviews about such matters was an extremely rare occurrence. Any idea that an artist might wish to talk about their connection to the world of UFOs and express their spiritual beliefs back in 1972 was simply one step too far for even their devoted fanbase and certainly caused heart palpitations in those record company executives who recognised the financial risk posed by any of their artists choosing to discuss such contentious ideas in public.

However, all this changed in the summer of 1972 when a young, fresh-faced, and relatively unknown British musician stepped forward and openly shared his personal perspective of the UFO mystery—both on and off his records. In so doing, he single-handedly changed not only the prevailing musical landscape but also dragged the dark, contentious topic of extraterrestrial life out and into the public arena.

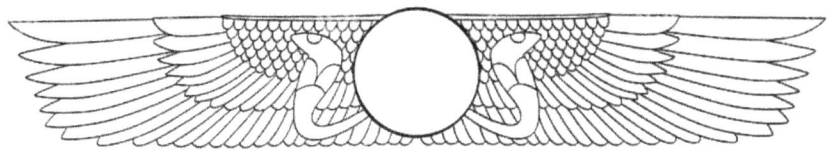

1. Ziggy Played Guitar

"This ain't rock 'n' roll, this is genocide."

Diamond Dogs by David Bowie (1947-2016).

On Wednesday, July 5, 1972, a young London-based singer-songwriter who performed under the stage-name David Bowie, strode into BBC Television Centre, West London, with his backing band. Their visit to the studios that afternoon followed an invitation from the national broadcaster for them to perform on the prestigious weekly TV music programme *Top of the Pops*.

Although Bowie enjoyed an unprecedented level of commercial success in the decades that followed, in the summer of 1972 he was struggling to establish himself as an artist. Since entering the music business in the early 1960s, he had attempted to establish himself as a solo performer. However, despite the success of his cleverly-crafted hit single *Space Oddity*[31] in July 1969–the same month Apollo 11 landed on the Moon–the creative hiatus that followed had given Bowie's critics an opportunity to write him off as a 'one-hit-wonder'. Despite the lack of commercial success throughout the years that followed, Bowie continued to redefine his on-stage persona–changing it from a solitary, guitar-strumming hippy into an artist with a more contemporary and flamboyant rock-star image. Three years of hard graft and personal transformation had passed and he was now ready–and hungry–for fame. This opportunity to appear on national, prime-time TV was one not to

---

[31] The BBC deemed *Space Oddity* too controversial to play on their national radio station; fearing its dark and tragic lyrics would "stoke up a degree of angst towards the Moon Landings that was the antithesis of the nation's mood." The decision was over-turned once the Apollo 11 crew returned safely. (Source: https://faroutmagazine.co.uk/bbc-banned-david-bowie-space-oddity-moon-landing/)

be missed and both Bowie and his band of seasoned musicians were aware they had to make it count—which they did, in no uncertain terms!

Quite what the show's producers, or the small crowd of young, mainly female, teeny-boppers who skipped school that day to appear on the programme expected to see and hear from this odd assortment of renegade musicians is unknown. It is entirely probable that the majority of the dewy-eyed, music-fans huddled tightly together in front of the small stage waiting to watch Bowie perform did not even know who this strange, rather emaciated-looking young man with red hair was. What is certain though is that nobody who was present that day; from the show's other performers through to members of the audience, sound engineers, and cameramen, could have known that from the moment Bowie and his band struck their first chord they were not only witnessing musical history taking place but were also participating in an event of cosmic proportions.

Within twenty-four hours of the programme's broadcast to an unsuspecting English nation the perception of Bowie as a whimsical entertainer—one who had a a questionable penchant for singing about gnomes and homesick astronauts—morphed into something akin to superstar status: a demi-god with an adoring and almost fanatical fanbase. The seismic shift that took place in the personal and professional fortunes of Bowie and his fellow musicians over a period of just a few hours in July 1972 was remarkable enough but their appearance on *Top of the Pops* was something of a social phenomenon for it also single-handedly changed the direction of modern pop culture for the following few decades.

Top of the Pops became an iconic British television program with a long and chequered history. Launched on Wednesday January 1, 1964, its opening show was presented by the now totally discredited BBC Radio One DJ Jimmy Savile (1926-2011). Savile, who had already become a national institution and a person who—as the country found out to its cost many decades later, should in fact should have been incarcerated in one—introduced a variety of artists during the programme; including a youthful Rolling Stones who had just reached number 13 in the national pop charts with a single titled I Wanna Be Your Man.

From its humble beginnings, audience ratings for *Top of the Pops* climbed steadily until, at its peak, the show had upwards of 15 million viewers tuning-in each week; with its extended Christmas edition being one of the most popular TV programmes aired by the BBC over the holiday period. The programme grew in such stature that, by the early 1970s, it had become so ingrained into the psyche of the English nation that each Thursday evening–immediately after the traditional English custom of 'teatime'–viewers all over the United Kingdom would settle down in-front of their television sets as a family to watch the show.[32]

The programme's immense popularity and widespread appeal was derived from a very simple formula. Each week the show incorporated a rundown of the singles charts, studio performances by a mixture of new and established acts, and a dance routine performed by a troupe of sexually-provocative, female dancers. This variety of audio and visual candy made the show essential viewing for multiple generations of viewers and for young, cash-struck music fans it often proved to be the closest they would get to seeing their musical heroes perform on stage.

While the status of the programme was immense, the environment used by the BBC to record it in was less impressive. Irrespective its massive success, few resources were made available for its production; which resulted in it being filmed in a studio that was cramped and claustrophobic. Throughout its recording, the stage, audience, lighting rigs, and several unwieldy studio cameras, all jostled for position in the limited amount of space available. This invariably led to conflict between all parties and most weeks audiences watching from home were treated to the rather comical sight of members of the audience being run down or unceremoniously brushed aside by over-zealous camera-operatives wheeling their monolithic equipment into position ready for a close-up shot. Nevertheless, despite the weekly commotion and chaos, *Top of the*

---

[32] By the beginning of the 1970s, *Top of the Pops* had become so ingrained within the national psyche that it was often described as a "national institution". At the point of its demise on July 30, 2006, it had become the world's longest-running music show.

Pops projected a cosy, friendly atmosphere; while its established format gave the program an air of warm familiarity with viewers.

An Alienated Landscape

Bowie's four-minute performance on the programme turned out to be the first time since Elvis Presley's notorious performance on America's Ed Sullivan Show on October 28, 1956, that a televised appearance by an musical artist resulted in a seismic shift in popular culture. Presley's hip-gyrating rendition of Hound Dog that day was considered by many Americans to be an overtly sexual routine—one that guardians of public morality felt might enflame the libidos of the most sedate American teenager. As a precaution, his performance was heavily censored by TV producers who instructed cameramen to focus on the singer from his waist upwards. This resulted in the bizarre situation in which throngs of teenage girls watching the show from their raised studio seating could be heard in the background screaming, panting, and wailing at the top of their lungs at the sight of Presley's crotch-thrusting; while at the same time only the performer's seemingly static, upper body could be seen by the estimated 60 million people who were watching him at home on their tiny black and white TV screens.

The fallout from Elvis' performance had a profound social impact. It divided middle-class Americans into those those who were shocked and appalled by Presley's "overt display of 'sexual depravity" (even though most of them had only heard about it afterwards) and those who caught the occasional sight of Presley's sweaty, pelvic thrusting and considered it to be the most exciting thing they had ever seen. Although nowhere near as contentious, Bowie's rather camp performance on *Top of the Pops* fell into a similar category. It too raised eyebrows with many conservative viewers criticising the BBC for broadcasting what they felt was an outward display of homoeroticism by Bowie towards his lead guitarist, Mick Ronson.

Today, the musicians close interaction appears tame and criticisms of it are manifestly puerile and inexplicable. Nevertheless, at the time they were deemed to be provocative and critics response to it is a clear indication of the puritanical environment so many musical artists had been openly challenging for over a decade. What is particularly odd though is that in their haste to castigate Bowie for his supposedly unfettered sexual advances they completely overlooked the most shocking aspect to Bowie's performance. It was not the flamboyant gesticulations of the two young men that should have been challenged but the lyrical content of the song they had chosen to perform.

A self-penned composition, *Starman* was originally recorded by Bowie at Trident Studios, London on February 4, 1972, during sessions for his *Rise and Fall of Ziggy Stardust and the Spiders from Mars* album. The musicians Bowie chose to record with him were collectively known as The Spiders from Mars.[33] They included Woody Woodmansey, Trevor Boulder, and Mick Ronson. As a band they had worked with Bowie on previous recordings but on *Ziggy Stardust* they were, for the first time, credited with a status equal to that of the main man.

As a cross-over mix of rock and pop anthems, *Ziggy Stardust* is often described as a concept album—a collection of songs bound together with a common story or theme. On it, Bowie chronicles the tribulations of a homesick extraterrestrial who has arrived on Earth; charged with the task of warning mankind of an impending ecological disaster and resulting societal collapse. Despite offering humanity salvation from its self-destructive tendencies, the home-sick alien discovers that his important message clashes with the zeitgeist of the poisonous world he finds himself trapped in.

The chilling apocalyptic and totalitarian environment Bowie imagined on *Ziggy Stardust* appeared on other albums during the same period. His 1974 record *Diamond Dogs* had also been planned as a concept album with a dystopian theme using a storyline based upon the

---

[33] The name of Bowie's backing band was taken from a mass UFO sighting that occurred on October 27, 1954, during a football match between Fiorentina and rivals Pistoiese at the Stadio Artemio Franchion. A silvery, cobweb type of substance was seen being exuded from the craft—hence the spider connection. Samples of it were analysed and found to contain boron, silicon, magnesium, and calcium. This material has manifested during other paranormal cases and not just those related to the UFO phenomena. It is often referred to as "angel hair".

classic futuristic novel 1984 by English writer George Orwell (1903-1950). Orwell's book portrayed a deeply claustrophobic England; wherein its citizens barely survive in a repressive, surveillance society whose government has systematically destroyed all personal freedoms and suppressed the natural instincts of its citizens. Bowie originally intended his interpretation of the book to be, among other things, a stage show but his plans were thwarted when Orwell's estate point-blankly refused him permission to use the author's material. For that reason his *Diamond Dogs* album avoided any direct reference to 1984; although it did portray the same dystopian environment characterised by Orwell.

On *Ziggy Stardust*, Bowie's homesick alien, Ziggy finds himself far from home, struggling to survive in a soul-destroying environment similar to the one described by Orwell. It was a theme Bowie touched upon in his hit-single *Jean Genie* which was released on November 24, 1972. Like *Starman*, this was also a catchy composition—one based upon a blistering Bo Diddley-style riff hammered out by Bowie's guitarist Mick Ronson. The song was a hit and subsequently appeared the following year on Bowie's 1973 *Aladdin Sane* album.

When another extraterrestrial-themed single titled *Life on Mars* followed, Bowie's legion of fans sensed that there was a recurring pattern in his songwriting. From *Space Oddity* through to *Prettiest Star*, Bowie had—over the space of just a few years—demonstrated an interest in a variety of fringe topics; such as space travel, flying saucers, and alien life. While this may have come as a shock to some of his fans, Bowie's handful of close friends—those who had known him more intimately over the years— were already aware that the musician had been interested in these subjects since a teenager when he was involved in editing a British UFO magazine. Nevertheless, very few were aware that Bowie's interest in UFO research was more than just notional. It had become very personal.

In a 1975 interview with Cream[34] magazine he spoke candidly about his UFO experiences.

---

[34] Thomson, Elizabeth and Gutman, David, *The Bowie Companion*, Da Capo Press, 1996.

1. Ziggy Played Guitar

> "About six years ago I made sightings, six or seven times a night for about a year when I was in the observatory. We had regular cruises that came over. We knew the 6:15 was coming in and would meet up with another one. And they would be stationary for about half an hour, and then after verifying what they'd been doing that day, they'd shoot off."[35]

Mad Mystical Mateus

It was against the background of his interest in alien life that Bowie formulated the concept of Ziggy; the alien character he unleashed upon an unsuspecting World in 1972. The character had been fermenting in his imagination for some time following a conversation he had with English rock and roll star Vince Taylor (1939-1991). Taylor had been one of a handful of young British singers who, inspired by American artists such as Jerry Lee Lewis and Bill Haley, helped establish rock and roll as a popular cultural and musical movement in the UK at the end of the 1950s. Taylor enjoyed notable success and personal acclaim in the early years of the following decade but his potential to become a major musical force went unrealised after he succumbed to the same temptations that eventually led to the premature demise of so many musicians in the 1960s.

Taylor, who was in his early twenties at the time, was completely unprepared for fame and the wealth that his success brought him. He unrepentantly haemorrhaged hard cash by spending his (and his band's) money on alcohol and hard drugs. Over a three or four-day period of a sell-out European tour Taylor took as many tabs of acid as he could get his hands on. He unceremoniously washed these down with copious amounts of Mateus rosé wine and this near lethal cocktail of stimulants resulted in the rocker slipping into an alternate reality in which he had a strange, mystical experience. He now saw himself not as Vince Taylor (Brian Maurice Holden) but as a grand, messianic figure that he later christened "Mateus Christ". This revelation was so lucid that Taylor was

---
[35] Bowie had several UFO sightings at White Sands, New Mexico in 1976 while filming the movie *The Man Who Fell to Earth*. (Source: Cameron, Grant, Tuned-In: The Paranormal World of Music, Itsallconnected Publishing, 2017).

convinced God had sent him into this World on a supremely important spiritual mission. Convinced this was his true calling in life, Taylor felt obligated to reveal his messianic status to his legions of adoring fans at the earliest opportunity.

The night following his religious conversion, Taylor was booked to perform at the first of two sell-out shows at La Locomotive club in Paris. However, his drinking and drug-taking binge had left him a mere shadow of his former self. When he arrived at the pre-show soundcheck Taylor was in such a poor physical and mental state that he was incapable of recognising much of his surroundings. Bobbie Clarke, a fellow band member and close friend of Taylor, described the moment he first saw the singer in Paris.

> "He had appeared the very morning of the first concert that we were to give at *La Locomotive*, unshaven, his clothes in tatters, his shoes, those of a tramp who had walked too much. We looked at each other in amazement before this pitiful picture."

After speaking to his friend, Clarke recalled that: "...he expressed himself strangely: "I am Vince Taylor, and I am not Vince Taylor. Vince Taylor is dead! My name is Matthew, I am the son of Jesus Christ!"

There is no record of how the show went that night but Clarke recalls that the following day Taylor re-appeared at the club for their second booking in what initially seemed to be better physical condition.

> "Vince showed up for the soundcheck, clean-shaven, clean-haired, and said, 'I'm sorry about last night, but you know, I was really tired. There, today I am ready to sing. It's going to be great, I'm in great shape!"

Clarke was greatly relieved to hear this. When he and Taylor returned to La Locomotive later that day he noted that the rock and roll star was still in a positive mood. Encouraged by this, he looked forward to what promised to be a memorable performance by the rocker but, to his

1. Ziggy Played Guitar

immense dismay, upon reaching the entrance to the venue Vince spotted a large poster pinned to the wall of the foyer which was advertising the gig. Vince immediately walked up to it, took out a pen and began to deface it by crossing out his own name and replacing it with the word "Jesus".

"I said to myself, it's off to a bad start." Clarke recalled in his memoirs while Ralph Danks, the guitarist in Taylor's band, also has tortured memories of that night.

> "We were all in a great mood, except for Vince who was constantly in and out of his mystical new persona. I had my eyes fixed on him, I did not trust him on this one, I measured that it was his last chance to revive his career in free fall. *The Locomotive* was jam-packed with Vince fanatics, and in the front row I spotted Sheila, his sister..."

During the prelude to the show—as the band stood in the wings waiting for the curtain to go up—they were alarmed to discover that Taylor had not yet appeared. Danks put down his guitar, rushed off to the backstage area and found the singer alone; slouched in a chair in the corner of his dressing room. The singer had a blank expression on his face and seemed deeply confused—completely lost in a world of his own making. The guitarist managed to bring him around whereby Taylor promised that he would join the band on stage once the instrumental intro had finished.

> "So, I ran up on stage, we played a quick version of C.L.A.N.K, a song I had composed with Bobbie, and then the guy said, "Ladies and gentlemen, the biggest star in the world... Vince." .... Taylor!!!!"

As the curtain rose, the packed audience rushed towards the front of the stage screaming wildly. Initially thrilled at the prospect of seeing their hero in the flesh they immediately fell eerily silent—stunned by the astonishing sight of Taylor peering down at them, wrapped in a potato

Left: Vince Taylor performing in Blokker (Netherlands) on May 23, 1963. Image copyright: Hugo van Gelderen (ANEFO)

sack with a water bottle and drumstick in his hand. The band launched into the intro to the first song—a cover of the Eddie Cochran song *C'mon Everybody*—but rather than joining in, Taylor leaned forward and began blessing his fans by firstly sprinkling them with water and then by throwing crumbs of bread over them in a mock Christian baptism. Taylor then turned to the band and brought the show to an abrupt halt. In front of the now completely stunned Parisian audience the singer announced over the PA that Vince Taylor was dead but had arisen as the "Son of Christ".

"I am Mateus." he repeated over and over before climbing down from the stage and then weaving his way through the packed audience, reaching out to touch each one and blessing them with the messianic greeting "Come, follow me. I am the way." Taylor's sister, Sheila, was so shocked by her brother's bizarre change of character that she panicked. Seeing her in such a troubled emotional state, Taylor tried to calm her down by assuring her that "I have prepared a plane for you and my disciples. Come with me and I will fly you to my Father's kingdom in Heaven. God will make it so." According to Ralph Danks "...the show was a complete disaster, an absolute shipwreck."[36]

MEN, MINDS AND A MAP

News of the Paris debacle spread far and wide and the bad publicity it

---

[36] Gaignault, Fabrice. *Vies et mort de Vince Taylor (Trans. Lives and Death of Vince Taylor)*, Fayard, 2014.

generated brought Taylor's career to a screeching halt. The singer was due to fly to Sans Francisco after the gig—courtesy of Sheila's financial generosity and support—but the plan now had to be cancelled and the singer, along with his weary and despondent band, had to return home. In the years that followed, Taylor performed only very occasionally; solely around the UK and with the number and size of venues prepared to host him diminishing rapidly.

It was while he was living in London that he accidentally bumped into Bowie one day outside Tottenham Court Road Underground Station. The two musicians were already acquainted for, as a young Mod[37], Bowie had occasionally frequented Taylor's London residence. Remembering that Bowie had once taken a keen interest in esoteric mysteries and strange conspiracies, Taylor felt drawn to share some of his divinely inspired insights with his one-time acquaintance. These included divulging what he insisted was "...highly sensitive and classified information".

Pulling Bowie to one side, Mateus reached deep into his inside pocket and pulled out a large map which he unfolded and handed to Bowie for closer examination. He awaited his response. Bowie carefully looked it over and found that it included hand-drawn marking which Taylor maintained were every one of a multitude of extraterrestrial bases concealed at various locations across the planet—sites he maintained that the UK government were aware of but which they were not disclosing to the public.

"Look, David, see...there are UFOs everywhere. the extraterrestrial is living among us." Taylor exclaimed.[38] According to other witnesses, he then pointed his finger at the northern regions of Iceland and exclaimed that the country was studded with fjords within which aliens had hidden armaments. "I know where the weapons are that the aliens are planning to use to invade Europe"[39] he asserted. Addressing Bowie

---

[37] 'Mod', or 'Modernist', was a 1950s subculture movement that started in London and spread throughout Great Britain. Followers tended to be keen on modern jazz—a precursor to rock n' roll.
[38] Vince Taylor: The Leather Messiah, https://dangerousminds.net
[39] Gaignault, Fabrice. *Vies et mort de Vince Taylor* (Trans. *Lives and Death of Vince Taylor*), Fayard, 2014.

directly, he then gave him a stern warning, "But be careful, it's between us, and you don't tell anyone!"

Even for a seasoned UFO believer, Bowie later admitted that he had found Taylor's behaviour and conspiratorial ideas extremely bizarre. Nevertheless, the chance meeting and the odd conversation they had left an enduring impression on him. A couple of years later Bowie mixed the concept of extraterrestrials with the image of Taylor as a burned-out rock star and created Ziggy Stardust; the predominant element in his song *Starman*, and the central character within his album *The Rise and Fall of Ziggy Stardust and the Spiders from Mars*.

SAVIOUR MACHINE

Ziggy, as a fictional character, was more than just an artistic creation employed by Bowie to embellish his songwriting. The psychological characteristics of his alien friend were complex for, as his creator envisioned him, he was an omnisexual alien rock star sent to Earth with a warning to humanity that they were living in a final, five-year period of existence. At the same time, Bowie portrayed Ziggy as a benevolent creature—one who was also bringing to the inhabitants of planet Earth a message of redemption. It was NOT too late for humanity to change its course of self-destruction.

The musician shared some of his conceptualisation of Ziggy in an interview with William S. Burroughs of *Rolling Stone* magazine.

> "Ziggy is advised in a dream by the infinites to write the coming of a starman ... this amazing spaceman who will be coming down to save the Earth. Ziggy starts to believe in all this himself and thinks himself a prophet of the future starmen. He takes himself up to the incredible spiritual heights and is kept alive by his disciples. When the infinites arrive, they take bits of Ziggy to make themselves real, because in their original state they are anti-matter and cannot exist on our world. And they tear him to pieces onstage

during the song 'Rock 'n' Roll Suicide.'"[40]

As chaotic as our World was in 1972, the five-year termination period Bowie referred to was not an accurate reflection of the state of the planet at that time: neither was it simply a number picked out of thin air. In 1972, while working on the *Ziggy Stardust* album, Bowie's late father[41] appeared to him in a dream and told his son that humanity had only five years in which to save the planet from destruction.[42]

As a character and extension of Bowie's alter-ego, Ziggy the alien survived as a part of his on-stage persona for a relatively short period of time. Following the release of the *Ziggy Stardust* and the Spiders from Mars album, Bowie and his band embarked upon a mammoth 191-date UK tour to promote it. At the end of it, Bowie fulfilled his own prediction regarding the fate of Ziggy when, at the climax of the final date of the tour held in Hammersmith Odeon, London, Bowie declared to a shocked and stunned audience that this was the last concert he would ever do.[43]

Many, including his own bandmates who had not been informed of his decision prior to his announcement, interpreted his comments to mean that Bowie was initiating a premature conclusion to his own professional musical career. In truth, he had simply become bored of the whole Ziggy persona and decided to kill him off prior to moving on and pursuing other musical projects.[44]

The 'death' of Ziggy occurred almost one year to the day after his induction into the societal zeitgeist during the transmission of Bowie's and The Spiders From Mars iconic *Top of the Pops* appearance. In the

---

[40] https://www.rollingstone.com/music/music-news/ziggy-stardust-how-bowie-created-the-alter-ego-that-changed-rock-55254/
[41] Bowie's father, Haywood Stenton 'John' Jones was born in Doncaster, Yorkshire, on November 21, 1912. He died on August 5, 1969. (Source: https://en.wikipedia.org/wiki/David_Bowie)
[42] Cameron, Grant, Castillo, Katarina, and Barnabe, Desta, *Tuned-In: The Paranormal World of Music*, CreateSpace Independent Publishing Platform, 2017.
[43] This was filmed by American documentary filmmaker Donn Alan Pennebaker (1925-2019) and released in cinemas as a documentary record of the concert in 1979.
[44] Ziggy made a momentary re-appearance at the Marquee Club in London during the filming of Bowie's *The 1980 Floor Show* on October 19, 1973.

intervening years the musician and his backing band had conquered England and had appeared at one sell-out show after another; to rapturous audiences comprised ecstatic teenage boys and fawning pre-pubescent girls. A cultural revolution had just taken place in popular entertainment and Bowie was posed to follow this throughout America and the rest of the World. He could, in many ways, have milked the Ziggy concept to its maximum throughout the rest of the decade and ensured the continuing stratospheric rise in his career but Bowie avoided these pitfalls and rather wisely called a halt to his cosmic pantomime prematurely. Ziggy's end came about just as Bowie predicted it would in the lyrics to the title track of his *Ziggy Stardust* album.

> *"Making love with his ego.*
> *Ziggy sucked up into his mind.*
> *Like a leper messiah.*
> *When the kids had killed the man.*
> *I had to break up the band."*

He could, in so many ways, have been describing the demise of either Ziggy or Taylor...or maybe both!

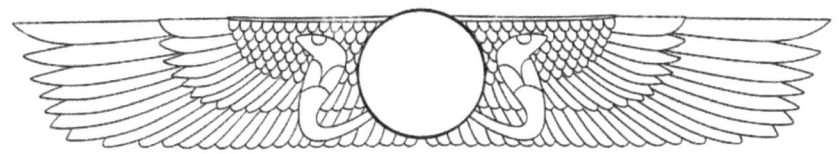

2. OPENING THE VORTEX

"Ritual may be vital to reaction, but it is also the life blood of revolution."

American anthropologist, historian, and academic David I. Kertzer (1948-present day).

The Rise and Fall of Ziggy Stardust and the Spiders from Mars album first appeared in record stores on June 16, 1972. It quickly entered the top 10 of the UK Album Chart in the second week of its release and by the end of 1972 had sold nearly 100,000 copies in the UK alone making it eligible for gold status.[45]

Ziggy Stardust proved to not only be popular with fans but it also received widespread critical acclaim with one reviewer writing for the monthly American music magazine Circus describing it as "...from start to finish ... of dazzling intensity and mad design... a stunning work of genius."[46] The stature of this legendary album has increased rather than diminished over the decades and is often acclaimed as one of the most influential records in rock music history.[47] From its eco-apocalyptical opener *Five Years* through to its commentary on rock n' roll excess and the seductive trappings of stardom in its closing track *Rock n' Roll Suicide* the record features an eclectic collection of electrically charged and mesmerising anthems which Bowie and his band delivered with intensity.

---

[45] The album peaked at number five on the UK charts in February 1973 and returned to the charts again in January 1981, following the success of the single *Ashes to Ashes*.
[46] *Ziggy Stardust*, Circus, June 1972.
[47] The album is considered so important in cultural terms that in 2017 it was described as "culturally, historically, and artistically significant" by the US National Recording Registry.

Several tracks on *Ziggy Stardust* were potential singles but record company executives chose *Starman* to promote which led to its release on April 28, 1972. *Suffragette City*—another Bowie original and one of the creative highlights from the same album—was included on its B-side. Although the song is an essential part of the album's core theme, *Starman* was very nearly omitted from it. Instead, its original track-listing featured a cover-version of the Chuck Berry song *Round and Around* but upon hearing *Starman* for the first time, RCA immediately recognised its commercial potential and insisted upon its inclusion.

Despite their initial optimism, *Starman* failed to attract immediate interest from either the music press or national radio who seemed to feel that their listeners were not ready for such an artistic oddity—particularly as the single had been released by a relatively unknown and unestablished artist. Consequently, *Starman* failed to crash into the singles chart as expected and was a further eight weeks before it made any sort of impression on the weekly record sales figures and even then it only just crawled into the Top 50 by charting at number 49 on June 24—an achievement resulting from BBC Radio One DJ Johnny Walker playing it on his lunchtime radio show.

The exposure Walker gave the song brought it to the attention of *Top of the Pops* executives. Their music show had a policy of featuring both established artists and less well-known acts whose singles had entered the lower echelons of the UK music charts. By late June 1972, *Starman* had received sufficient interest from the public to justify the BBC inviting Bowie to perform it on television.

Difficult Questions

The edition of the show Bowie and the Spiders were booked to appear on was presented by the hideously saccharine BBC Radio 1 DJ Tony Blackburn (the BBC sure knew how to pick them!) Once the inanely grinning and utterly fatuous presenter had introduced Bowie with his usual patronising and inauthentic manner the studio camera panned away and focused on Bowie strumming the opening chords to *Starman* on his Egmond, twelve-string, acoustic guitar.

2. Opening the Vortex

It was an impressive start but, as the camera moved back from its opening close-up shot, a small percentage of home viewers—those who could afford a colour TV—were treated to the remarkable sight of Bowie's blond-haired guitarist Mick Ronson dressed in a golden, one-piece outfit and then of the equally arresting sight of Bowie wearing a body-hugging, multi-coloured leotard. The song Bowie and his Spiders from Mars band was performing must have been equally astonishing to many TV viewers. With a catchy melody and soaring chorus it was the sort of song you could enjoy without much recourse to an appreciation of musical composition. However, for those who wanted to engage more fully with it—and specifically with its lyrical content—then it was apparent that not only did the song's cosmically inspired and well-crafted lyrics sublimely capture the public's mood at that moment but they also posed a deeply philosophical question—a conundrum that had been swimming around on the edges of polite society ever since NASA's initial foray into outer space but particularly since the 1969 Moon landing. In an sense, *Starman* was conceptualising the forbidden.

By the year of the song's release, 1972, billions of inhabitants on this planet had been exposed to several years of intense, daily, media coverage of the NASA space missions. The further out into space their spacecraft traveled, the more the minds of observers back on planet Earth were forced to quietly consider the possibility (or even probability) of the occupants of the craft accidentally encountering other lifeforms out in the dark void. Had the 1969 NASA Moon landings taken place fifty years later then the World's media would be full of speculation regarding the existence of extraterrestrials but this was definitely NOT the case back in 1972! Through a fear of being being ridiculed for believing in "little green men", there was no serious discussion of the subject of alien life by any pundit or commentator in any branch of the mainstream media. The topic was, in so many regards, avoided at all costs: maybe for reasons that were social, or political, or even religious. In an era when science fiction was dominant in all areas of the entertainment industries; including, film, TV, and literature, discussion of alien life-forms, civilisations, or the detection and interception of inter-galactic communications seemed to many to be a

Left: Picture sleeve edition of the 7" single Starman by David Bowie

glaring omission. These were areas of debate and analysis that the 'establishment' seemed to want to avoid but David Bowie had no such qualms. Within the lyrics of *Starman* he not only posed a number of these difficult and uncomfortable questions but also proffered equally challenging answers. In his opinion, extraterrestrials not only exist but that at that very moment there was an unknown off-planet civilisation covertly observing humanity from very close quarters.

As his performance of *Starman* reached a climax, a studio camera turned and focused upon the singer. This time Bowie was visible with one arm draped around the neck of his guitarist Mick Ronson in a warm embrace. As Bowie and his arachnid band broke into the song's chorus, the young, visually stunning, twenty-five-year-old musician, turned directly to the camera and peered deeply into its lens. With a cheeky look on his face and knowing twinkle in his eyes, he bore deep into the soul of the nation and intoned in unequivocal terms that ET would "*...like to come and meet us...but he thinks he'd blow our minds.*" It was a spine-chilling moment that must have caused the blood of millions of TV viewers all over the UK to run cold!

Regular UFO Sightings

Bowie's appearance on *Top of the Pops* was an unparalleled success. England—a well-known repository of eccentricity in most fields of endeavour—immediately took Bowie to their hearts. Up until the musician's darker and more introspective period during the late 1970s when he was recording in Soviet-controlled Berlin, Bowie added much needed colour and excitement to what was a grey and dispirited nation. In a contemporary musical landscape which had become dominated by

2. OPENING THE VORTEX

Tolkien-inspired 'prog rock' here at last was a working-class hero who was offering an exciting new genre of music that teenagers could directly identify with. The musician also carried an aura of 'street-cred' with him for it was through the carefully-crafted lyrics of his songs that Bowie engaged with issues that reflected the daily lives of his fans; including such real-life challenges as, urban decay, a personal search for freedom of expression, and the innate desire by so many youngsters to break free from state, church, and parental control.

Fans saw in Bowie personal characteristics that his close friend John Lennon might have referred to as those of a "working-class hero". On the face of it he appeared to be speaking their kind of language but how many of his legions of followers fully appreciated the deep level of interest Bowie had in the language of philosophy, psychology, and cosmology? It is highly probable that, back in 1972, very few of them paid too much serious attention to this or to to the fact that Bowie was involved in the fringe world of UFO research. Bowie was keenly aware of this and was aware that this was a subject that made people feel uncomfortable.

Through the lyrics of *Starman* he sought to breakdown preconceptions regarding the topic by having a little bit of fun with it. It was almost as if he was attempting to lighten up the debate on extraterrestrial life and make it more palatable for people to digest without diluting its significance. As he saw it, the phenomena presents humanity with a mystery that deserves the time and respect of everyone and should not simply be considered a comedic form of entertainment. Indeed, his take on the subject went far beyond the commonly held perception of flying saucers as nuts-and-bolts craft. The musician, who by 1972 had already been studying UFOs for several years, believed that a direct link exists between the sighting of regular them and the level of psychic or psychospiritual awareness held by their observers. Although this connection had first been proposed by the Swiss psychologist Carl Jung(1875-1961)[48] it was, the time. a contentious position to hold but Bowie felt confident in expressing this perspective.

---
[48] Jung, C. G., *Flying saucers : a modern myth of things seen in the skies*, London Routledge & Kegan Paul, 1959.

What made Bowie think that there was more to the UFO enigma than simply interpreting it in terms of pure nuts-and-bolts craft? Author and UFO researcher Peter Koening quoted Bowie from an interview he gave around this time in which he revealed the reason behind his this insight into the phenomena.

> "A friend and I were traveling in the English countryside when we both noticed a strange object hovering above a field. From then on, I have come to take this phenomenon seriously. I believe that what I saw was not the actual object, but a projection of my own mind trying to make sense of this quantum topological doorway into dimensions beyond our own. It's as if our dimension is but one among an infinite number of others."[49]

Hunting UFOs

Someone who was only too aware of Bowie's fascination in UFOs was the American actress and journalist Mary Angela (Angie) Barnett. Angie met Bowie in London in 1969 when she was 19 years of age. The two forged a close relationship and they married on March 19, 1970, at Bromley Register Office in Beckenham Lane, Kent. Theirs was an odd and unlikely coupling and the marriage did not last long for they divorced on February 8, 1980.

During their time together, Angie accompanied her husband on tour, played a pivotal role in helping him establish his career as a Glam Rock superstar, and was instrumental in developing his striking visual on-stage appearance during the Ziggy era. In her biography, *Backstage Passes: Life on the Wild Side with David Bowie*, she revealed the degree to which Bowie had become fascinated in UFOs and extraterrestrial life. In one of her recollections of their time together, she describes how, during his 1974 tour of America, the couple travelled from one venue to another in a limousine that was driven by Tony Macia. Once they escaped the light pollution created by large cities, David would roll back

[49] Beckley, Timothy Green, *The Authentic Book of Ultra-Terrestrial Contacts*, Global Communications, 2012.

2. OPENING THE VORTEX

the sun-roof of the car, extend the lens of a powerful telescope up through it, and enthusiastically scan the night sky for signs of alien craft.

Not a bad way to pass the endless years spent driving from one gig to another you might think but Angie suggests that David's enthusiasm for ufology was more than just that of a hobbyist. He seemed to take it almost as seriously as his musical career.

> "David believed very strongly that aliens were active above our planet, and so did (do) I. That's why we were so alert in the limo on the way to Minneapolis, watching intently for signs of further UFO activity in the bright night sky. It was mostly David who had his eye pressed to the telescope (purchased by Corinne Schwab, his personal assistant, during a lightning shopping spree in Detroit). I don't know quite what David expected, because by now he'd moved beyond his manic-monologue mode into his silent, non-communication state, but I suspect he wouldn't have been surprised at all if the aliens had come right down to the limo and tractor-beamed him up for an exchange of ideas. He was feeling pretty much like the center of things here on Earth at the time, after all, and it probably seemed obvious to him that some right-thinking human should take on the job of Man's ambassador...."[50]

Angie's idea that Bowie felt himself to be at the heart of ET contact was succinctly captured in the third verse of *Starman*:

> *"Look out your window I can see his light,*
> *If we can sparkle, he may land tonight."*

A similar references to Bowie's uncanny ability to observe—and to possibly initiate their appearance—also appears in the lyrics to his seven-miniute long song *Memory of a Free Festival* which he recorded in

---

[50] Bowie, Angie, *Backstage Passes: Life on the Wild Side with David Bowie*, The Berkley Publishing Group, 1993.

34

September 1969 for his *Space Oddity* album but then reworked in March-April 1970 at the request of Mercury Records who felt it would make a good single.

> *"We scanned the skies with rainbow eyes and saw machines.*
> *Of every shape and size.*
> *We talked with tall Venusians passing through.*
> *And Peter tried to climb aboard but the Captain shook his head.*
> *And away they soared,*
> *Climbing through the ivory vibrant cloud."*

AMBASSADOR FOR A PHENOMENA

Looking back at the events surrounding Bowie during the period 1972-1974, it is difficult to imagine how one song could have had such a profound cultural effect but it did. In the decades that followed, several musicians—mavericks who spearheaded a new wave of pop/rock music—recalled the impact seeing Bowie on TV that evening had on them. Each one asserts that they were immediately filled with an implacable desire to become musicians themselves or, as Rolling Stone magazine put it in an online article in 2016:

> "Every future legend in the British Isles was tuned in. Morrissey was watching. So was Johnny Marr. Siouxsie was watching. Robert Smith was watching. Duran Duran were watching. So were Echo and the Bunnymen. Dave Gahan. Noel Gallagher. U2. Bauhaus. Jesus, Mary, and their Chain. Everybody.

It's no coincidence that there was a boom of English rock stars born between 1958 and 1963 – these were the kids stuck at home on a Thursday night in 1972, watching an otherwise depressing hour of *Top of the Pops*. As Bono told Rolling Stone magazine in 2010, "The first time I saw him was singing *'Starman'* on television. It was like a creature falling from the sky. Americans put a man on the moon. We had our own British guy from space – with an Irish mother."[51]

---
[51] www.rollingstone.com/music/news/how-david-bowie-became-the-starman-

2. Opening the Vortex

Analysis of the *Starman* performance has appeared in so many books, magazines, and articles over the decades that one might assume that every aspect of the event has received in-depth analysis of one kind or another; but this is not the case. There have been notable omissions in their commentaries which need addressing.

From the perspective of ufology it is important to pose the question: to what degree did the performance—and the song *Starman* in particular—give the topic of aliens a degree of credibility within the general public? The number of teenagers who were inspired to become musicians as a result of watching Bowie and Ronson on *Top of the Pops* have been catalogued at length but no ufologists have admitted to being encouraged to research the phenomenon after hearing the lyrics of *Starman*.[52] This is unfortunate and leaves Bowie's notable contribution to ufology going unrecognised. There is no doubt that several elements within the Ziggy album introduced young music fans to the concept of ET contact and encouraged them to engage with the subject. Not only did songs on this, and several other albums, feature titles and lyrics that referenced life in the the cosmos but more significantly it was through his creation of Ziggy that Bowie seeded humanity with a new archetype/mythological construct—one formed around the image of the lonesome cosmic-traveller, trapped on our planet, and struggling to survive in an environment not of their liking or choosing.

Bowie gave further weight to the personification of this archetype when he starred in the 1976 film *The Man Who Fell to Earth*. This was one of his most iconic screen appearances for he took on the lead role of an alien visitor to this planet. The film was well-received, Bowie was credited as a accomplished actor, and its storyline helped establish this powerful archetypal construct within the zeitgeist. It re-emerged in other films, the most notable being Steven Spielberg's (1946-present day)1982 blockbuster, *E.T., the Extra-Terrestrial*, which received nine nominations at the 55th Academy Awards.

Although created by Bowie, his own use of this archetype peaked during the years 1969 to 1974 and this was followed by a decline in his
20160706

[52] The author happens to be an exception!

Left: Film poster for The Man Who Fell to Earth starring David Bowie.

use of UFO/ET-inspired lyrics shortly after the release of *Aladdin Sane* in 1973. The term "alien" did re-emerge in the title of his hit-song Loving the Alien on his 1987 album Tonight but it made no reference to extraterrestrials. Instead, it featured a series of references to a 12th-century Catholic military order known as the The Poor Fellow-Soldiers of Christ and of the Temple of Solomon (more commonly known as the Knights Templar). When asked about the lyrics to *Loving the Alien*, Bowie explained that it "...came about because of my feeling that so much history is wrong – as is being rediscovered all the time – and that we base so much on the wrong knowledge that we've gleaned."[53] This is an interesting comment for him to make for it reveals that Bowie was still engaged in the study of fringe topics during a period when esoteric references in his lyrics had dried up. Bowie's biographer David Buckley noticed this as well for he called the song "...the only track on the album with the gravitas of much of his earlier work." [54]

Bowie constantly challenged the art of songwriting throughout his career. Despite the semi-comedic qualities of songs like *Jean Genie*, *Space Oddity*, and *The Laughing Gnome*, he demonstrated that he was capable of crafting lyrics that included references to a wide range of esoteric ideas. At the time, most critics, commentators, and fans, failed to pick-up on them—in much the same way that they had also missed the importance Bowie paid to the idea of extraterrestrial life. Maybe this is not too surprising. Fans who enjoyed his catchy, hit-singles were not necessarily the same as those who studiously explored the lyrics printed on the inner sleeves of long-playing records in minute detail. If they had been then they might have noticed that within a handful of songs— particularly on his albums *The Man Who Sold the World* (1970) and

[53] *Let's Talk, A Conversation with David Bowie*, Rolling Stone, October 25, 1984.
[54] Buckley, David, David Bowie: *The Music and The Changes*. Omnibus Press, 2015.

Hunky Dory (1971)–Bowie not only revealed his fascination with ufology but also hinted at an interest he had in an even darker realm–one which very few of his fans would have been able to either accommodate or conceptualise.

Psychomagickal Ritual?

Although the lyrics to Bowie's early songs demonstrate that the had an interest in metaphysics, at the time of the broadcast of *Starman* on *Top of the Pops*, millions of TV viewers were completely unaware that dark dynamics were at play–themes specific to the dark world of occultism[55] and mysticism.[56] While cultural history marks it as a spontaneous and light-hearted affair–one that featured an unapologetic air of flamboyance and the theatrical–not all is as it first seems. While most viewers presumed they were witnessing performance-art, they were in fact unconsciously resonating to a field of psychomagickal[57] energy that was being harnessed and disseminated by Bowie and Ronson.

Effective rock-and-roll performances are predicated upon several well-established theatrical presumptions. For example, rock bands showcase their musical talents on a pre-prepared stage and direct to a receptive audience using such audio-visual props as lighting and costume to enhance the impact of their performance. However, anyone with knowledge of the Western Mystery Tradition[58] should have noticed the distinct parallels between Bowie's appearance on *Top of the Pops* and pre-scripted actions of a kind used in magickal ritual. These include

---

[55] The term 'occult' is derived from the Latin 'occultus' meaning hidden', or 'secret'. James Webb, author of *The Occult Underground* (1974) described the occult as an "Underground of rejected knowledge, comprising heretical religious positions, defeated social schemes, abandoned sciences, and neglected modes of speculation."

[56] Mysticism, on the other hand, is more indicative of a direct experience of the divine as opposed to occultism which is more closely related to the exploration and practical engagement with Universal Law.

[57] The term 'psychomagickal' is an amalgamation of psychological functioning at a spiritual level and traditional occult or magickal practice. The letter 'k'; is added to the word magic to indicate that it has an occult context and does not refer to the type of illusionary, or sleight-of-hand, practiced by stage entertainers.

[58] The Western Mystery Tradition encompasses a wide range of esoteric traditions including that of the 'Law of Correspondences' which proposes that actual, as well as symbolic, associations exist which connect all things in our Universe and beyond.

Left: Jacques de Molay (c. 1300). The last Grand Master of the Knights Templar, who joined the order at the age of twenty-one.

the use of specific colours, tonal invocation, and the application of a willed focus. Not only were each of these key occult elements evident on the day but the date and the time of its broadcast was not accidental.

All magickal operations require precise timing if it is to be successful and a magus will always ascertain the most favourable moment to perform it. The timing of Bowie's appearance falls into this category; for it appears to have been deliberately timed to synchronise with specific planetary and stellar conditions. The combination of these factors resulted in an injection of cosmic energy into the collective unconscious[59] of the English nation.[60] Something powerful, archetypal, and fundamental occurred that day—as events during the weeks and months that followed demonstrate—but to understand exactly what took place we need to take a closer look at David Bowie and his occult influences.

---

[59] The term 'kollektives Unbewusstes' (trans. 'collective unconscious') was coined by Swiss psychoanalyst Carl Gustav Jung (1875-1961) who stated that ancient primal symbols, or 'archetypes', common to everyone reside deep within human unconscious.
[60] The encoding of occult information within music and is not a modern phenomenon. Beethoven and Mozart infused Masonic elements into their compositions.

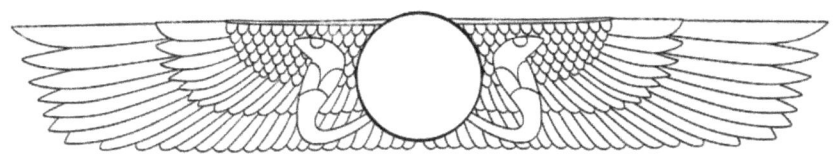

3. Beyond Good and Evil

"Without music, life would be a mistake."

Twilight of the Idols by Friedrich Nietzsche (1844-1900).

David Bowie (real name David Robert Jones) was born in Brixton, London, on January 8, 1947. After leaving school in 1963 he studied art, music, and design at Bromley School of Art in southeast London with the intention of either entering the world of performance art or taking up a career as a professional musician. His creative instincts eventually led him into songwriting and at the time of his death in 2016 he had sold over 100 million records worldwide which made him one of the best-selling artists of all time.[61]

In addition to being a musical legend, Bowie was also acclaimed as an actor: starring in over 30 films, television shows, and theatrical productions. His success in each of these vocations has been extensively documented by biographers but what is not so well known is that Bowie had a lifelong interest in philosophy and metaphysics; including practical magick and the Jewish Kabbalah.[62]

Bowie's maternal half-brother, Terry Burns, was a major influence on his philosophical leanings. Terry, who was ten years older than Bowie, had schizophrenia and was prone to seizures leading him to spend time between his home and hospital. It was through his influence that Bowie was guided into perusing several lifelong interests; including modern jazz, Buddhism, Beat poetry, and the occult.

---

[61] https://en.wikipedia.org/wiki/David_Bowie
[62] O'Leary, Chris, *Rebel Rebel: All the Songs of David Bowie from '64 to '76*, Winchester: Zero Books, 2015.

Bowie's underlying thirst for deeper personal meaning and a greater understanding of the mysteries of the universe turned him into an avid book-reader. This became most apparent in 1975 when he was cast as the central character in Nicolas Roeg's (1928-2018) film *The Man Who Fell to Earth*. The role required him to travel to New Mexico in preparation for the filming where, despite being in the grip of cocaine addiction, Bowie was said to have been:

> "...diligent and engaged, happy to banter with the crew and work on his lines with co-star Candy Clark. He had, rather ambitiously, promised not to use drugs for the duration of the shoot, so when he wasn't needed, he would take himself off to his trailer and indulge in an altogether less harmful pastime: reading books."[63]

The British newspaper *The Sunday Times* reported that because of his hatred of air travel Bowie traversed the United States by train; hauling a "mobile bibliothèque" which was stored inside a modified trunk. It was said that this opened out to reveal a stack of books neatly displayed on shelves. They were, according to the newspaper, Bowie's favourite titles with several publications written about the occult and the dark side of human consciousness.

In March 2013, London's Victoria & Albert Museum (V&A) held a career retrospective which included over five hundred items from Bowie's archive. These included examples of his personal stage costumes, artwork, handwritten lyrics, and video storyboards. The exhibition was so popular with the public that it toured the World before eventually closing at New York's Brooklyn Museum five years later. In Ontario—the show's first destination after leaving London—the V&A presented a list of one hundred books that Bowie considered to be the most important and influential in his life. They were not necessarily his favourites but included titles that he felt had made the greatest impression on him. The list included several novels with an apocalyptic,

---

[63] Connell, John, *Bowie's Bookshelf: The Hundred Books That Changed Bowie's Life*, Gallery Books, 2019.

dystopian, isolationist theme. These included *The Waste Land* by T.S. Elliot, *1984* by George Orwell, *The Outsider* by Colin Wilson, *Inferno* by Dante Alighieri, and *A Clockwork Orange* by Anthony Burgess. The collection also contained a few titles on various religious, spiritual, and psychological topics. These included *The Divided Self* by R. D. Laing, *The Origin of Consciousness in the Breakdown of the Bicameral Mind* by Julian Jaynes, and *The Gnostic Gospels* by Elaine Pagels.

While most of these books would be considered 'fringe' by bibliophiles, the oddest title on the list was the 1856, occult classic *Dogme et Rituel de la Haute Magie* (trans. *Transcendental Magic, Its Doctrine and Ritual*) written by Alphonse Louis Constant—the French esotericist and Kabbalist more commonly referred to as Éliphas Lévi.

Astral Light of Mendes

Left: French esotericist, poet, and writer Éliphas Lévi Zahed, (born Alphonse Louis Constant (1810–1875)

Eliphas Lévi (1810-1875) was the son of a Parisian shoemaker. From an early age he developed a fascination with religion and this led him to pursue a career in the Catholic Church. However, at the age of twenty-six he alienated church authorities and was forced to relinquish his position in the priesthood. From that point forward life took him down a completely different path. In 1850, at the age of forty— following a personal financial and spiritual crisis—Lévi explored the rich vein of esoteric and occult thinking that permeated the Parisian intelligentsia during the middle of the 19th-century. Lévi became a writer and ceremonial magickian and his deep understanding of the subject resulted in the publication of more than twenty books on magick, Kabbalah, alchemy, and occultism.

Paris was a hot-bed of occult practice and study towards the end of the 19th-century but Lévi's spiritual philosophy and occult theories more than any of that period that escaped the confines of the French capital. These crossed the physical and literary barrier created by the English Channel and had a deep impact on the teachings of the London-based secret society known as the Hermetic Order of the Golden Dawn[64] and in particular upon the work of ex-Dawn members Aleister Crowley (1875-1947)–who believed himself to be the reincarnation of Lévi– and Arthur Edward Waite (1857-1942) who translated Lévi's *Dogme et Rituel de la Haute Magie* into English in 1923. The teachings of the French magickian also crossed the Atlantic and influenced Helena Blavatsky (1831-1891) and the Theosophical Society[65] which she founded.

Unlike several other occultists from America, France, and England who rose to prominence during this period, Lévi's work has successfully navigated the passage of time. His work's on magick are often cited but his most notable contribution to the subject was his remarkable rendering of the Baphomet, or Sabbatical Goat, which has become an iconic image in modern occultism. This strange and beguiling demon-like figure creates what we might call a composite 'ideagram'[66] and as such draws upon a variety of esoteric and philosophical principles. However, the figure has been misappropriated and degraded by many amateur occultists–most notably by Devil-worshiping cults such as the

---

[64] The Hermetic Order of the Golden Dawn (1887-1903) was an English secret society based in London. It was founded by William Wynn Westcott (1888-1897), Samuel Liddell MacGregor Mathers (1897-1903) and William Robert Woodman (1828-1891). The society was based on an initiatory framework like that found in Masonic lodges, although unlike Freemasonry it did admit women. The society also included traditional occult practices such as astrology, tarot divination, Kabbalah, and geomancy.
[65] The Theosophical Society was a religious movement founded in New York City in 1875 by Helena Blavatsky with Russian mystic Henry Steel Olcott as its president. The society drew upon several spiritual philosophies including Neoplatonism, occultism, Hinduism, Buddhism, and Islam.
[66] An 'ideagram' can be defined as a visualised concept which promotes "A uniquely evolutionary approach to thinking, concentrating and developing visual diagrams to convey the inherent wisdom and content of concepts and narrative material." (Source: www.ideagram.co)

3. Beyond Good and Evil

Satanic Temple[67] whose members credit Lévi's Baphomet with being a representation of the Devil. This is also the public's perception of it—a confusion that arose after English writer Dennis Wheatley (1897-1977) appropriated it to represent a malevolent figure in several of his occult novels. It was also used by A. E. Waite who erroneously designated the Baphomet as the central figure on Arcana 15 of his tarot—a card he titled THE DEVIL. Despite this, the notion that the Baphomet can be directly linked to Diabolism is completely unfounded and without merit. It is certainly not the context that Lévi originally had in mind when he designed the Baphomet ideogram for, as he said in his book *The Mysteries of Magic*:

> "What is more absurd and more impious than to attribute the name of Lucifer to the devil, that is, to personified evil. The intellectual Lucifer is the spirit of intelligence and love; it is the paraclete, it is the Holy Spirit, while the physical Lucifer is the great agent of universal magnetism."[68]

Another noted occult researcher, J. Strube, described the Baphomet as a "representation of Lévi's magnetistic-magical concept of the Astral Light." Lévi qualified this description in the following way:

> "There exists in nature a force which is much more powerful than steam. ... This force was known to the ancients: it consists of a universal agent whose supreme law is equilibrium, and whose direction is concerned immediately with the great arcanum of transcendental magic. This agent, which barely manifests itself under the trial and error of the disciples of Mesmer[69], is exactly what the adepts of the Middle Ages called the first matter of the great

---

[68] Lévi, Eliphas and Waite, A. E., *The Mysteries of Magic*, George Redway, 1886.
[69] Franz Anton Mesmer (1734-1815) was a German physician who believed in the existence of a natural, all-pervading energy which he said could be used for healing via the hands. The term 'mesmerism' was coined after his discovery that this energy could be emitted via the human eyes and used to hypnotise.

> work. The Gnostics represented it as the fiery body of the Holy Spirit, and it was the object of adoration in the secret rites of the Sabbath or the Temple, under the hieroglyphic figure of Baphomet or the Androgynous Goat of Mendes."[70]

The central principles of Lévi's magickal philosophy consist of three primary components. These are; a belief in the existence of the invisible force he called the "Astral Light"[71], a recognition of the importance of the human imagination, and the efficacy of the application of the human 'Will' in magickal practice. These theories permeate a great deal of the modern spiritual movement and are particularly prevalent in most strands of New Age thinking and practice.

STRENGTH THROUGH WILL

Eliphas Lévi was not the only occult philosopher to impress Bowie during the early 1970s. Another explorer of the dark side of the human experience was the German philosopher Friedrich Nietzsche (1844-1900). Nietzsche was also a believer in the application of 'will-power' and even coined the term "der Wille zur Macht" (Trans. "the Will to Power") when describing a fundamental, but largely undeveloped, aspect of human nature which he likened to that of self-determination, or the process of actualising one's Will and utilising it to impact the physical world.[72] Bowie was specifically drawn to Nietzsche's concept of the Übermensch (trans. Superman or Overman). In what is undoubtedly Nietzsche's best-known work, *Also sprach Zarathustra: Ein Buch für Alle und Keinen* (trans. *Thus Spoke Zarathustra: A Book for All and None*), the philosopher tells of how Zarathustra's gift of the Overman is given to mankind in the form of the Übermensch—the formulator or creator of new social and cultural values.

The Übermensch is said to have avoid following the oppressive mores of the average citizen since he believes this results in a "mediocrity of

---

[71] Strube, J., *The 'Baphomet' of Eliphas Lévi: Its Meaning and Historical Context*, Correspondences IV, 2016.
[72] Leiter, Brian, *Nietzsche's Moral and Political Philosophy*, 2021.

3. BEYOND GOOD AND EVIL

character". Instead, he strives to elevate himself above the notion of good and evil and consequently become detached from the base concerns of the majority.[73] It is through this process that Zarathustra proclaims his goal as the journey towards the state of the Übermensch. His primary motivation is a desire to trigger spiritual evolution by applying self-awareness and by overcoming superstitious beliefs rooted within the Christian notion of God and religion.[74]

Left: German philosopher Friedrich Nietzsche in 1875.

Nietzsche was deeply critical of society and its constructs. He also felt deeply antagonistic towards those whom he felt were responsible for defining its parameters. To him, all religion—particularly the Christian church, the press, and mass-culture in general—were attempting to force an individual into a state of complete conformity: something he felt contributed to the suppression of an individual's natural intellectual and psychological development. To Nietzsche, these forces were so detrimental to an individual's psyche that accumulatively they result in an irreversible decline in the core values of the human species. Nevertheless, he maintained that there is an upside to this slide into degeneration. Those individuals who were able to recognise these obstacles to growth were presented with the opportunity to circumnavigate them. It was believed that through the application of will-power anyone could transform themselves into superior human being so that, because of their efforts, society might produce higher, brighter, and healthier offspring.[75]

Bowie was so impressed by the philosophical ideas associated with

---

[73] Nietzsche, Friedrich, *Master and Slave Morality from Beyond Good and Evil*, Penguin Books, 1973.
[74] van der Braak, Andre, *Zen and Zarathustra: Self-Overcoming without a Self*, Journal of Nietzsche Studies, 2015.
[75] Kellner, Douglas, *Nietzsche's Critique of Mass Culture*, International Studies in Philosophy, 1999.

the Übermensch that he referenced them in his song *The Supermen* which he recorded in 1970 for his *The Man Who Sold the World* album. Bowie was savvy enough to avoid quoting Nietzsche's directly in his lyrics[76], preferring instead to employ the term "homo-superior". Despite this subtle change, the musician clearly references Nietzsche's theory that humanity can attain a heightened state of being. In his song Quicksand from his *Hunky Dory* album he sings "*I'm not a prophet or a stone age man, just a mortal with potential of a superman.*" Although Bowie was appearing to redefine Nietzsche's terminology here in the book *The Man Who Sold the World: David Bowie and the 1970s* author Peter Doggett suggests that Bowie's reference to the term "homo-superior" originally appeared in a 1935 novel by the science fiction author Olaf Stapledon (1886–1950) titled *Odd John*. In it, the author refers to the concept of a "homo superior"—an idea that pervades Stapledon's later works and which culminated in his book *Sirius* (1954) wherein the subject appeared in the form of a dog.

As an extension of Nietzsche's concept of the 'superior man', Bowie also referenced what he described as a coming super-race of powerful spiritual warriors in his 1971 song *Oh! You Pretty Things* with the line:

> "*Let me make it plain.*
> *You gotta make way for the Homo Superior.*"

Referencing the idea of a 'superior human race': something he evidently felt was already starting to emerge in society through its younger generation. Later on in the same song Bowie advises members of the generation about to be superseded to..:

> "*Look out at your children.*
> *See their faces in golden rays.*
> *Don't kid yourself they belong to you.*
> *They're the start of a coming race.*"

His belief in an up-coming generation of psychically and spiritually advanced children also appeared in his song *Changes*—which also

---

[76] Frederich Nietzsche was for a long time—and still is in some quarters—linked to German National Socialism and Hitler's Nazi Party.

appeared on *Hunky Dory*.

> *"And these children that you spit on*
> *As they try to change their worlds*
> *Are immune to your consultations.*
> *They're quite aware of what they're goin' through."*

In 1972, in an interview with the weekly UK music paper Melody Maker, Bowie was asked to reveal his thinking behind the lyrics to these songs.

> "We have created a new kind of person in a way. We have created a child who will be so exposed to the media that he will be lost to his parents by age 12. All the things we can't do they will."

In their book *Bowie: An Illustrated Record*, music journalists Roy Carr and Charles Shaar Murray summarised the essential concept that underpins Bowie's *Changes* and *Oh! You Pretty Things* songs. In their opinion, Bowie's lyrics herald "the impending obsolescence of the human race in favour of an alliance between visiting aliens and the youth of the present society."[77] This references a new form of hybrid youngster who, like Ziggy, originates from another place in time and space.

The Era of Indigos

Around the same time that Bowie was morphing into a superstar, Nancy Ann Tappe (1931-2012) was rising to prominence in the rapidly-expanding New Age spirituality movement. Tappe had developed a unique analytical process which she felt could be used in the field of human psychology. She called it "colorology"—the study and interpretation of the human personality through an application of the science of colour. Tappe had spent years working with a large clientele in both the United States and Switzerland where she taught students

---

[77] Carr, Roy; Murray, Charles Shaar, *Bowie: An Illustrated Record*, Eel Pie Publishing, 1981.

The Sirius Mythos - Book 1: GOD*STAR

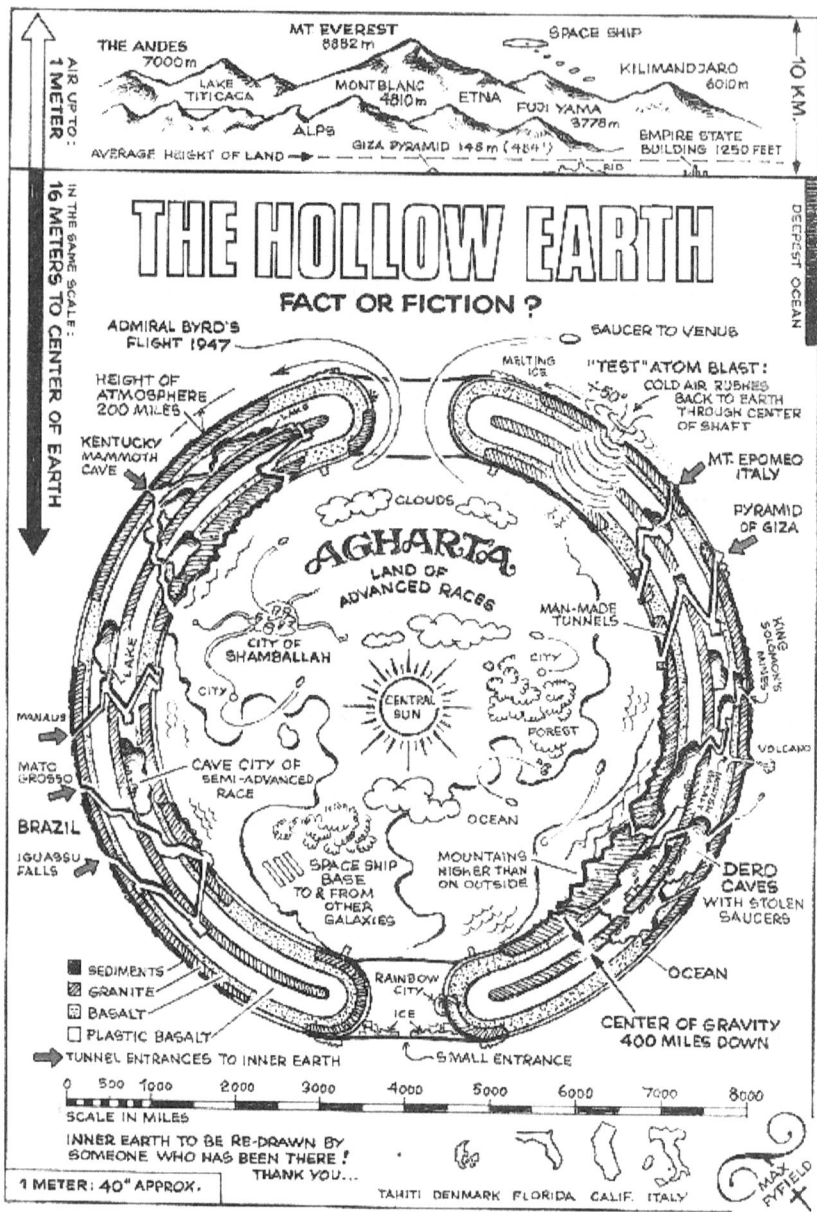

Above: A representation of the structure of Agartha. Proponents of the hollow Earth theory included Edmond Halley (1656-1742), Pierre Bouguer (1698-1753), and Charles Hutton (1737-1823).

how to develop new paradigms of consciousness.[78] It was through the application of her own protocols that she encountered a new breed of extraordinary human beings—young people with exceptional skills whom she referred to as Indigo Children by virtue of the colour of their auras or personal electromagnetic fields.

Tappe's theories regarding the nature and origins of these children were subsequently developed by Lee Carroll—an American channeller and author who has authored thirteen books including transcripts from conversations held with an extra-dimensional intelligence called Kryon who originates from the star Sirius. Like Bowie, Carroll believes that this new generation of incarnating children is reflective of a major evolution currently taking place in human consciousness—one which encompasses characteristics of high intelligence, natural psychic ability, empathy, curiosity, and a strong will. Sadly, as a result of living in a society that fails to understand the significance of these qualities, these traits tend to isolate Indigo Children from their peers and this often results in their family and peers classifying them as 'strange' or 'out-of-the-ordinary'.

Because of their inherent spiritual nature, Indigo Children are said to be difficult to control. Bowie seems to have predicted this aspect to their nature in the lyrics of *Oh! You Pretty Things* when he sings:

"Oh, You Pretty Things.
Don't you know you're driving your Mamas and Papas insane."

High Noone

Bowie was evidently predicting the imminent appearance of fledgling "homo-superiors". Although Nietzsche's and Stapledon's ideas regarding a super-race were instrumental in forming his beliefs, Bowie was also influenced by the popular science-fiction writer and the author of *2001: A Space Odyssey*, Arthur C. Clarke (1917-2008) and specifically by his third novel *Childhood's End* which he published in 1953. In it, Clarke tells of a race of mysterious aliens he called "The

Overlords"[79] who arrive on Earth with the intention of ending war, hunger and unrest. Their role is said to be that of "midwives" who are charged with the task of supervising the birth of the next iteration of humanity.

Clarke's story ends with a final generation of homo-sapiens who lived out their days in empty peace while their children roamed and explored the stars.

> "You must face the fact that yours is the last generation of homo sapiens. As to the nature of that change, we can tell you very little. All we have discovered is that it starts with a single individual—always a child—and then spreads explosively, like the formation of crystals around the first nucleus in a saturated solution. Adults will not be affected, for their minds are already set in an unalterable mould.
>
> In a few years it will all be over, and the human race will have divided in twain. There is no way back, and no future for the world you know. All the hopes and dreams of your race are ended now. You have given birth to your successors, and it is your tragedy that you will never understand them..."[80]

Back in 1971, the concept of a superior race coming to replace old and tired genetic stock remained a fanciful science fiction notion. Despite the popularity of Childhood's End the concept resided only within the minds of a fringe readership for many decades. When it eventually emerged and became infused into the national lexicon of the

---

[79] UFO researcher Timothy Good, documented the case of Swedish man Richard Hoglund who was contacted by an extraterrestrial called "Father Ra Paz" or "Rapas" who said that he represented a group called "The Overlords". The alien gave Hoglund a metal plate measuring 4.5cm. in size and about 1cm. thick made of an aluminium-type material, engraved with three rows of cryptic or hieroglyphic-type symbols. (Source: Good, Timothy, *Earth: An Alien Enterprise*, Pegasus, 2013.) The term "Overlord" was also used by the English contactee Ray Logan to describe a group of Sirian extraterrestrials that he met in the 1980s. (Source: Logan, Ray, *The Sirius Papers*, Overlord Communications, Year unknown.)

[80] Clarke, Arthur C., *Childhood's End*, Ballentine Books, 1953.

English nation it did so not through Bowie, Nietzsche or Clarke but via a cover version of *Oh! You Pretty Things* which was performed by pop heartthrob Peter Noone (1947-present day). The one-time lead singer of the English pop group Herman's Hermits had a major hit with it and took it to number 12 in the UK singles chart.[81]

A Coming Race

In *Oh! You Pretty Things* Bowie's inclusion of the term "start of the coming race" references a specific strand of esoteric philosophy. The term originally appeared in an 1871 novel by the English Member of Parliament, Edward Bulwer-Lytton (1803-1873). Titled *Vril, the Power of the Coming Race*[82] the book tells the story of a vastly superior master-race of fundamentally peaceful beings which are said to live within, and not upon, planet Earth[83] where they survive on a form of universal energy called 'Vril'. Bulwer-Lytton's description of this energy is comparable to that of Lévi's "Astral Light" and is said to be employed by the Vril-Ya[84] for a wide range of objectives—from the destruction of physical matter through to advanced healing.[85] The book also maintained that this invisible force can be harnessed and directed using a staff or through an application of mental concentration (Will). Eastern and Oriental mystics have always maintained that a similar chi-

---

[81] Peter Noone's cover of *Oh! You Pretty Things* featured Bowie on piano. It reached number 12 in the UK music charts in early 1971.
[82] Another classic Rosicrucian-inspired work by Edward Bulwer-Lytton is his 1842 novel *Zanoni* which was featured in Bowie's Top 100 books that most influenced him. The novel tells the story of its protagonist Zanoni who possesses occult powers and knows the secret to eternal life. (www.nypl.org/blog/2016/01/11/david-bowies-top-100-books)
[83] *The Coming Race* states that in time the Vril-ya will run out of habitable space underground and start claiming the surface of the planet, destroying mankind in the process should it proves necessary to do so to protect their idyllic world of peace and happiness.
[84] There is a suggestion that the Vril-Ya, who Bulwer-Lytton described as the descendants of an antediluvian civilisation called the Ana, could be related to some of the priests of the Mystery Schools of Atlantis who sought refuge underground at a time when their civilisation was destroyed by a great cataclysm such as the Great Flood.
[85] Occult theory states that the source of the power behind Vril is the "Black Sun"—an unseeable energy that operates behind Sol and which is believed to originate from the star Sirius. (Source: Young, Karl, *Third Reich Pilgrim: Part One - The Ruins of Power*, Hermitage Helm Corpus, 2012.}

like force exists and that it can be controlled and directed by an initiate using their Third Eye, or pineal gland. This is a principle which many believe to be represented by the classic all-seeing eye symbol employed by many historical and occult traditions but particularly by secret societies such as Freemasonry.[86] Bowie could well have been thinking about the Vril-Ya and their immense capacity to kill or cure using Vril energy in the lyrics to his song *The Supermen*.[87]

> *"Where all were minds in uni-thought.*
> *Power weird by mystics taught.*
> *No pain, no joy, no power too great*
> *Colossal strength to grasp a fate.*
> *Where sad-eyed mermen tossed in slumbers*
> *Nightmare dreams no mortal mind could hold.*
> *A man would tear his brother's flesh.*
> *A chance to die.*
> *To turn to mold"*

The themes Bulwer-Lytton wove into *The Coming Race* captured the imagination of several 19th-century occultists and was even taken to be factually correct by prominent members of Blavatsky's Theosophist Movement. This included Rudolf Steiner (1861-1925) who contended that Bulwer-Lytton had set his account of Inner-Earth dwellers around already established mystical philosophies: such as those related to Agartha[88] and Shambhala.[89]

A belief in the existence of an antediluvian society—one that is said to living alongside of humanity but independent of human civilisation—remains as popular today as it did in Bulwer-Lytton's era. A strand of

---

[86] The modern origin of the symbol is said to have been used by the 17th-century Bavarian secret society the Illuminati.
[87] Some commentators have also detected the influence of American horror writer H. P. Lovecraft (1890-1937) and his description of "dormant elder gods" in the same song. (Source: Carr, Roy and Shaar Murray, Charles *Bowie: An Illustrated Record*, Eel Pie, 1981)
[88] Theosophists conceptualised Agartha as a vast complex of caves beneath Tibet and that they are inhabited by demi-gods, called Asuras.
[89] Blavatsky claimed that she was in contact with a "Great White Lodge" comprised of Himalayan Adepts living in a mystical realm known as Shambhala.

modern ufological research believes that there is evidence that proves that certain types of flying saucers do not come from the stars but originate from within our Inner Earth. These craft are said to be controlled by entities who are very similar in character to that of the Vril-Ya.

The concept that the interior of our planet is home to an advanced civilisation is not a concept limited to modern conspiracy theorists[90]– although it is worth noting that many Inner Earth theories only became established after science-fiction writers such as Jules Verne (1828-1905) used it in their stories. In Verne's case it resulted in his timeless 1865 fiction story *Journey to the Centre of the Earth*.[91]

STRANGE DAYS - LIKE THESE!

In a final look at Bowie's iconic *Oh! You Pretty Things* song, it is worth examining its possible origins. Bowie claims that it spontaneously surfaced from somewhere deep within his consciousness while he was asleep. When he woke, he forged it into a more coherent form while seated at his piano.[92]

Is it common for musicians to access inspiration in this way and, if so, how many other songs have been pulled from the same astral realm? The answer is many, with notable examples being the classic hit-songs *Yesterday* by Paul McCartney (The Beatles), *Satisfaction (Can't Get No)* by Keith Richards (The Rolling Stones), *#9 Dream* (John Lennon), and *Purple Haze* by the legendary rock-guitarist Jimi Hendrix. Each of these

---

[90] See www.loc.gov/rr/scitech/SciRefGuides/hollowearth.html for a list of academic references to the Hollow Earth theory.
[91] In 1974, Rick Wakeman (1949-present day)–a classically-trained pianist who studied the piano and orchestration at the Royal College of Music in London– released a live recording of a performance of his interpretation of Verne's *Journey to the Centre of the Earth* using a narrator, choir and orchestra performed at a concert at the Royal Festival Hall, London. The album reached number 1 in the UK album charts and was a multimillion-dollar seller in six weeks of its release. Wakeman appeared on several Bowie's iconic songs including *Changes*, *Life on Mars?* and *Oh! You Pretty Things* but turned down an offer from Bowie to become a permanent member of the band preferring instead to join the prog-rock band Yes.
[92] A 2005, academic paper titled *Music in Dreams* in 2005 revealed that musicians dream about music twice as much as non-musicians leading the authors to conclude that "the recalled music was non-standard, suggesting that original music can be created in dreams." (Source: https://pubmed.ncbi.nlm.nih.gov/16243543/)

musicians have admitted that their compositions emerged from within the subconscious artist while asleep and appeared in the form of one or more dreams and the frequent way in which these timeless classics appeared suggests that the doorway to a sphere of creative and inspiring music swung open in the decade between the mid-1960s and mid-1970s. For many musicians with long term careers this period proved to be the highlight of their creative output. For Bowie, the early 1970s marked a phase of sustained creativity and it is entirely possible that a large percentage of his music emerged as a direct consequence of his ability to engage directly with the same inner-plane realm.

An example of a musical legend who drew inspiration for his work through psychic channels was referenced on Bowie's composition *Song for Bob Dylan*.[93] Although essentially a poet at heart, Dylan (1941-present day) is recognised as the spokesperson of 1960s counterculture. His method of songwriting centred upon adding music to his poetic compositions—a process that Bowie's admits formed his preferred method of composing. In *Song for Bob Dylan* he mentions the singer directly; albeit in a somewhat oblique way which led many to wonder whether he was praising or critiquing the artist[94].

Despite, or maybe because of, his monumental success, Dylan became a recluse and for many years shied away from all publicity. However, in 2004 TV personality Ed Bradley (1941-2006) managed to interview him for the popular CBS program 60 Minutes.[95] It was the first interview Dylan had given for nearly twenty years. When Bradley quizzed the singer-songwriter about the source of his inspiration—something which he pointed out had netted him a back-catalogue of over 500 songs recorded on more than forty albums—Dylan answered, "I don't know how I got to write those songs." This surprised Bradley who

---

[93] Bowie premiered *Song for Bob Dylan* on June 3, 1971, during a BBC concert session, with George Underwood (King Bees bandmate and school friend) singing lead vocals. (Source: Pegg, Nicholas (2011). The Complete David Bowie, London, Titan Books.)

[94] During the 1970s, David Bowie and Bob Dylan met on several occasions and whilst not buddies they appeared to be friendly towards each other. It has been alleged that Dylan wanted Bowie to produce his 1983 album Infidels. During 1975 and 1976, Dylan embarked upon his Rolling Thunder Revue—a 57-date, tour of North America and Canada. His band included Bowie's guitarist Mick Ronson.

[95] www.youtube.com/watch?v=hOas0d-fFK8

3. BEYOND GOOD AND EVIL

was deeply confused by the musician's response. "What do you mean you don't know how?" he asked. Dylan paused for a moment before replying:

> "Well, those early songs were like almost magically written.... Darkness at the break at noon. Shadows even the silver spoon. The handmade blade, the child's balloon."[96] Well, try to sit down and write something like that...there's a magic to that and it's not "sick freedom roy kind of magic", you know it's a... it's a different kind of a penetrating magic and, you know, I did it, I did it at one time."

John Lennon (1940-1980) also held a similar belief regarding his own creative songwriting. The ex-Beatle is widely quoted as having once said that:

> "When the real music comes to me - the music of the spheres, the music that surpasses understanding - that has nothing to do with me because I am just the channel. The only joy was for it to be given to me and to transcribe it, like a medium."[97]

Like Dylan, both Bowie and Lennon grew increasingly disillusioned with the trappings of their own success. In 1974, Lennon was being hounded by the US authorities who considered him a threat to the fabric of society following the musician's very public opposition to the Vietnam War. Following a temporary split with his girlfriend, Yoko Ono, Lennon moved out of Los Angeles and took up residence in a penthouse apartment in New York.

Bowie was also living in New York at the time and the pair often met and jammed together. This led to a one-day session at the Electric Lady

---
[96] Here Dylan is quoting from his song *Its Alright Ma (I'm Only Bleeding)*.
[97] After falling into a half-sleep one day, Lennon heard a mysterious voice that spoke t was o him across the void. It in a language that Lennon did not recognise or understand. When he was jolted awake, the words, "Ah! böwakawa poussé, poussé" filled his head around which Lennon wrote the rest of the song, *#9 Dream* which he included on the 1974 *Walls and Bridges* album.

Studios in Greenwich Village in January 1975 where the hit song Fame was written—a collaboration that led to Bowie's first single to top the Billboard Hot 100 in September 1975. The composition was an acerbic commentary on the two musician's intense dissatisfaction with the music industry which Bowie felt included "...money-grabbing managers, mindless adulation, unwanted entourages and the hollow vacuity of the limousine lifestyle...". [98]

Left: John Lennon in 1974

Like so many of Bowie's friends and acquaintances, Lennon was also deeply fascinated in the subject of UFOs. His belief in the phenomena intensified at 9:00 p.m on August 23, 1974, when he observed one at close quarters from his New York apartment. The object flew so close to the window that he said he was sure he could have thrown a brick at it!

"I was standing, naked, by this window leading on to that roof... just dreaming around in my usual poetic frame of mind... as I turned my head, hovering over the next building, no more than a hundred feet away was this thing with ordinary electric light bulbs flashing on and off round the bottom, one non-blinking red light on top. It was coasting, very quietly, like a tourist! So, I just watched. After about twenty minutes it disappeared over the East River and behind the United Nations building."[99]

Lennon was living with his 22-year-old assistant May Pang at the time and she was also able to corroborate Lennon's version of events.

---

[98] Pegg, Nicholas. *The Complete David Bowie*, Titan Books, 2016.
[99] Zabel, Bryce, *There's UFOs Over New York*, Medium, 2021.

"As I walked out onto the terrace, my eye caught this large, circular object coming towards us. It was shaped like a flattened cone, and on top was a large, brilliant red light, not pulsating as on any of the aircraft we'd see heading for a landing at Newark Airport. When it came a little closer, we could make out a row or circle of white lights that ran around the entire rim of the craft – these were also flashing on and off. There were so many of these lights that it was dazzling to the mind."[100]

Lennon referenced their UFO sighting on his *Walls and Bridges* album—released by Apple Records on September 26, 1974. The inner sleeve of the LP featured one of John's doodling which he created as a way of both illustrating his UFO experience and documenting its lasting impression upon him. It also included a whole host of other mystical symbols; including, Yin/Yang. Eye in the Triangle, Swastika (with a line through it), and I-Ching hexagrams—all of which leads one to wonder whether Lennon was also deeply interested in the occult evidenced by his reference to "Druid", "magic", and "Grail" in his 1973 song *Mind Games*.

---

[100] Ibid.

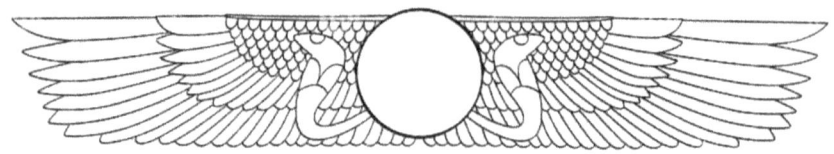

4. Stellar Atune-ment

"The spacecraft that are appearing today are under the direction of the Hierarchy of their own planets and are working in close harmony with the masters and mystery schools of the Hierarchy on Earth... Thus, we see that there is a definite connection between the mystery schools and the UFO. They are really one and the same force in operation..."

UFOs Confidential, George Hunt Williamson (1926-1986).

On July 6, 1972–the day of the broadcast of Bowie's *Top of the Pops* performance–a supremely important and portentous event took place in the heavens. On this date, the Sun arrived at a point marked by 14 degrees of the zodiac sign Cancer placing it in direct alignment (an aspect referred to in astrological terms as a 'conjunction') with the star Sirius. The two heavenly bodies had been closing in on one another from around the time that Bowie and his band walked into the BBC television studios. Twenty-four hours later–at the very moment that millions of viewers were watching him openly question the possibility of the existence of cosmic intelligences on their TV screens–our Sun and Sirius completed their consummation.

Within the annals of ancient occult and cosmological theory, this pairing had always been seen as highly portentous; for it highlights the unification of the two most influential stellar influences in our sector of the galaxy. The ancient Egyptians deemed it to be so important that they established their annual calendar around the event. Even today, remains of the ancient practice of venerating Sirius at this time of the year can be seen throughout where it is often commemorated by national public holidays. The countries of Algeria, Portugal, France, Malawi,

Philippines, Solomon Islands, and Venezuela are just a few territories that hold national holidays on or around the fourth of fifth of July each year in celebration of the concept of freedom (which astrologers maintain is underpinned by the dynamics of Sirius) or by way of commemorating their emancipation from a colonial power. The most widely known celebration of this 'Spirit of Freedom'[101] is of course celebrated in the United States as 'Independence Day' or by the 'Fourth of July' celebrations.[102]

So, what exactly is it about this Sun-Sirius conjunction that is so important from an occult or mystical perspective and what role did it play in the apparent timing of the broadcast of Bowie' *Starman* performance on *Top of the Pops*? Before we answer that let's take a closer look at the star itself.

THE GREAT PROVIDER

The star Sirius, ('Sothis' to the ancient Egyptians and 'Seirios' to the Greeks) can be easily located by extending an imaginary line downwards through the belt of Orion until it meets a bright, iridescent luminary. Astronomically speaking, the star sits within the constellation Canis Major (trans. 'big dog') and for this reason Sirius is often referred to as the 'dog star'. Not only is it the brightest star in the heavens being roughly twenty-five times the luminosity of our Sun and twice its size but it is also one of our nearest neighbours at just 8.6 light years.[103]

Sirius does not stand alone. It forms part of a binary star system with its neighbour (classified as Sirius B): an extremely dense, white-dwarf companion. While Sirius B is not visible to the naked eye its presence was detected by Alvan Clarke (1832–1897) at Dearborn Observatory in 1862 while he was testing out a new type of telescopic lens. Since then,

---

[101] Of all its esoteric associations, Sirius is most closely associated with the process of individual or collective freedom, the process of individualisation or 'coming into wholeness'.
[102] As a result of the precession of the equinox the exact date of the Sun/Sirius alignment now falls around the fifth or sixth of July each year.
[103] In the Arabic world the prominence of Sirius in the night sky made the star invaluable for guiding caravans, establishing the dates of pilgrimages, regulating calendars, and even forecasting the weather. (Source: Nogués, Miquel Forcada, Treatise on the Anwa and the Times of Ibn 'Asim, C.S.I.C., 1993.)

astrophysicists have noted the effect of what appears to be a third companion known as 'Sirius C' which romulates a rare 'trinary star system'. Sirius C is said to have been 'observed' over twenty times between 1920 and 1930)

Although modern astronomy has a great deal to discover regarding the Sirius star system, astrophysicists are, in many ways, way behind understanding star and the fact that there is also a direct connection between it and our own solar system towards which it is said to be advancing at speed and that it will will continue to do so for the next 210,000 years.[104] While this is a relatively recent scientific theory references to the existence of a binary relationship between our Sun and Sirius was recorded within many ancient sacred texts: particularly within those written in the Far and Middle East.

Not only does an orbital relationship exist between the two stellar bodies but an important metaphysical link connects them. The intense elctromagnetic energy given off by Sirius radiates to Earth via its connection to our Sun and this relationship underpins one of the most fundamental secrets to the dog-star. Many sacred teachings refer to Sirius in its role as a master behind our slave Sun by using such terms as; 'The Sun behind the Sun', 'The Midnight Sun', 'Our Spiritual Sun', the 'God Star', and 'The Black Sun'.

The pivotal role Sirius is said to play in guiding our solar system caused it to be designated the 'Source of all Things' or, as French Egyptologist Schwaller De Lubicz (1887-1961) put it:

> "The double star of Sirius - which for Pharaonic Egypt played the role of central sun to our entire solar system - today suggests the existence of a cosmic system of atomic structure whose nucleus is this 'Great Provider,' the Sothis [spd.t] of the ancients. There might well be a need to revise our cosmology in the not-so-distant future."[105]

---

[104] Cruttenden, Walter, *The Lost Star of Myth and Time*, St. Lynn's Press, 2005.
[105] Schwaller de Lubicz, R.A., *Le Roi de la Théocratie Pharaonique* (trans. *Sacred Science: The King of Pharaonic Theocracy*), published privately, 1958.

4. Stellar Atune-ment

From the perspective of our planet, Sirius has a very interesting orbital period. Because of its displacement from the ecliptic, the star exhibits a remarkably regular cyclic period which lasts exactly 365.25 days. The ancient Egyptians noted this fact and integrated it into their annual calendar starting with the first month that was said to be ruled by the god Thoth. The ancient Egyptian New Year was timed to start when the heliacal rising of Sirius was observed from Cairo astronomical observatories: sometime around July 19 in our Julian calendar. Coincidently, this date also coincided with the seasonal melting of mountain snow in the north of the country. This huge volume of freshwater flowed into the Nile which resulted in the flooding of large areas of land adjacent the banks of the river.[106] The rich, alluvial soil left behind once the flood had abated contributed greatly to the fertility of large tracts of arable land; the produce from which stimulated the wealth of the whole country. This natural wonder led to the ancient Egyptian's associating Sirius' associated deity, the goddess Isis to become known as 'The Great Provider'.

Ancient Mystery Schools

The observatories of Cairo were not the only centres which were used to track the motion of Sirius (often referred to as the 'Sothic Period'). Many different cultures over many millennia did similar and as a result collected vast repositories of ancient astronomical knowledge about the star. Much of this has been lost over the passage of time but many of their insights can still be found encoded into their architecture. The ancient Egyptians, for example, integrated a great deal of stellar gnosis into the fabrication of their temples as well as in many their wall paintings.

However, it was not common practice to record advanced astronomical data in such a way—only stellar mythology and important astronomical events. Deeper understanding of ancient knowledge related to the Sirius was jealously guarded by the elite who secured it within libraries of advanced occult learning. The only initiates with access to this sacred teaching were those who had be admitted to one of

---

[106] The original name for Egypt is 'kemet' which means 'black lands'. This is a direct reference to the rich alluvial soil that was deposited on its banks following the annual flooding of the river Nile.

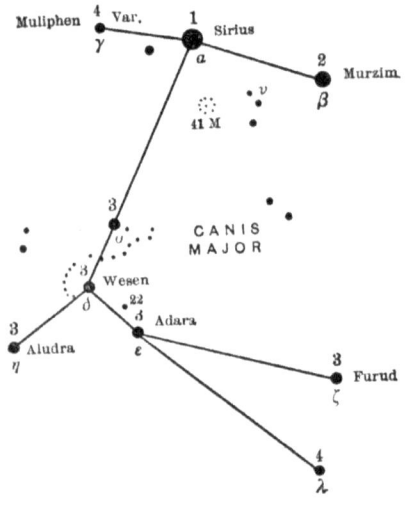

Left: Sirius: the alpha majoris of the Canis Major (Big Dog) star-grouping.

several ancient 'Mystery Schools' which were scattered throughout regions within southern Europe, the Mediterranean, as well as throughout the more northerly regions of the United Kingdom, Northern Europe, and Scandinavia.

The origins of these storehouses of arcana have been dated as far back as the time of Atlantis (around 10,500B.C.) but most of them are believed to have been destroyed—along with the rich repository of information they contained—during a great flood which is said to have engulfed and sunk Plato's legendary land. As a result of this and similar tragedies (including the burning down of the Library of Alexandria by Christians in 391A. D.) most of the written knowledge pertaining to the Sirius star system were lost. Fortunately, we can still find a proof of their existence encoded within the teachings of modern secret societies; particularly those of the Rosicrucians and Freemasons as well as in such early mystery religions as Mithraism, Zoroastrianism, and Islam.[107]

Although physically lost, some ancient star knowledge is being rediscovered by mystics, psychics, and dedicated occult researchers. Their discoveries and insights suggest that the Atlantean mystery schools had two primary components. Not only were they physical repositories of esoteric knowledge but they also had a complimentary system of education which was located in the higher-dimensional realms of Sirius itself. A conduit between the two schools of learning was

---

[107] The Theosophical Glossary quotes Helena Blavatsky's references to Sirius. "Thus Sothis-Sirius had, and still has, a mystic and direct influence over the whole living heaven and is connected with almost every god and goddess,; Being connected with the Pyramid, Sirius was, therefore, connected with the initiations which took place in it."

4. Stellar Atune-ment

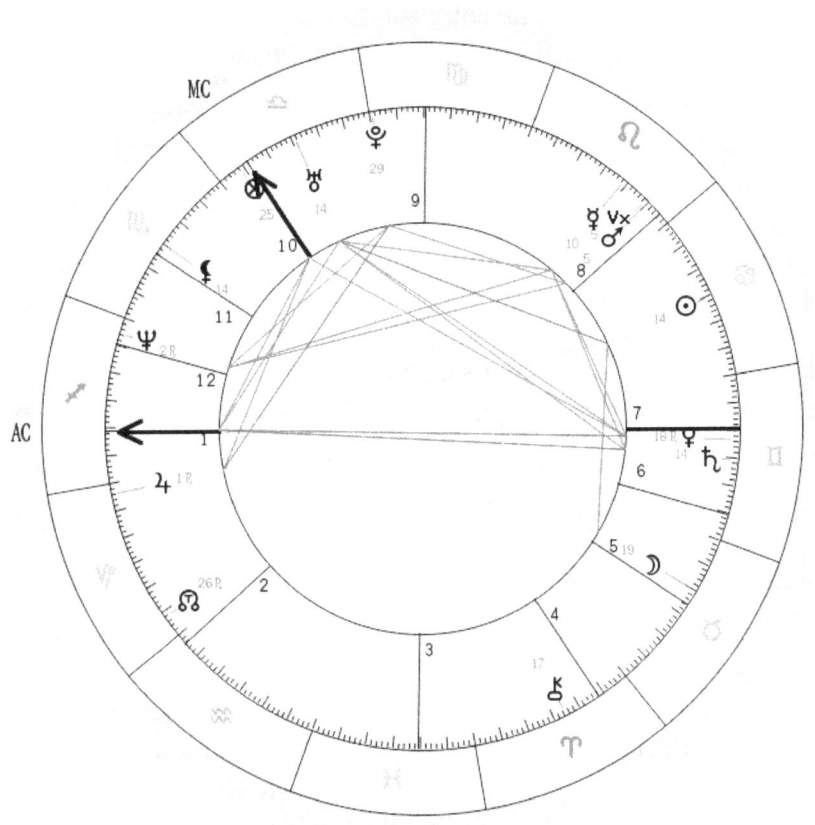

Above: Astrological chart for Bowie's Top of the Pops performance of Starman broadcast by the BBC on July 6 7:30pm. The Sun (indicated by a dot inside a circle) is at 14 degrees of Cancer and exactly conjunct the star Sirius.

Note: The Part of Fortune is conjunct the M.C.–i.e. directly overhead at the time. This position denotes a great potential for the realisation of career opportunities or "This aspect suggests that your personal goals and aspirations align with the opportunities for growth and abundance that the universe presents to you." (Source: www.astromatrix.org) Might this explain the phenomenal rise to fame Bowie experienced shortly after the programme's transmission?

established via an 'energetic link'; one that connected the Earth-based schools of spiritual teaching with their etheric counterparts. [108]

There is a good reason why these secret repositories of learning are often referred to as ancient 'mystery' schools for they jealously guarded their arcane secrets from access by the profane. The schools vast repository of knowledge were only made accessible to those initiates who proved themselves 'worthy' and had attained a certain level of spiritual attainment—a heightened, energetic state initiated through years of spiritual development and enlightenment. The Mystery Schools adopted a strict graded system of initiation to help facilitate the development of a student as they attained occult insight.

The same graded system also operated on what was an astral counterpart to a school and this was located on Sirius where esoteric knowledge was stored not in the form of dusty scrolls and parchments but as light-energy held in crystalline containers within temples.[109]

A residue of this graded system of initiation can be found in modern Freemasonry and particularly in its 33rd Degree. Very few Masons ever reach this point of attainment and so little is known regarding the form of metaphysical teaching disseminated at this level. However, as we shall see later on, there is very good reason to believe that 33rd Degree Masonry is based upon contact with Sirius and/or Sirians.

The ancient system of initiation once used by Freemasonry has unfortunately lost much of its occult/magick potency. How relevant this ancient system of Sirian initiation would have been in today's Masonic tradition is open to debate but the monopoly it and similar secret societies once held over sacred Sirian teachings has largely faded now that so much of it is re-emerging via the psychic, archeological, and historical channels of research.

---

[108] A common feature believed to have been central in securing this 'magnetic' or 'astral' link is the pyramid, or cone-shaped hill, such as the Great Pyramid of Egypt, Silbury Hill in England, the Aztec temples, and the Bosnian pyramids.
[109] Several of these star temples remain in existence today and occultists or 'astral travellers' who can access them have described seeing them as huge crystalline structures which, once entered, are found to contain vast libraries of esoteric knowledge being administered by librarians.

4. STELLAR ATUNE-MENT

Nevertheless, not all of the knowledge contained in the Halls of Learning on Sirius is accessible via intellectual study, psychic perception, or through years of 'spiritual atunement'. Some of the scientific or metaphysical information contained in these academic repositories helped to establish our modern civilisation and these were disseminated by spiritually-advanced teachers from Sirius. These Sirians were (and still are) occasionally 'sent' to our planet with the specific task of seeding humanity with knowledge and information geared towards an advancement in the human race. Many of them work unseen and unrecognised within established institutions but the work of other Sirian guides is rather better known. Many great inventors, artists, and musicians—people such as Leonardo da Vinci, Nikola Tesla, and Mozart—have been found to have utilised knowledge drawn from a sphere that exists far beyond the scope of human intelligence. In fact, all the great 'creatives' demonstrate a link to what we might refer to as 'stellar ancestry'.

Certain extra-dimensional groups closely aligned to Sirius have also been involved in the dissemination of scientific and technical knowledge but in somewhat unorthodox ways. In this regard it is interesting to note that the famous Roswell UFO crash took place on July 5, 1947: exactly twenty-five years prior to the day of the Bowie broadcast on July 5, 1972. Over the intervening period ufologists have suggested that some of the wreckage from the downed craft was recovered and back-engineered by the US military which resulted in a vast array of technological innovations in common use today. If this is true, then the alien occupants of the Roswell craft may have deliberately downed their own vehicle as a way of passing on technological information to humans.

THE CREATIVE WORD

The graded systems of initiation used by the mystery schools were cloaked in symbolism and allegory: disguised in such a way that it made this knowledge inaccessible to the uninitiated. This system is used today by all secret societies but their efforts to safe-guard their teachings have often been breached. One of those who published meaningful and specific information related to the metaphysical qualities of Sirius was the English occultist Alice A. Bailey (1880-1949). Bailey became a leading-light in the modern spiritual movement due to her claim that she had a direct connection to what are referred to as 'Hidden Masters' from whom she received important insights into mystery school teachings.

Left: Esoteric writer and channeller Alice A. Bailey (1880-1949).

Born in Manchester, England, Alice moved to the United States in 1907 where she established herself as a spiritual teacher and metaphysical writer. Her journey into esotericism started at the age of fifteen when one day, while her family were attending the local church, a tall, Eastern-looking man dressed in a turban inexplicably appeared in her room.[110]

The stranger identified himself as Djwhal Khul (D.K.) He explained that he was one of the 'Ascended Masters'—or 'Secret Chiefs' as the Order of the Golden Dawn came to call them; an initiate of what the Theosophical Society termed 'The Ageless Wisdom' or 'Perennial Philosophy'.[111]

He explained that Alice had been chosen by 'them' to fulfil a great spiritual mission but that her ability to follow this path depended upon her moving away from her current mental and emotional focus on petty, personal concerns. Alice agreed and her contact returned every seven years to give her spiritual instruction. Most of the spiritual information Bailey received from D.K. was delivered telepathically between 1919 and 1949 and with guidance from her 'Master', Bailey eventually completed a series of twenty-four books of occult wisdom which were

---

[110] The Hidden Masters often appear to be of eastern descent which causes many researchers to associate them with India, Tibet, and even the Lost City of Shambhala.
[111] The "Perennial Philosophy" views the world's religious traditions as sharing a single, metaphysical truth or origin from which all esoteric and exoteric knowledge and doctrine has emerged. (Source: https://en.wikipedia.org/wiki/Perennial_philosophy)

4. Stellar Atune-ment

published by the Lucis Trust. These covered a wide range of metaphysical topics; including; an in-depth assessment of the dynamic energies and interaction between stars, planets, and zodiacal signs; discussion of the cosmic laws that underpin their motion; the advanced practices of meditation, healing, and psychology; and well as advice on how human society can restructure itself around more spiritual principles. They also revealed a great deal of metaphysical information related to The Sirius Mythos and its modern iteration.

In their discussions, D.K. explained to Alice that there are a series of 'paths' which an occult initiate can take. One of these he referred to as the 'Path of Sirius' but she was given very little additional information about it. In *Initiation, Human and Solar*[112] she wrote:

> "Very little can be communicated about this Path. In the mystery of this influence, and in the secret of the sun Sirius, are hidden the facts of our cosmic evolution, and incidentally, therefore, of our solar system. First and foremost is the energy or force emanating from the sun Sirius. If it might be so expressed, the energy of thought, or mind force, in its totality, reaches the solar system from a distant cosmic centre via Sirius. Sirius acts as the transmitter, or the focalizing centre, whence emanate those influences which produce self-consciousness in men."

D.K. explained that the influence of Sirius does not reach Earth directly but it is first transmitted to the planet Saturn prior to being redirected to our planet. This, in a sense, enables its power to be 'stepped down' or reduced in potency so that it does not burn through and destroy the cellular structures within life-forms on this planet.

That being said, he also explained that, should an initiate so choose, it is possible to partly circumnavigate this protection and take what Bailey described as a sequence of "initiations" into the Siriun current.

---

[112] Bailey, Alice, *Initiation, Human and Solar*, Lucis Press, 1922.

These enable a neophyte to acclimatise themselves to the originating power radiated by the star. At these points of transformation—which have the effect of upgrading the energetic field (aura) or light codes within the DNA of the human body/psyche—the energised field momentarily intensifies and is, as Bailey put it, "...applied to the centers of the initiate with terrific force."

The "centers" she references are unseen energy points located within the human body. They are referred to in Hinduism as 'chakras'—a Sanskrit word meaning 'wheel' or 'cycle'. They are said to number between seven and twelve depending upon the level of spiritual development of an individual. They are positioned along the length of the spine; spreading from the bottom (anus) up to the top of the head. In a healthily functioning individual these wheels of electromagnetic energy are in perfect alignment and well-balanced causing them to rotate and disseminate energy between one another.[113] Bailey stated that the path that leads to Siriun initiation requires the initiate to step up, or refine, each of these centers so that the star's energy can be attuned to and safely infused into their spiritual body.

D.K. stated that the nature of this Siriun influence is predominantly comprised of 'mind-energy' and is experienced "...primarily in the throat center"—something she described as "the great organ of creation through sound." This is an interesting statement for it may partially explain why some singers and musicians have an ability to intone the energy of Sirius during a vocal performance.[114] On this specific subject Bailey wrote:

---

[113] Psychic healers maintain that physical ailments within the human body can be attributed to one or more centre being out of alignment, damaged, or clogged with accumulated dark astral material.

[114] Lou Reed (1942-2013) of the American rock band Velvet Underground is said to have been a devotee of Bailey and was impressed with her book *A Treatise on White Magic* which author Ryan H. Walsh suggests influenced the Velvet Underground's second album, *White Light/White Heat* released in 1968. Bowie and Reed were close friends, and he recorded a version of *White Light/White Heat* during the 1973 *Pin Ups* album recording sessions. It was not included on the album, but the backing track was used on Mick Ronson's second solo album, *Play Don't Worry*, released in 1975 with Ronson adding new vocals. Bowie included the song in his live performances between his 1972 *Ziggy Stardust* Tour through to his final tour in 2003-4.

> "The throat center is the organ specifically of the creative WORD. It registers the intention or creative purpose of the soul, transmitted to it by the inflow of energy from the ajna center; the fusion of the two energies, thus brought about, will lead to some type of creative activity. This is the higher correspondence to the creativity of the sacral center. In that center the negative and the positive creative energies are embodied in the separate male and female organisms and are brought into relation in an act of creation, consciously undertaken, though as yet without much definite purpose."[115]

The Three Centers

I have already touched upon sleep and dream incubation as a method by which creative individuals have been able to access an unconscious stream of inspiration—some of which appears to include ideas, concepts, and inspired wisdom that extends beyond the consciousness of most individuals on this planet. Bailey confirmed that this is a process that the ancient mystery schools used to connect to the Sirian temples of learning while in an active astral state,

In *Letters on Occult Meditation*—a collection of conversations held with D.K. from May 16, 1920 and October 20, 1920, she mentions that spiritual work often occurs during sleep when the astral body is open to a wide range of cosmic influences.

> "By work done on the emotional body at night under the direction of more advanced egos, working under the guidance of a Master. Stimulation of vibration or the deadening of vibration follows on the application of certain colour s and sounds. At this particular time two colour s are being applied to many people for the specific purpose of keying up the throat and foremost head center, namely, violet and gold."[116]

[115] Bailey, Alice, A., *Esoteric Healing*, Lucis Press, 1953.
[116] Bailey, Alice A., *Letters on Occult Meditation - Letter X - The Purification of the*

Throughout her works Bailey reiterates her belief that the throat center is one of three primary chakras in the human body which, if and when they are unified, results in the development of a major "Triangle of Force". The chakras in question are those positioned in the throat area, within the human heart', and at a location said to be the 'head center'. When these are correctly activated, they are said to work in unison and create a powerful triad of force. This is centred in an area of the brain commonly referred to as the 'Pineal Gland'. For thousands of years, mystics have referred to this small organ as the 'Third Eye'[117]—a point through which the human soul can manifest.

Under normal circumstances the Third Eye is inert and inactive. The level of psycho-spiritual work required to fully develop and awaken this faculty of inner illumination is not easy to attain and the complete unification of the three centers is only achieved by those initiates who manage to divert enough of the energy residing in the four lower centers of the body up the spine and into the Heart Centre. Bailey explains the process in the following way:

> "Before the three physical head centers awaken, man is largely subjected to force flowing through the four minor etheric centers; later the three major centers - the head, the heart, and the throat - begin to vibrate, gradually assuming a greater sweep of activity, till their energy tends to negate that of the lower centers, to absorb their vitality and deflect the direction of their vitality, until the three higher wheels are in full fourth dimensional activity."[118]

This may well be a process that many modern rock musicians go through and there is circumstantial evidence to suggest Bowie was one of those who was able to create the reality he desired by developing a

---

Vehicles, Lucis Trust, 1922.
[117] Secret societies have long since symbolised this process of unfoldment and subsequent Third Eye activation with a symbol denoting an eye positioned in the centre of an equilateral triangle. The eye in the triangle motif appears in connection with advanced degrees of Freemasonry and the US Dollar bill.
[118] Bailey, Alice A., *A Treatise on Cosmic Fire*, Lucis Press, 1925.

similar 'triangle of force' within himself. In fact, it is not difficult to find within his lyrics and various important stages in his life to an energisation of these three centers.

1: Heart Center

Bowie was well-aware of the esoteric importance of the human heart—and not just as an organ used for pumping blood around the vascular system. He understood its powerful role when activated as an energy center and referenced this in the lyrics to his song *Fill Your Heart* recorded for his *Hunky Dory* album.

> *"Fill your heart with love today.*
> *Don't play the game of time.*
> *Things that happened in the past.*
> *Only happened in your Mind*
> *Love cleans the mind.*
> *And makes it Free."*

2: Throat Center

Being a singer, the throat was the primary center through which Bowie found artistic expression—his way of communicating his vision of the World.[119] Regarding this chakra, Bailey states:

> "This center is to be found at the back of the neck, reaching up into the medulla oblongata, thus involving the carotid gland, and down towards the shoulder blades. It is an exceedingly powerful and well developed center where average humanity is concerned."[120]

Bowie not only used his throat center as a conduit via which to

---

[119] Early on in his career as an entertainer, Bowie was trained in the art of mime by choreographer Lindsay Kemp (1938-2018). T. Rex front-man Marc Bolan invited Bowie to open for him during their UK tour of 1969. Bowie performed a one-man, silent, mime routine, which is said to have depicted China's invasion of Tibet. His performances were met with derision from the audience at most of the gigs. (Source: https://faroutmagazine.co.uk/david-bowie-t-rex-one-man-mime-act/)
[120] Bailey, Alice A., *Esoteric Healing*, Lucis Press, 1953.

express his art but he also used it to employ an ancient technique known as 'in-toning' or 'vibrating'—an occult practice which harnesses and increases the energy emitted from this center. The tone, or frequency, used can vary according to the preference of the student but when Bowie practised it he utilised the sacred 'AUM'[121] which is an ancient sacred mantra used to clear the energy fields surrounding an individual prior to any magickal, spiritual, or religious work. Primarily an Eastern practice, Alice Bailey maintained that the AUM mantra had become corrupted in the West through its over-use by Christianity which had incorrectly turned it into the traditional 'Amen' uttered at the end of most prayers or religious rituals. This shift from its intended function caused D. K. to refer to it as "...the lowest aspect of the originating Sound."[122] He later added:

> "The use of the Amen in the ritual of the Christian Church will eventually be discouraged, because it is basically a materialistic affirmation, being usually regarded by the average churchgoer as setting the seal of divine approval upon his demand to the Almighty for protection, or for the supply of his physical necessities; all this is, therefore, related to the life of desire, of aspiration, of dualism and of request."

Regarding this insight into the Western misuse of the Eastern AUM sound, it is interesting to reference the lyrics to Bowie's 1969 song *Cygnet Committee* which includes the line "We slit the Catholic throat" which is suggestive of an attempt to suppress the church's intonation of 'Amen'.) The title of the song from which these lyrics are referenced is also of some relevance. A cygnet is, of course, the name given to a young swan and Bailey maintains that there is a connection between the AUM and the ancient star constellation Cygnus[123]—a word that forms the

---

[121] White, Timothy. Musician, May 1983 - https://www.moredarkthanshark.org/eno_int_musician-may83.html
[122] Bailey, Alice A., *The Rays and the Initiations*, Lucis Trust, 1960.
[123] Cygnus was among the 48 constellations listed by the 2nd century astronomer Ptolemy, and it remains one of the 88 modern constellations.

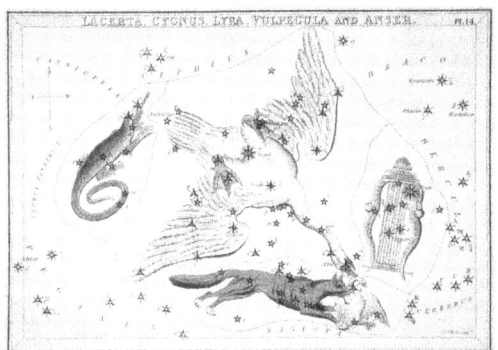

Left: The constellation Cygnus (the Swan) depicted on cards published in London c.1825. Surrounding it are the stars Lacerta, Vulpecula and Lyra—which features highly in the history of extraterrestrial contact.

Latinized Greek name for 'swan'. The writer also draws the attention of readers of her book *The Labors of Hercules* to the fact that H. P. Blavatsky—the founder of the Theosophical Society—says of the swan, or what she described as "the great bird":

> "And then thou canst repose between the wings of the great bird. Aye, sweet to rest between the wings of that which is not born, nor dies, but is the AUM[124] throughout eternal ages".[125]

Cygnus—the swan—is the stellar symbol of the 'bird of spirit' in the Nada-Bindu Upanishad (Rig Veda). The Kumbakonam Theosophical Society states that the sacred word is connected to the swan in the following way.

> "The syllable A is considered to be its (the bird Hamsa's) right wing, U, its left, M, its tail, and the Ardha-matra (half metre) is said to be its head."

3: Head Centre (Inner Eye)

Energisation of the head chakra has a profound effect. Bailey maintained that it activates a triad of power which in turn awakens the Pineal Gland which is linked to the Third, or Inner eye..

---

[124] The letters A. U. M. are also believed to represent the Latin term 'Artifex Universus Mundi' which translates to "The Great Architect of the World"—a term which is extensively used in Freemasonry.

[125] Blavatsky, H. P., *The Voice of the Silence*, The Theosophical Publishing Society, 1889.

> "When the triangle of force that these three physical centers form is in circulatory effect, the greater triangle can be seen in circulation; it then becomes a "wheel turning upon itself. The major etheric centers are in full action, and the man is nearing the moment of liberation."[126]

The Third Eye also regulates energies within the human eyes and it is interesting to note that Bowie had an particular relationship with his organs of vision.

1. Bowie had a distinct set of eyes of differing colours, brought about through an altercation he had as a youngster over a girl called Carol Goldsmith. Some sources maintain that Bowie was also afflicted with a condition known as 'anisocoria' which resulted in the pupils of his eyes being different sizes.

2. Eyes are referenced in several of Bowie's music videos. In one of his final video productions, for his song *Lazarus* he appears with bandages covering his eyes with two small holes—where his eyes should be— marked by small black buttons.

3. On the cover of his album *Aladdin Sane*, Bowie poses with a red and blue lightning flash descending from the top of his head down, across his face, and which encompasses his right eye. Bowie's right eye was also highlighted in 1974 when he created a character he called 'Halloween Jack'—a sort of space pirate character employed for his *Diamond Dogs* album. Press photos taken to promote the musician dressed in his character appeared that year in the teen music magazine *Top Pop Scene*. Here, Bowie was shown sporting a black patch over his right eye. In the same publication, the artist was also shown performing live and can be seen sporting a large, colourful patch

---
[126] Bailey, Alice A., *A Treatise on Cosmic Fire*, Lucis Press, 1925.

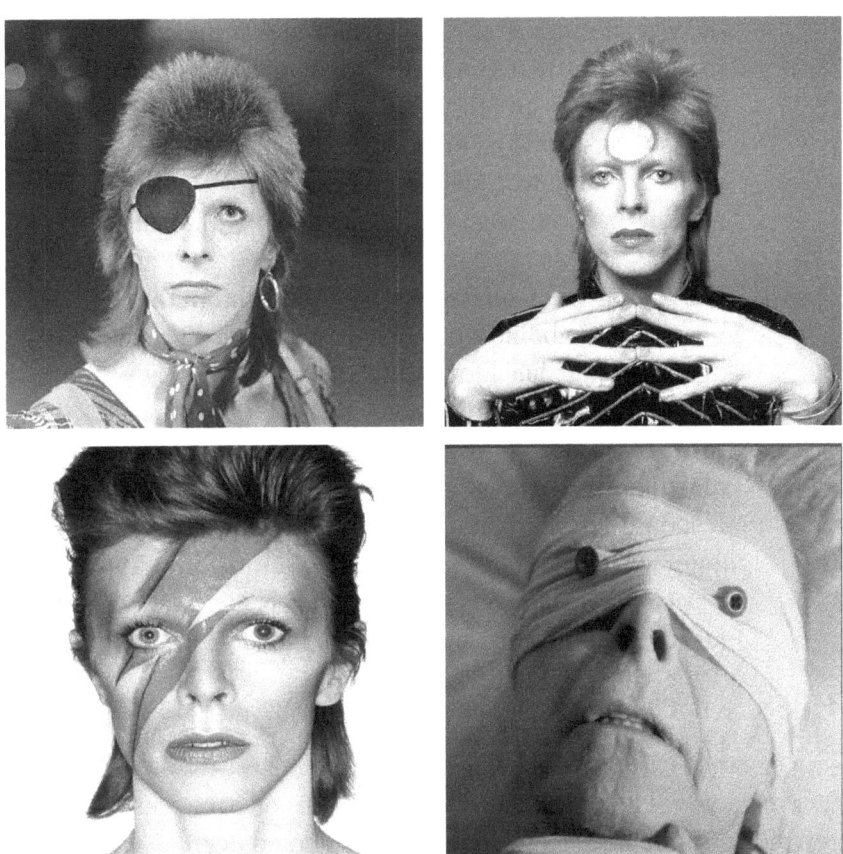

Above: Artistic expression or occult symbolism? David Bowie and his many references to his made throughout his career.

located in the centre of his forehead and directly over the location of his Third Eye. Regarding the esoteric significance of the eyes, Bailey stated that...

"The stage of the "awakening urge." Of this stage, the half-opened eye is the symbol. The neophyte, just admitted into the Ashram, becomes (as the Book of Instructions for Neophytes expresses it) "the victim of a dual sight. With the right eye he sees a shaded way into the central Ashram; from point to point, from light to dark and dark to light as the pillars point the way, he sees a narrow corridor and at the end a room; within that room the passing figure of the Master appears and disappears. With the left eye, a world of mist and fog, of gloom and shadowy forms is seen - a land of woe and dire distress, with light and shadow moving back and forth. From within that gloomy land a cry comes forth: We need your aid. We cannot see. Come hither with the light. In these phrases is embodied the first reaction of the new disciple to the dual life to which his admission to the Ashram has committed him - the life of ashramic instruction and of steady approach to the Master, plus the life of outer service which must come as a response to need and not as a fulfilment of an enjoined duty. He sees in neither direction with clarity. Remember ever that approach and service must be self-initiated and self-implemented."[127]

ETs: Sons of God?

The range of topics Alice Bailey published in here twenty-four books was immense. They included every facet of modern occult work and revealed esoteric knowledge to an unprecedented degree. Said to form part of the "ancient wisdom teachings", D.K. and Bailey's intention was that they would establish a library spiritual teachings that would guide humanity into what they foresaw as a "New Age". They proved to be correct in their assumption for their body of work has continued to grow in importance within the Western esoteric movement during the past few decades—an era which saw a dramatic rise of interest in UFOs.

Although their corpus of work covered contemporary topics such as alternative healthcare, future education, and in-depth psychology, they make no specific reference to flying saucers or unidentified flying objects. Considering that it was so future-centric this does appear to be a strange omission. Were extraterrestrials even thought of by Bailey and D.K. as forming an important part of a new spirituality movement? It

---
[127] Bailey, Alice A., *Discipleship in the New Age II*, Lucis Press, 1955.

was, but to find evidence of their awareness of extraterrestrials one has to study their work from a different perspective.

Back in the 1940s UFO terminology had yet to find its way into the English lexicon—or anyone else's for that matter. Nevertheless, it is apparent that Bailey and D.K. were aware of the 'ageless teachings' which often describe anomalous aerial objects. Bailey characterised them not as flying saucers but as 'craft' connected to higher-dimensional "Ascended Masters" who utilised vehicles of etheric light-energy as their transportation system. In September 1940, Bailey and D.K. specifically referred to these off-planet visitors in her book *The Externalisation of the Hierarchy*.

> "There still remains one mode of intervention which is still more mysterious, illimitably more powerful, and definitely more difficult to evoke and subsequently to contact. This is the emergence, response, or appearing of great Sons of God Who dwell in sources far removed from our planetary life altogether..."

The same publication also included veiled comments Bailey made in 1935 regarding the form and function of these "Sons of God" or ultra-dimensionals. On page 25 she points to "...the regenerative forces of Those extraplanetary Beings Who offer Their Help at this time." In *The Externalisation of the Hierarchy* she included transcripts of further conversations conducted with D.K. between April and May 1940.

> "Hovering today within the aura of our planet are certain great spiritual Forces and Entities, awaiting the opportunity to participate actively in the work of world redemption, re-adjustment and reconstruction.... the waiting extra-planetary Forces."

If Bailey was correct in her assertion that certain UFOs are balls of heightened consciousness operated by extraterrestrials who are

"...awaiting the opportunity to participate actively in the work of World redemption", then it is interesting to compare her statement with the many reports submitted by World War Two airmen who claimed to have been followed by balls of plasma-like, light-energy while flying aerial missions. They referred to these mysterious lights by a variety of names including 'Foo Fighters', 'Balls of Fire', 'Ghost Fliers', and 'Ghost Rockets'. Pilots reported seeing them over an area that stretched from Scandinavia to North Africa and from the Bay of Biscay to the Russian Front. Not only were they observed by the crews of aircraft operated by the Allies but also by opposing forces which led to the strange situation in which all sides involved in the war believed they were witnessing advanced technology owned by their enemies.

In describing these strange lights, pilots often stated that they exhibited flight characteristics which gave them the distinct impression of being operated or controlled by an external intelligence. Not only did the orbs fly alongside aircraft but they also demonstrated an uncanny ability to accelerate and decelerate at high speed; thereby enabling them to stay close to the planes they were following. Whenever circumstances required it, they would swerve in any direction to avoid being hit when fired upon by air and ground-based gunners.

In April 1943, D.K. drew Alice's attention to what he described as "Certain great Energies of extra-planetary significance Who stand ready to intervene...". It is difficult to think of what wartime circumstances might have had to occur to force them to become involved in the conflict. Perhaps D.K. was suggesting that the intelligences were considering stopping innocent lives from being lost through aerial bombardments, by trying to limit the impact of Nazi deployment of V2 rockets fired at London, or the carpet-bombing of German industrial cities by the Allied forces but this appears not to have been the case. When viewing the worst atrocity of the World War Two—namely America's decimation of the Japanese cities of Hiroshima and Nagasaki using atomic bombs—there is no indication that they made any sort of effort to stop the innocent slaughter of hundreds of thousands of Japanese citizens.

To many, D. K.'s comments will therefore appear somewhat

incongruous. UFO history records accounts given by many 1950s contactees who said that they had been personally assured by the extraterrestrials they interacted with that they WOULD intervene in the case of a full-scale nuclear war. In the case of the dropping of the atomic bombs on Japan, this does not seem to have been the case although to counter this argument it is worth noting that there have been numerous reports of UFOs appearing at nuclear weapons facilities[128] whereby they directly took over and controlled launch sequences in a way that seems to be a concerted reminder to truculent humans of just who is really in charge of things down here.

World War Two was, like all conflicts, a dirty affair. Bailey addresses this in her book *The Reappearance of the Christ* (1947) and stated that the cause of the war was partly due to "A welling up of magnetic force on Sirius, which produces effects upon our solar system and particularly upon our Earth, via the Hierarchy."[129] She also made an interesting reference to the possible intention of the Sons of God (i.e. extra- or ultra- terrestrials).

> "I have made two affirmations during the past years anent the Hierarchy. One was that as a result of the cleansing of the Earth through the medium of the world war (1914-1945) and through the suffering to which humanity has been subjected (with a consequent purifying effect which will demonstrate later), it will be possible for the Hierarchy to externalize itself and function openly upon the physical plane. This will indicate a return to the situation which existed in Atlantean days when (using the Biblical symbolism) God Himself walked among men - divinity was present in physical form because the Members of the Hierarchy were guiding and directing the affairs of humanity as far as innate free will permitted. On a higher turn of the spiral,

---
[128] Hastings, Robert L., *UFOs Nukes Extraordinary Encounters at Nuclear Weapons Sites*, Createspace, 2017.
[129] Bailey, Alice A., *Esoteric Astrology*, Lucis Publishing, 1951.

> this again will happen. The Masters will walk openly among men. Secondly, the Hierarchy will then restore the ancient Mysteries, the ancient landmarks so earnestly preserved by the Masonic tradition, and which have been securely embalmed in the Masonic ritual, awaiting the day of resurrection."

This sounds as close to the idea of a mass-landing by extra-terrestrials on planet Earth as it is possible to get and her reference to what she called the "Hierarchy" is somewhat reminiscent of the graded structure used by secret societies. She wrote:

> "These ancient Mysteries were originally given to humanity by the Hierarchy and were - in their turn - received by the Hierarchy from the Great White Lodge on Sirius. They contain the clue to the evolutionary process, hidden in numbers and in words; they veil the secret of man's origin and destiny, picturing for him in rite and ritual the long, long path which he must tread. They provide also, when rightly interpreted and correctly presented, the teaching which humanity needs in order to progress from darkness to Light, from the unreal to the Real and from death to Immortality."

Bailey believed Freemasonry to be the conduit through which the lost knowledge of the ancients could be disseminated. She also stated that the astral connection between Masonic temples on Earth and the "Great White Lodge of Sirius" will be re-established in a form more closely reflective of the way they operated in Atlantean times.

> "Any true Mason who understands, even if only to a slight degree, the implications of that in which he participates will recognize this most ancient of Oriental prayers, giving the key to the three degrees of the Blue Lodge. I mention here the Masonic purpose because it is closely related to the

> restoration of the Mysteries and has held the clue - down the ages - to that long-awaited restoration, to the platform upon which the restored teaching can be based, and the structure which can express, in powerful ritual and in organized detailed rites, the history of man's moving forward upon the Path of Return."

And finally, regarding the nature of the ancient knowledge brought by the "Wise Ones" Bailey stated:

> "The Mysteries will be restored in other ways also, for they contain much besides that which the Masonic rites can reveal or that religious rituals and ceremonies can disclose; they contain within their teaching and formulas the key to the science which will unlock the mystery of electricity - that mystery of which H.P.B. spoke[130]; though much progress has already been made by science along this line, it is as yet only embryonic in nature, and only when the Hierarchy is present visibly on Earth, and the Mysteries of which the Masters are the Custodians are given openly to man, will the true secret and nature of electrical phenomena be revealed."[131]

The central ethos behind the work of of Alice Bailey is perhaps summed up in this statement; for it references a central premise that, while mankind has the potential so make huge spiritual advancements through its own effort, it will only truly understand the workings of the cosmos from advanced knowledge brought by external teachers. This is also a central theme that permeates the message extraterrestrials often try to impress upon contactees right across the World.

---

[130] Blavatsky maintained that "there are no blind and mechanical forces in the cosmos. Everything is an expression of some kind of intelligence. Even electricity is said to be a manifestation of the elementals i.e., angels etc." (Source: Blavatsky, H. P., *The Secret Doctrine*,Theosophical Publishing House, 1993.
[131] Bailey, Alice A., *The Reappearance of the Christ*, Lucis Press, 1947.

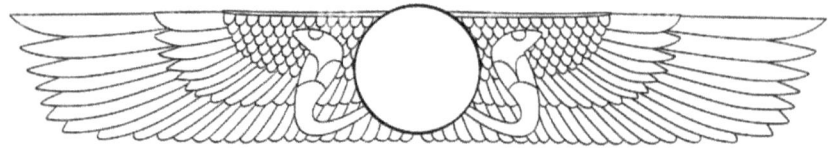

5. Songs of Revelation

"And when comets are to be seen in the neighborhood of the Star SIRIUS, then there will be great difficulty in the house of kings, and brother will rise up against brother, and there shall be war and famine. And in these things the worshippers of the Dog will rejoice, and reap the spoils of these conflicts, and will grow fat."

The Necronomicon, Abdul Alhazred.

In 2014, the highly-respected ufologist Grant Cameron was contacted by extraterrestrial experiencer Chris Bledsoe: author of the book UFO of GOD. Bledsoe explained that members of an ET group identifying themselves as "The Guardians" had contacted him and asked him to pass on a message to Cameron.

According to African ufologist and contactee Kwame Adapa, this group of extraterrestrials originate from Sirius B and that they have been mandated to help "manage life, growth and spiritual advancement for all beings in this galaxy." Adapa describes them as "the wardens, the 'referees', the shepherds of the galactic incarnation game."[132]

Bledsoe is not the only person to have been in contact with this particular group of aliens. Another pioneer in the field of UFO study, the American author and researcher Budd Hopkins (1931-2011), also had first-hand experience of them. Hopkins—a pioneer in the field of alien abduction research throughout the 1980s and 1990s— authored several critically-acclaimed books on the subject. When Steve Boucher visited him at his Manhattan studio in 1982 to discuss his own ET

---

[132] Adapa, Kwame, *The Guardians, Earth, Humans and Ascension*, CreateSpace, 2020.

experiences he found its interior decorated with artwork depicting angelic-looking figures which Hopkins had painted to represent The Guardians.

The communiqué Bledsoe passed to Cameron was simple and concise. It simply read, "The message is in the music." This intrigued Cameron and in 2017 he published *Tuned-In: The Paranormal World of Music*[133] in which he catalogued a host of famous musicians who not only admitted to having a close connection to UFOs but who also credit an external intelligence with helping them to compose music. *Tuned-In* was not the first publication to examine the connection between UFOs and music. Twelve years earlier Michael C. Luckman, the director of the New York Center for Extraterrestrial Research published *Alien Rock: The Rock 'n' Roll Extraterrestrial Connection.*[134]

In each of their respective books, Cameron and Luckman demonstrated that during the 1960s and 1970s a number of well-known musicians claimed to have been influenced by benevolent entities originating from higher cosmic planes. Analysis of their song lyrics very often reveals an interest in a handful of recurring themes that mirror issues raised by extraterrestrials during their interactions with contactees as far back as the late 1940s and early 1950s. In many contact cases, the occupants of landed craft warned the humans they spoke to of a dire need for humanity to end atomic warfare, to take better care of their increasingly sick planet, and to work towards raising the collective vibration of society (i.e. to make it more spiritual and less materialistic).[135] Although a handful of these early UFO contactees came to public prominence and enjoyed a massive following all over the United States, the messages they relayed from their cosmic visitors fell on deaf ears. Nobody in any position of power or authority paid the slightest attention to their concerns regarding the accumulation of

---

[133] Cameron, Grant, *Tuned-In: The Paranormal World of Music*, Itsallconnected Publishing, 2017.
[134] Luckman, Gary, *Alien Rock: The Rock 'n' Roll Extraterrestrial Connection*, Gallery Books, 2006.
[135] There were no warnings from ETs in the 1950 regarding issues negatively impacting mankind this century; such as authoritarianism, corporate greed, surveillance states, and over-population. These and other issues are addressed by the Sirian High Council via contactee Patricia Cori in her *Sirian Revelations* series.

radioactivity in the upper atmosphere as a direct result of the atomic bomb tests that were being carried all over our planet.[136] However, it did resonate with the Hippy Generation who found a close resonance between the extraterrestrials messages and their utopian dream of a world of love, light, and peace.

Such youth movements were clearly able to accommodate radically-new concepts—no matter what their source—but for 'normies' (i.e. the rest of mainstream society), the idea that flying saucers from the stars were roaming freely in our skies was difficult enough to grasp without having to accommodate the philosophical, political, and environmental questions their occupants brought with them. Nowhere was their messages a greater threat than within the hallowed halls of such establishment administrations as those connected to government, orthodox religion, and further education. Outside of these layers of society, the alien messages were treated with a degree of respect but within them they were (and still are) seen to be a diabolical threat. Those who lived and worked outside the confines of orthodoxy—such as rock musicians—felt more comfortable in embracing both the paranormal world of ufology and the sociopolitical issues the subject presents humanity with.

Many of these artists were, rather strangely, associates of David Bowie. Including; John Lennon (with whom Bowie co-wrote the song *Fame*), Mick Jagger (with whom Bowie collaborated for the *Live Aid* charity event in 1984), and long-time friend Marc Bolan (the T. Rex lead singer with whom Bowie shared a manager in the early days of their careers). Each of these artists experienced their own UFO sightings during the 1970s but, unlike Bowie, they chose not to reveal their experiences directly through their songs. Others, some of whom were not so closely connected to Bowie, seemed less reticent about referencing extraterrestrials and UFOs in their songwriting.[137]

---

[136] Many researchers have postulated the theory that the exploding of nuclear bombs rented a hole in the etheric fabric of our planet and sent a wave of radioactivity out into the Solar System which was threatening other planetary ecosystems. This could have been partly the reason for the extraterrestrials deep concerns.
[137] In the post-1970s era, the number of musicians who have referenced UFOs in the lyrics of their songs has diminished substantially with a few notable exceptions being;

5. Songs of Revelation

One example of a song that also drew upon Bowie's visual concept of an 'ambassador from the skies' was *A Spaceman Came Travelling*: by British-Irish singer-songwriter Chris de Burgh (1948-present day). Released on his 1975 album *Spanish Train and Other Stories* its first verse establishes the song's context in clear terms.

> *"A spaceman came travelling on his ship from afar.*
> *'Twas light years of time since his mission did start.*
> *And over a village he halted his craft*
> *And it hung in the sky like a star, just like a star."*

Within the lyrics in *Spaceman*, de Burgh referenced a fringe theory that was held by an increasing number of researchers in the UFO community. This centred on the theory that the Biblical description of the Star of Bethlehem—which was said to have guided the three Magi, or kings, to the location of Christ's nativity— mirrors many modern reports of UFO sightings. To those record-buyers who were not aware of the Christ/UFO theory this appeared to be a strange subject. Some even felt that the song bordered on the sacrilegious and was a deliberate attempt to eviscerate core Christian teachings.

This had not originally been de Burgh's intention for he had strong Christian convictions of his own—albeit that they were tempered with a deep mistrust of organised religion.[138] When music critics asked him in interviews about the inspiration for writing *Spaceman*, the musician explained that he had written the song after reading of a copy of the classic ancient aliens book *Chariots of the Gods?* by German ufologist Erich von Däniken (1948-present day) which he had borrowed from a friend and found fascinating.

A Spaceman Came Travelling is, like *Starman*, a quirky, slightly tongue-in-cheek composition with a catchy tune. Rather ironically, it is often featured on Christmas 'pop-hits' compilations and lists of top Yuletide songs.[139] It also highlights, or challenges, some interesting

Subterranean Homesick Alien by Radiohead, *Aliens Exist* by Blink-182, *Rosetta Stoned* by Tool, *E.T.* by Katy Perry, and *Space Invader* by Ace Frehley (Kiss).
[138] Chris de Burgh: *Still High on Emotion,* Inside World Music, 2004.
[139] https://en.wikipedia.org/wiki/List_of_Christmas_hit_singles_in_the_United_Kingdom

metaphysical concepts. For example, verse three features the lyrics:

> *"Then the stranger spoke, he said, do not fear.*
> *I come from a planet a long way from here.*
> *And I bring a message for mankind to hear.*
> *And suddenly the sweetest music filled the air".*

It is interesting to note comments de Burgh made in a BBC interview years after his song had been a hit when he said "What if the star of Bethlehem was a space craft and what if there is a benevolent being or entity in the universe keeping an eye on the World and our foolish things that we do to each other?"

Not only was de Burgh fascinated by the work of Erich von Däniken but he is a self-confessed fan of the works of fellow Irishman William Butler Yeats (1865–1939)[140] whose poetry expressed a similar apocalyptic vision of the future to that enunciated by Bowie when, in his 1919 poem *The Second Coming* he wrote:

> *Things fall apart; the centre cannot hold;*
> *Mere anarchy is loosed upon the world,*
> *The blood-dimmed tide is loosed, and everywhere*
> *The ceremony of innocence is drowned;*
> *The best lack all conviction, while the worst*
> *Are full of passionate intensity.*[141]

The Second Coming reflects Yeats assertion that human history can be marked as a series of epochs or periods which he called "gyres". He believed that we are currently witnessing the end of a thousand year cycle which has been dominated by Christianity. Yeats expanded upon the metaphysical concepts underpinning his poem by publishing a book-length study of various philosophical, historical, astrological, and poetic topics. Titled *A Vision: An Explanation of Life Founded upon the*

---

[140] In 1885, William Butler Yeats was involved in the formation of the Dublin Hermetic Order. He attended his first séance the following year then studied Theosophy and Hermeticism, He was a member of The Hermetic Order of the Golden Dawn with Aleister Crowley.

[141] *The Second Coming* has been widely quoted from by several musical artists including Lou Reed, Joni Mitchell, Hozier, and The Roots.

Writings of Giraldus and upon Certain Doctrines Attributed to Kusta Ben Luka, it was privately published in 1925.¹⁴²

Left: William Butler Yeats in 1923.

Chris de Burgh saw the birth of Christ as the beginning of one of Yeats cycles. He imagined "...the nativity scene, the thing hovering over, and I could see the shepherds in the fields and this weird, ethereal music was drifting into the air and they were "what the heck is that?"¹⁴³

Within account story of de Burgh and *A Spaceman Came Travelling*, we see a recurring pattern—one which is expressed by so many who believe in the existence of UFOs and aliens. De Burgh believes in the existence of a numinous 'Vril-like' energy¹⁴⁴ which he believed a psychic was capable of accessing and utilising as an alternative form of healing. He even claimed to be able to cure people directly by using his hands to access this energy which he said could be generated through prayer.¹⁴⁵

In the same year that de Burgh released his album that contained *A Spaceman Came Travelling*, the Canadian rock band Klaatu wrote and recorded *Calling Occupants of Interplanetary Crafta*—for their debut album *3:47 EST*. They released the song as a single a year later but it went completely unnoticed by the public and quickly fell into obscurity. According to John Woloschuk—a founder member of Klaatu and one of the song's composers—the song was inspired by a public event that was held in March 1953 when an organisation calling itself the International Flying Saucer Bureau (IFSB) conducted a psychic experiment on

---
[142] https://en.wikipedia.org/wiki/The_Second_Coming_(poem)
[143] Allen, Liam, *The Stories of the Christmas Hits*, BBC News, 2010.
[144] It is difficult to accurately define what 'psychic power' actually is. I lean towards the theory that it describes the application—through extra-sensory skills—of a naturally-occurring and all-pervasive field of energy similar to that of Vail.
[145] *De Burgh Tells of 'healing' hands*, BBC News. 2006.

Left: The picture sleeve version of Calling Occupants of Interplanetary Craft by Richard and Karen Carpenter.

"World Contact Day". At a predetermined time members of the group entered into a meditative state and sent out a telepathic message to any cosmic beings who might be receptive to their transmissions.[146]

Their collective message read:

> "Calling occupants of interplanetary craft! Calling occupants of interplanetary craft that have been observing our planet EARTH. We of IFSB wish to make contact with you. We are your friends and would like you to make an appearance here on EARTH. Your presence before us will be welcomed with the utmost friendship. We will do all in our power to promote mutual understanding between your people and the people of EARTH. Please come in peace and help us in our EARTHLY problems. Give us some sign that you have received our message. Be responsible for creating a miracle here on our planet to wake up the ignorant ones to reality. Let us hear from you. We are your friends."[147]

The song might have ended its days in the bargain bin of record-stores but *Calling Occupants* rather surprisingly re-emerged in 1977 when it was covered by the popular American brother/sister duo The Carpenters. Despite the song being an unwieldy seven minutes long, widespread radio station air-play turned the single into a major hit. It entered the Top 10 in the United Kingdom and Canada and became

---

[146] Woloschuk, John, *Klaatu Track Facts*, Official Klaatu website.
[147] Bender, Albert K., *Flying Saucers and the Three Men*, 1968.

number 1 in Ireland.[148]

Klaatu's legacy has been somewhat memorialised in rock history by their song becoming one of The Carpenters most enduring successes and by the public's awareness of World Contact Day which continues to be held every year on March 15. In 2013, by way of commemorating the event's 60th year of operation, the experiment was extended from one day to a whole week!

Music From the Ethereal Realms

In the 19760s and 1970s, bands, singer-songwriters, and musicians of all kinds drew inspiration from a vast spectrum of literary sources. Bowie referenced Nietzsche; de Burgh read von Daniken; the Beatles integrated the humour of Edward Lear; and Tolkien's *Lord of the Rings* trilogy seemed to inspire everyone at some stage in their musical career!

However, musicians not only looked outwards for lyrical ideas, they also peered inwards and investigated the veil that separates our mundane consciousness from that of the higher realms. While many musicians have deliberately used drugs and other artificial stimulants to thin the veil it does sometimes lift of its own accord and in so-doing facilitates access to an infinite well of archetypal energies—some good, some bad, but all worth their weight in gold to an artist or musician.

David Bowie, John Lennon, Paul McCartney, Keith Richards, and Bob Dylan are just a few rock stars who have spoken publicly about their ability to tap into this invisible force and extract creative ideas from it for their songwriting. The barrier that curtails everyone's ability ability to tap into a world of diverse concepts and abstract ideas does lift during the course of sleep but it can be rent asunder by other means. Meditation, ritual, prayer, and drugs are all effective and are methods by which artists of many kinds have been able to access advanced occult knowledge, new musical ideas, and insights into the Divine. The Western musical tradition upon which contemporary music became established from the 1920s onwards was fertile ground upon which spiritual impulses derived from this 'intelligent universe' could express

---

[148] https://en.wikipedia.org/wiki/Calling_Occupants_of_Interplanetary_Craft

itself.[149] The world of popular music is not unique in this regard and music infused with impulses from the Divine can be traced back by several centuries. Many early classical composers acknowledged the existence of the same creative conduit via which they too drew inspiration. A good example is Johannes Brahms (1833–1897) who when once asked about his composing style said:

> "After all, it may be of some interest to posterity to know how the Spirit speaks when the creative urge is upon me. I immediately feel vibrations that thrill my whole being.... These are the Spirit illuminating the soul-power within, and in this exalted state, I see clearly what is obscure in my ordinary moods; then I feel capable of drawing inspiration from above."[150]

Giacomo Puccini (1858-1924) said his opera *Madama Butterfly* was dictated to him by God and that he was "...merely instrumental in putting it on paper and communicating it to the public."[151] German composer Richard Wagner (1813-1888) stated that he once slipped into a mystical state in which he saw himself at the bottom of the River Rhine when the opening music of Das Rheingold came to him.[152]

Another German composer, Richard Georg Strauss (1864–1949) admitted to relying upon his ability to tap into "...the source of Infinite and Eternal energy from which you and I and all things proceed." He spoke of what he called an "afflatus" (a word which can be translated to mean "to be blown upon by an all-inspiring, divine wind") that appeared to be without limit in its capacity to respond to anyone who felt a desire to express the creative urge within themselves. The source of the inspiration he experienced when composing seems almost extraterrestrial for he admitted to being "aided by a more than earthly Power" and that he had musical ideas dictated to him by what he called

---

[149] Blues and rock music is based upon the pentatonic sequence–a five-note scale which can be symbolised by the pentagram. This perhaps partly explains the commonly held belief that: "The Devil has all the best music!"
[150] Abell, Arthur M., *Talks with Great Composers*. London: Psychic Book Club, 1955.
[151] Ibid.
[152] Ibid.

"Omnipotent Entities".

Giacomo Antonio Domenico Michele Secondo Maria Puccini (1858–1924) was an Italian composer famous not just for having an inordinately lengthy name but also for writing popular classical operas. Puccini revealed his belief in what he referred to as a "supernatural influence" which he said, "qualifies me to receive Divine truths.". He also spoke about the "vibration to pass from the dynamo, which the soul-center is, into my consciousness, and the inspired ideas are born" and how "that higher Power we call God" allowed him to access energetic forms which he was able to translate into music.[153]

One of the World's best-known composers, Ludwig van Beethoven (1770–1827) was said by writer David Tame to be, "...a musical avatar, born to initiate new and higher vibrations of thought and feeling in the hearts of the people of his own day, of our day, and of untold centuries to come"[154]. In 1823, Beethoven was asked by Louis Schlösser what the source of his inspiration was. He replied:

> "That I cannot say with any degree of certainty: they come to me uninvited, directly or indirectly. I could almost grasp them in my hands, out in Nature's open, in the woods, during my promenades, in the silence of the night, at earliest dawn. They are roused by moods which in the poet's case are transmuted into words, and in mine into tones that sound, roar and storm until at last they take shape for me as notes."

Although composers of all kinds have managed to enter the realm of creative ideas there has been no real indication so far that any of these musicians were specifically tapping into an energetic field of energy emanating from Sirius. However, there are examples of artists from our modern era who have made incidental reference to the star; or to elements that are directly related to its mythos. These include Yoko Ono (1933-present day)—the wife of ex-Beatle singer-songwriter John Lennon. On her 1985 album *Starpeace*—a record that opens with her

---
[153] Ibid.
[154] Tame, David, *Beethoven and the Spiritual Path*. Wheaton: Quest, 1994.

sharing an imaginary conversation with an extraterrestrial—she included lyrics which includes the phrase "blue star people from outer space"—a term often used to describe Sirians.

Other contemporary artists who have briefly referenced Sirius in their songs include Nick Cave (*We Real Cool* and *King Sized Nick Cave Blues*), Bob Seger (*I Wonder*), and Robbie Williams (*Arizona*). Other rock musicians have revealed an even deeper awareness of Sirius but before exploring who they are it is worth returning to the world of modern classical music first for within it we encounter a composer whose music inspired many famous rock musicians and who not only admitted to having a Sirian pedigree but claimed to produce music originating from the star.

THE MUSIC OF SIRIUS

Karlheinz Stockhausen was born on August 22, 1928, near Kerpen-in-the-Cologne in Germany. At the age of seven he received his first piano lessons from the organist of the Altenberger Dom—the former church of Altenberg Abbey. In January 1942 Stockhausen became a boarder at the teacher training college in Xanten where he continued piano training and studied oboe and violin.[155] He furthered his musical education at the Hochschule für Musik Köln (trans. Cologne Conservatory of Music) between 1947 and 1951.

Although classically trained, Stockhausen avoided becoming a stereotypical composer and outwardly refused to follow established musical norms. Over a period of nearly sixty years, he worked up to 16 hours per day and produced 370 individual works with later ones challenging the idea of what classical music should be. Before wandering off the beaten-track Stockhausen's works were relatively orthodox in nature and included a series of nineteen piano pieces, a ten-instrument composition titled *Kontra-Punkte* (1952-1953), *Stimmung* (1968) for six vocalists, *Aus den sieben Tagen* (trans. *From the Seven Days*) (1968), Mantra (1970) for two pianos and electronics, and Inori (trans. Adorations) which he wrote for soloists and orchestra around 1973–

---

[155] Kurtz, Michael, *Stockhausen: A Biography*, Faber and Faber, 1992.

74.[156]

In total, the composer's catalogue of work included miniatures for musical boxes through to works for solo performers, chamber and choral music, traditional orchestral music of many forms, and even full-length operas but by the mid-1970s Stockhausen had broadened his repertoire even further when he started to infuse cosmological themes into his work. This begun with *Tierkreis* (trans. Zodiac) (c.1974–75)–a composition consisting of twelve melodies with each one sonically describing a sign of the zodiac. A series of compositions referencing spiritual or metaphysical concepts followed including one of his better-known works *Licht* (trans. *Light* and subtitled *The Seven Days of the Week*) and which was a cycle of seven operas which he composed between 1977 and 2003. These were based these on the spiritual teachings contained within The Urantia Book.[157]

Jonathan Harvey in his book *The Music of Stockhausen* recalled just how involved the composer was in the world of metaphysics.

> "I once went to Stockhausen's house in Kürten, Germany. A maid showed me in and there, in the hall, was an Egyptian mummy in a sarcophagus. I had the very strong impression that it was Stockhausen himself. The place, which he had designed, did seem haunted by an extraordinary presence. In fact, he was upstairs asleep and came down half an hour later. I found him a charming if strong personality. We talked about spiritual matters. He felt he was in contact with the angels, like William Blake, as well as with higher intelligences, beings who had evolved

---

[156] https://en.wikipedia.org/wiki/Karlheinz_Stockhausen
[157] *The Urantia Book*, *The Urantia Papers*, or *The Fifth Epochal Revelation* is a spiritual and philosophical publication said to have originated in Chicago sometime between 1924 and 1955. Its authors have never been confirmed but they state that the aim of the book is to "unite religion, science and philosophy." In addition to Stockhausen, other figures in the music industry who have said that the book has been highly influential in their lives include Stevie Ray Vaughan, Jimi Hendrix, Randy California, Jaco Pastorius, Pato Banton, and Jerry Garcia. In 2001, a jury decreed that the English-language book's copyright was no longer valid in the United States after 1983 and deemed it to be a public domain work.

Above: Electronic music pioneer Karlheinz Stockhausen at WDR studios in 1994 - the same location used to record his Sirius suite.

more, maybe on other planets. He talked a lot about Sirius. He often had dreams - visions - that made decisions about pieces for him. He trusted them implicitly. I thought of him as a sort of shaman: once or twice, I saw strange things in his face - other faces than his own."[158]

In 1971, shortly after composing *Sternklang* (trans. Star-Sound), Stockhausen's five-year-old daughter, Julika asked if she could have a dog as a pet. He agreed and a puppy was obtained for the child which they named 'Sirius' after the Dog Star. Shortly afterwards, Karlheinz happened to come across a passage in a book written by Christian mystic and visionary Jakob Lorber (1800-1864) in which he described Sirius as the "Sun at the center of our Universe"[159].

This triggered subconscious memories within Stockhausen and he subsequently experienced a series of revelatory dreams in which

---

[158] Harvey, Jonathan, *The Music of Stockhausen*, Faber & Faber, 1975.
[159] Lorber, Jakob, *Der Kosmos in geistiger Schau*, Lorber-Verlag, Bietigheim, 1961.

5. Songs of Revelation

snippets of vitally important personal insights came through.[160] In a later interview he said that these were "Crazy dreams; from which it emerged that not only did I come from Sirius itself, but that, in fact, I completed my musical education there." Stockhausen now had come to believe that he was unconsciously drawing creative inspiration from the star and was destined to continue doing so throughout his current incarnation. He explained his musical connection to it in the following way:

> "(On Sirius) everything is music, or the art of coordination and harmony of vibrations...the art is very highly developed there, and every composition on Sirius is related to the rhythms of nature...the seasons, the rhythms of the stars."[161]

As a direct consequence of his cosmically-activated consciousness Stockhausen set about putting his Siriun insights into a musical context[162]. This project began at the studio of the West German radio station WDR in Cologne during July 1975 and continued until March 1977. This composition was his most challenging and ground-breaking of his career and his intention was that it would be part autobiographical, part science-fiction; a composition that told the story of four emissaries from the star Sirius who visited Earth with the intention of teaching humanity about the form of music Sirians create back on their star.[163] The result, *Sirius*, was a musical drama that comprised of four parts or sections. Each one reflected the energies of the four seasons and was underpinned with a reference to the astrological periods that govern each portion of the solar year. This was a highly complex piece of music over which Stockhausen laboured day and night for nearly two years to perfect. Rehearsals for its public performance were conducted in rooms

---

[160] Tannenbaum, Mya, *Conversations with Stockhausen*, Oxford University Press.
[161] Patrick, Justin, *Music from Sirius: The Dreams of Karlheinz Stockhausen*, 2010.
[162] Marconie observed that Sirius could be understood as a "...covert tribute to the visionary protagonist of L'Astronome, a planned but never executed musico-dramatic narrative from 1928 concerning an astronomer who contacts intelligent life on Sirius but is publicly vilified for exposing the world to the dangers of invasion by a superior intelligence." (Source: Marconie, Robin, *Other Planets: The Complete Works of Karlheinz Stockhausen (1950–2007)*, Rowman & Littlefield, 2016.)
[163] Stockhausen remained adamant that his Sirius composition was a direct communication from his home star of Sirius—even through to the very end of his life.

fitted with specially modified 8-channel tape-recorders, unique types of microphones, and modified loudspeakers.[164] As Stockhausen later explained in an interview with Albrecht Moritz:

> "The exact synchronisation by means of earphones, without conductor, alone requires a completely new technique of hearing, singing and playing. By listening to this music, in particular to the WHEEL, one perceives how the newly discovered means and structural possibilities of electronic music can awaken in us a completely new consciousness for revelations, transformations, and fusions of forms, which would never have been possible with the old musical means and become increasingly similar to the art of metamorphosis in nature."

Immediately following *THE WHEEL* section of the suite, Stockhausen's musicians replicated a radio broadcast message using words and phrases taken directly from *Der Kosmos in Geistiger Schau* (trans. *The Cosmos in Spiritual Vision*) by the aforementioned Jakob Lorber. It said:

> "Only this period of creation has the virtue – still undiscernible for you – that in the entire eternal infinite it is the only one in which I, creator of all worlds, have completely taken on the nature of the human flesh. I have chosen for Myself within the entire, immense Universe, this particular capsule, and within this, the local universe whose central sun is SIRIUS, and among the 200 million suns rotating around SIRIUS, I have chosen just your Earth where I would incarnate as human being…Here I will raise, for all times and eternities to come, children completely similar to Me, who, together with Me, will

---

[164] The beginning of Stockhausen's *Sirius* composition utilised a special rotating loudspeaker and electronic tape to simulate the descent and landing of spaceships from Sirius.

5. Songs of Revelation

reign over the entire infinite..."[165]

The first section of the *Sirius* suite had its opening performance in front of a specially invited audience at the unveiling of the Albert Einstein Spacearium in Washington D.C on July 15, 1976. Stockhausen added further sections to *Sirius* and these were performed at various venues around the World later the same year.

During the media promotion of the composition, Stockhausen was completely forthcoming with information about about his own personal connection to Sirius, the star. In an interview with Stefan Holmström[166] he was asked what qualities he thought designated a Sirian spirit.

> "Musicality; extreme musicality and extreme openness for unknown musical forms, and what is most important is that the musical forms must always be related to natural, organic events on this planet, which means to the elements – the four elements – to the movements that we can experience in nature - to the rhythms – and to the harmonic principles that one should study very much; the ecology of this planet, and human bodies; the rhythms of the organs of the human body etcetera – so this is a typical sign that the spirit tries to relate music to the natural laws of musical parameters; melody, harmony; rhythm in particular."

Later on, in an interview held just after the World premiere of *Sirius*, the composer made the following statement.

"The spirit of it is that it is music from Sirius, which

---

[165] In Stockhausen's 1975 sketchbook, Kompositions Kurs über SIRIUS, the composer wrote that during a period spent n hospital following a bout of severe exhaustion brought on by overworking on his Sirius composition, he had a vision that children born during the period July 25 to September 5 when the Sun and Sirius rise together – were "beings (musically gifted) from Sirius, traveling on rays of light to get here."

[166] Stefan Holmström was a reporter and producer at the Swedish Broadcasting Corporation who interviewed Stockhausen at the Electronic Music Festival in Skinnskatteberg, Sweden in June 2000.

is transposed on this planet and [reveals] the possibilities of this planet, because I think that the culture of this planet has been mainly formed by visitors from Sirius, especially in the time between 9000 and 6000 B.C., [as have] most of our modern concepts of cultural achievements, as far as these are still available, because, as you know, an enormous amount has been burned in the library of Alexandria, where all the secret knowledge of architecture, of mathematics, of astronomy and of the arts, and of the magnetism of the Earth, of ecology, etc., has been destroyed voluntarily by the Christian orthodox administration.

But I think that our main sources of present-day culture, as decadent as it may be in most parts of the planet, stem from visitors from Sirius whose main representatives (leaders) were Isis and Osiris. Through a series of revelations which were at first quite nebulous but have become more clear during the past few years, I know (as little as I know about details) that I have come from Sirius, myself. And I know that the highest kind of language that can exist for this highly developed culture is music. As long as we're inclinated toward the bodies and possibilities of the body of this planet Earth, then everything from Sirius appears as music. It is structured in a direct harmony with the forming principles of the universe, of the rotations, of the seasons, of different aspects of youth, man, woman, the friend, of the elements earth, fire, water, air, of states of growth, etc.

All of these characteristics stem basically, and have been made conscious, from this culture, and there are many other planets which have been influenced by these universal principles, which are communicated best through sound in music that is the best and most universal way."¹⁶⁷

Stockhausen died of heart failure on December 5, 2007, in Kürten, Westphalia, aged 79. He was posthumously described as "one of the great visionaries of 20th-century music".¹⁶⁸ The wording on his gravestone is unknown but could well include one of his more famous quotes: "I was educated at Sirius and want to return to there."

THE SIRIUN MOON OF NEIL PEART

Stockhausen's ground-breaking use of electronic sound had a significant influence on a handful of prominent rock musicians—±artists who were keen on expanding the boundaries of modern Western music. They included the German avant-garde bands Can and Tangerine Dream, the French electronic composer Jean-Michel Jarre, and the English rock band Pink Floyd. The Beatles paid homage to Stockhausen by including his face among the collage of famous people they respected on the cover of their *Sgt. Pepper's Lonely Hearts Club Band* album.

Although not basing their compositions around the use of electronics, a group who did tear down established musical barriers was the Canadian three-piece band Rush. Formed by Geddy Lee (bass, vocals) and Alex Lifeson (guitar) in 1968, they underwent several line-up changes prior to Neil Peart (1952-2020) replacing their original drummer. Born in Hamilton, Ontario, Peart grew up in Port Dalhousie where he developed an early interest in music. His membership of Rush in 1974 proved pivotal to the band's career for he led them to become one of the biggest acts in rock history: releasing nineteen studio albums of which ten exceeded sales of over a million copies in the United States.

Peart was not only a highly accomplished drummer but from Rush's *Permanent Waves* (1980) album onwards, he was also their primary lyricist. Primarily deriving lyrical inspiration from fantasy, science fiction, mythology, and philosophy he also tackled a range of social

---
¹⁶⁷ *Stockhausen Interview* - www.music.buffalo.edu
¹⁶⁸ Hewett, Ivan, *Karlheinz Stockhausen: Both a Rationalist and a Mystic, the Composer's Influence Stretched from Boulez to the Beatles,* Guardian Unlimited, 2007.

topics which others deemed contentious. In addition, he also tackled humanitarian issues, questioned the 911 terrorist attacks, faith, and orthodox religion. As a result, Rush met with widespread criticism in 1976 after the release of their *2112* album—the liner notes of which included a credit to the Russian-born American writer and philosopher Ayn Rand (1905-1962).[169]

Rand attained prominence in the literary world following the publication of her 1943 novel *The Fountainhead* and then *Atlas Shrugged* in 1957. The novelist also advocated "Objectivism"—a philosophy based on reason as a method of acquiring knowledge rather than that offered through faith and religion. This somehow led the music press into labelling Rush as fascist: acting as a tool of Nazi propaganda. What they failed to pick up on was the fact that these were the very subjects the band were railing against in the lyrics of their song *2112*. The press also failed to inform their readership that Peart was actually an active member of the Canadian charity Artists Against Racism.[170] The furore over his political interests did not stop Peart from continuing to challenge the status quo. As an extension of this he also became involved in political movements such as those irelated to environmentalism.

At some point along his spiritual and philosophical journey, Peart encountered the star Sirius. In his song *Dog Years*, he wrote:

> *"In the dog days*
> *People look to Sirius.*
> *Dogs cry for the moon*
> *But those connections are mysterious.*[171]*"*

In these few, short lines, Peart rather mysteriously identified the position of the Moon in his astrological birth-chart. Although his actual birth date, September 12, 1952, is known, the exact time—which is important when drawing up a natal chart—is not. In such circumstances the accepted practice in Western astrology is to substitute midday (i.e.

---

[169] See Sciabarra, Chris Matthew, *Rand, Rush and Rock*, The Journal of Ayn Rand Studies (Volume 4, Number 1), 2002.
[170] https://en.wikipedia.org/wiki/Neil_Peart
[171] Lyrics to *Dog Years* by Neil Peart from the Rush album *Test for Echo* (1996)

12:00hrs.) as an approximation. By this method the position of Neil Peart's Moon is 7 degrees of the sign of Cancer. The Moon moves very quickly and if an astrological chart is drawn for slightly later in the day it would create an exact conjunction with Sirius: located at 14 degrees of the same sign. Such an alignment would explain why the musician was an extra-ordinary talent and such a deeply caring individual. There is no evidence that Peart had a deep interest in astrology but the coincidence is important enough to be mentioned.

Sadly, following a series of deeply personal tragedies, Peart passed away from a type of brain cancer called 'glioblastoma' on January 7, 2020. He was 67 years of age.

GOJIRA AND THE WHALES

Another rock group engaged in challenging musical boundaries is the French progressive death-metal band Gojira. Founded by brothers Joe and Mario Duplantier in 1996, the brothers have, like Peart, consistently written music infused with lyrics referencing spirituality, philosophy, and the environment. Their first two albums, *Terra Incognita* (2001) and *The Link* (2003), helped established them as a dominant force in rock music. In 2005, they released their third studio album titled *From Mars to Sirius*—a concept album that incorporated space-travel and environmentalism. It received widespread acclaim with the music-paper Rolling Stone adding it in their 2017 *100 Greatest Metal Albums of All Time* list.

Thematically, the lyrics of From *Mars to Sirius* recount an imaginary transition from a state of conflict and war to one of peace and serenity with the star Sirius as the ultimate destiny, or culmination, of the transitional journey. It also includes references to a widespread New Age belief that the cetaceans of our planet (whales, porpoises, dolphins etc.) are sentient creatures who maintain a close psychic connection to their natural home on Sirius B.[172] It is also said that they are capable of telepathically transmitting spiritual insights to sensitively attuned humans.[173] It is a theory that Gojira expressed in their song *Flying*

---

[172] http://askingangels.com/healing/earth/incarnated-dolphins.php
[173] Newman, Hugh, *The Psychic Children: Dolphins, DNA & the Planetary Grid*,

Whales; wherein its writers state "*I have to find the whales. That once did guide us.*" In addition to Sirius B, Gojira also referenced the dark-star companion Sirius C. On the album's track *To Sirius*, they sing:

> "*I come to Sirius C.*
> *To learn from you friends of old.*
> *And wish to come into being.*"

And finally, from the track *Global Warming*, Gojira recognises the existence of Sirians along with their possible involvement in the evolution of our planet:

> "*Four hundred thousand years ago,*
> *They came from outer space,*
> *And gave us life here,*
> *And we are just taking everything for granted,*
> *I don't think we should do this now.*"

As dark and bombastic as Gojira's brand of heavy metal is, the album closes with a sense of optimism and by predicting that a collapse in the old order will initiate a brighter future for humanity.

> "*I had this dream, our planet surviving.*
> *The guiding stars always growing.*
> *And all the worlds, the fates all the countries*
> *They're all rebuilding at the same time.*
> *I never fell and always believed in*
> *We could evolve and get older.*
> *Open thy eyes and let all this flow in*
> *Now see a new hope is growing inside*".

It is through their environmentalism that Gojira have been most effective in initiating change. As dedicated environmentalists they have focused a great deal of time and money on such projects as those which attempt to deal with climate change, marine pollution, and the

---

Avalon Rising Publications, 2007 and Wyllie, Timothy, *Dolphins, Extraterrestrials, Angels*, Bear & Company, 1993.

deforestation of the Amazon rainforest.[174] Their fervent ecological stance initially started out through the brother's exposure to the sea as children. Mario Duplantier often recalls how the effect of seeing the devastation of oil-spills in the nearby ocean as children left them deeply concerned about the plight of marine life.[175] Brother Joe Duplantier has even gone so far as to state that had he not become a musician, he would have worked for either Greenpeace or the Sea Shepherd Conservation Society.[176]

BLUE OYSTER CULT

The story of Gojira demonstrates how only a thin line spearates the world of Music, metaphysics, and spirituality. One of the strangest examples of a relationship between a group of rock musicians and the occult, however, is found in the story of an American hard rock band who originated from Long Island, New York, called Blue Öyster Cult (BOC)

BOC released their self-titled debut album in January 1972 after which they quickly rose in musical stature to become one of the biggest rock acts in the business by selling 25 million records Worldwide; including 7 million in the United States alone. Initially called Soft White Underbelly—a term taken from a World War Two speech given by British Prime-minister Winston Churchill (1874-1965)[177]—the band were initially the brainchild of American manager and record-producer Samuel 'Sandy' Pearlman (1943-2016) when, in 1967, he gathered together a group of musicians who could provide the music for his *Imaginos* poems.

Although they were not essentially a singles band, BOC did enjoy commercial success a few years later with their classic song *(Don't Fear) The Reaper* which peaked at No. 12 on the Billboard Hot 100 singles chart. Taken from their 1976 album *Agents of Fortune* it became a platinum-seller, peaking at No. 29 on the U.S. Billboard chart.

It was the cover of *Agents of Fortune* that revealed the band's occult

---

[174] https://en.wikipedia.org/wiki/Gojira_(band)
[175] Andersen, Eric, *Gojira Spreading Eco-Friendly Message*, The Daily Iowan. 2009.
[176] *Gojira: Entretien Avec Joe Duplantier*, Radio Metal, 2008.
[177] https://en.wikipedia.org/wiki/Sandy_Pearlman

interests by featuring artwork that depicted a stage magician with his arm raised and a hand clutching four cards of the tarot's Major Arcana. With his other hand, the magician is shown making what is known in occultism as the "Mark of St. John"—a raised thumb and primary finger which is pointing at a symbol similar in style to that of an inverted ankh.

The band also revealed their interest in ufology by including a song on the album titled *E.T.I. (Extra Terrestrial Intelligence)*. It contained the somewhat cryptic lyrics:

"I hear the music, daylight disc,
Three men in black said, "Don't report this.
Ascension," and that's all they said.
Sickness now, the hour of dread.
All praise.
He's found the awful truth.
Balthazar.
He's found the saucer news."

The reference to Balthazar in these lyrics is interesting. According to Christian tradition he was one of the three Magi (the other two being Caspar and Melchior) who travelled to the scene of the birth of baby Jesus in Bethlehem. Balthazar[178] is traditionally referred to as the King of Arabia and is believed to be the one who specifically brought Mary and Joseph the gift of myrrh.[179]

Earlier we saw how, through the lyrics of his hit song *A Spaceman Came Travelling*, Chris de Burgh tapped into a theory held by some occult researchers hat the star that guided the Three Kings, or Magi, to Bethlehem was actually Sirius and not a UFO. This line of cosmological theory also proposes that the trio represented the three stars thaht make up the Belt of Orion and which were always considered important in Arabian astronomy for their rising always marked the close appearance of Sirius on the horizon. Regarding the symbolic significance of Balthazar in particular, it is worth noting that the numerical value of the

---
[178] The Feast Day of Balthazar is January 6—a date that commemorates his death in 54AD. It is a date that pays an important role in modern conspiracy theory.
[179] https://en.wikipedia.org/wiki/Balthazar_(magus)

5. Songs of Revelation

word 'Balthazar' is 713 –the same value as the term 'Sirius rising'

Pearlman's attempt to bring his occult-inspired poetic writings to life proved for be a tortuous experience for everyone involved. It was originally planned to be a musical project which was to be co-ordinated by the ad hoc bands' drummer Albert Bouchard (1947-present day). However, his subsequent departure from the group–closely followed by a breakdown in the relation between Pearlman and BOC–meant that a more fully fleshed-out version of the poet's literary work did not appear until the band's eleventh studio album titled *Imaginos* in 1988.

Pearlman's poetry, it should be said, defied convention. It not only reflected his fascination with the occult, extraterrestrials, and with the obscure stories of American horror writer H. P. Lovecraft (1890-1937), but it was also peppered with numerous veiled references found within the spiritual enigma presented by Sirius. The most notable example of this appeared in the BOC song *Astronomy* which they included on their 1974 album *Secret Treaties*–and which includes lyrics based upon Pearlman's poem *The Soft Doctrines of Imaginos*.

In a 1988 interview conducted with the UK heavy-metal magazine *Kerrang*, Pearlman described his poem as "an interpretation of history – an explanation for the onset of World War I, or a revelation of the occult origins of it...a combination of horror story and fairy tale."[180] In it, he tells the story of a group of aliens called the "Les Invisibles" who were said to have been guided throughout history by a genetically-altered type of human called the 'Imaginos' (also referenced in his poetry as "Desdenova").[181]

In BOC's song *Astronom*, the primary character of Imaginos realises his role as an altered human whereupon he is raised from the dead and transformed into the female persona of Desdenova–a character who also appeared on the rear cover of the *Secret Treaties* album and in the BOC

---

[180] *Blue Oyster Cult*, Kerrang Magazine, Issue 206, September 24, 1988.
[181] Pearlman created the word "Desdenova". Its numerical value is 899, the same as "The Light that is not Light". This phrase refers to the dark energetic emanation of Sirius known as 'The Midnight Sun' which emits a light that cannot be seen. The term "Spiritual Sun" also carries the value 899.

song, *I Am the One You Warned Me Of.*

> "*Call me Desdenova, eternal light.*
> *These gravely digs of mine*
> *Will surely prove a sight.*
> *And don't forget my dog, fixed and consequent.*
> *Astronomy...a star."*

The lyrical reference to "My dog, fixed and consequent" is a direct reference to Sirius—the dog star[182] and the stellar home of Pearlman's Les Invisibles.[183]

Imaginos was conceived of as a rock opera and in order to fully accommodate Pearlman's prolific poetic output, the intention had been to record it as a trilogy of double albums. This was a challenging project in anyone's eyes but as a musical project it surely tested the patience and capabilities of everyone involved. At the core of the challenges lay Pearlman's immense range of esoteric interests. These included mythology, sociology, alchemy, science, and occultism; all of which were wrapped up in part-horror and part-fairy tales, were replete with references to ancient civilisations, conspiracy theories, and included what he felt to be the deliberate manipulation of the course of human history by external forces that replicated those described by H. P. Lovecraft in his Cthulhu Mythos.

Despite clocking in at nearly an hour in length, the first iteration of *Imaginos* proved to be less than the sum of its rather complex parts. The album was not universally acclaimed upon its release and even its cover proved problematic. It featured an old picture of the legendary San Francisco restaurant Cliff House; taken around the turn of the twentieth century and immediately prior to it being burned down and reconstructed. The original concept for the artwork—as conceived by by Pearlman and Greg Scott—was more ambitious than this for, as the artist later explained in an interview:

> "So, what might have Imaginos become graphically?

---

[182] https://en.wikipedia.org/wiki/Astronomy_(song)
[183] Swartz, John, 4.6: What is the story told by the album, Imaginos?, Hotrails.

> Well, the front cover was Imaginos himself, a very kind of apocalyptic image of him, standing in front of a stormy sky with the ship and the pyramid in the background, holding a mirror out towards you. His Doberman pinscher, which appeared in various versions of my other artwork, was in front of him. That was a very intense and spooky kind of image. The back cover was basically all the same elements rearranged. It was Imaginos as a young boy, and he's standing waist-deep in the water with a model boat, and the dog is behind him in a constellation. So, there's this drawing of the dog, where the constellation Sirius is coming through him. So, it was basically all the elements; there was a kind of farmhouse, in place of the pyramid. So, each of the elements of the front cover were translated in the back cover in different places and in different ways."[184]

Lovecraft's *Cthulu* series of stories refer to the "Great Old Ones"– alien creatures who were said to originate from other dimensions in time and space and who once ruled the Earth but were defeated and expelled by opposing cosmic forces. Lovecraft believed that they would return at a point when "the stars are right" or when they were conjured back into our dimension as a result of human cults performing ceremonies said to include a variety of "blasphemous incantations". The abode of the Great Old Ones is deemed to be Sirius.

Rather than being the mere creations of a troubled and haunted mind (Lovecraft suffered from severe depression) many believe that his stories and novels contain hidden meanings and magickal formulae which Lovecraft had not been consciously aware of. The Esoteric Order of Dagon (EOD) is an occult society that took its name from Lovecraft's story *The Shadow Over Innsmouth* which he wrote in November/December 1931 and then published in 1936. The occult order worked

---
[184] Popoff, Martin, *Agents of Fortune: The Blue Oyster Cult Story*, Wymer Publishing, 2016.

on what they refer to as "Lovecraftian magick"[185] from 1981 using a form of magick which descends from the esoteric traditions practised by the Sirius mystery cults of ancient Egypt and Sumeria. Despite drawing their magickal current from literature, the EOD considered themselves to be a serious occult fraternity with bona fide use of occult symbolism and ritual. Their use of three dots in their logo,[186] for example, was something that the society said was derived from:

> "...the very old Masonic connections of some occult orders and signifies that an esoteric meaning is involved. The true hidden reference is to the Sirius system, of three stars, including our own sun. The ancient Sumerian/Egyptian Mysteries of Oannes (or the Philistine Dagon, Lord of the Deep Ones) and the stellar gnosis of the All Seeing Eye of Sirius, concealed in the Hermetic Freemasonic Traditions, forms the basis of the 23 Current that informs the secret society."[187]

Whether the inclusion of such dark, occult elements as those espoused by the Esoteric Order of Dagon resulted in Blue Öyster Cult's career coming to a grinding halt is unclear but their fourteenth studio album, *Curse of the Hidden Mirror*–released on June 5, 2001–was poorly received and its lacklustre sales led to the band being dropped by their record label.

The band did not release another studio album for nearly 20 years but their 2020[188] album titled *The Symbol Remains* was more positively received by fans and critics alike. Once again it featured the same occult perspective that permeated most of their career for it contained an interesting track titled *The Old Gods Return* which is a clear reference

---

[185] Another proponent of the theory that Lovecraft was in touch with authentic occult forces was Kenneth Grant, the British occultist and head of the Typhonian OTO who also attached deep occult significance to the stories of Lovecraft.
[186] The group also explained their use of the symbolism of an amphibian- being in their motif as "...a creature evoluted to travel between two worlds."
[187] www.esotericorderofdagon.org
[188] https://en.wikipedia.org/wiki/Curse_of_the_Hidden_Mirror

to H. P. Lovecraft and his dark mythos.

> *"Now is the time the old gods return.*
> *Exactly when the world is not expecting it.*
> *Exactly when we're sure of ourselves.*
> *That's exactly when the old gods return.*
> *And sweep our cities back into hell."*
> *An Eye in the Sky*

VISION FROM AFAR

The lyrical reference within BOC's *The Old Gods Return* to "*An Eye in the Sky*" highlights an important aspect to the sacred teachings inherent within the Sirius Mythos. It highlights a jealously-guarded secret which several prominent secret societies have striven to keep concealed from the general public for thousands of years. Nevertheless, it did surface in its symbolic form as the "All-Seeing Eye" during the 1970s with its most evident expression being via the English audio-engineer, songwriter, musician, and record-producer Alan Parsons (1948-present day).

In October 1967, at the age of just 18, he was employed at the famous Abbey Road Studios, London, where he assisted the Beatles and Pink Floyd in the recording of their classic *Abbey Road* and *Dark Side of the Moon* albums.[189] He was a restless individual and, despite the highly placed position he held in the music business, he struck out on his own in 1976 and released the first of several solo albums under the name The Alan Parsons Project. Titled *Tales of Mystery and Imagination*, the first release contained an interpretation of the macabre stories of Edgar Allan Poe (1809-1849)—who, alongside H. P Lovecraft, was one of the earliest practitioners of the horror-fiction genre. It was partly as a consequence of his study of Poe that Parsons followed up his critically acclaimed *Tales* album with *I Robot* (1977) which Parsons described as:

> "The story of the rise of machine and the decline of man, which paradoxically coincided with his

---
[189] http://en.wikipedia.org/wiki/Alan_Parsons

discovery of the wheel...And a warning that his brief dominance of this planet will probably end, because man tried to create robot in his own image."

Subsequent albums included *Pyramid* (1978) and *Eve* (1979)—both of which featured a deep exploration of esoteric symbolism—and his next album, *The Turn of a Friendly Card* (1980), contained similar esoteric elements to those used by Blue Oyster Cult on their *Agents of Fortune* album, While these albums sold in relatively modest numbers, Parson's career took off following the release of his 1982 album *Eye in the Sky* which reached number 7 in the US album charts. The following year it was nominated for the Best Engineered Album award at the annual 25th Grammy Awards and in 2019 won a Grammy in the Best Immersive Audio Album category.[190]

From an occult perspective, *Eye in the Sky* is an interesting record. Its opening track is a two-minute instrumental titled *Sirius* and this segues into *Eye in the Sky*—a song that has subsequently achieved almost legendary status throughout the United States; where it is still used at a variety of sporting events: particularly basketball[191]. Its lyrics includes the following lines:

"I am the eye in the sky.
Looking at you
I can read your mind.
I am the maker of rules."

The term "*eye in the sky*" is an ancient reference to the star Sirius. In many cultures there is a belief that the star is a sentient being (a 'deity' or 'god') and that through its singular "eye" it has the capacity to look down upon us all and to monitor our actions. This same eye is a universal symbol and one that emerges at the core of many esoteric traditions, within popular culture, and forms as essential symbol within the teachings of many secret societies.

---

[190] https://en.wikipedia.org/wiki/Eye_in_the_Sky_(album)
[191] It was popularised by the Chicago Bulls in 1990 when Michael Jordan was in the team.

5. Songs of Revelation

Above: All-Seeing Eye on the gate of Aachen Cathedral

Above: The Eye of Providence as depicted on the U.S. $1 bill.

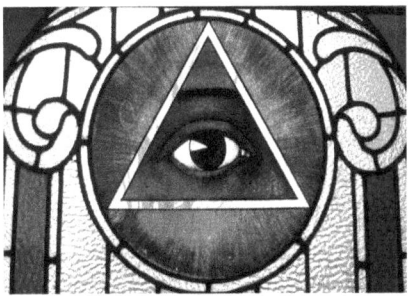

Above: The All-Seeing Eye or 'Eye of Sirius in a stained glass window at Saint Raphael Catholic Church, Springfield, Ohio.

Above: A modern interpretation of the Masonic all-seeing eye, square and compasses.

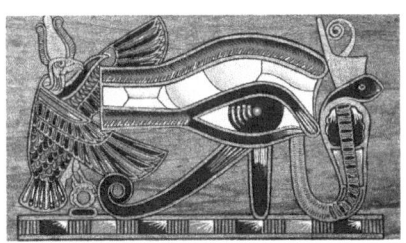

Above: The 'widget' or Eye of Horus found throughout ancient Egyptian religious teachings.

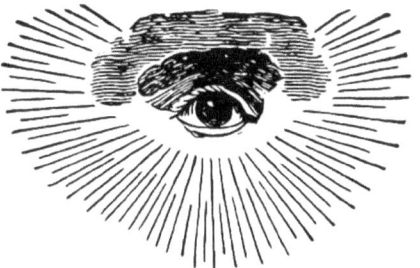

Above: An early Masonic depiction of the Eye of Providence radiating the Glory of God.

Parsons references this later in the lyrics of the same song.

> *"Dealing with fools*
> *I can cheat you blind.*
> *And I don't need to see any more.*
> *To know that*
> *I can read your mind; I can read your mind".*

This 'all-seeing eye' was symbolised by the ancient Egyptians as the Eye of Horus motif which Parsons employed as a single image on the cover of the *Eye in the Sky* album.[192]

In fact, this symbol appears to have had personal significance to Parsons. In 2006 he was photographed wearing a distinctive Eye of Horus pendant: twenty-five years after the *Eye in the Sky* album was first released.

An interesting coincidence emerges in the story of Alan Parson's musical history. A musician who became an integral element in the formation of his Alan Parsons Project was Eric Norman Woolfson (1945–2009). A talented Scottish songwriter, lyricist, vocalist, executive producer, and pianist, Woolfson wrote songs for other artists during the 1970s; including for Peter Noone, the ex-member of Hermans Hermits who had a hit with Bowies' *Oh! You Pretty Things*. Woolfson also pursued a career in musical theatre and his first production was a stage musical based on the Austrian neurologist and founder of psychoanalysis Sigmund Freud (1856-1939) with whom he was said to be deeply fascinated.[193]

STAR OF SIRIUS

The opening track on Alan Parson's 2019 album *The Secret*—a record he told interviewers included "musical and lyrical themes that are very close to my heart and my own interests and passions"[194]—is *The*

---

[192] The cover was designed by Hipgnosis - the same London artwork house that designed the album covers of Pink Floyd and many other legendary artists of the 1970s.
[193] https://en.wikipedia.org/wiki/Eric_Woolfson
[194] https://www.loudersound.com/news/new-alan-parsons-album-the-secret-to-be-released-in-april

5. SONGS OF REVELATION

Sorcerer's Apprentice—a part-collaboration with the legendary Genesis guitarist Steve Hackett (1950-present day). Although now a solo artist, Hackett's first record under his own name was recorded at a time when he was still in his former band. Released in 1975, *Voyage of the Acolyte* reached number 26 in the UK and 191 in the US album charts.[195]

Voyage was a concept album inspired by Hackett's interest in tarot cards and in their ability to foretell the future. This is reflected in each track on his album which featured a reference to a card. They included such titles as *Ace of Wands*, *Hands of the Priestess*, *A Tower Struck Down*, *The Hermit*, *Shadow of the Hierophant*, and *The Lovers*. Although Hackett is not known for having deep occult beliefs on *Voyage* he demonstrated an awareness of esoteric teachings related to tarot Arcana number 17 which is titled THE STAR. In the lyrics to his song *Star of Sirius* he states:

> *"He who knows love knows who you are.*
> *Worlds you may find lit by a star.*
> *Again, renewed by the vessels of Isis.*
> *You're ready to fly".*

Even today, very few tarot readers are aware of the deep esoteric connection that exists between Arcana 17 THE STAR, Sirius, and the ancient Egyptian goddess Isis whose spiritual dynamics are encoded into the tarot card's imagery. Known as "The Great Provider", Isis (in her role as the star Sirius) was credited with replenishing Egypt by inundating the Nile river. The connection between Isis and THE STAR card—which usually pictures a naked woman pouring water from a jug into a river—is not very often referenced by tarot researchers but they were referred to in a tarot deck published by the English occultist A. E. Waite who was an important figure in the Western Mystery Tradition and who played a significant part in the unfolding, or unveiling, of the Sirius Mythos.

---

[195] Although a solo album, it also featured guest contributions from Genesis bassist Mike Rutherford and drummer Phil Collins.

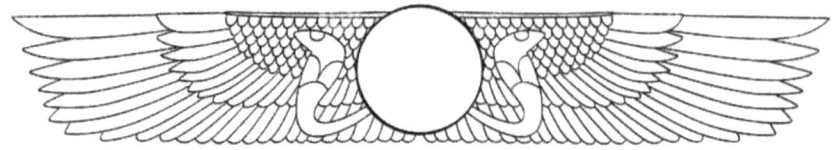

6. Mystical Union

"Remember that the Tarot is a great and sacred arcanum - its abuse is an obscenity in the inner and a folly in the outer. It is intended for quite other purposes than to determine when the tall dark man will meet the fair rich widow."

American rocket scientist Jack Parsons (1914-1952).

Arthur Edward Waite (1857-1942) was born in Brooklyn, New York. His father died at sea when he was very young and this resulted in his mother returning to her home country of England where Arthur was educated at a small private school in North London. The death of his sister, Frederika, in 1874, led Waite to study psychical research and then esotericism. His interest in metaphysics deepened further following frequent visits to the archives of the British Museum and in January 1891 he joined London's famous occult secret society, the Hermetic Order of the Golden Dawn, as an Initiate. In 1899 he entered the society's Second Order and in 1902 joined the Masonic fraternity Societas Rosicruciana in Anglia.[196]

Waite became a prolific writer on magick and the occult. Between 1886 and 1938 he published a succession of books on alchemy, the Holy Grail, black magick, Freemasonry, and Rosicrucianism. However, his most noted achievement took place in 1910 when he collaborated with artist Pamela Coleman-Smith (1878-1951) to produce a deck of tarot cards based upon imagery drawn from the symbols, themes, and colour associations used in the Golden Dawn's secret teachings. The result—commonly known as the Rider-Waite Deck—subsequently became the most important and enduring interpretation of the tarot ever

---
[196] https://en.wikipedia.org/wiki/A._E._Waite

produced. It remains the best-selling deck in the World today and established the foundation upon which many thousands of inferior imitations are based.

At the time of the release of Waite's deck the tarot was still a largely unknown divination system. It was one of the founders of the Golden Dawn, Samuel Liddell MacGregor Mathers (1854-1918), who introduced it into the society but it was Waite who took their astrological, Hermetic, and Egyptian correspondences and single-handedly infused them into a tarot deck that was popular with a much wider audience than that found within occult circles. Its engaging simplicity offered students and non-students of the occult an accessible gateway into a rich and deeply fascinating world of mythology, archetypal imagery, cosmology, and the Kabbalah; but it was Pamela Coleman-Smith's colourful and vibrant imagery that helped popularise the cards in the 1960s and 1970s—a period during which it was one of only a handful of decks available at regular bookstores.

One of those often found sitting alongside Waite's on booksellers shelves was the *Book of Thoth*—a deck developed in 1943 by fellow Golden Dawn associate Aleister Crowley and illustrated by artist Lady Marguerite Frieda Harris (1877-1962). It too incorporated Mather's Golden Dawn tarot attributions but also infused elements of Crowley's own perspective on magick and those of the French occultist Eliphas Lévi. The *Book of Thoth*'s accompanying manual—which was published under the same title—remains a classic textbook on magick and Kabbalistic theory.

BEAST 666

Edward Alexander Crowley, more commonly known as as Aleister Crowley (his spelling), was born on October 12, 1875, to an affluent business family located in the English town of Royal Leomington Spa, Warwickshire. His father, Edward Crowley (1829–1887), was originally trained as an engineer but he established and ran a lucrative brewing business called Crowley's Alton Ales. Following his death, Aleister inherited a sizeable fortune from his father's estate which

Left: Aleister Crowley: The Philosopher—one of his many personas.

allowed him the freedom to indulge in his passions. These included mysticism, the occult and, most importantly of all, magick.

Despite a deep distrust of formal education, Aleister Crowley was a highly-intelligent individual who became an accomplished poet, painter, master chess player and mountaineer—a field in which he held several records. This impressive catalogue of intellectual and artistic achievements is largely ignored and it is his occult activities that has turned him such a controversial and divisive figure. Even today he is erroneously regarded by non-occultists to be the consummate Satanist and Devil worshipper—the most prevalent perception of him—but it is largely an inaccurate reflection of the man and one which has partially become established in the minds of the public through the writer Dennis Wheatley[197] who mischaracterised Crowley as a heartless Devil-worshipper called "Mocata" in his 1934 novel *The Devil Rides Out*. This bad-boy image—which Crowley enjoyed promoting himself when ever the opportunity arose—is unfortunate as his contribution to modern occultism is unparalleled.

Like Waite, Crowley was a prolific writer on many occult and metaphysical topics but his extensive body of work has also been misinterpreted—mainly by those who attempt to judge it through their ignorance of the principles of occultism. Nevertheless, even the most fervent follower of the magus concedes that his philosophy—one based upon his belief that science and magick can co-exist—can be difficult to comprehend.

---

[197] Wheatley's private library included a copy of Aleister Crowley's book *Magick in Theory and Practice* which included a personal dedication of a photo of Crowley. Wheatley's birthdate was the same as Bowie's.

6. MYSTICAL UNION

Left: The Ancient Egyptian Stele of Revealing believed by Crowley to depict the three primary deities in the Book of the Law; namely Nuit, Hadit, and Ra-Hoor-Khuit.

Of all his indecipherable works, Crowley's most inaccessible is *Liber AL vel Legis*–or *The Book of the Law*. This convoluted manuscript of occult illumination was 'transmitted' to the occultist in Egypt in 1904 while he was on honeymoon with his newly-wedded wife Rose. Following a meditation held in the Kings Chamber of the Great Pyramid, a discarnate entity called Aiwass[198] appeared to them in their Cairo hotel room and dictated a three-part, futuristic, and apocalyptic document which Crowley later believed formed the basis of a new religion which he called Thelema.

While the World has failed to succumb to Thelema in the way Crowley predicted, its central tenet, "There is no law beyond do what thou wilt; every man and woman is a star; the word of sin is restriction."[199] nestled very comfortably into the collective ethos of many 1970s rock stars.

One could even argue that it became its mantra for it led to many rock musicians interpreting Crowley's as a license for debauchery. They were wrong. To Crowley, the phrase "Do What Thou Wilt" was an exhortation to his students to follow what he called their true "Magickal

---

[198] Aiwass describes himself in Liber AL as the "minister" of Hoor-paar-kraat, the True Self. Thelemites identify him with the Egyptian god Horus who governs the Aeon of Horus–a new era Crowley maintains was initiated in 1904 with the *Book of the Law*.
[199] Crowley, Aleister, *Liber II: The Message of The Master Therion*, The Equinox Volume III, independently published in 1919.

Will": which references the concept of the "Great Work" within Western Mystery Tradition teachings.

Rather than offering an easy, chilled-out, and trouble-free existence of the sort exhorted by the Hippy generation, the development of the Magickal Will is actually a deeply challenging process that requires a period of intense introspection on the part of the initiate before one's spiritual destiny becomes revealed to him or her. Thelemites invariably find this a difficult path to follow for it requires the sort of hard work, devotion, intense discipline, and focused application which few people living in this modern, fast-paced, technological society have the practical resources to develop.

For this, and many other reasons that are too complex to explore in this book but will be in a subsequent volume in this series, Crowley's Thelemitc philosophy failed to attract a strong following; even among students of the occult. However, it became popular with a small number of well-known rock-stars who saw through the nihilistic elements many felt were inherent in Crowley's philosophy. One of the most famous Thelemites was Led Zeppelin guitarist Jimmy Page (1944-present day) who at one-time possessed an extensive collection of Crowley memorabilia; including the magickian's former home Boleskine House near Loch Ness in Scotland.

Like Vince Taylor, Page also indulged in hard drugs but the guitarist did manage to escape from its grip relatively unharmed; without feeling a need to cloak himself in a self-destructing messiah-complex—a condition many magickians contract—and to remain relatively grounded. It is not difficult to trace a history of occultists who lose their minds (and souls) through close engagement with magick. A common feature of this 'affliction' is a morbid adherence to a bloated, self-aggrandising, ego. Several examples of this can be found throughout the music industry but the following accounts that illustrate just how destructive an interest in occultism can be should act as a warning to anyone in this field of research and to impress upon them the need to progress very carefully before dabbling with dark forces.

6. MYSTICAL UNION

MAGICK, MUSIC AND MADNESS

On March 14, 2012, the UK's leading weekly music paper, *New Musical Express*, published an article titled *50 of the Greatest Producers Ever*. It was, as its title suggests, a run-down of the most important or influential music-producers in the history of rock and pop music.[200] Its author, Tim Chester, placed the recording pioneer Joe Meek at number one and ranked him higher than Brian Wilson, Phil Spector, and George Martin.

Meek's reputation as a primary driving force in 1960s popular culture was borne from his unique approach to recording music. Meek saw himself as an artist and always played a vital role in the composition of the songs that he was recording. The unorthodox, electronics-based methods he employed when capturing and creating sound resulted in some of the most memorable hits of the period and for that he is regarded today as a maverick—someone whose methods challenged the established recording industry and its strict working practices. Meek pursued his goals regardless and worked himself so hard that, along with an unhealthy interest in the paranormal and a dependency on drugs, the price he paid was not only to his finances, reputation, and business interests—all at the cost of the sanity of himself and others that he collaborated with.

Robert George "Joe" Meek (1929-1967) was born at 1 Market Square[201], in the small town of Newent, Gloucestershire. He developed an interest in electronics at a very early age and very quickly filled his parents' garden shed with an odd assortment of electronic components, circuit boards, and radios which he repaired, modified and experimented with.

Joe also developed a deep love for music. In 1934 he asked his parents for a toy gramophone as a Christmas present upon which he endlessly played a small collection of children's records. Not content with using the device simply for entertainment, he experimented with its

---
[200] https://www.nme.com/list/50-of-the-greatest-producers-ever-1353
[201] The number of the house Meek lived in is significant. Tarot Arcana 1 (THE MAGICIAN) governs electronics, communications, and vibratory sound. A 'market is a place of commerce and this is also governed by Mercury—the card's ruler.

limited capabilities to an unexpected result. Later on in life he reflected upon the exact moment he became drawn into recording sound.

> "At this time I used to be fascinated with making things out of shoe boxes like puppet shows and slot machines and all sorts of things, and I used to try and experiment with my gramophone, and I discovered if you played the record at the end on the run-out groove you could shout down the sound chamber and the sound would be imprinted in the grooves. And I thought that I'd discovered something marvellous, and of course I was really doing just what Edison had discovered years before."[202]

Another area of the arts that interested Joe was theatrics. Inspired by a local amateur dramatics performance, he staged Saturday afternoon shows for friends in Newent. The stories he enacted were usually improvisational but the themes they were based upon were very often macabre: focussed on his interest in paranormal mysteries and witches.

In his 2011 book, *The Legendary Joe Meek*, John Repsch speculates on the probable source of Joe's darker interests. He suggests that the young boy was greatly influenced by a commonly held belief in and around his home town that the heavily wooded area of the Forest of Dean which surrounded his home was a hotbed for the practice of Witchcraft.

> "...there are said to have been hangings and burnings in the area – some as close by as Newent Market Square where Joe was now living. Stories of mystery proliferated, mainly of ghosts still keeping up regular appearances ever since the Civil War: the man in the old Tan Yard who was seen walking around without his head; the woman in white who caused a car crash on Ross Road; of nearby Conigree Court, where "all sorts of things have been seen."

---

[202] Repsch, John, *The Legendary Joe Meek: The Telstar Man*, Cherry Red Books, 2011.

6. Mystical Union

The following Christmas Joe asked for a year's subscription to *Practical Wireless*—a monthly magazine that included articles and projects aimed at the budding electronics enthusiast. Using its circuit diagrams, Joe constructed a crystal radio and later on built a television set with a 12" screen. This made the Meeks the first family in the area to own one but it proved useless as there were not yet any TV masts transmitting television signals in the Newent area.

In all regards, Joe's head was in a completely different space to that of friends and family. His exploration of electronics consumed him: even to the extent that it jeopardised his academic studies. His brother, Eric, recalled that:

> "Joe was a dreamer. I mean, he'd sit and be miles and miles away, and the world was in oblivion to Joe, like. You could talk to him and he didn't take no notice. Joe tended to live and think in the different world he'd be in. He didn't live in our reality world."

In 1948, Joe received his call-up papers for National Service and he opted to join the Royal Air Force who, once they recognised his advanced knowledge in radio and electronics, sent him to RAF Yatesbury, Wiltshire, where he spent two months in technical training. He emerged as a radar mechanic and was posted to an assortment of radar installations located around the West Country. Night after night Joe sat alone in one small hut or another—usually perched on the edge of a cliff—scanning the night sky visually and on screen for any signs of aircraft movement. It was hard and tedious work but it fomented within him a deep interest in outer space.

Following his demob in 1950, Joe returned to his home town intending to consider his future career on 'civvy street'. Keen to get out of the narrow social confines of Newent, he found employment as a salesman at the electrical retailers Currys in the nearby city of Gloucester. It was uninspiring work and he quickly moved on to become a TV serviceman at the nearby MEB store where he had a much closer, hands-on, relationship with electronics.

While working for the MEB, Geoff Woodward—a engineer who was working in the same workshop—introduced him to sound recording using a tape-recorder. This enthralled Joe and he soon began recording and mixing popular tunes which he took from the radio and later spliced onto tapes. Woodward remembered that:

> "These tapes he would often play at fetes and Saturday evening dances where once again he was in demand. He only charged expenses though, being quite content with all the applause. When he was not dancing he would often introduce the records and may well have been one of the first ever mobile disc jockeys. For outdoor events he would use two huge speakers, and in Newent the sound could be heard all over town."

In the summer of 1953, Joe took the next evolutional path by cutting his first recording using sound effects he built at the MEB workshop. The company had played a pivotal role in his early career as a record-producer but Joe grew restless and left to work at Broadmeads: Gloucester's largest electrical firm. A year later he started to record local dance bands and in the same summer cut his first vocal record featuring Newent schoolgirl, Marlene Williams (she later married Joe's brother, Eric). Around the same time, Joe came across an job advert which had been placed in one of the national newspapers by an established London film studio. He applied, was accepted, and quickly prepared to move to the big city.

ENGINEERING SUCCESS

The hustle and bustle of London was a world away from his sleepy and unsophisticated home county of Gloucestershire but Joe adjusted well to the change and soon found his recording skills in high demand by everyone from Radio Luxembourg to the jazz musician Humphrey Lyttelton (1921-2008) for whom he engineered the single *Bad Penny Blues* in 1956.

6. MYSTICAL UNION

Left: Joe Meek in his home studio in the early-1960s.

Buoyed on by his success, Joe set up his own production company, RGM Sound Ltd., which he operated from a tiny, home studio at 304 Holloway Road, Islington: a three-floor flat positioned above a shop that sold leather goods. From within thi cramped and chaotic premise—which was located in a dark, dirty, and noisy district of North London—Meek rather miraculously produced records by some of the biggest names in the music business. These included Shirley Bassey, Cliff Bennett and the Rebel Rousers, Mike Berry, Petula Clark, Jess Conrad, Lonnie Donegan, Billy Fury, Tom Jones, Tommy Steele, Big Jim Sullivan, Screaming Lord Sutch and Gene Vincent.

With these and other minor names in the music business, Meek produced hit after hit on the UK singles chart and in September 1962 really hit the big-time with his best known composition, *Telstar*—an instrumental recorded by The Tornados. The song—which Meek named after the first NASA communications satellite, launched on July 10, 1962—remained in the charts for 25 weeks: five of them at the number one spot. *Telstar* was a Worldwide success; reaching the number one position in the charts of Belgium, Ireland, New Zealand, South Africa and the United States where it became the first single by an English group to top the Billboard Hot 100.

The Tornados followed up their success with three more top-20 singles and Meek had another number-one in July 1964 with *Have I the Right?* by The Honeycombs. It seemed that Joe could do no wrong, but by April 1966 the hit singles were starting to dry-up dry-up. As a result the record-producer experienced deepening financial problems. Further legal matters put additional pressure on his company's accounts and led him to become harassed by the Official Receiver for related unpaid liabilities. As it was, his monetary woes were the least of his problems. Joe also became caught up in the dark criminal world of the

Kray Twins, suffered increasingly from his bipolar disorder, and was even developing schizophrenia.

In his book *Great British Eccentrics*, Steven Tucker described the rapid decline in Meek's life at that time.

> "Meek started experiencing psychotic delusions, culminating in his refusal to use the studio telephone for important communications due to his belief that his landlady was eavesdropping on his calls through the chimney, that he could control the minds of others with his recording equipment, and that he could monitor his acts while away from the studio through supernatural means."[203]

By late 1966, Joe had fallen badly behind on his rent for the flat/recording studio. The lease on the building was coming up for renewal and he felt that his long-suffering landlady—who lived in the same premises and complained constantly about the noise Meek's recording sessions were creating—was trying to get rid of him. Meek was effectively flat broke. His personal bank account was overdrawn and he faced the very real prospect of having his recording equipment taken by bailiffs in lieu of his mounting debts.

With declining record sales and royalties for his work not finding its way to him (including for his *Telstar* composition for which he received a copyright claim. (This was settled in Joe's favour three months after his death. It amounted to some £3m in today's money.) Joe Meek was now fast losing his grip on reality—a condition brought on by creative burn-out, mental exhaustion, and a reliance on barbiturates and amphetamines to keep him going.

A Hidden Life

Joe's paranoid state kept growing. He firmly believed that his flat was being bugged by unknown persons: traitors both in and out of the music business he felt were attempting to steal his ideas and recordings.

[203] Steven, Tucker, S. D., *Great British Eccentrics*, Amberley Publishing, Stroud, Gloucestershire, 2015.

6. MYSTICAL UNION

Whether Joe Meek was truly surrounded by spies and enemies as he believed is unclear but what is evident is that he was most certainly a man with secrets—not least of was the fact that he was gay. Although it had long since been accepted that homosexuals frequented all areas of the performance arts, the practice was widely frowned upon by the rest of society: even in the late-1960s. In fact, not only was male homosexuality deemed socially unacceptable but was illegal in the United Kingdom.

In 1963, Meek was arrested and subsequently convicted of "importuning for immoral purposes" in a London public toilet for which he received £15 fine. The publicity that the trial generated had a profound impact on Meek's personal psychology. For many years, he had striven to hide his sexuality from everyone: particularly from his family and mother in particular. His criminal record also left him feeling vulnerable to what he saw as 'bad actors'. In an interview with his brothers, Eric and Arthur, featured in a BBC documentary in 1991, it was maintained that Joe was never the same person after his conviction. Arthur even admitted that Joe had once told him that he was being blackmailed over his sexual preferences—though he did not say by whom.[204]

For such an energetic, out-going, and buoyant personality, Joe did appear to start attracting a string of dark influences. One of these was focussed on the occult and the paranormal which, as we saw earlier, first began as a child in Newent. A particular strand of modern spiritualism that peeked Meeks interest the most was known as "Electronic Voice Phenomenon" (EVP). This relatively unknown strand of psychic research unexpectedly emerged in 1959 after Swedish painter and film producer Friedrich Jürgenson recorded birds singing. When he played back the tape, he was astounded to discover that, in addition to the natural sounds he expected to hear, he detected the voice of his dead father and deceased wife calling his name from the spirit world.[205] Subsequent recordings included what he believed to be was a message from his late mother.[206] Along with Latvian psychologist Konstantin

---
[204] *The Very Strange Story of Joe Meek*, Arena, BBC, 1991.
[205] Senkowski, Ernst, *Analysis of Anomalous Audio and Video Recordings, presented before the Society For Scientific Exploration*, US, June 1995
[206] Cardoso, Anabela, *TC Voices: Contact with Another Reality?*, ParaDocs, 2003.

Raudive (1909-1974)—who popularised EVP throughout the 1970s—he eventually accumulated a library of over 100,000 recordings which featured a series of communications with discarnate people.[207]

Meek was intrigued by this research and the unorthodox use of a technology he had a close affinity with. He decided to try and replicate their results by setting-up a portable tape-machine in local graveyards in the hope of capturing the voices of dead spirits. His results were mixed. (though he did maintain that he had recorded a conversation with a distressed cat). Nevertheless, his lack of tangible results did not stop Meek from wanting to delve deeper into the world of the paranormal; so he paid for a subscription to to the popular periodical *Psychic News* from which he learnt more about the world of psychism and psychics.

SOUNDS OF SPACE

Left: Geoff Goddard (1937-2000)—classically-trained hit-maker.

In the late summer of 1961, Meek commissioned a 22 year-old songwriter from Reading called Geoff Goddard (1937-2000) to write a memorable song for the popular British actor Johnny Layton (1936-present day). Goddard was had just graduated from the Royal Academy of Music as a concert pianist but he grew increasingly inclined towards composing popular melodies. Joe asked him to write something with Leyton in mind over the coming weekend and on the Sunday, Goddard was inspired to draft a song about a man who heard the voice of his dead lover calling to him from her ethereal abode. He titled it *Johnny Remember Me* and presented to Joe at his flat the next day. Meek was impressed and the two men worked together in the studio to flesh-out the idea. The result was Meek's first UK number one record—an achievement he attained despite the single being

---

[207] Raudive, Konstantin, *Breakthrough: An Amazing Experiment in Electronic Communication With the Dead*, Taplinger Publishing Co. 1971.

considered a rather tasteless topic by the clergy and subsequently banned by the BBC.[208]

The success of *Johnny Remember Me* cemented Meek and Goddard's professional relationship. Together they had a string of hit singles but the two men discovered they had more than a mutual interest in writing and recording music. They were also fascinated in metaphysics.

Bob Kingston worked with them both during his time at the Islington recording studio and developed a unique insight into Meek's inner psyche.

> "I think basically he must have been a religious man because he was searching constantly. He was not a devout church-goer but within himself I think he was very much a lost individual. I always thought he was a very lonely person but you could never really get to know him.
>
> They (Meek and Goddard) became really close. These two very strange personalities worked like magic together. I think they were very similar in make-up and temperament; both very mystical.[209] They didn't think and live on normal planes as the average person.
>
> They were constantly searching for something and I believe that this is very largely the reason why their sensitivity was so attuned to outer things that they were capable of creating what they did."[210]

The spiritual influence that was pervading the two men was expressed through one of their musical collaborations—the song *Magic Star* which was a vocal version of Meeks international hit record *Telstar*. Sung by a

---

[208] https://en.wikipedia.org/wiki/Johnny_Remember_Me
[209] It is interesting to note that the Gematria value of the Meek/Goddard hit *Johnny Remember Me* is 1410–the same as the term "A Twin Soul"
[210] Repsch, John, *The Legendary Joe Meek: The Telstar Man*, Cherry Red Books, 2011.

15-year-old, unknown singer called Kenny Hollywood (real name Kenny Plows), it was released by Decca Records in 1962. Its lyrics revealed Goddard's mystical philosophy.

> *As the stars light up the sky*
> *And I kneel and pray*
> *Guide the footsteps*
> *Safe and sound*
> *Back home again to stay*

Goddard clearly believed in the existence of a sentient and benevolent cosmos. He was also of the opinion that it was possible to forge a link with some sort of 'universal intelligence' and to use the results of this connection in the creative process. The songwriter spoke about this process as it impacted his own songwriting and in a recognition of Meek's creative talents.

> "I believe one can mentally attune oneself to an infinite knowledge or this unknown thing in infinity. It can be done. I believe that inventors, scientists, great creators in the Arts are really totally devoted people who work this single course in life and totally attune themselves to becoming receptive to available things from outer space somewhere. I believe that Joe was, like Geoff, one of these very sensitive people, lonely people – complete loneliness, total individuals; totally different sets of values in life, but nevertheless had great creative ability and this mental attuneness which enabled them to draw on something to enhance this creativity, and therefore do what they were doing."

In 1959–in a way that is reminiscent of the classical composer Karlheinz Stockhausen–Meek composed a "sonic landscape" which was intended to be a reflection of his personal perception of the cosmos.[211] The result was a ground-breaking piece of music titled *I Hear*

---
[211] Sub-titled *An outer space music fantasy* it was, as its composer put it, an attempt

6. MYSTICAL UNION

a New World which he recorded at Lansdowne Studios, Holland Park, London, using a five-piece skiffle band called the Blue Men. It was released by Meek's own record label *Triumph* the following year.

I Hear a New World is a remarkable and mesmerising aural adventure, one that was ground-breaking at the time and established, or pre-heralded, the emergence of the psychedelic and space-rock a decade later. Although predominantly an instrumental album, its opening track, *I Hear a New World*, included vocals and the lyrics "*I hear a new world. Calling me, calling me.*" accompanied by strange backing-vocals that replicated the ethereal voices of aliens far off in time and space. Meek clearly had an interest in extraterrestrials (which he referred to on his album by such strange names as "Globbots", "Saroos", and "Dribcots") but did not speak openly about his clear belief in the existence of extraterrestrial life outside of his close circle of friends.

WHERE MUSIC AND MAGIC MEET

The aspect of Meek's and Goddard's spiritual leanings that did emerge into the public arena came about in a most bizarre way. Meek and Goddard shared a deep admiration for the legendary American singer/songwriter Buddy Holly—a musician who was a seminal influence in the emerging rock and roll scene of the mid-1950s. Unfortunately, Holly's career was cut short when he tragically died in a place crash in early 1959. The aircraft he, Ritchie Valens and The Big Bopper (Jiles Perry "J.P." Richardson Jr.) were traveling in, crashed into a cornfield five miles northwest of Clear Lake, Iowa, shortly after takeoff.[212]

Geoff Goddard was keen on finding out whether the spirit of Buddy Holly had survived the musician's death. Learning that Meek had some experience contacting the dead via a ouija board, they started to hold twice-weekly seances. They eventually made contact with a number of dead spirits and these included Joe's father, the famous tenor singer Mario Lanza (1921-1959), and Lithuanian-born American singer/actor Al Jolson (1886-1950).

"to create a picture in music of what could be up there in outer space."
[212] The cause of the accident was placed on the plane's faulty gyroscope.

Following one of their psychic sittings, Goddard returned home and later that night had a dream in which Buddy Holly appeared to him. The following morning Goddard awoke and felt inspired to write a song about the singer's untimely death. He called it *Tribute To Buddy Holly* and played it to Joe who was thrilled with the composition which he felt should be sung by British singer and actor Mike Berry (1942-present day).

Following its recording, Meek and Goddard felt it was only right that they should ask Holly what his impressions were of the song. They held another séance and made contact with him. Geoff later explained what happened next.

> "And we sat and put our hands on the tumbler and it started moving round and spelt out Buddy's name and mine. And Joe asked if '*Johnny Remember Me*' would be a hit, and it spelt out that it would go to No.1. And he asked if the tribute to Buddy Holly that I'd written – would that be a hit, and the answer was: 'See you in the charts'."

Holly's prediction turned out to be entirely correct. *Tribute To Buddy Holly* reached number 24 in the UK singles charts in October 1961. As it was riding up the charts, Geoff held a number of interviews with the music press during which he spoke about the contact he and Meek had established with the spirit of Holly. The story caught the attention of the spiritualist newspaper *Psychic News* who wrote a lead article based on the seances and Goddard's belief that the source of his earlier song *Johnny Remember Me* came from the inner planes. He explained to them that:

> "I am sure I receive my inspiration from the spirit world. When I wrote '*Johnny Remember Me*' it was early morning and I had just opened my eyes. I always keep a tape recorder by my bed, and I sang that song into it without working on it at all.[213]

---

[213] *Does Dead Rock Star Guide Song Writer: 'Johnny Remember Me Sensation,*

Goddard expanded a little further on his comments and on his belief that creative ideas can come from the heavens.

> "I intend to go on with my songwriting although it seems I must wait for inspiration from the spirit world. I find I can sit at the piano for hours without being able to write a note of music – and yet after a dreamless sleep I can produce a bestseller in practically the time it takes to sing it!"

Goddard was also interviewed by the music paper *Disc*. He told their interviewer that he was convinced that Buddy Holly had not only inspired the song but had become a guiding, or steering influence in his songwriting career.

> "Every Monday night I attend seances with a development group and this first message was passed on to me from someone who received it and who knew I was a songwriter. Since then I've had several more, this time directly to me from Buddy, and these talks with him have given me the encouragement and inspiration I need. Buddy said he would help me and soon after that I started getting better ideas. I wrote my first recorded song, 'Lone Rider', which was cut by the Fleerakkers and then I wrote 'Johnny Remember Me'. I remember writing that song. I woke up on a Sunday morning and within ten minutes it was completed, words and music. Buddy said it would reach No.1 – I believed him; he said it was a great song and would be the start of good things for me. He is a constant inspiration to me"

The success of *Tribute to Buddy Holly* came as something of a relief to Mike Berry as it revived his singing career. He had, for some time, been the lead vocalist for Meek's house-band The Outlaws but the musicians had developed a career of their own and even attained a

---

Psychic News, September 8, 1961.

respectable level of success with two instrumentals which entered the lower reaches of the UK singles charts in March and June 1961 respectively.

The Outlaws were, in many ways, a seminal group. Its members included; Chas Hodges (1943-2018), who was better known later on as one half of the duo Chas and Dave; Bobby Graham (1940-2009), who played on thirteen number one singles and was touted as a replacement drummer for Beatles; and Mick Underwood (1945-present day), who later worked with a variety of artists before joining the Ian Gillan Band in the 1980s. However, its most famous member was the iconic guitarist Ritchie Blackmore (1945-present day), who was a member of the hard rock band Deep Purple and then the founder of Ritchie Blackmores Rainbow with singer Ronnie James Dio.[214]

Outlaws and Graves

Although Meek's interest in the paranormal seems to have been fairly mundane and low-level something occurred around this time that deepened his fascination in the darkside of the human experience. During a visit to Highgate Cemetery, North London, late one night (presumably to record the discarnate voices of any spirits lurking about) he happened to encounter the famous (or infamous) occultist David Farrant (1946-2019). Farrant was President of the British Psychic and Occult Society at the time and came to the attention of the national news media following his trial held at London's Old Bailey in 1974 for practicing Witchcraft. He was found guilty and received a jail sentence of 4 years and 8 months.

The occultist was not only unpopular with the British establishment but he was also a contentious figure in the world of psychic research as he expressed a deep interest in esoterica, the rites and tenets of the Old Religion, Wicca and High Magick: something he incorporated into his

---

[214] Blackmore, like Dio, has long since had a reputation for being interested in spirituality and the occult—something he seemed to have developed early on during his career as a session musician. is even worth considering whether it was as a direct result of his joining the Joe Meek organisation in 1960 that he became exposed to the psychic world frequented by Meek and Goddard.

6. Mystical Union

more traditional methods of psychic research.[215]

Is it possible that, either during or following their meeting, Farrant influenced Meek's spiritual development by introducing him to darker elements of occultism? This is unclear but it is interesting to note that in his biography of Meek, John Repsch maintained there were rumours in the 1960s that the record producer was not only engaged in psychic activities but that he also practised Black Magick with Goddard–the intention being to use the dark power they raised to push their careers forward to greater heights. Repsch even maintained that they were specifically attempting to make contact with the "Great Beast" Aleister Crowley.

Did Farrant introduce Meek and Goddard to these aspects of the dark arts? Farrant disputes this and in a 2013 article titled *A Life In The Death of Joe Meek* he described the train of events that followed his unexpected meeting with Meek in Highgate Cemetery.

> "We met on about three occasions after this, and had long discussions in my Highgate flat and at a local café which basically involved him wanting to become involved in my group. Sadly this never happened, as Joe also had other ongoing problems at the time, mainly involving personal disputes with other songwriters and singers involved in the record industry. I was also concerned that Joe's desire to become involved in occult matters would have been somewhat dangerous to encourage due his fragile emotional state at the time..."[216]

Either way, around this time there was a dramatic increase in paranormal activity within Meek's flat/recording studio. Repsch described such occurrences as Meek hearing:

> "...footsteps went round the bed and the spirit

---

[215] https://davidfarrant.org/about\](https://davidfarrant.org/about%5C
[216] Farrant, David, *A Life In The Death Of Joe Meek*, https://davidfarrant.org/a-life-in-the-death-of-joe-meek/, 2013.

tripped over the cord of his electric fire, pulling out the plug, and another occasion when he came downstairs at 3 o'clock in the morning to find the chairs and tables all dancing round the living room, he imparted his news in a state of extreme nervous excitement.

Playing back tapes of the day's sessions on his own he would sometimes hear voices that should not have been there, and once told the press that on the fade-out of a Riot Squad record, 'I Take It That We're Through', "A phantom voice mutters 'hello' or something like that". The mutter is barely audible but is in there somewhere amongst the last guitar twangings. Late at night when the house was empty he was sure he could sometimes hear people talking in the studio..."

Strangest of all, for some reason Meek had painted the classic Illuminati/Masonic symbol of the All-Seeing Eye on his apartment wall[217] and then reported hearing voices coming from it warning him about certain associates in his life.

The Appearance of Rameses

What started out as an inquisitive foray into occultism had now developed into something more sinister. On occasions, quite dark paranormal activity took place in Meek's flat which appears to have coincided his deepening fascination with Black Magick, Some sources maintain that he was inspired to study occultism after reading the works of Dennis Wheatley and Aleister Crowley.

Despite this unwelcome ethereal intrusion, regular seances continued to be held and, following the success of connecting with the spirit of Buddy Holly via paranormal means, Meek's psychic interests expanded greatly and he began to visit fortune-tellers in Soho. This was

---

[217] Some cultures around the World believe that the All-Seeing Eye motif protects them from evil spirits.

6. MYSTICAL UNION

followed by a trip to a medium based in Essex, known only as "Mrs. Smith" who was able to predict the most favourable days for him to record. During the course of one consultation she informed him that a Red Indian chieftain had starting acting as one of Meek's spiritual guides. Another spirit had joined him on the inner planes whom she identified as the ancient Egyptian Pharaoh Rameses the Great. This thrilled Meek who immediately began to collect as much literature as he could find on pharaohs, mummies and Egyptology.[218]

CONTROLLING ALIENS?

By 1966, Meek's fascination with the subject had completely taken over his life but at the same time, the immense success he had enjoyed as the UK's premier hit-maker waning and the stress that declining sales brought, further exacerbated his declining mental health. Meek was completely convinced that there were poltergeists living in his flat and that photographs hung on the walls of his recording studio were attempting to communicate with him. Most extraordinary of all, was his conviction that aliens were controlling his mind and that on occasions they even controlled what he was saying.

Was Meek's conviction that extraterrestrials had infiltrated his life correct or was it simply an indication of his growing paranoia? He certainly believed in extraterrestrial life: as his LP *I Hear a New World* demonstrated. It also seems to have been a topic that he discussed with his friend Geoff Goddard who was also extremely reticent about his interest in the subject of ufology. However, the story of his brief musical career reveals some intriguing insights that can be traced back a few years prior to teaming up with Meek.

When Goddard decided to pursue a musical career within popular music rather than follow the trail set by his classical music training, he composed a large catalogue of material. Some of this was later recorded by several well-known 1960s artists; including Heinz, Mike Berry, The Tornados, The Outlaws, Freddie Starr, and the original shock-rocker

---

[218] Repsch, John, *The Legendary Joe Meek: The Telstar Man*, Cherry Red Books, 2011.

Screaming Lord Sutch.[219]

Although he was happy writing for Joe, Goddard initially had aspirations to become a pop-star in his own right. In an effort to establish himself he released a string of singles between 1961 and 1963. They all flopped and his final attempt to conquer the hit-parade occurred in October 1963 when he released a self-penned song titled *Sky Men*. The single was backed by another of his compositions, *Walk With Me My Angel*. It was produced by Meek—which makes its alien-inspired theme even more indicative of the two men's common interest in aliens. It contained the following lyrics:

> *Sky Men, Sky Men, where do you come from?*
> *Where are you going to, Sky Men?*
> *As I was walking out one night, me and my darlin'*
> *We saw in the sky a flashing light, me and my darlin'*
> *And as it hovered overhead*
>
> *And as the sun was turning red*
> *We heard a voice and that voice said:*
> *"Children of Earth, be not afraid, for we come in peace"*
> *Sky Men, Sky Men, where do you come from?*
> *Where are you going to, Sky Men?*
>
> *If you are ever out at night, you and your darlin'*
> *And if you see this flashing light, you and your darlin'*
> *Don't be afraid and run away*
> *For soon there's going to come a day*
> *When all the world will hear them say:*
> *"Children of Earth, be not afraid, for we come in peace"*

The failure of *Sky Men* as a commercial single scuppered Goddard's desire for fame and fortune. It was one of the last occasions that he

---
[219] https://en.wikipedia.org/wiki/Geoff_Goddard\](https://en.wikipedia.org/wiki/Geoff_Goddard%5C

contributed a song to Joe Meek's stable of recording artists and within a year the two men had fallen out; resulting in Goddard being so burned by the music industry that he left it altogether and returned to Reading.

Unmanaged Decline

The reasons for Meek and Goddard falling out are not clear but in all probability it was at least founded on Meeks descent into paranoia which had become so bad that his conviction that he was being spied upon led him to insist that his musicians and co-workers communicated with one another using hand-written notes which then had to be burnt once read. The poor state of Meek's mental health is reflected in an account given by one of his most avid supporters.

Although the Holloway Road flat Meek lived/recorded in was small, he also held the lease on an apartment a short distance away and rented it out to one-time Outlaws guitarist Ritchie Blackmore. At one point, when he was on tour, his German wife Margaret, occasionally visited Joe and spent the evening with him during which they had in-depth discussions about mysticism and the paranormal. One evening, she visited Meek, knocked on his door and was met by the mere shadow of the man.

> "I got a shock of my life because he was white in his face and it was like the eyes coming out of his head. Actually he looked like a devil and when I talked to him he didn't answer me. He was like a madman, saying somebody stealing something. He was dressed completely in black: black trousers and a very shiny shirt and black shoes. We went in the living room and he started running in the room like an idiot; he didn't sit, he stood and was running from one corner into the other – very restless – and was keeping his hands on his head and always said, 'I don't understand it, I don't understand it. I don't know what's happening".

Margaret believed that his poor mental state was due to his prolonged exposure to the dark arts.

> "I think it must have been either this [Aleister] Crowley or somebody through black magic who disturbing his way to live. And this is what he always told me: 'I'm not by myself'. I said, 'Why, you're sitting there by yourself?' 'No,' he said, 'There's somebody around me – I can feel it. There's somebody in the air.'
>
> (Meek felt this to be a negative spirit that had taken possession of him.) I said, 'Tell me why are you so restless, why are you always shouting and get so mad about things. And he always said, 'Listen. There's somebody in me. I can't help myself, I can't get him out. I feel sometimes I'm not myself; I'm talking but it's not my voice.' He told me that in his life before, he was a nice person but in this life he's evil: 'I have to get everybody back for what they've done before in this life.' What I think was that he was doing black magic. I think in his black magic he was wishing some other producer very bad luck. I don't know any names but I know he was wishing him failure..."[220]

Meek's visitor that night made another startling connection.

> "Another thing which he always said to me, and said that night, 'Margaret, you are so much like Lady Harris.' And I said, 'Who is she?' – 'No, no,' he said, 'It's OK, it's OK.' She was the girlfriend of Aleister Crowley."

Lady Frieda Harris was, of course, the artist who illustrated Crowley's *Book of Thoth* tarot deck.

---

[220] In the well-researched biopic *Telstar: The Joe Meek Story* (2008) Joe is shown performing an occult ritual in his flat by incanting Latin while seated inside a pentagram that he had drawn in chalk on the floor of his front room.

6. Mystical Union

The Day the Music Died

Meek spent Christmas 1966 with his family in Newent. The rest improved his mood, partially restored his self-confidence, and encouraged him to make plans for the future. On New Year's Eve, his brother drove Joe back to London where he felt well enough to see the New Year in with his landlady, Violet Shenton. His optimistic mood continued throughout the weeks that followed and on January 23, 1967, Joe wrote to John Ginnett—a solicitor tasked with over-seeing Meeks strained financial affairs—in which he laid out his plans for the coming year.

> "I have a couple of really hot disc's to offer Ive recorded with new groups so a really solid arrangement can be made with E.M.I. for world rights and publishing, after Ive met there man in charge Im going to ask for a certain amount of guaranteed promotion, you may feel Im going to far at times, but let me have a go."

Joe explained that he was planning a trip to Egypt with his studio assistant Patrick Pink (aka Robbie Duke) and that they were intending to spend a fortnight in Cairo where they intended to visit ancient Egyptian antiquities and significant sites of archeological significance. Meek failed to mention to his solicitor that his primary goal in making this trip was to discover more about the former life of Ramses—his inner-plane guide.

However, despite the sense of optimism Meek was now experiencing, events behind the scenes were taking a very dark turn. On January 16, a tractor driver ploughing a field near to the remote Suffolk village of Tattingstone, uncovered two suitcases that contained the dismembered remains of a young man. This triggered an intensive police hunt int what the national newspapers called the "Suitcase Murder". The bodily remains were identified as those of Bernard Oliver, a 17-year-old youth from Muswell Hill. Oliver was a homosexual and as a consequence, all male gays in the North London area were investigated by the police for possible information leading to the arrest of the killer.

In the weeks that followed, their net of investigation drew closer to the home of Joe Meek. Now, Patrick Pink believed that he was also being spied on but by the police (which lends some credence to Meek's belief he was being surveilled and that his phone calls were monitored.) When four, nearby, North London addresses were raided, Meek feared that he might be next...and he had too many secrets that he was desperate to protect from any number of prying eyes. This added to the intense psychological pain building up in Meek and a few weeks later he called an end what, as Repsch put it, was a "...hopeless war with the 1,001 bogeymen inside him."

Joe awoke one morning and was in a particularly bad mood. He had a small breakfast and then went upstairs to his studio to begin work. Prior to powering up his recording equipment, Meek shouted down to Patrick and told him to ask Mrs. Shenton to come up and see him. Violet answered the call and, upon hearing of Meek's bad emotional state from Patrick, climbed up the short flight of stairs hoping to improve Meek's poor emotional state.

Once she reached the upper landing, a brief, somewhat heated, exchange took place between her and Joe regarding his rent-book. The terse discussion ended and, as Violet turned to head back down the stairs, Meek grabbed a single-barrelled shotgun he was borrowing from former Tornados bassist Heinz Burt, loaded it with a single cartridge, pointed it at his landlady, and shot her in the back.

Upon hearing the explosion from the downstairs office, Patrick came rushing out to see what had happened. As he began to climb the stairs, the body of Mrs Shelton came tumbling down and landed face-down in his arms. She had sustained a fatal injury. Patrick shouted back up the stairs "She's dead." and then, having laid her body to one side, he tentatively started to climb the stairs towards Joe's studio. He had not progressed very far when he heard a second gunshot. He arrived on the landing to find Joe covered in blood and body tissue. Meek had turned the shotgun on himself and blown his own head off.

The date of his suicide was February 3, 1967–the exact same day that Buddy Holly died in his plane crash in 1959.

GRAHAM BOND ORGANISATION

Another eccentric Englishman who also fell under the spell of magick and drugs was the '60s jazz/rock musician Graham Bond (1937-1974) who was a major influence on the UK rhythm and blues scene in the 1960s. Born in Romford, Essex, Bond studied music at the Royal Liberty School in Gidea Park, East London. His first public performance took place in 1960 with the Goudie Charles Quintet with whom Bond continued playing for the following twelve months prior to joining the highly-influential band Alexis Korner's Blues Incorporated. Bond did not settle and left to form the Graham Bond Quartet with ex-Korner members Ginger Baker (1939-2019) on drums and Jack Bruce (1943-2014) on double bass—both musicians found fame playing with Eric Clapton in the late 1960s supergroup, Cream.[221]

Bond's band morphed into the Graham Bond Organisation soon afterwards but the musician's constant use of hard drugs contributed to such a decline in his mental and physical health that it led to the band's dissolution in 1967. Even after the break-up, Bond exhibited further serious mental disorders; including manic episodes interspersed with periods of intense depression. During this period he became so ingrained in the study of Aleister Crowley and Thelema that he started to believe he was his illegitimate son. Bond felt obligated to continue his 'father's' work and embraced the Satanic role he believed Crowley espoused.

Bond's fascination with Crowley bled over into his music. After moving to America, he recorded two solo albums. The first, released in 1968, featured the Crowley-inspired title *Love is the Law*[222] with its follow-up appearing in 1969 under the name *Mighty Grahame Bond*. The album did not sell well and the success Bond craved for continued to elude him. Within a year of its release the result of his constant drug

[221] https://en.wikipedia.org/wiki/Graham_Bond
[222] The phrase "Love is the Law, Love Under Will" is a central tenet to all of Crowley's disciples or followers. In addition to being a form of social greeting it is also the formula for an important occult principle.

Left: Graham Bond the Magician. Photographed with his magic staff and a five-pointed star (the Ancient Egyptian symbol for Sirius) around his neck.

abuse hit the musician hard. With his career floundering and his marriage now dissolved, the years of commercial failure had left his financial affairs in complete ruin. A catalogue of personal problems caused another mental breakdown and he spent January 1973 in hospital.

Bond never fully recovered from his health issues and, on May 8, 1974, he died after falling under the wheels of a train while it passed through Finsbury Park Station, London. The musician was just 36 years of age when he died and his immense potential as a musician went unrealised. Given his fragile mental state, it was widely assumed by the music press that the cause of Bond's death was suicide or simply the result of a tragic, careless accident. Pete Brown (1940-2023) worked with the musician on his last musical project, the *Two Heads Are Better Than One* LP in 1972. He spoke candidly about Bond's death.

> "Right at the end, Graham said to me: 'I'm giving all the magic stuff up and I'm just going to play. I'm not going to do anything influenced by that anymore'. Then a few days later he was dead."[223]

---

[223] https://www.loudersound.com/features/the-apocalyptic-story-of-graham-bond

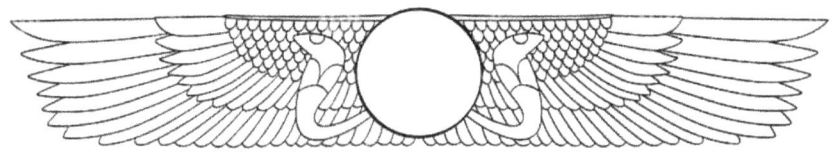

7. Conjuring the Demonic

"The pursuit of Mystery and the practice of Magic can change your life as few other activities can, for good or ill. Some things that you considered important in the past now seem trivial, and vice versa. You've transformed yourself into a wiser being, a more compassionate person, a more complex entity, and, we hope, into an eager explorer of illusions and realities."

Nema, Wings of Rapture.

While the mixing of drugs and the occult is clearly a dangerous cocktail, one must consider whether Graham Bond's death came about as a direct result of his withdrawal from magick rather than his engagement with it. The spirits, once conjured to life, are unforgiving if subsequently ignored.

As we have now seen on several occasions, a strong case can be made for a link between the escapist use of hard drugs and a desire to manipulate reality through magick. The same practices certainly appears to be attractive to similar types of individuals. An example of this can be seen in the life of the legendary Led Zeppelin guitarist Jimmy Page (1944-present day) who, like Bond, was also a devoted practitioner of the magickal tradition developed by Aleister Crowley—a magus who was also addicted to a cocktail of narcotics[224]—albeit that this was partially due to a serious medical condition.

The possibility of a causal link between the avaricious consumption of drugs and the practice of Crowley's magick was also evident when, in

---

[224] Crowley's was prescribed heroine by a medical professional at a time prior to the implementation of the Dangerous Drugs Act (DDA) in 1920. He wrote an honest, but fictional account, of his narcotics use in the novel *The Diary of a Drug Fiend* which he published in 1922.

a series of interviews conducted with Bowie from 2000 onwards, he maintained that he felt his fascination with Crowley was in part fuelled by the cocaine habit he had developed at the time.[225] How taken in he was by Crowley's religion is open to conjecture but it is clear that he certainly never considered himself to be a 'Thelemite' (i.e., an adherent to the principles and philosophies of Crowley's new religion). He was much too free a spirit for any long-term commitment to a particular spiritual philosophy. Neither is there any evidence to suggest that he was ever a member of a recognised secret occult society. Instead, Bowie should be classified as a sole practitioner, preferring to use magick and occultism as a tool to breakdown the indoctrination he had been subjected to while growing up in a society dominated by archaic religious dogma.

The song-writer made his opinion on religion clear in his 1971 song *Quicksand* in which he sings: *"Don't believe in yourself, don't deceive with belief."* and *"Can't take my eyes from the great salvation. Of bullshit faith."* In so-doing, the musician highlighted what became a lifelong struggle for self-illumination and a desire to eradicate years of psychospiritual indoctrination at the hands of the established Christian church: a cause which, like Lévi and Nietzsche, he pursued up until the time of his death.

In an interview published in the May 1983 edition of *International Musician and Recording World,* Bowie was more specific regarding his occult interests as a young man.

> "I had this more-than-passing interest in Egyptology, mysticism and the Kabbalah. At the time it seemed transparently obvious what the answer to life was. My whole life would be transformed into this bizarre nihilistic fantasy world of impending doom, mythological characters and imminent totalitarianism."

---

[225] This statement was undoubtedly a deviation from the truth as magickal work requires a clear head and strong psychic constitution—conditions heavy drugs fail to create. Also, Bowie's initial fascination in Crowley predated his use of cocaine. (Source: FHE Health, 2020)

7. CONJURING THE DEMONIC

Back in 1970, his belief in "mythological characters and imminent totalitarianism" actually predates his cocaine habit so can not be put down to any sort of self-inflicted paranoia brought on by his use of narcotics. Instead, the current that fed Bowie's thirst for arcane and mystical knowledge came from an external rather than internal source.

Although his personal search for occult insight and revelation appeared within his lyrics, Bowie's spiritual quest went largely unrecognised by music critics and fans alike. A few fans might have recognised an oblique reference to Aleister Crowley in the lyrics of his song *Quicksand*, or recognised him as another of the many faces featured on the Beatles iconic 1967 album *Sgt. Pepper's Lonely Hearts Club Band*, but unless you were a student of occultism the deeper connections between Thelema and rock music went largely unnoticed. It would have remained that way if it were not for the fact that the veil that shielded Bowie's occult interests from public gaze started to wear thin towards the end of the 1970s. The music press—who for the most part would have had little understanding of the occult references within Bowie's music—began to suspect that there was another, previously unrevealed aspect to the rock superstar character and started to question the musician's involvement in the dark arts.

In 1997, during an interview with the UK's premier weekly newspaper *New Musical Express*, Bowie was specifically asked about his occult practices earlier in his career. "So were you involved in actual devil worship?" an interviewer once asked pointedly. "Not devil worship, no," replied Bowie, "it was pure straightforward, old-fashioned magic." "The Aleister Crowley variety?" asked the journalist to which Bowie replied "No, I always thought Crowley was a charlatan."

While Bowie was clearly trying to distance himself from his earlier fascination with Crowley he later admitted to having had a deep interest in the teachings of Crowley's early occult society the Order of the Golden Dawn, and in particular with two of its most famous members.

> "There was a guy called [Arthur] Edward Waite who
> was terribly important to me at the time. And another

146

called Dion Fortune who wrote a book called 'Psychic Self-Defence'."

DEMON IN THE POOL

Left: Dion Fortune (dressed in her magical regalia) pioneered a resurgence of interest in the Mystery schools of the Greeks and Egyptians, the Kabbalah, and esoteric Christianity.

Dion Fortune (1890-1946)[226] was a British occultist and ceremonial magician. She was best known as the co-founder of the Fraternity of the Inner Light—a Mystery School which she based upon teachings she claimed were shared with her by the Ascended Masters. Fortune joined the Alpha et Omega Lodge of the Hermetic Order of the Golden Dawn in 1919 and in 1922 published information gleaned from the Masters in a publication titled *The Cosmic Doctrine*. [227]

In a subsequent book, Dion Fortune revealed additional information about her contact with them; describing them as "being dressed in either an indigo, blue, or white robe." She also explained that she had came to know them by their proper title name: the "Lesser Masters under the Jurisdiction of the Most Wise, Lord of the Blue Ray, a ruler of Hermetic Wisdom. The ancient and sacred knowledge they presented her with was transmitted telepathically but in order to receive it she first had to complete an intense period of preparation—a trial she described in the following way:

---
[226] Dion Fortune died of leukemia at the Middlesex Hospital, London on January 8th, 1946—exactly one year to the very day that marked Bowie's birth. (Source: www.innerlight.org.uk)
[227] Fortune, Dion, *Cosmic Doctrine*, Rider & Company, 1949.

> "To tell the full story of the training that led to the power to bring through the teaching contained in these pages would take too long, moreover, there are parts of it of which I am not at liberty to speak; I may say this, however, that after the experience I have narrated, I found that certain powers had awakened within my soul, certain capacities had been added to consciousness, and that, although I have never again had such a transcendent vision as the meeting with the Masters on the mountain, I found that I began to receive, or conceive, ideas such as had never come to me before, that formulated themselves in my mind as clearly as if a voice had spoken.
>
> At first, I could only obtain fragments of teaching in this way, but with practice, the power increased, and it seemed as if information on any subject, even those with which I was quite unacquainted, could be obtained by this method. The process seemed to be exactly the same as that of telepathy, but the communicators gave me to understand that they did not possess physical bodies but were discarnate minds which had advanced beyond the stage of evolution which is conducted in matter."[228]

Dion Fortune wrote about a variety issues related to magick and the occult but the book Bowie cited as the most significant to him in his 1983 interview was *Psychic Self-Defence*. It was published in 1930 by the same company that released A. E. Waite's popular rendition of the tarot.[229]

For several decades *Psychic Self-Defence* was the definitive treatise on the practise of "astral protection"–an essential skill all occultists need to develop in order to protect themselves against dark, malevolent forces that appear in the life of an occultist once they begin exploring the

---
[228] Ibid.
[229] Fortune, Dion, *Psychic Self-Defence*, Rider & Company, 1933.

inner realms. As we saw in the story of Graham Bond, magick is a very potent force and is not, as many teenagers and amateur practitioners foolishly presume, a toy to be played with for amusement purposes. It can, and does, produce powerful effects and for this reason requires careful handling at all times.

Bowie, as skilled as he was in magick—or thought himself to be—appears to have failed to take sufficient care during the course of his magickal work and ended up being 'bitten' by something unpleasant on several occasions. The ramifications of his opening of the spatial gateways and not closing them again properly can be seen in events that took place around him during 1972/3 when he experienced a series of paranormal events while planning and recording the *Ziggy Stardust and the Spiders from Mars* album. These were strange days in the life of the young musician and those closely connected to him. One of those who were impacted by these unseen forces was Angie Bowie. She spoke openly about the dark aura of mystical craziness that surrounded David during this pivotal period in his life and professional career.

> "Some interesting, even mind-blowing things happened, events and signs and phenomena worthy of the deepest thought and most intensive investigation."[230]

Spiders from Mars guitarist Mick Ronson was more specific when it came to describing the same aura of paranormal weirdness. Michael Luckman stated that these events had been taking place for some time. "David became convinced that he was being stalked by men from Mars in 1969 or 1970." he said in his book *Alien Rock*.[231]

As if extraterrestrial contact is not weird enough, Bowie's occult practices also appeared to have made daily life for those around him even more bizarre. American film producer Cameron Crowe (1957-present day) was a rock journalist working for *Rolling Stone* magazine.[232] He

---
[230] Bowie, Angie, *Backstage Passes: Life on the Wild Side with David Bowie*, The Berkley Publishing Group, 1993.
[231] Luckman, Michael, *Alien Rock: The Rock N' Roll Extraterrestrial Connection*, Gallery Books, 2005.
[232] http://othersidepodcast.com/blog/2016/01/18/75-starman-david-bowies-

interviewed David several times from the mid-1970s onwards and recalled a very odd experience he had while in the company of the rockstar during the time that Bowie was living in New York.

> "Suddenly – always suddenly – David is on his feet and rushing to a nearby picture window. He thinks he's seen a body fall from the sky. "I've got to do this," he says, pulling a shade down on the window. A ballpoint-penned star has been crudely drawn on the inside. Below it is the word "Aum." Bowie lights a black candle on his dresser and immediately blows it out to leave a thin trail of smoke floating upward. "Don't let me scare the pants off you. It's only protective. I've been getting a little trouble from ... the neighbours."

The exact nature of the "neighbours" Bowie refers to remains unclear but one can surmise that he was referring to the sort of negative astral beings that Dion Fortune warned against tangling with. Angie was more specific than her husband when it came to identifying them. She maintained that David was referring to one specific malefic entity: the Devil. In her biography, she recalls how she and David watched in horror as a beast-like form rose up from the bottom of their indoor swimming pool. It alarmed them so much that they immediately performed an exorcism; at which point the water started to bubble. Forcing herself to peer down into the water, Angie caught sight of a large shadow lurking at the bottom of the pool. She said that it took on the shape of:

> "...a beast of the underworld; it reminded me of those twisted, tormented gargoyles screaming silently from the spires of medieval cathedrals. It was ugly, shocking, malevolent; it frightened me."

In a subsequent interview with Bowie in 1983 he recalled that there were other occult influences at play during the same period.

legacy-of-ufos-and-the-occult/

> "I was living in L.A. with Egyptian decor. It was one of those rent-a-house places, but it appealed to me because I had this more-than-passing interest in Egyptology, mysticism, the cabala, all this stuff that is inherently misleading in life, a hodgepodge whose crux I've forgotten. But at the time it seemed transparently obvious what the answer to life was. So, the house occupied a ritualistic position in my life."[233]

The musician was then asked about comments he had made in his earlier *Rolling Stone* interview.

> R.S: "What's the story on that incident Cameron Crowe wrote about in 1976, in which you interrupted your interview with him to pull down a window shade, which had a star and the word "Aum" drawn on it, and light a black candle, claiming you'd just seen a body fall from the sky?"
>
> Bowie: "That used to happen all the time. I was one of those guys that you see on the streets who suddenly stops and says, "They're coming! They're coming!" Every day of my life back then I was capable of staying up indefinitely. My chemistry must have been superhuman. I'd stay up for seven or eight days on the trot! By the end of the week, my whole life would be transformed into this bizarre nihilistic fantasy world of oncoming doom, mythological characters and imminent totalitarianism. Quite the worst."

MAGICK IN THE CARDS

While it is not clear whether Bowie ever possessed a copy of either Crowley's seminal work on practical occult work titled *Magick*, or his

---
[233] Timothy White, Musician, May 1983.

enigmatic sacred text *The Book of the Law*, he did own a copy of Crowley's *Thoth* tarot. Why he chose this deck over the one designed by his preferred occultist A. E. Waite is unclear but it might have been due Crowley's greater use of magickal symbology which made it useful both in regular divination and in the practice of Thelemic magick.

Crowley deliberately designed his tarot deck as a magickal tool and in this regard the *Book of Thoth* should be approached with a degree of care. It can be a highly potent tool in the hands of an expert. That being said, it is unlikely that the demonic entity that appeared in Bowie's New York swimming pool was conjured-up by using the tarot. Spirits of the type described by Angie require a more determined and sophisticated effort on the part of a magickian to evoke.

The tarot is, in all regards, a fascinating device but for anyone who may be unfamiliar with it and its powers it is worth explaining a little about what it is and how it works. Originally called 'tarrochi', its early history remains somewhat obscured. Most historians suggest that it originated as a card game in Italy during the 15th century before evolving into a popular fortune-telling device around two hundred years later. The cards popularity increased dramatically shortly afterwards and they became widely used throughout Europe; predominantly by the upper and ruling classes.[234] The cards continue to evolve and today are not only used in the practice of divination but are increasingly employed as a tool of self-analysis and psychological development.

A traditional tarot deck is comprised of 78 cards. Twenty-two of them—known as the Major Arcana—are particularly significant in relation to understanding the metaphysical principles that underpin Western Mystery Tradition teachings. Some of the card's titles (e.g., THE WHEEL OF FORTUNE, DEATH, JUDGMENT and THE WORLD) are mundane, but others, such as the first card in the numbered sequence[235] commonly known as THE MAGICIAN, or MAGUS, hints at something much deeper and more occult.

---

[234] The tarot Court Cards feature a hierarchical sequence of royal positions. i.e. King, Queen, Knight, and Page.

[235] The tarot has a card numbered 0, THE FOOL but it has a unique role to play in the system that will be explored in depth a subsequent volume in *The Sirius Mythos* series.

Left: THE MAGICIAN tarot card conceived by Freemason Edward Arthur Waite and drawn by artist Pamela Coleman-Smith.

Waite characterised his version of this card by employing the image of a flamboyant young man, standing at a table/altar upon which rest four small implements. This central figure is, of course, the magickian him/her self. The figure (of slightly indeterminable gender) is shown with one arm raised, pointing a sceptre or wand skywards with the other arm lowered and pointing towards the ground. This symbolises the process of 'earthing' or 'grounding' into 3D reality any cosmic power that is derived from a Magickian's connection to higher realms. The four tools—which are carefully laid out on the magickian's table—represent the metaphysical principles of 'Fire', 'Air', 'Water', and Earth. These are easily identifiable by all strands of occultism to represent the building blocks of (meta-) physical reality.

In this regard, the Magician's action as illustrated on this card not only illustrates the preferred environment for any magickal work but also reveals the concerted action of deliberate, controlled, or willed manifestation.[236] As all Harry Potter fans will tell you, wherever a magus figure is seen brandishing a stick, baton[237], or cane he or she is applying, focussing, and directing magickal power using willed intent.

Walking Through Astral Walls

Crowley's interpretation of THE MAGICIAN tarot card is a slight variant of Waite's theme. His version featured the same four tools but

---

[236] "The principal characteristic of Tahuti, or Thoth (the Egyptian representation of Mercury) is that he has the head of the ibis. The ibis is the symbol of concentration, because it was supposed that this bird stood continuously upon one leg, motionless." (Source: Crowley, Aleister, *The Book of Thoth*, The Equinox III:5, 1944.)

[237] In French medieval decks the title of Arcana 1: THE MAGICIAN is 'Le Bâteleur' (trans. The Bearer of the Baton).

floating in the air—an element attributed to Mercury which has rulership over the processes of magick and communication. Crowley also associated it with the ancient Egyptian god Thoth who was said to have calculated the framework for the establishment of the heavens, stars, and Earth. Crowley made this association because the ancient Egyptians also credited him with being the author of all works of science, religion, philosophy, and magick. This he felt best describes the potential the tarot has "to reveal all things." Lévi's own conclusions regarding the importance of this occult divination system mirrored those of Crowley.

> "Of all oracles, the tarot is the most astounding in its answers, because all possible combinations of this universal key of the Kabbalah give oracles of science and of truth as their solutions. Without the Tarot the Magic of the ancients is a closed book, and it is impossible to penetrate any of the great mysteries of the Kabbalah. So arranged, the Tarot is a veritable oracle and replies to all possible questions with more precision and infallibility than the Android of Albertus Magnus. An imprisoned person with no other book than the Tarot, if he knew how to use it, could in a few years acquire universal knowledge, and would be able to speak on all subjects with unequalled learning and inexhaustible eloquence."[238]

Crowley saw the role of his tarot as a magickal tool for future generations: to be used by those working under the auspices of the mercurial energies of the Aquarian Age. He was far less-interested in the alchemical tradition favoured by Waite and felt that his tarot deck should represent the "pure" ancient mystery wisdom tradition. One can easily imagine why Crowley's approach to the occult tarot might have piqued Bowie's curiosity but did the musician actually use Crowley's *Book of Thoth* deck in the practice of magick? This does appear appear to have

---

[238] Lévi, Eliphas, *Dogmé et Rituel de la Haute Magie*, (Trans. *The Ritual of Transcendental Magic*), Translated by A. E. Waite, Rider & Company, England, 1896.

been the case for Doggett observed that, during the period David and Angie were living in New York, Bowie was:

> "...reported to be drawing pentagrams on the wall, experimenting with the pack of tarot cards that Crowley had created, chanting spells, making hexes, and testing and investigating the powers of the devil against those of the Jewish mystical system, the Kabbalah."[239]

In the same *New Musical Express* interview cited earlier, Bowie confirmed Doggett's assertions by stating:

> "I drew gateways into different dimensions, and I'm quite sure that, for myself, I really walked into other worlds. I drew things on walls and just walked through them and saw what was on the other side!"

The magickal skills required to achieve this are difficult to perfect and while Bowie might have been trying to downplay his interest in occultism—and in Crowley in particular—it appears he was trying hard to access and experience the inner worlds at this pivotal stage in his career.

The Musickians

Given the all-consuming undercurrent of occult and metaphysical influences that were flowing through and around Bowie between 1970 and 1975, it is worth returning to his legendary performance of *Starman* on *Top of the Pops* in 1972 and to consider it not only in terms of its cultural impact but also with regards to the magickal and occult dynamics at play at the time. Given that Bowie seems to have found the *Thoth* deck to be an effectual magickal tool, it is fitting that we should consider the degree to which the musician might have personally identified with the arcane imagery featured in Aleister Crowley's representation of Arcana 1 THE MAGICIAN. Indeed, comparing the card's pictorial imagery with the circumstances surrounding his

---

[239] Doggett, Peter, *The Man Who Sold the World: David Bowie and the 1970s*, Vintage, 2012.

7. CONJURING THE DEMONIC

appearance on *Top of the Pops* some very odd similarities can be found.

Firstly, it is interesting to note that the environment in which the performance took place—namely the *Top of the Pops* television studio—operated as an enclosed, sonic temple. The stage he performed on can be seen to have replicated an altar or working magickal environment and the four musicians (Bowie, Ronson, Woodmansey and Boulder) to represent the four primary elements[240] which a magickian unifies in order to attain the required goal. In addition, the technological equipment used during the recording (i.e., cameras, lights, sound etc.) all fall under the umbrella of the planet Mercury; as is Wednesday which was the day of the *Starman* recording.

Where the connection between Bowie and THE MAGICIAN tarot card is particularly noticeable is in in its colouring. When designing his tarot deck, Crowley had his artist Frieda Harris tincture it with just two colours. These were electric blue and yellow/gold which are, as we have already seen, the very same colours that dominated the opening televised sequence of *Starman*. (i.e. Bowie's electric-blue guitar and Ronson's gold-coloured outfit).[241] The colours blue and gold are by no means arbitrary. They are highly significant within Crowley's *Book of the Law* where they are specifically referred to by the astral entity who channelled the sacred text to Crowley and his wife. In chapter I, verse 60 Aiwass stated, "My colour is black to the blind, but the blue & gold are seen of the seeing."[242] If you take an occult perspective of the *Starman* transmission it is easy to interpret Aiwass's reference to the colour "black" and to "blindness" as a characterisation of those viewers who

---

[240] The numerical value of the term "Spiders from Mars" is 705: the same value as the term 'Tetragrammaton'— the four-letter Hebrew theonym for Jehovah (YHVH). It is means "to be, to exist, to cause to become, or to come to pass". The term is often used in ritual magick to initiate a state of 'coming into being', or the 'process of spiritual manifestation'. The four-fold qualities of YHVH are associated with the four elements.

[241] In ritual magick, correspondences play an essential role in expressing or conceptualising customarily inexpressible fields of energy. It is by using a specific colour—one known to carry the frequency of the planet being worked in a ritual—that its core energy can be tapped into and utilised. In the case of the Starman performance the prevailing astrological energy at the time was the Sun and Sirius.

[242] Crowley, Aleister, *Liber AL* vel Legis, (Chapter I, Verse 60), privately published, 1909.

were not spiritually acclimatised enough to recognise the true essence of what they were watching on their television screens that evening. On the other hand, those who might have recognised the occult dynamics of the moment (i.e., the spiritually aware and those viewers who instinctively understood how the occult underpins our reality[243]), probably were, as Aiwass put it, resonant to the "blue and gold" of the "seeing".

It is also worth reminding ourselves that at the point of the *Starman* transmission, our Sun was in direct alignment with Sirius. In occultism, the colour yellow/gold is assigned to the Sun while electric-blue denotes the energy of Sirius—a fact that will become even more pertinent later on.

Ritual Robes

When analysing Bowie's *Top of the Pops* performance with reference to occult principles it is even more intriguing to discover that in the verse in *The Book of the Law* that follows Aiwass's reference to the colours "blue and gold" there appears the line "I charge you earnestly to come before me in a single robe, and covered with a rich headdress." In his song *Quicksand*, Bowie makes a tantalising reference to the use of colour and ritual garments when he admitted that:

> *"I'm closer to the Golden Dawn.*
> *Immersed in Crowley's uniform.*
> *Of imagery."*

The secret teachings of the Order of the Golden Dawn paid close attention to the colour of the ritual robes that their initiates used while performing magick. The colour associations employed by them were specifically designed in accordance with ancient Egyptian iconography. Bowie became fascinated with the magickal attire that was worn by Crowley and the other members of the G.D. and this became most apparent following the publication of a series of photographs taken in 1971 by his publicist Brian Ward. The intention was to use them on the cover of his *Ziggy Stardust* album but this did not occur. Nevertheless,

---

[243] Probably those youngsters listed earlier who emerged as musicians in a new generation of rock-stars.

the photographs Ward took that day are telling for they show Bowie dressed in an Egyptian-inspired outfit that was comprised of a single, white robe, with a headdress redolent of the Egyptian Sphinx. In addition, it was adorned with an assortment of mystically inspired jewellery.[244]

This was not the first occasion that Bowie had been photographed by Ward while wearing clothing that reflected the artist's esoteric leanings. In 1969, Canada's most widely read daily newspaper, *The Globe and Mail*, reported that Bowie had recently been photographed by Ward while, as they put it, "...dressed as an initiate into one of Crowley's quasi-Masonic cults for a photo shoot." Once again, the plan had been to use the photographs in the artwork of an upcoming album but this idea was also shelved.[245]

The importance of wearing specific garments when performing magickal or initiatory ritual can be found within all secret societies— particularly within those ancient brotherhoods who are connected to the teachings of the Western Mystical Tradition. According to Murry Hope, their use dates back to the era of the ancient Mystery Schools. In her book Practical Atlantean Magic she explained that:

> "The priestly hierarchy was easily distinguishable to the general public by its apparel, each branch displaying specific symbols, colours and robes. So, just as we, today, are able to recognise an officer of the Law by his uniform, or a gentleman of the cloth by his collar, the Atlantean people knew whether the priest they were passing in the street was a Healer, Magi, first-year novitiate, and so forth, and would respond accordingly."[246]

Hope also referred to the specific colours used.

"The use of colour featured strongly in the Atlantean

[244] http://thosegirlss.blogspot.com/2015/05/mcm-david-bowie-as-sphinx.html
[245] http://www.theglobeandmail.com/arts/art-and-architecture/in-pictures-back-to-the-seventies-with-david-bowie/article14425283/
[246] Hope, Murry, *Practical Atlantean Magic*, The Aquarian Press, 1991.

ethos, and Plato's description of the blue and white robes of the Atlantean priests evidence the fact that this tradition was carried right through to the latter days, blue, white and gold being the sacred colours of the Atlantean priesthood."

In another odd correlation between Bowie and Crowley's *Book of the Law*, a verse in the text states that "Blue am I and gold in the light of my bride: but the red gleam is in my eyes..."[247] Bowie's eyes are alternatively coloured blue and reddish-brown.

Lights of Sirius

Although it may appear strange that Bowie and Ronson appeared on television in July 1972 exhibiting colours associated with the energies of our Sun and the star Sirius at the very moment they were forming an alignment to one another; the Sirius-related associations do not end there.

Firstly, on several occasions during the broadcast, the TV cameras focussed in on the two musicians from such an angle that a powerful studio light shone directly into the camera lens. Clearly this was meant to represent a star; which we now understand to be Sirius.[248]

There is a strange connection between studio lights and the star Sirius. In the 1998 film *The Truman Show*[249] its main character–which was played by the actor and conspiracy theorist Jim Carrey (1962-present day)–is shocked to see a large studio light fall from the sky outside his suburban home. He picked it up, looked it over, and found that it was labelled "Sirius (9 canis major)". What is the symbolic relevance of this? Well, the Gematria value of the term i "Sirius (9 canis major)" is 1382–the same value as the phrase "The Matrix Has You". This is strangely ironic for *The Truman Show* is the story of a middle-aged man (Carrey) who discovers that he is trapped within a controlled

---

[247] Crowley, Aleister, *Liber AL vel Legis*, Chapter II, Verse 50, privately published, 1909.
[248] Bright lights shone directly into a TV camera lens was generally avoided due to the potential damage it can cause to its internal electronics.
[249] https://en.wikipedia.org/wiki/The_Truman_Show

7. CONJURING THE DEMONIC

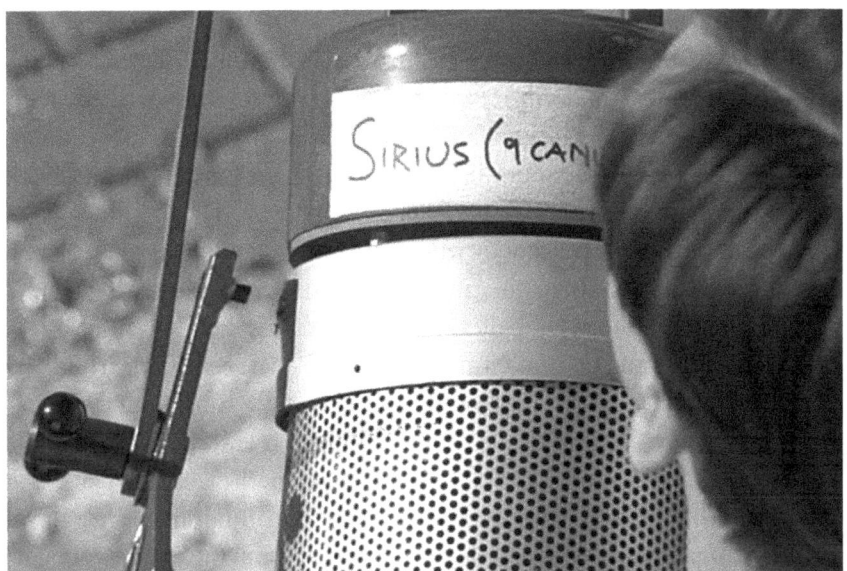

Above: A Light from the sky: Truman Burbank (Jim Carrey) makes a strange Sirius-related discovery in the film The Truman Show.

reality from which he tries to escape. This is often referred to in modern spiritual parlance as "The Matrix" (after the 1999 science fiction film of the same name)—a field of energy that has the effect of keeping the consciousness of humanity fed by an endless sea of false, corporate-generated, narratives.[250]

Secondly, following the shot of the BBC studio light, the TV camera panned to a view that included the whole band whereby a second light—positioned alongside the first—could be seen. It too was shining directly into the camera lens. Unlike the first, this was not white in colour but was bright, golden-yellow: reflective of the rays of our Sun. The use of the studio's lights—which were mounted on a fixed lighting gantry high above the stage—was unusual in any edition of *Top of the Pops* and clearly their use on this particular occasion was unusual, which leads one to assume that they were clearly meant to act as an additional visual prop.

Throughout the 1960s and early 1970s, *Top of the Pops* was a fast-

---

[250] The soundtrack for The Truman Show was written by Philip Glass (1937-present day); a close friend of David Bowie who reinterpreted versions of Bowie's late-1970s albums Low, Heroes, and Lodger from a classical music perspective.

moving and extremely stripped-down affair—one which relied upon a quick turnaround of performers during a day's filming. Other than at the recording of Christmas editions of the programme, there was normally insufficient time to introduce much in the way of visual enhancement. For this reason it was somewhat irregular to see that effort had been made to enhance Bowie's performance in this way. The significance of this became even more evident when the TV cameras panned back and revealed for the first-time other items suspended from the ceiling. These included two, spherical, balloon-like objects joined together—as if unified in one grand conjunction. One of these featured a ring around its centre which gave it the appearance of the planet Saturn with whom, as we saw earlier, Sirius has a quite specific relationship.[251] As the performance drew to a close, the TV camera drew right back and revealed Bowie—along with the rest of his band—illuminated by a third, white, elongated object which was also hanging from the ceiling. A visual representation of the ongoing solar alignment with the binary star system of Sirius, along with its third, companion star, was complete and the magickal psychodrama concluded.

Magickal Essence

Taking a step back from this somewhat challenging hypothesis that what was unknowingly witnessed by British TV viewers on July 5, 1972, was a carefully orchestrated occult ritual for a moment, it is worth reminding ourselves that there is definitive, scientific evidence that over the course of just two days prior to its transmission, two major luminaries conjoined and, according to ancient texts, this alignment invariably results in cosmic energies streaming into our planet. For millennia occultists have taken advantage of this ancient knowledge and used this date to harness such powers for any number of different reasons. In the case of Bowie's iconic performance, these powers were directed into the nation's collective psyche and had the effect of radically altering the course of musical history by virtue of its energisation of several aspiring musicians. However, as we shall soon discover, this period of just 48 hours was more significant in determining the future of

---

[251] The energy of Saturn underpins the field holding the "Matrix" in form.

7. Conjuring the Demonic

humanity than we can even begin to imagine.

Given the bizarre and mysterious catalogue of 'synchronous' connections revealed so far, it is perhaps time for an even deeper examination of the *Starman* performance. One method for determining whether a sacred dynamic is at play during a physical plane event is mathematics. Like colour associations–which reveal or capture the frequency of electromagnetic energies at play–numbers can reveal the vibratory rate of such features as symbols and words. In the field of occultism, there are several numerological systems which have proven to be tried and tested methods but the one preferred by Aleister Crowley and the Order of the Golden Dawn is called 'Gematria'. This system calculates values based upon the Jewish Kabbalah and, given that Bowie was closely acquainted with this occult philosophy in the 1970s, it would seem to be the most appropriate system to apply here.

The online encyclopaedia Wikipedia defines Gematria as "the practice of assigning a numerical value to a name, word or phrase according to an alphanumerical cipher." This is a somewhat simplistic explanation of a system which can become extraordinarily complex in the hands of an expert. However, the aspect to Gematria that is most relevant here refers to the principles of 'occult correspondence'. This states that if two or more terms have the same numerical value then a connection of significance exists between them–at some level.

To understand why this is important in metaphysics it is worth repeating the Nikola Tesla quote used earlier in which he stated that "If you want to find the secrets of this universe think in the terms of energy, frequency, and vibration."[252]

Having already evaluated Bowie's *Starman* performance with reference to colour, symbol, and ancient Mystery School teachings, we can now perform a numerical evaluation of its key components which reveals several fascinating insights.

1. The term 'BBC Television Centre' has a Gematria

---

[252] For thousands of years, sacred music and sanctified sound–the quintessential expression of "energy, frequency, and vibration"–have been used as a medium through which to express cosmological concepts.

value of 1268. This is the same as the phrase 'Goddess of the Heavens'—an expression often used to describe the ancient Egyptian deity Isis who was represented in the heavens by the star Sirius.

2. The numerical value of the word 'Starman' is the same as the word 'Thoth'—the Egyptian god who governed magick and who gave his name to the Crowley tarot deck used by Bowie.[253]

3. The frequency of the opening chord to *Starman* is B-flat. This resonates at the frequency of 466hz. In Jewish Gematria the value 466 equates to the phrase "Her Name is Isis"—another reference to the goddess of Sirius.

4. The *Starman* single is officially timed at 4m. 16s. in length.[254] 416 is the Gematria value of the term "I am a Starseed". The term 'starseed' is widely used in New Age parlance to define an extraterrestrial entity, soul, or a being with a heightened level of spiritual consciousness, who has chosen to incarnate on planet Earth in order to carry out a quite specific role or task. Bowie described his Ziggy alien character playing this role.

5. The value of the word 'Bowie' is 966 which is the same as the phrase 'The Sun and Sirius'—a reference which can be applied to the conjunction that occurred on July 5, 1972.

6. Evaluating the phrase 'David Bowie' via Gematria creates the value 1684 which is the same as the phrase "And There Fell a Great Star from Heaven". This phrase is taken from the King James version of the Bible and forms part of the Book of Revelation (ch.8

---

[253] The date of the transmission was the first day of the month of Thoth in the Ancient Egyptian calendar.
[254] https://en.wikipedia.org/wiki/Starman_(song)

v.10). Theologians maintain that the name of the star that fell was Wormwood.[255] Some historians have proposed that the star Wormwood is Sirius. The number 810–as in ch.8 v.10–is the value of the phrase 'Dog Star Sirius'.

Aleph	Bet	Gimel	Dalet	Hey	Vav	Zayin	Chet	Tet	Yud	Kaf
א	ב	ג	ד	ה	ו	ז	ח	ט	י	כ
										ך
1	2	3	4	5	6	7	8	9	10	20
Lamed	Mem	Nun	Samech	Ayin	Pey	Tsaddi	Kuf	Resh	Shin	Tav
ל	מ	נ	ס	ע	פ	צ	ק	ר	ש	ת
	ם	ן			ף	ץ				
30	40	50	60	70	80	90	100	200	300	400

Above: Table of correspondences for the Kabbalstic Gematria system of numerology.

When viewed as a whole, this set of numerical associations–and there are more to follow–appears to suggest that a hidden, highly intelligent, 'undercurrent' permeated the environment surrounding Bowie in July 1972. There is also a strong suspicion that this 'intelligence' formulated, or manipulated, many of the key elements surrounding his *Top of the Pops* performance. It also appears to have been at work, weaving its magick and authority, even earlier than this and that it had been generating a sympathetic mode of consciousness within Bowie in the years prior to 1972.

An example of it at work can be found in Bowie's song *Oh! You Pretty Things*; the basic framework of which emerged rather unexpectedly while he slept. In Bowie biographer Paul Trynka's 2011 book *David Bowie–Starman* the author includes the transcript of a conversation

[255] https://en.wikipedia.org/wiki/Wormwood_(Bible)

Bowie had early one morning in January 1971 with Bob Grace—the publishing manager of Chrysalis Music:

> "I woke up at 4 o'clock. Had this song going in my head and I had to get out of bed, work it out on the piano and get it out of my head so I could go back to sleep."
>
> "What's it called?" asked Grace.
>
> "*Oh! You Pretty Things*" said Bowie.[256]

Bowie seemed reluctant to claim the credit for a song which had apparently formed deep within his subconscious that night. It is particularly interesting to note that he was not only aware of the songs structure but also its title which leads one to presume that it must have come through as 'a part of the package' or 'download'. But where did *Pretty Things* originate from? What, or who, was it that woke him during the night to recall it? We will probably never know the answer to these questions but the song's full title may hold a clue regarding its source:...

...the Gematria value of the term "Oh! You Pretty Things" is 1707—the same number as the phrase 'Sirius, Our Spiritual Sun'.

---

[256] Trynka, Paul, *David Bowie – Starman: The Definitive Biography*. New York City: Little, Brown and Company, 2011.

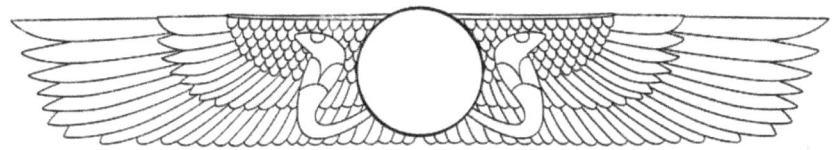

8. Black Stars & White Robes

> "My life was an unending, unchanging midnight. It must, by necessity, always be midnight for me. So how was it possible that the sun was rising now, in the middle of my midnight?"
>
> **Midnight Sun, Stephanie Meyer.**

David Bowie's record company, Sony Music Entertainment's Legacy Recordings, released *Blackstar*—the artist's twenty-sixth, and final studio album—on January 8, 2016—just a few days before the musician passed away. The record was yet another significant departure in musical style by an artist who had spent his career continually redefining both himself and his music. This time Bowie took inspiration from such electronic musicians as Boards of Canada and hip-hop artists such as Kendrick Lamar and Death Grips. Bowie rarely kept to the same musical formula from one album to the next so yet another change in musical direction came as no real surprise to his fans. Even so, *Blackstar* was an audio challenge with Bryan Wawzenek of *Ultimate Classic Rock* magazine reflecting the opinion held by so many that this was "...his most experimental album in years."[257]

Despite its limited appeal, *Blackstar* was a massive commercial success. Within its first year of release it had sold nearly two million units—a remarkable achievement in an age of file-sharing and music downloads. Although Bowie's inclusion of occult, spiritual, and philosophical themes had waned greatly since the 1970s they partially resurfaced on *Blackstar* with the most evident examples being the

---

[257] Wawzenek, Bryan, *David Bowie Albums Ranked Worst to Best*, Ultimate Classic Rock, 2016.

record's cryptic title and occult-referenced cover design which featured a single black pentagram on a white background. This raised the eyebrows of a few critics but then again, so had previous album covers by the artist.[258]

In today's more liberal music scene the use of pentagrams by artists of all musical persuasions has become so commonplace that it is rarely commented upon. However, Bowie's stark use of the symbol—which in the minds of the general public remains closely associated with Black Magick and Devil worship—runs counter to the non-occult persona Bowie had been striving to exhibit during the mid to late 1970s. So why this resurgence of interest in the use of occult iconography; one which is indelibly connected to—as Bowie himself once put it—"the wrong side of the brain"?

All occult symbols, whether it is the pentagram, swastika, or even the Baphomet, should be evaluated within a deeper context than that ascribed to by society. This is particularly true of the five-pointed star which is not Satanic at all but which is actually a representation of the magickal process. Each point simply represents one of the four metaphysical elements (i.e. earth, air, fire, and water) surmounted by a fifth, all-pervading principle which is known as Akasha—a Sanskrit word used by Western occultists to denote the concept of 'Universal Spirit'.[259] In this context its inclusion on the cover of *Blackstar* would appear incongruous but it should be remembered that Bowie had been writing and then recording the album at a time when he knew it would almost certainly be his final studio recording. His cancer diagnosis came as a blow but rather than capitalise on any sympathy his fans might display towards him Bowie made the decision to keep news of his declining health from the public; preferring instead to avoid the inevitable media interest and to focus on writing, recording and producing his *Lazarus* stage show.

---

[258] The most notable being the contentious image of Bowie reclining in a dress on the early covers of *The Man Who Sold the World*, the bizarre image of the artist as half-man and half-dog on the cover of *Diamond Dogs*, and who can forget the spectacularly awful cover for The Next Day which alienated critics and fans alike.
[259] An inverted pentagram (one with its apex pointing downwards) signifies the grounding of the four elements into physical reality, or the earth-plane.

8. BLACK STARS & WHITE ROBES

At a very rudimentary level the cover design of *Blackstar* symbolised the closing chapter in a long and illustrious career. Following his death, the record's producer, Tony Visconti (1944-present day)–someone who worked with the musician on his early RCA albums–explained that Bowie had intended *Blackstar* to be his swan song and a "*parting gift*" for his fans prior to his passing.[260] Given the tragic circumstances surrounding Bowie at the time of its recording, the use of the colour black on his album cover was appropriate given its close occult and cultural associations with the process of death and decay.

BLAZING STARS

The cover for *Blackstar* was partly designed by British graphic designer, filmmaker, and typographer Jonathan Barnbrook (1966-present day). He had worked with Bowie on previous album artwork including *Heathen* (2002), *Reality* (2003), and *The Next Day* (2013). However, rather than simply being a contractual arrangement his input on the *Blackstar* album was a collaboration with its creator. In an interview with Barnbrook in 2013 he stated:

> "Working with a strong and creative artist like David Bowie is actually very free and very personal – it's not like it's a famous pop star at all. And because it's very direct and we don't think about the record company a great deal. If a record company marketing department had been involved, we wouldn't have done that cover. They would have said, 'It looks like a Greatest Hits', or something like that. They wouldn't have got the symbolism that myself and David wanted."[261]

It is entirely probable that the decision to include a pentagram on the cover was, at the very least, a joint decision but we can safely credit Bowie with the idea given that Barnbrook has no history of incorporating

---

[260] Renshaw, David, *Producer Tony Visconti*, New Musical Express, January 11th, 2016.
[261] *Designing Bowie – Jonathan Barnbrook*, Clash, www.clashmusic.com, March 2013.

occult symbolism into previous artwork. However, there is an intriguing mystery to the story of how the cover artwork came about. Some who have explored the cover's bleak and minimal design have discovered previously hidden elements within it that are only evident after closer scrutiny. Because they were discovered after Bowie passed away he was clearly not in a position to answer questions regarding his use of a pentagram on the album. Nevertheless, in an interview with Mary Anne Hobbs conducted for the BBC 6 Music radio station in November 2016, Barnbrook spoke about *Blackstar* and the rudimentary design of its cover. He confirmed that the artwork was not as plain and self-evident as it first appeared and that there are additional elements concealed within it that owners of the album had yet to discover.

> "There are a number of black stars on the album, it's not just the five on the front – and they do symbolise different things in life," said Barnbrook.
>
> For instance, there's the rosette that looks a little bit like a price ticket; this is still a commercial product, you still buy it. There's the guiding star; that idea of person you follow in your life, the idea of something spiritual that music gives you. There are a lot of other things going on that aren't completely at the surface, but I do hope people see them – not necessarily straight away."[262]

Hearing this, Bowie fans immediately re-examined the *Blackstar* cover with a renewed sense of intrigue and found that if you exposed it to direct sunlight then the black pentagram reveals a collection of individual stars; leading to the assumption that the single star on the album cover had a cosmic relevance. After placing the album cover under ultra-violet light, the black star changes colour and glows a luminous blue: as if it represented the iridescent twinkling of Sirius.

A deeper analysis of *Blackstar* from a metaphysical perspective reveals that in the first chapter of Crowley's *Book of the Law* the

---

[262] www.bbc.co.uk/programmes/p04g55l3

8. BLACK STARS & WHITE ROBES

Egyptian star-goddess Nuit[263] (sometimes referred to as 'Nut' or 'Nuith')—a deity depicted as a naked woman covered in stars—specifically identifies herself as a star. "I am the blue-lidded daughter of Sunset; I am the naked brilliance of the voluptuous night-sky." Once again, a possible link to Sirius is suggested here but to re-enforce the connection even further, it can be noted that Nuit also says of herself that "I am Infinite Space, and the Infinite Stars thereof" (i.e., 'I.S.I.S,' or 'Isis'). In other verses of *Liber Al vel Legis* she is called the 'Queen of Heaven' and 'Queen of Space'—terms often used to describe the goddess Isis.

These are tantalising threads of conjecture but it is important to emphasise that there is no clear evidence that Bowie was deliberately encoding occult references lifted from Crowley's 1904 text *The Book of the Law* into the artwork of his *Blackstar* album. However, if we put this to one side for a moment and follow the accepted occult principle that a five-pointed star references Sirius, then it is worth considering the possibility that something much deeper is at play here. In this regard it is worth noting that Alice A. Bailey believed that the 'Ray of Sirius' is encapsulated within the tenets of Freemasonry. This is borne out by the noted Freemason and scholar Albert Pike (1809-1891) who, in his seminal work of Masonic philosophy titled *Morals and Dogma*[264], stated that "The Ancient Astronomers saw all the great Symbols of Masonry in the Stars. Sirius glitters in our lodges as the Blazing Star."[265]

This possible Masonic perspective is interesting considering that Bowie had no direct connection to the Craft. The only, extremely tenuous link between the musician and Freemasonry, exists in his temporary appreciation of the Freemason Arthur Edward Waite. However, while Bowie might not have joined Waite's fraternity there is

---

[263] In the Thelemic system, 'Nuit' is one-third of a triadic cosmology that underpins the three chapters of *The Book of the Law*. The other two includes her masculine counterpart, 'Hadit' and 'Ra-Hoor-Khuit', also known, as Aiwass put it, the 'Crowned and Conquering Child'. A literal interpretation of the name 'Ra (who is)' is 'Horus of the Horizon'.

[264] French philosopher René Guénon (1886-1951) noted that a large amount of *Morals and Dogma* was taken from Dogme et Rituel de la Haute Magie by Éliphas Lévi". (Source: Guénon, René, Theosophy: History of a Pseudo-religion. Sophia Perennis, 1921.)

[265] Pike, Albert *Morals and Dogma*, Supreme Council, 1871.

further evidence to support the idea that a ray of 'Masonic Influence' was interested in him![266] There is a dedicated "David Bowie Meeting Room" in the Masonic Temple in Toronto.[267] One has to question why this should be. What exactly was it about David Bowie that the Canadian Masons felt should be celebrated in such a prestigious way?

LAZARUS

Throughout the eighteen-month period Bowie was battling cancer he continued working on two major musical projects. The *Blackstar* album was the first and the second involved the writing and production of a stage show titled *Lazarus*–a musical inspired by an Enda Walsh (1928-1984) book titled *The Man Who Fell to Earth*. Yet again we see the Ziggy archetype in operation for the story featured Thomas Newton as a humanoid alien trapped on Earth: unable to either die or return to his home planet. It was a role Bowie knew well through his role in the film's adaptation of the book in 1976.

Lazarus had its World premiere at the New York Theatre Workshop on November 18, 2015 and then played through to January 20, 2016. At this point it transferred to the West End, London and appeared at the King's Cross Theatre between October 25, 2016 and January 22, 2017.[268] The production featured several of Bowie's classic songs; including *The Man Who Sold the World*, *Changes*, and *Heroes* as well as four new songs from Bowie including *Lazarus:* which subsequently appeared as the third track on his *Blackstar* album. This was released as a single on December 17, 2015, and became his first Billboard Top 40 hit in more than 28 years when it landed at number 40 in the week following his death.[269]

The official music video used to promote *Lazarus*[270] was uploaded to

---

[266] Once again, numerology reveals another strange relationship here. The value of the term 'Blackstar' is 307–the same value as the word 'Freemason'.
[267] https://en.wikipedia.org/wiki/Masonic_Temple_(Toronto)
[268] https://en.wikipedia.org/wiki/Lazarus_(musical)
[269] Trust, Gary, *David Bowie Scores First Top 40 Hot 100 Single Since 1987 With 'Lazarus'*, Billboard, January 2016.
[270] In Gematria the word 'Lazarus' has a value of 892 which is the same as the term 'Lucis Trust'–the name of the publishing house that released Alice Bailey's twenty-four volumes of occult teachings.

the YouTube video-sharing platform on January 7, 2016. Directed by Johan Renck (1966-present day)[271] it focused solely upon Bowie who, in its opening shot, was shown lying on what appears to be his deathbed with a bandage covering his face and black buttons where his eyes should have been. The video ends with an emaciated-looking Bowie retreating into a dark wardrobe dressed in a diagonally-striped suit. This was a direct reference to the rear cover of the 1991 CD reissue of his *Station to Station*[272] album wherein Bowie (who was wearing a very similar suit) is observed squatting on the floor, drawing the Kabbalistic symbol of the Tree of Life. Bowie referenced this esoteric map of magickal consciousness in the lyrics of the *Station to Station* album's title track.

> *"Here are we, one magical moment.*
> *Such is the stuff, from where dreams are woven.*
> *Bending sound, dredging the ocean*
> *Lost in my circle.*
> *Here am I, flashing no colour.*
> *Tall in this room overlooking the ocean.*
> *Here are we, one magical movement.*
> *From Kether to Malkuth*
> *There are, you drive like a demon.*
> *From station to station."*

By referencing the spheres of Kether and Malkuth in his lyrics, Bowie demonstrated an understanding one of the of basics to the Kabbalistic doctrine; which is the Tree of Life ideagram—a magickal map of consciousness consisting of ten, interconnected spheres, or Sephiroth. Twenty-two paths connect them together and this led Éliphas Lévi to associate each one with a Major Arcana of the tarot.[273] The pathway that

---

[271] Renck also directed the music video for Bowie's previous single *Blackstar* in November 2015.

[272] *Station to Station* was Bowie's tenth studio album and was originally released on January 23, 1976.

[273] Three tarot Arcana connect Kether to Malkuth. These are 21: WORLD, 14: TEMPERANCE, and 2: HIGH PRIESTESS. Their accumulative Kabbalistic value is 400 + 60 + 3 = 463 which is the same as the term "Übermensch" as coined by Friedrich Nietzsche.

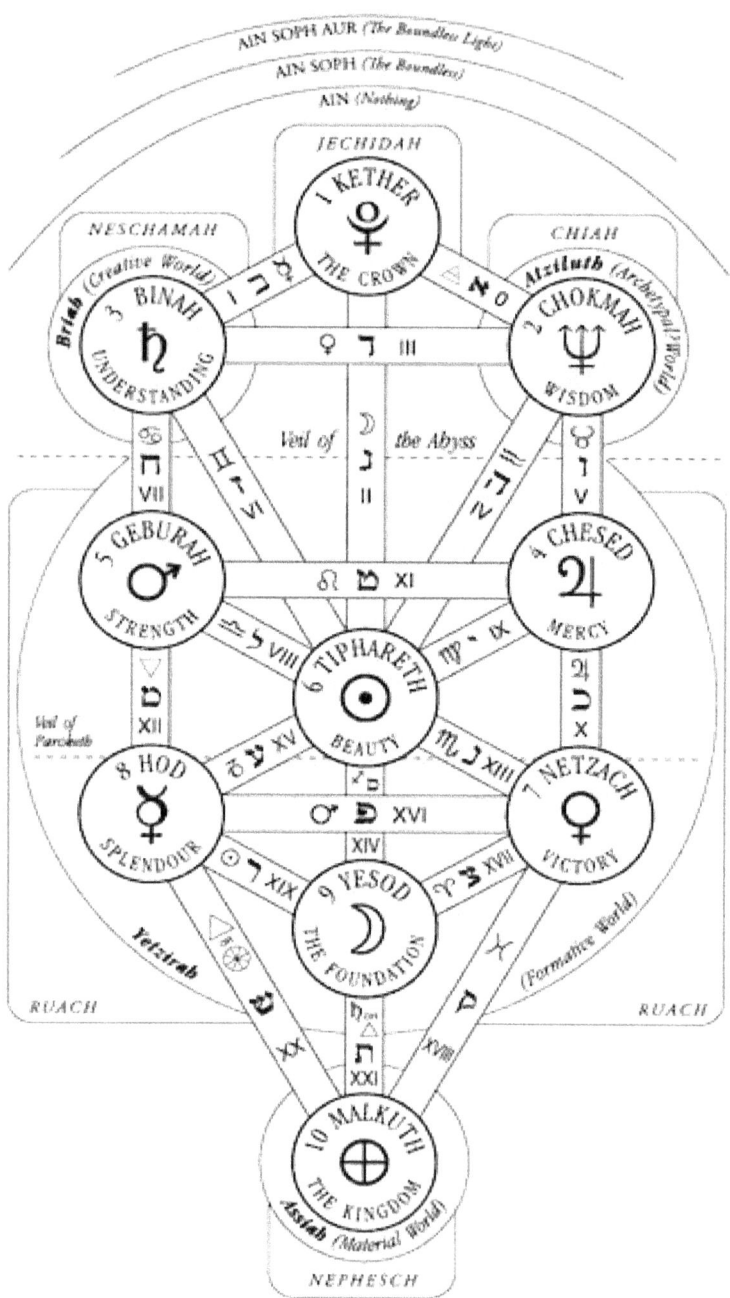

Above: Tree of Life - The Kabbalistic map of consciousness

connects Kether to Malkuth denotes the journey of the neophyte during their incarnation as they steadily work their way through progressively heightened states of consciousness from that of the Earth plane (Malkuth) to the highest spiritual realm (Kether). In some traditions Kether is associated with the star Sirius.

Bowie oblique reference to the Tree of Life with his video for *Lazarus* infers that he knows he is ending his progression through life and that he was now ready to pass on through to an ethereal kingdom. In fact, the opening line in his *Lazarus* song says it all:

"Look up here, I'm in heaven...
I'm so high it makes my brain whirl."

The central theme to the *Lazarus* video highlighted Bowie's weakening physical condition and strengthening spiritual consciousness. The strands of these two dynamics are crossing in his final hours and so he plays the role–if indeed it was an act–of a man having who has come to terms with his fate but who is confounded by his ever-deepening state of psychospiritual confusion.

At one point in the video, Bowie is seen struggling to raise himself up off his (death) bed and to drag himself to a writing desk where, in his weak and confused state, he tries to draw-from his mind thoughts he so desperately wants to record in an old journal.[274] Eventually, through great pain and anguish, he manages to commit his ideas to paper. This is a somewhat harrowing scene but it is also riddled with symbolic occult references leading one to question whether Bowie truly had given up occultism as he so often maintained. In addition to the aforementioned bed, table and wardrobe, there were other artefacts on display in the video. They included a human skull–which is found extensively throughout Freemasonry rituals and teachings where it symbolises mortality, death and rebirth into a renewed state–and a candle, which is extensively used by numerous spiritual disciplines to denote the light of the human Soul which survives human death. The old journal Bowie

---

[274] This scene is redolent of the twelfth grade of the Ancient and primitive Rite of Memphis- Misraim–a ritual structure that focuses upon preserving the Egyptian mysteries.

records his thoughts in also made an appearance in his video for his song *Blackstar* where he can be seen holding it out at arm's length. As he does so it reveals a black pentagram embossed upon the book's worn and creased cover. The same video features additional occult elements but most significantly it opens with the image of an eclipsed sun. Is this meant to represent Sirius in its guise as the 'Sun at Midnight'?

A Search for Meaning

Irrespective of how you interpret the occulted aspects to Bowie's life, his songs, or on-stage persona, it is clear that similar occult threads underpin the careers of friends, artists, and musicians he was associated with. The symbol of the 'black-star' is a good case in point for it is found in connection with one of the World's most successful and inspirational musical entertainers; Elvis Aaron Presley (1935-1977)—an artist of such stature that he was often simply referred to as 'The King'.[275]

Presley was born on January 8, 1935, in Tupelo, Mississippi to Vernon Elvis (1916-1979) and Gladys Love (née Smith, 1912-1958) who were members of the local Assembly of God—a strict Christian faith who are the World's largest Pentecostal denomination.[276] It was through an exposure to their teachings that young Elvis received his early Christian education but later on in his life he found these incapable of satisfying his emerging thirst for personal enlightenment. Although expressed only in private, Presley was so engaged in discovering a personal spiritual truth that it brought him into conflict with some of the people he worked with. In the end, it was his hairdresser Larry Geller (1939-present day) who steered him towards esotericism as a possible source of spiritual sustenance. He obtained a variety of publications for Elvis covering a wide range of topics. Gary Tillery catalogued some of the books that interested Presley the most in *The Seeker King: A Spiritual Biography of Elvis Presley*.

"He read *Isis Unveiled* and *The Secret Doctrine* by

---

[275] Presley is estimated to have sold around 500 million records worldwide during his career making him one of the best-selling music artists of all time. (Source: https://en.wikipedia.org/wiki/Elvis_Presley).
[276] https://en.wikipedia.org/wiki/Assemblies_of_God

> Helena Blavatsky, George Gurdjieff's *Meetings with Remarkable Men,* and P. D. Ouspensky's *The Fourth Way.* He read *The Urantia Book,* Manly Palmer Hall's *The Mystical Christ* and *The Secret Teachings of All Ages, The Chakras* by C. W. Leadbeater, and Jiddu Krishnamurti's *You Are the World.* He read *Pyramidology: The Science of the Divine Message of the Great Pyramid* by Adam Rutherford, *The Holy Kabbalah* by A. E. Waite, and Hermann Hesse's *Siddhartha.* A lifelong student of the Bible, he was fascinated by books that gave him new insights into its texts. He read *The Hidden Wisdom in the Holy Bible, Volumes I and II,* by Geoffrey Hodson, *The Aquarian Gospel of Jesus the Christ* by Lévi, and *Old Testament Wisdom* by Manly Palmer Hall. He also enjoyed books that broadened his view of Christianity, such as *The Gospel According to Thomas* and *The Lost Books of the Bible and the Forgotten Books of Eden* by Rutherford H. Platt."

Although there is no evidence that they ever swapped reading matter, Tillery clearly identified a remarkable degree of commonality between Presley's and Bowie's literary interests; with the writings of A. E. Waite and Éliphas Lévi being the more notable examples. The two superstars also shared an interest in Frederich Nietzsche.[277]

SIGN OF BIRTH

Bedtime reading apart, David Bowie and Elvis Presley had more in common with one another than the fact that their careers rose stratospherically following an iconic and controversial TV performance. They also shared the same birthdate–January 8.[278] This fact may seem

---

[277] *Also sprach Zarathustra,* was a musical interpretation by Richard Georg Strauss (1864-1949) of Nietzsche's classic work of the same name. It featured in the 1968 Stanley Kubrick directed film *2001: A Space Odyssey* and Presley used it as an introduction to his Las Vegas shows from the late 1960s to his death in 1977.

[278] Another notable individual born on the same date was the occult novelist Dennis Yeats Wheatley (1897-1977). His 1934 book *The Devil Rides Out* tells a disturbing

merely coincidental but astrologers believe that every birthdate (i.e., the angular degree the Sun makes in the heavens or zodiac) acts as a unique doorway into a specific area of the spiritual realm. This has the effect of establishing the character, underlying dynamics, and framework, of an individual's incarnation. Consequently, those born on the same day of the year are liable to express similar personal characteristics. Given this long-held astrological theory to be correct then it is perhaps not too surprising to find that there were close psychospiritual connections between the two musicians and that they were intellectually compatible as evidenced by their joint interest in books on philosophy, spirituality, and the occult. This point of intersection did not come easily for either men and Gary Tillery recounts a time when Elvis struggled to find a worthwhile spiritual philosophy.

> "Fascinated by secret orders and their rituals and symbols, Elvis became aware of an out-of-print book by Manly Palmer Hall[279] titled *An Encyclopedic Outline of Masonic, Hermetic, Qabbalistic, and Rosicrucian Symbolical Philosophy*. Unable to find one, he paid to reprint it and obtained two copies autographed by the author—one for himself and one for Dr. Nichopoulos".[280]

Where the two musician's esoteric interests really overlapped though was in their mutual fascination with ufology. In fact, according to Larry Geller, Presley was utterly obsessed with the subject and had been ever since he had a telepathic exchange with an alien when he was just eight years old. This early exposure to the UFO phenomenon continued story of black magic and the occult with the main character, Duke de Richleau, being modeled on the occultist Aleister Crowley.

[279] Manly Palmer Hall (1901-1990) was a Canadian author and mystic who authored over 150 volumes of esoteric teachings. His 1928 book *The Secret Teachings of All Ages* is widely recognised as the most comprehensive encyclopedia on the esoteric teachings of the mystery schools. Hall was made a Knight Patron of the Masonic Research Group of San Francisco and in June 1954, was initiated as a Freemason into Jewel Lodge No. 374, San Francisco. On December 8, 1973, he was recognised as a 33° Mason—the highest honour conferred by the Supreme Council of Scottish Rite Masonry. (Source: https://en.wikipedia.org/wiki/Manly_P._Hall)

[280] Tillery, Gary, *The Seeker King: A Spiritual Biography of Elvis Presley*, Quest Books, 2013.

throughout his lifetime and Geller—who effectively became Presley's spiritual guru—maintained that during the period they were working together both he and Presley observed unidentifiable objects flying through the sky on a regular basis. His recollections include a sighting the two men had while in the desert and another one when several UFOs appeared above Graceland—Presley's palatial home. Apparently, Geller once gave Elvis a book on ufology and a week later he experienced another UFO event while travelling through on Route 66 through New Mexico. This time he saw an object streak across the sky, stop abruptly, make a right-hand turn, and then accelerate away at an incredible speed.

These UFO encounters convinced Elvis that sentient beings live in our Universe. In *Elvis: What Happened?*, Australian journalist Steve Dunleavy recorded conversations with Sonny West[281] (1938-present day) —a friend of Presley who was given the challenging job of protecting the star from 1954 up until his death in 1977. West maintained that:

> "Elvis firmly believed there was life on other planets. He believed that there are flying saucers and that there are visitors from other planets that come down to Earth."[282]

He was not alone. It is common for UFO sightings and ET abduction to run through multiple generations of a family and this was the case for Elvis as his father, Vernon, had an equally remarkable UFO sighting on the night Elvis was born. According to Jon Taysom:

> "His father told us he'd gone out to have a cigarette at 2 a.m. during the delivery, and when he looked up into the skies above their little shack, he saw the strangest blue light. He knew right then and there that something special was happening."[283]

---

[281] Wests' influence on Presley regarding the topic of UFOs might well have been more profound than it appears. He was born on that 'fateful' date of July 5 (1938) and so has Sirius conjunct his Sun in his natal birth-chart.
[282] Dunleavy, Steve, *Elvis: What Happened?*, Ballantine Books, 1977.
[283] Taysom, Joe, *From Elvis Presley to John Lennon: 6 legendary musicians who claim to have seen UFOs*, https://faroutmagazine.co.uk/musicians-that-spotted-ufo-john-lennon-elvis-presley/

Dark Saturn

Both Bowie's and Presley's thirst for spiritual truth was spurred on by their mutual rejection of orthodox Christian teachings and a strong desire to escape the dogma it had imposed upon them from an early age. Both men were also exposed to the UFO phenomena at an equally early age in their life: leading to a conflict between personal religious and philosophical beliefs. Experiencers often attempt to resolve this by investigating mysticism, occultism, and alternative theologies but escaping early religious conditioning is a difficult process; for it requires a continual state of internal probing and self-analysis. This is not a path for the faint-hearted for, as the theologian, historian, and activist for Native American rights, Vine Victor Deloria Jr. (1933-2005) once put it "Religion is for people who're afraid of going to hell. Spirituality is for those who've already been there."

The process of discovering for oneself an authentic spiritual path or, as Crowley put it, "finding one's True Will", can take a lifetime confronting personal traumas. This presents immense challenges to 'lesser mortals' but for super-rich and highly successful superstars such as Bowie and Presley the pressure of work and the lack of privacy that accompanies stardom invariably creates additional barriers to self-development but they both had specific challenges in this regard. Being born under the zodiac sign of Capricorn, they came under the powerful influence of the planet Saturn—the sign's designated planetary ruler. In his song *Oh! You Pretty Things*, Bowie referred to the Earth as a "bitch", but he could equally have applied the term to Saturn—a dark, opposing force often associated with the practice of the Dark Arts.

Analysing the astrological birth-charts of each musician reveals the Moon—which astrologers believe governs a native's emotional and introspective nature—is positioned very close to Saturn in both Presley and Bowie's horoscopes. This is a difficult pairing and is indicative of deep-rooted emotional pain which can, if left unresolved, lead to melancholia, paranoia, and depression.[284] Depending upon an

---

[284] Severe depression afflicts not only musicians and those with malignant Saturnian influences. It is a common feature to many occultists or spiritual seekers. Crowley, Nietzsche, Bond, are just a few examples of those who were struck down by the

individual's ability to cope with the isolation and the karmic retribution Saturn inflicts, the result of ignoring its lessons can often lead to a dependence upon drugs as a way of dulling psychological pain. Both Bowie and Presley used narcotics and alcohol as emotional crutches for extended periods of their lives. In the case of Presley, overeating also proved to be his coping mechanism and this eventually led to a severe deterioration in his physical health during the final years of his life.

For all its negative connotations, Saturn has a powerful spiritual aspect to its nature. It is through its imposition of limitation on an individual that it functions as both guide and teacher—albeit a harsh and unforgiving one. The UK astrologer Liz Greene once described Saturn as, "The membrane which separates the personal unconscious from the collective unconscious."[285]. In this regard, the influence of the planet can be seen underpinning Presley's attempt to attain personal illumination and escape what Nietzsche might call 'group-think'. Saturn initiates this process by breaking down the psyche. Once this has been achieved a previously unrecognised strata of the personality emerges—identified by Jung as "the personal Shadow"—from deep within an individual's unconscious. This is the only way in which true spiritual revelation and personal insight into the True Will can be attained.

Saturn effectively creates, but also strips back, the veil that separates us from the illusions imposed upon by religion, governments, education, and society. Ironically it both constructs the "Matrix" and offers the opportunity to dissolve it. Bowie sensed this duality and was aware of an invisible power that worked upon him from behind the scenes. Presley held the same opinion and often described what he felt were "guiding forces" which he felt were determining the direction his musical and acting career took.

Larry Geller stated in his biography that Elvis once said to him "I always felt an unseen hand behind me."[286] He qualified this remark by adding that Presley believed he was working under the aegis of highly

---

affliction. In the case of Alice Bailey, she suffered so badly from depression in her early life that she seriously contemplated suicide.
[285] Greene, Liz, *Saturn: A New Look at an Old Devil*, Weiser, 1976.
[286] Geller, Larry, *If I Can Dream: Elvis' Own Story*, Avon Books, 1990.

advanced spiritual masters known in Theosophical circles as the 'White Brotherhood'.

Elvis was convinced that he was in direct psychic contact with them and that "they had helped him". Geller explained to his readers—who were not necessarily disposed towards spiritual terminology—that this group of advanced masters and illuminated beings were "...enlightened entities that have existed since time immemorial.".

Presley became so enamoured by the interest that the Brotherhood were showing in him that, like Vince Taylor, he is said to have:

> "...truly felt he was chosen to be here now as a modern-day saviour, a Christ."

As we saw earlier, Bowie was also a firm believer in this clandestine group of ageless entities and that they wield a hidden influence throughout our World. In *Oh! You Pretty Things* he sang

> *"I think about a world to come...*
> *Where the books were found by the Golden Ones."*

References to the Great White Brotherhood are littered throughout occultism. Exactly who these mystic teachers are can be left for later discussion but at this point it is interesting to reference Bowie's take on them in the lyrics to his song *The Supermen*

> "When all the world was very young.
> And mountain magic heavy hung.
> The supermen would walk in file.
> Guardians of a loveless isle
> And gloomy browed with superfear
> Their endless tragic lives
> Could heave nor sigh.
> In solemn, per serenity

This is a classic description of the Ageless Ones—a race of advanced humans who have been known by a variety of names throughout the history of the World. Bowie reflects upon their possible nature in the same song.

> *Wondrous beings chained to life.*
> *Strange games they would play then.*
> *No death for the perfect men*
> *Life rolls into one for them*
> *So softly a supergod cries."*

Although they were not close personal friends, Bowie had a deep admiration for Presley and once admitted that "Elvis was a major hero of mine."[287] It is said that the Londoner first encountered his music after seeing his cousin, Kristina, dance to Presley's classic song *Hound Dog* shortly after its release in 1956.[288]

The two Capricornian musicians met for the first time in 1972 when Bowie, despite his fear of flying, crossed the Atlantic by plane to watch Elvis perform in New York. On the night of the concert Bowie sat close to the front of the stage dressed in his Ziggy gear; sporting his flaming red hair which apparently caught Elvis's attention![289] It is said that the two momentarily met back-stage after the concert to exchange pleasantries but there is little doubt that had the opportunity arisen Bowie and Presley would have conversed for hours about their mutual spiritual interests.

At the core of their inquisitive minds was a mutual philosophy regarding life, society, and the future of mankind. Both of them were of the opinion that, despite the darkening world of the early 1970s, humanity was on the cusp of experiencing a profound spiritual renaissance. Neither musician believed that this mystical regeneration of the World Soul would express itself through orthodox religion but it would manifest outside of its strict and dogmatic structure.

Throughout Bowie's formative years, the ethos of the Church of England had permeated the whole of the English, middle-class society

---

[287] https://theblast.com/167213/how-are-elvis-presley-and-david-bowie-connected/
[288] Sandford, Christopher, *Bowie: Loving the Alien*, Time Warner, 1996.
[289] Ibid.

he had grown up in. Its Christian philosophy underpinned religious studies throughout the state-run education system; including that of Burnt Ash Junior School, Bromley, where Bowie received most of his early education.

For Presley—who was born and brought up in the Bible-belt region of the American South—similar levels of religious control was no less oppressive, However, from the late-1950s onwards, the monopoly once held by orthodox Christianity was beginning to wane. By the start of the 1960s, large numbers of American Christians were experiencing a similar degree of antipathy towards established religion and an opportunity to escape from its clutches emerged when a new form of 'pseudo-Christianity' emerged in the form of TV evangelism.

As attractive as this less austere form of religious worship was to many of those living in the American South, Presley refused to be taken in by any of it. He believed all prevailing strands of orthodox Christian teaching were corrupt and that they were never going to find an authentic place within what a newly-emerging "golden era of spirituality" which he believed was just over the horizon.

In his biography on Presley, Larry Geller quoted Elvis on the subject.

> "Someday in the near future we'll see how the so called ministers of God react as they see their worn out ways and the whole 'old age' start crumbling...They'll all get theirs. I can't wait till this NEW AGE comes..."[290]

EVERY MAN HAS A BLACK STAR

Although there was a notable degree of philosophical commonality between Bowie and Presley, they were quite different musically. Presley was a traditional musician with roots firmly grounded in gospel and country music while on the other hand Bowie established his early musical style upon some of the great crooners—artists such as Jacques Brel (1929-1978) and Anthony Newley (1931-1990).

---

[290] Geller, Larry, *If I Can Dream: Elvis' Own Story*, Avon Books, 1990.

8. BLACK STARS & WHITE ROBES

There is, however, a fascinating musical connection between the songs of Bowie and Presley that reveals the strange, mystical environment that surrounded the two artists up to the time of their untimely deaths.

On August 8[291], 1960, Presley recorded *Black Star*. It was a song that was going to be featured in an upcoming movie he was starring in. In the end, it was not used but was posthumously released on Presley's *Collector's Gold CD* which was released in 1991. The lyrics to the first verse of *Black Star* are interesting.

> *"Every man has a black star.*
> *A black star over his shoulder*
> *And when a man sees his black star*
> *He knows his time; his time has come."*

During the time Bowie was facing his own demise he expressed similar sentiments in the lyrics to his own *Blackstar* song.

> *"Something happened on the day he died.*
> *Spirit rose a metre and stepped aside.*
> *Somebody else took his place, and bravely cried.*
> *(I'm a blackstar, I'm a blackstar).* "[292]"

The "Black Star" motif in occultism works in a variety of different ways. At an immediate level it represents the planet Saturn which, as we saw earlier, became the governing planetary energy within their sun-signs and which underpinned the chthonic elements to their inner psyches.

In regards to the Sirius Mythos, the black star (i.e. a luminary that emits no visible light) can be associated with Sirius and with Sirius C in particular. In a subsequent volume in this series I will focus on the myth surrounding the Egyptian god Set and his role as "The Hidden God"

---

[291] This date is important for it is referred to in New Age circles as the "Lions' Gate". It will be discussed in greater depth in Chapter 9.
[292] In a line in the first verse of his song *Blackstar* Bowie sings "at the centre of it all" which references a line in a Crowley ritual titled *The Star Sapphire*. The Greeks believed that sapphires were associated with the god Apollo, the god of music.

which the English occultist Kenneth Grant (1924-2011) believed was closely connected to the Sirius star-system but for now it is worth noting that Set, or Seth, was later merged into Christian theology as "The Opposer" or Devil. and his associate with all that is evil in this World is unfortunate for it this resulted in the loss of so many of this deity's important attributes as teacher and initiator in occultism. Once again, it is the 'black star's' role as the symbol of Saturn—portrayed as the Greek god Kronos, the god of time—that controlled the process during Bowie's final two years of his life. As the Grim Reaper, his scythe finally fell and Bowie passed away in his New York City apartment on January 10, 2016. He was aged 69. The musician did not have a funeral and his ashes were scattered during a Buddhist ceremony held in Bali, Indonesia.[293]

Accolades flowed in following news of his passing but of all the achievements the musician attained during his professional career the one that would have impressed the 1972 version of Bowie the most was his stellar immortalisation. In honour of his memory, astronomers have designated a sequence of stars to him. These include the luminaries Sigma Librae, Spica, Alpha Virginis, Zeta Centauri, SAA 204 132, and the Beta Sigma Octantis Trianguli Australis which is located in the vicinity of Mars. Together these formulate the iconic lightning flash which Bowie used as a facial decoration on his 1973 *Aladdin Sane* album.[294]

Ziggy had finally made his way back home to his abode in the stars!

---

[293] https://en.wikipedia.org/wiki/David_Bowie
[294] *David Bowie: astronomers give the Starman his own constellation*, The Guardian, Monday January 18, 2016.

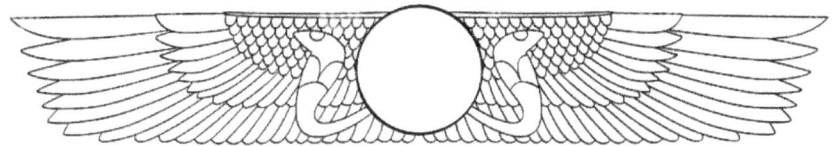

9. Golden Plates

"And with the greater Wisdom of the Kolob the Righteous shall walk with God as Enoch, and God shall wipe away all their tears and they shall put on the Crown of Light, for they shall become the Lamb who has faithfully carried the Cross of Creation unto Salvation."

The Keys of Enoch, J. J. Hurtak

Exploring the worlds of occult, mysticism, and spirituality was an intense, highly personal mission for Éliphas Lévi, Friederich Nietzsche, Aleister Crowley, David Bowie and Elvis Presley. Each one of them set out questioning the validity of the religious dogma of the prevailing established church and ended up falling down spiritual rabbit-holes! At great risk to themselves and their careers, they explored previously unchartered waters and discovered an inner darkness which, although cold and inhabited with malevolent powers, often resulted in divine revelation, personal illumination, and some extraordinary flashes of creative brilliance.

Both Bowie and Presley were less reticent than most when it came to sharing their spiritual beliefs and insights with members of their professional and personal circle but the response their received differed quite markedly. Presley met fervent opposition when attempting to spiritually engage with the people he worked with and this led him to a point where he only trusted his hair-stylist with his intimate spiritual thoughts. When Bowie began to express his occult leanings he found that most of the musicians he was working with had spiritual convictions of their own.

Keyboard player, Mike Garson (1945-present day), worked with Bowie throughout his career and is best known for his piano parts on Bowie's *Aladdin Sane* album and for providing keyboard accompaniment on his *Ziggy Stardust* tour of 1972/73. After being introduced to the teachings of the Church of Scientology by jazz musician Chick Corea (1941-2021), Garson decided to join the organisation as a full-time member in 1970. Prior to leaving it in 1982, Garson was still advocating the religion to other members of the 'Spiders'. It was their drummer, Mick 'Woody' Woodmansey (1950-present day), who took to Scientology teachings became fully committed to the organisation. He even held his wedding service at a Scientology church located in Sussex.[295]

Early 1970, pre-Spiders member Rick Wakeman (1949-present day) played keyboards on the classic Bowie songs *Life on Mars*, *Space Oddity*, *Changes*, and *Oh! You Pretty Things*. After leaving Bowie's backing band he became well-known for his innovative solo albums which included a musical interpretation of the story of King Arthur and his Knights of the Round-Table. Wakeman is also known for his strong Christian beliefs; although he freely recognises other denominations as being equally valid.[296] Despite the Church of England's traditional rejection of Freemasonry, he joined the organisation and was inaugurated at Chelsea Lodge No. 3098.[297]

There is no evidence that the fourth member of the Spiders, bassist Trevor Boulder (1950–2013), held particularly strong religious views but Bowie's guitarist Mick Ronson did—and they were the same as those which that once interested Elvis.

Michael Picasso

Michael 'Mick' Ronson was born in Kingston-upon-Hull on May 26, 1946. He was classically trained as a child in piano, recorder, violin, and harmonium but a deep love of the electric guitar emerged after he encountered the music of American guitarist Duane Eddy (1938-

---

[295] Woodmansey, Woody, *My Life With the Spider from Mars*, Sidgwick and Jackson. 2016.
[296] https://www.innerviews.org/inner/wakeman.html
[297] https://en.wikipedia.org/wiki/Rick_Wakeman

present day).

In November 1963, at the age of 17, Ronson joined his first band, The Mariners before leaving to join another local Hull group called The Crestas who had built a solid reputation by playing in pubs in the local area. In 1965, Ronson left and moved to London where he took up a part-time job as a mechanic. He continued playing guitar and joined a group called The Voice but his new life in the city proved unsatisfying and Ronson returned to Hull in 1966 and joined the city's most popular band The Rats. When its drummer John Cambridge left the group he was replaced by Mick "Woody" Woodmansey. Cambridge also moved to London but in early 1970 he returned to Hull in search of Ronson who he felt might be interested in playing in David Bowie's new backing band called The Hype. Ronson was very reluctant to return to the capital initially but eventually agreed and two days later, on February 5, 1970, he made his debut with Bowie on John Peel's national BBC Radio 1 show.

The Hype played their first gig at The Roundhouse in London two weeks later. It featured Bowie, Cambridge, and Bowie's long-term studio producer Tony Visconti on bass. John Cambridge did not remain long and left in March where he was replaced by Woody Woodmansey. In April 1970 Ronson, Woodmansey, and Visconti started recording Bowie's *The Man Who Sold the World* album at Advision Studios in London.

The line-up of The Hype changed once again and the band now included Trevor Bolder who was brought in to replace Visconti on bass guitar and then keyboardist Rick Wakeman who later joined The Strawbs and then the prog-rock band Yes. This slightly ad-hoc collective was also employed by Bowie for the recording of his next album, *Hunky Dory* with Ronson taking over the task of musical arranger for the string parts on several tracks: including the seminal *Life On Mars*? Wakeman subsequently left and the backing band became known as The Spiders from Mars with Ronson once again playing a key role in the orchestral arrangements and other instrumentation on *The Rise and Fall of Ziggy Stardust and the Spiders from Mars* album.

Ronson found his musical skills in high demand. In 1972, through a connection to Bowie, Ronson provided strings and brass arrangement on Mott the Hoople's Bowie-produced album *All the Young Dudes* during which Ronson established a long-term working and personal relationship with Mott's lead singer and primary songwriter, Ian Hunter. Ronson also co-produced Lou Reed's album *Transformer* with Bowie, played on a few tracks on the Dana Gillespie album *Weren't Born a Man*, and appeared on the 1972 country rock album *Bustin' Out* by Pure Prairie League where he created musical arrangements for a string ensemble and contributed guitar and vocals on several tracks on the record.

Ronson played on Bowie's next two albums, *Aladdin Sane* and the 1973 covers album *Pin Ups* but his working relationship with him soured on that fateful night at the Hammersmith Odeon in 1973 when Bowie killed Ziggy off. Now that he was free from the shackles of the Spiders, Ronson went on to enjoy a prolific musical career. He released three solo albums and joined Mott the Hoople for a short while before working on a more permanent basis with their lead-singer Ian Hunter by joining his band and operating as an arranger on his albums. Ronson later worked with a slew of other artists including David Cassidy, Roger Daltrey (The Who), Ellen Foley, John Mellencamp, Roger McGuinn, Slaughter & The Dogs (who took their name from the Ronson album *Slaughter on 10th Avenue*), Morrissey, The Wildhearts, Rich Kids, and Elton John. He was also a permanent member of Bob Dylan's Rolling Thunder Revue band.

In 1991 he produced and added backing vocals and guitar overdubs on several tracks of *Nun Permanently* by the Swedish cult band Leather Nun but at the end of its production the musician was diagnosed with cancer. Ronson continued working and the following year produced Morrissey's album, *Your Arsenal* but his health was failing and his final live performance was at the Freddie Mercury Tribute Concert held at Wembley Stadium, London, on April 20, 1992; where he played alongside Hunter and Bowie on the classic Mott the Hoople song *All the Young Dudes*. The musician died of liver cancer at the age of 46 on April 29, 1993.

9. GOLDEN PLATES

ELVIS AND THE LDS

Mick Ronson did not publicly discuss his religious interest or the fact that he had been raised in The Church of Jesus Christ of Latter-day Saints (LDS) (otherwise known as the Mormons). Very few Ronson biographies or obituaries have revealed the reasons behind his involvement: other than suggesting it was simply as a result of being brought up in the religion by his parents. Some accounts maintain that Mick had grown disenchanted with the LDS sometime prior to his death and that he has even been cited as a "former Mormon".[298] Other sources contradict this by maintaining that Ronson remained a Mormon Elder until his death.[299] Either way, his funeral was conducted as a Mormon ceremony.

While Ronson was a permanent member of the Mormon Church, Elvis was not—although he had a profound interest in the religion and at one point came close to joining. Presley's friend, martial arts expert Ed Parker—a close companion he often referred to as "my second daddy"—had been raised a Mormon and as a result of their friendship Presley became curious about the LDS and their teachings. This led Parker to give Elvis a series of books about the church, one of which is still on display at Elvis' Graceland home. Elvis found the publication so intriguing that he often questioned his mentor about his faith during their limo drives to and from concerts.[300]

On one occasion the two men were driving from Las Vegas to Pasadena in a brand-new Cadillac Elvis had given Parker. They arrived Parker's home in California early in the morning. His Mormon associate invited Elvis to meet the other members of his family which included two young daughters. Elvis was immediately taken by the friendliness of Parker's family, their simple home life, and strong adherence to what he saw as core, or authentic, Christian values. Despite Elvis' rejection of orthodox Christianity he remained a firm believer in Christ as a spiritual figurehead. The girls were due to attend their LDS church later that morning and they asked Elvis if he would like to join them. He agreed

---
[298] en.wikipedia.org/wiki/Mick_Ronson
[299] Ibid.
[300] Skousen, Paul B., *Brother Paul's Mormon Bathroom Reader*, 2005

and he was warmly welcomed as one of the congregation. It is said that from that point on attendances reached capacity every weekend with churchgoers fervently hoping that 'The King' might return one day.[301]

In addition to his conversations with Parker regarding the Mormon Church he also discussed them with Olive Osmond, the mother of the famous Mormon family musical group The Osmonds. Olive, it is said, was always keen on spreading the Mormon message wherever she went and often handed out copies of the *Book of Mormon* to many musicians and celebrities; including Queen Elizabeth II–the head of the Christian Church in England![302]

CAVE OF SECRETS

So, who are the Mormons, what do they believe and what was the nature of its spiritual dynamics that was so attractive to Ronson and Presley?

The history of the church begins with Joseph Smith Jr. who was born on December 23, 1805, in Sharon, Vermont. Sometime prior to 1814 the family relocated to the western side of New York–an area that was a hub of intense religious revivalism during the Second Great Awakening in the early 19th-century, Essentially a Protestant revival led by Baptist and Methodist churches it was felt by those who were involved in it that it was pivotal to the future of America for it heralded the onset of a new religious era.[303] To others who were kindly disposed towards the movement, it was seen more as a political crusade via which a 'Golden Age' in America could be initiated using religion as a tool to bring about changes to current laws and thereby force the American citizenry human behaviour into creating an improved society.[304] These new religious groups supported, among other causes, The Temperance Movement–who were fighting for a blanket-ban on the manufacture and sale of

---

[301] Latter-Day Saints Living - https://www.ldsliving.com/the-day-elvis-presley-attended-early-morning-seminary/s/77866
[302] https://latterdaysaintmusicians.com/music-news/mother-osmond-elvis-presley-queen-elizabeth-and-the-book-of-mormon
[303] https://en.wikipedia.org/wiki/Second_Great_Awakening
[304] Foner, Eric, *Give Me Liberty! An American History. Vol. 1*, W. W. Norton & Company, 2006.

9. Golden Plates

alcohol—and abolitionists who were pressing for an end to slavery.

Although the Smith family were Christian fundamentalists they also practised 'religious folk magic'—a strand of occultism traditionally practised within the closed confines of small American communities. Joseph's father, Joseph Smith Snr., was widely considered to be a proficient medium and the metaphysical skill he was particularly known for involved the divining rod. Although considered a fringe psychic science today, the use of a rod, or rods, for finding water sources and other mineral deposits was a regular practice in remote areas of agricultural America—particularly during times of drought. Father Joseph extended this range of uses by using his rods to search for lost treasure.

It appears that the whole of the Smith family was both extremely psychic and highly spiritually attuned for it is said that both parents and his maternal grandfather experienced visions and dreams which they firmly believed to be direct messages and communications from God.[305]

Around 1816, the Smith family left Vermont and moved to Palmyra, New York. It was here that Joseph Jr. started to apply some of the metaphysical practices he had learned from his father and was soon divining for water and buried treasure. However, the young man's interest in occultism extended beyond this. On September 22, 1823—at the age of 18—he conducted his first operation of ceremonial magick. Up to this point, he had started using what is called a 'shew stone' or 'seer stone' which he first placed inside a hat and then then into prior to receiving visions. On the day of his first ritual, Smith Jnr. operated his seeing-stone and from within one of his visions emerged an angel called "Moroni" who told him that a set of golden plates could be found buried in a cave on nearby Hill Cumorah.[306] Smith was intrigued by this revelation, collected his magickal implements together and left for the cave where, at the stroke of midnight, he performed an evocation. As Moroni promised, the location of a set of plates were revealed to him.

---

[305] Quinn, D. Michael, *The Mormon Hierarchy: Origins of Power*, Signature Books, 1994.
[306] Lavenda, Peter, *The Angel and the Sorcerer, The Remarkable Story of the Occult Origins of Mormonism and the Rise of Mormons in American Politics*, Ibis, 2012.

Smith said that...

> ".... under a stone of considerable size, lay the plates, deposited in a stone box. This stone was thick and rounding in the middle on the upper side, and thinner towards the edges, so that the middle part of it was visible above the ground, but the edge all around was covered with earth. Having removed the earth, I obtained a lever, which I got fixed under the edge of the stone, and with a little exertion raised it up. I looked in, and there indeed did I behold the plates, the Urim and Thummim[307], and the breastplate, as stated by the messenger. The box in which they lay was formed by laying stones together in some kind of cement. In the bottom of the box were laid two stones crossways of the box, and on these stones lay the plates and the other things with them."

Just as Smith stooped down to remove them from their hiding place, he was set-upon by what he described as an "amphibious creature" which transformed into a man and struck him on the back of the head leaving him dazed. Evidently there had been a change in plan and was being denied access to the plates Moroni had promised him. Smith was confused by this turn of events but later surmised that the reasons behind the change of plan was because his "motives were not pure". He freely admitted that his original intention when making the trip to the hill had been purely financial but that his greed had blinded him to the plates true value; which he later realised was entirely spiritual.

Moroni reappeared in the cave and told Smith to return the same day each year; which he did faithfully for four years until, on September 22, 1827, Smith, performed another magickal ritual,[308] made contact with

---

[307] The first Biblical references to the 'Urim' and the 'Thummim. appears in Exodus 28:30, where they are named for inclusion on the breastplate to be worn by Aaron in the holy place. Other books within the Bible describe their uses: especially 1 Samuel.

[308] Owens states that: "Through his associations with ceremonial magic as a young treasure seer, Smith contacted symbols and lore taken directly from Kabbalah. In his

9. GOLDEN PLATES

Left: Artist's illustration of the moment the Angel Moroni handed over the Golden Plates to Joseph Smith.

Moroni, and was finally given permission to remove the plates from their hiding-place.[309]

Now that Smith had them in his possession he was able to examine them more closely. He was surprised to discover that the sheet-metal plates were thinner than he had expected and were held together with three rings which created a book measuring roughly 6" (15cms.) wide, 8" (20cms.) tall, and 6" (15cms.) thick. Smith found that he was able to flick through the first third of the metal sheets but the rest were "fused together into a single block" resulting them being—as Smith described it—"sealed."[310]

Smith took the plates home for closer examination and found that they were inscribed in a form of hieroglyphic writing which he was able to translate. Grant Hardy summarised Smith's method for achieving this." Smith looked at a seer stone placed in his hat and then dictated the text of the *Book of Mormon* to scribes" he said.[311] Other observers of

---

prophetic translation of sacred writ, his hermeneutic method was in nature Kabbalistic. With his initiation into Masonry, he entered a tradition born of the Hermetic-Kabbalistic tradition." (Source: Owens, Lance, *Joseph Smith and Kabbalah: The Occult Connection*, Vol. 27, No. 3, Fall 1994.)

[309] Quinn states that: "Whether by command of the treasure-guardian Moroni or by Joseph Smith's own choice, every circumstance of his September 1827 visit conformed to astrological traditions and to an occult handbook on sale in his neighbourhood." (Source: Quinn, Michael D., *Early Mormonism and the Magic World View*, Signature Books, 1998.)

[310] von Däniken, Eric, *History is Wrong*, New Page Books, 2009.

[311] Hardy, Grant, Ancient History and Modern Commandments: *The Book of Mormon in Comparison with Joseph Smith's Other Revelations*, Ashurst-McGee & Hauglid, 2020.

this process maintained that during the translation Smith distanced himself from his scribe with a blanket placed between the two of them.

In 1828–while aiding her husband in the transcription of the plates–Lucy Harris (1792–1836) repeatedly asked Smith to loan her their working manuscript. Smith reluctantly agreed but within weeks she had lost it. The most likely explanation for their absence was that they had been stolen from her by another member of Smith's extended family.[312] Smith was devastated by their loss. He believed that Moroni had subsequently taken them back into hiding and that his ability to translate the writing on the plates went with them. It is not clear what happened next but Smith stated that God had allowed him to resume his work but directed that he continued where he left off with what is called the *Book of Mosiah*–without having to retranslate the original, lost manuscript.[313]

Smith eventually recommenced his translations with his wife and brother between September 1828 and April 1829. Keen to avoid any further unnecessary interruptions, the group moved in with neighbours the following month and continued their work on the manuscript.[314]

At this time, Smith said he obtained permission–presumably from either God or Moroni–to permit eleven other individuals to see the golden plates and in certain cases to handle them.[315] Each of the chosen participants later signed written testimonies to the authenticity of Smith's working protocols with three of the group describing how they saw the plates in a visionary encounter with an angel and the other eight maintaining they had undertaken a physical examination of a few plates handed to them by Smith.

The group finally completed their translation in June 1829[316] and the manuscript was subsequently published as *The Book of Mormon: An Account Written by the Hand of Mormon upon Plates Taken from the Plates of Nephi* by E. B. Grandin Palmyra, New York, prior to going on

---

[312] Givens, Terryl, *By the Hand of Mormon: The American Scripture That Launched a New World Religion*, Oxford University Press, 2002.
[313] Remini, Robert V., *Joseph Smith*, Viking Penguin, 2002.
[314] Bushman, Richard Lyman, *Joseph Smith: Rough Stone Rolling*, Alfred A. Knopf, 2005.
[315] IBID.
[316] IBID.

sale in his bookstore on March 26, 1830.[317] Smith was only 24 years of age but by the time of his death on June 27, 1844, he had attracted tens of thousands of followers and founded a religion that has grown globally to a membership of nearly 17 million.[318] The *Book of Mormon* remains the church's central text and has subsequently been translated into at least 112 languages.[319]

THE NEW JERUSALEM

Joseph Smith had a pessimistic and apocalyptic view of the World. He believed that humanity would become increasingly irredeemable unless it resolved its deep-rooted tendency towards destruction and self-annihilation. If this decline was to be reversed then he felt it would have to take place in his home country and that America must play an active role in its redemption—a process that he asserted was only possible through the acceptance of what he referred to as "the true teachings of Christ". To this end, the LDS founder was determined to establish a Mormon church in every city and town in the country with each one directly connected to a central hub into which they could draw those who wanted to be 'saved'.

The Church of Christ—later named the Church of Jesus Christ of Latter-day Saints (LDS)—was formed by Smith and a handful of followers on April 6, 1830. Within six months of its formation they had instructed missionaries to travel to remote locations in America and to identify sites suitable for the construction of a City of Zion, or New Jerusalem. Theirs was to be no ordinary city for Smith's intention was it would initially accommodate fifteen to twenty thousand residents who would attract even more converts. Every family within its jurisdiction would qualify to receive an inheritance of land and be offered open access to the temple from they could receive religious instruction.[320]

---

[317] Kunz, Ryan, *180 Years Later, Book of Mormon Nears 150 Million Copies*, Ensign, 2010
[318] https://en.wikipedia.org/wiki/Membership_history_of_the_Church_of_Jesus_Christ_of_Latter-day_Saints
[319] *Translations of the Book of Mormon*, www.LDS365.com
[320] Lessee, Dean C., Esplin, Ronald K., and Bushman, Richard Lyman, *The Joseph Smith Papers, Volume I 1832-1839*, The Church Historian's Press, 2008.

Smith envisioned that his utopian metropolis would become a refuge from the chaos he felt would ensue during what he called "the last days". It would operate as a closed community within which the sick, poor, and needy could be administered as well as a place wherein everyone had equal rights before God. Most of all, Smith believed it would be a location from which Christ could establish his new ministry following his expected imminent return to Earth.

In short, he saw his new metropolis as a wholly sacred environment and to this end he intended it to be constructed with reference to cosmic proportions (i.e. based upon mathematics and ratios that reflected planetary motion). These esoteric values were to be applied when determining the exact width of the streets and even the size of building plots. [321] At its heart, it was going to reflect the "Creation of the heavens descending from the sky at the last day." Smith literally wanted to create heaven-on-earth for, as he said later on in his life:

> "That same sociality. which exists among us here, will exist among us there only it will be coupled with eternal glory."[322]

In the summer of 1831, Joseph Smith travelled to Missouri for a personal revelation had suggested to him that the little village of Independence, Jackson County, would make an ideal location for his visionary city. Despite believing he had been divinely guided to perform God's work, his plans met with strong local opposition. In 1833, two years after a City of Zion was started, the LDS were ejected. Undaunted by their rejection the church's founders soldiered on but just five years later, in 1838, Smith and his followers were also ejected from Kirtland; forcing them to relocate to Far West, Missouri, where, once again, they were expelled following an order by its governor.

Their next attempt to build their religious community was at Nauvoo,

---

[321] Building with regard to sacred measurements is not unique but it was common practice throughout ancient Egypt. More recently the same process was used by Freemasons in the founding of Washington D.C.1 (Source: Ovason, David, *Secret Architecture of Our Nation's Capital: The Masons and the Building of Washington, D.C.*, HarperCollins Publishers, 2002.)

[322] Howe, E. D., *Mormonism Unvailed*, privately published, 1834.

Illinois, and this began in 1839. This project was a little more successful and it expanded until it became home to 10-12,000 inhabitants. Unfortunately for the Mormons, history repeated itself once again and they were driven out. Their expulsion caused the outcasts to try again–this time in Utah where they finally found a permanent settlement in Salt Lake City.

A Godlike State

The sacred teachings under-pinning LDS philosophy is The *Book of Mormon* but is not a typical religious manuscript. It was forged from a collection of writings that are said to have been compiled by ancient prophets who were living on the American continent between 600B.C. and 421A.D. They were, according to Smith, a select group of individuals whom God had led out of Jerusalem prior to the birth of Christ.

The book that angel Moroni had provided them with has been described as a "brief sketch of the origin, progress, civilisation, laws, governments ...righteousness and iniquity" of the "aboriginal inhabitants of the country".[323] It is also said to contain theological discussions regarding the story of the Fall of Adam and Eve, the nature of the Christian atonement, eschatology, redemption from physical and spiritual death, baptism, communion, personal revelation, economic justice, and the nature of God, spirits and the angels. It also includes details regarding the proposed organisation of the Latter-Day Church. Even back in the day it proved to be a contentious text with Smith attracting criticism by asserting that Jesus Christ had appeared in the Americas following his expected return or resurrection.[324]

Occult Roots?

Mormon teachings and moral codes have been analysed, dissected, and critiqued more intrusively than any other contemporary American

---
[323] Davis, William L., *Visions in a Seer Stone: Joseph Smith and the Making of the Book of Mormon*, University of North Carolina Press, 2020.
[324] Hardy, Grant, *Understanding the Book of Mormon with Grant Hardy,. Journal of the Book of Mormon and Other Restoration Scripture (Interview)*. Vol. 25, Interviewed by Blair Hodges, 2016.

religion; with the only possible exception being The Church of Scientology with whom the LDS shares a common link: they both derive their origins from similar arcane beliefs and practices.

Scientology founder L. Ron Hubbard (1911-1986) formed his religion around occult work he performed with Aleister Crowley devotee and the famous rocket scientist Jack Parsons (1914-1952). The two magickians utilised the same occult practices as Smith prior to his receipt of his "Golden Plates". These were based upon the philosophies of Cornelius Agrippa (1486-1535),[325] Solomon (c.800 BCE), and Francis Barrett (1770-c1802).

Given the somewhat occulted history of Mormonism, it is perhaps not too surprising to discover that the *Book of Mormon*—as well as other seminal LDS texts—include esoteric information of a type which regular churchgoers might not be aware.[326] With more than a passing nod to Frederick Nietzsche's 'Übermensch and Bowie's 'Homo-Superior', Mormonism teaches that even as mere mortals, humanity has an opportunity, or even obligation, to grow into a spiritually advanced, Godlike status. Smith believed that:

> "Here, then, is eternal life—to know the only wise and true God; and you have got to learn how to be Gods yourselves, and to be kings and priests to God, the same as all Gods have done before you, namely, by going from one small degree to another, and from a small capacity to a great one; from grace to grace, from exaltation to exaltation, until you attain to the resurrection of the dead, and are able to dwell in everlasting burnings, and to sit in glory, as do those who sit enthroned in everlasting power."[327]

---

[325] Sirius was one of the fifteen fixed Behenian stars mentioned by Cornelius Agrippa in his *Three Books of Occult Philosophy* published in 1531. Agrippa also formulated an astrological glyph to represent the star.

[326] A full exposition of the magickal methods used by Joseph Smith and a full analysis of the occult threads running through the history of the Mormons, can be found in *Early Mormonism and the Magic World View* by D. Michael Quinn, Signature Books, 1998.

[327] Smith, Joseph Fielding (ed.), *Teachings of the Prophet Joseph Smith*, Deseret Book, 1938.

9. GOLDEN PLATES

According to Mormon teachings, God experienced this dramatic transformation process for himself or, as Mormon scholar McConkie stated: "God used to be a man on another planet."[328] This statement reveals Joseph Smith's belief in extraterrestrial life and this was confirmed by Oliver B. Huntington who wrote in a Mormon magazine:

> "As far back as 1837, I know that he (Joseph Smith) said the moon was inhabited by men and women the same as this earth, and that they lived to a greater age than we do—that they live generally to near the age of a 1000 years."[329]

Huntington also maintained that:

> "The inhabitants of the moon are more of a uniform size than the inhabitants of the earth, being about 6 feet in height. They dress very much like the Quaker style and are quite general in style or the one fashion of dress. They live to be very old, coming generally, near a thousand years. This is the description of them as given by Joseph the Seer, and he could 'See' whatever he asked the Father in the name of Jesus to see."[330]

While Mormon teachings might appear to be isolated from mainstream religion and spirituality there is an interesting connection between it and Freemasonry. Joseph Smith received his first degree as a member of the Craft at the Nauvoo Lodge on March 15, 1842, and the next day he was elevated to the degree of Sublime[331] Master of the Royal Secret. His progress through the first three degrees was equally rapid and just six weeks later, on May 2, 1842, Smith was claiming Masonic secrets as his own revelations to Mormon leaders. It was from

---

[328] McConkie, Bruce R, *Mormon Doctrine*, Bookcraft, 1966.
[329] *The Young Woman's Journal*, Vol. 3, Brigham Young University, 1891.
[330] *The History of Oliver B. Huntington*, Marriott Library, University of Utah.
[331] The third or Master Mason Degree in Blue Lodge Masonry is referred to as "the sublime degree of Master Mason". The archaic usage of the word "sublime" is "elevate to a high degree of moral or spiritual purity or excellence".

Freemasonry that Joseph Smith invented the basic ceremonies and symbols known as the "Endowment". McCormick stated that "Into the fabric of Freemasonry he wove his own peculiar brand of occultism, claiming it to be 'revelation' from on high."[332] A strong Mormon/Masonic connection remains evident today for the exterior of the LDS Temple in Salt Lake City is adorned with several Masonic designs; and even some Sirius-related symbols such as the All-Seeing Eye and the inverted 5-pointed star (pentagram).

THE END?

The rotten stench of impending apocalypse has permeated religion for a very long time. It is a philosophy that puts 'bums on seats' by drawing the sad and most isolated members of a community into a church; thereby providing it with its primary life-blood and recurring source of revenue. However, religion is far from having a monopoly on nihilism and the pervading sense of impending apocalypse that emerged within 1970s rock music, the Cold War, and geo-political events, did not emerge from the teachings of Joseph Smith or Friedrich Wilhelm Nietzsche. A residual sense of impending doom exists at the heart of all cultures and can be seen to rise and falls on a relatively regular basis.

The world of ufology is not immune from the same dark cloud of impending doom either. A number of well-established UFO cults came to embrace it ever since the first regular appearance of extraterrestrials in the 1950s. Their interpretation of it is a little more complex for most UFO cults intermingle the concept of 'apocalypse' with ET contact and group 'salvation'.

A belief in impending global catastrophe often proves to be nearly as dangerous as apocalypses themselves. In 1956, American sociologist Professor Leon Festinger proved this to be the case when he published a study titled *When Prophecy Fails*.[333] He based his analysis on a psychological investigation into a bizarre flying saucer cult based in

---
[332] McCormick, W. J., *Christ, the Christian, and Freemasonry*, Great Joy Publications, 1984.
[333] Festinger, Leon; Henry W. Riecken; Stanley Schachter, *When Prophecy Fails: A Social and Psychological Study of a Modern Group that Predicted the Destruction of the World*, University of Minnesota Press, 1956.

9. Golden Plates

Chicago called "The Seekers"

Festinger referred to their main spiritual leader as "Madame Keech" but this was merely a pseudonym. Her real name was Dorothy Martin (1900-1992); although she was also know by her magickal name "Sister Thedra". Martin was predominantly influenced by Theosophy but she had previously been involved with Scientology and drew inspiration fore her ideas from L Ron Hubbard's Dianetics movement. While practising automatic writing, Martin received messages from a high-level spiritual instructor she came to know as "Elder Brother" and then later on with a group of spiritual beings called "The Guardians" who were said to originate from the planets "Clarion" and "Cerus".

The Seekers were led to understand that these "Guardians" were benign spiritual teachers of humanity. They taught a range of metaphysical ideas and led the group to believe that there would shortly be a dramatic increase in the number of extraterrestrials visiting the planet. However, The Guardians also brought a dark message. They warned the group that they should prepare themselves for a imminent cataclysmic event that would bring with it widespread destruction to the Earth prior to its purification.

The date given for this was December 21, 1954, when a large flood would destroy Lake City, large portions of the United States, Canada, Central America, and Europe. They were also told that at the last minute, all true believers would be rescued by The Guardians in their spaceships which would take them off-planet and to safety on 'Clarion'.

Festinger discovered that when the tragic event failed to transpire as predicted there was no decline of cult members faith in their leaders. In fact, he found a remarkable strengthening of their commitment with the majority believing that it was their pious devotion that convinced God to spare the World from catastrophe. This was utterly irrational to Festinger and he formulated what is now known as 'Festinger Syndrome'–a theory which seeks to explain the reasons why prophetic failure is not normally fatal to cult-like religious groups.

Martin later left The Seekers and travelled to Peru where she became a pupil of George Hunt Williamson's (1914-1986) "Brotherhood of the Seven Rays".[334] After meeting other inner-plane 'Masters'—which included Joseph Smith's angel Moroni—Sister Thedra developed her own spiritual philosophy. In 1961, she returned to the United States where, in 1965, she established the Association of Sananda and Sanat Kumara at Mount Shasta, California. Around the same time, she announced that Moroni would soon reincarnate as a child and would begin to manifest his spiritual powers around August 1975. Disciples awaited his appearance but Moroni failed to turn-up and, once again, Festinger Syndrome struck leading her to continue growing the organisation based upon her channelled spiritual messages.[335]

The UFO mystery is a broad church. It encompasses a wide range of meta-philosophical ideas which many on the fringes of the topic have chosen to weave around a religious narrative. The geographical collapse predicted by The Seekers in 1954 was said to destroy society, eradicate civilisations, and presage the appearance of spiritual masters (i.e. ETs). All this was against the backdrop of rising tensions between America and Russia and the threat of all-out nuclear war.

However, this was not the apocalyptic scenario envisioned by Bowie. His version centred primarily upon societal collapse, urban decay, de-humanisation, and the imposition of authoritarian control systems. In many ways, it was a more accurate evaluation than that of The Seekers for he effectively foresaw the World as it became following the 9/11 'terrorist' attacks with its subsequent clampdown on personal freedoms. Its seem that Bowie was not too far off the mark when peering into his crystal ball[336]—just a little ahead of his time. Unless, of course, there happens to be another, more esoteric explanation for the deep trepidation Bowie felt regarding the future of humanity?

---

[334] Syzygy, *The Beast and the Prophet: Aleister Crowley's Fascination with Joseph Smith*, *Journal of Alternative Religion and Culture*, Vol. 3, No. 1-2, Winter/Spring 1994.
[335] Ibid.
[336] This is a hypothetical ball. There is no proof that Bowie ever actually owned a crystal ball-although he did hold one in the film *Labyrinth* (1986).

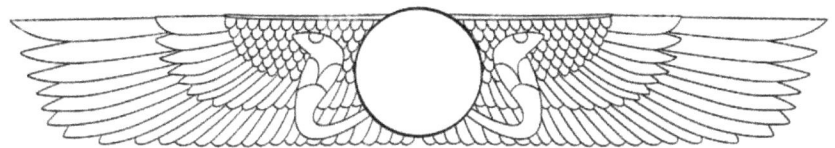

10. Tune in or Burn Out

"...the world we thought we knew no longer exists; in fact, hasn't existed since 1972. She can stop anticipating the end of the world, it has already come and gone."

The Gathering, William Gammil.

One month after Bowie's *Top of the Pops* appearance in July 1972, the predicted 'apocalypse' arrived. At 15:19 GMT on Monday, August 7, 1972, cosmic forces of immense magnitude were released after the surface of our Sun erupted in a way never seen before. As a result, a vast band of radiation was expelled far out into the Solar System—a discharge of such magnitude that it is credited by astronomers as the most powerful solar flare ever recorded. The electromagnetic wave it created was so intense that when it hit our planet it caused widespread damage by knocking out long-distance phone communication in several American states. At 22:30 UT the US communications company AT&T reported a surge of 60 volts on the coaxial (i.e., shielded) telephone cable between Chicago and Nebraska, creating an outage that subsequently forced the telecommunications company to redesign its power system for their transatlantic services.

In addition to causing AT&T problems, the electromagnetic field also shut down the phone service on Bell's cable link between Plano, Illinois, and Cascade, Iowa for a 30-minute period. Both the Canadian Overseas Telecommunications Corporation and the Canadian National Tele-Communications Company reported that the surges on their cables was so intense that it had burnt out several important components in their control systems.

In their analysis of the solar event, astronomers Marcos E. Machado and David M. Rust reported that the dynamic radio spectrum of the three powerful flares that took place over a span of 15 hours comprised Type II and type IV bursts. This was a sort of a piston-driven shockwave which travelled at a velocity of around 1500 km/s.[337] This seismic wave of energy was felt even farther afield than our planet when, at 11:24 UT, the Pioneer 9 spacecraft detected a shock wave from the first of the flares. This was accompanied by a sudden change in the solar wind speed from 350 to 585 km/sec. The intensity of these flares, classified as 'X2', was near the limits of the scale used to determine solar-flare X-ray power. They created an atmospheric aura visible to residents living in all states between Illinois and colour ado.

While the intensity of the solar storm sent recording equipment into a frenzy, the impending event had not been entirely unexpected–just its size and intensity! Weather forecasters at the Space Environment Services Center in Boulder, Colorado, had already issued an alert regarding the imminent arrival of an electromagnetic storm on August 4. According to *Science News*:

> "The early days of August saw a severe disturbance on the sun that produced four major flares between August 2 and August 7.... The ones recorded in early August were among the most major ever recorded.... The August 7 flare ran the X-ray sensors off the scale..."

The solar wind, which is reported to have had an average velocity of 500 km/sec.–or a million miles per hour–later reached the unheard-of speed of 2.5 million miles an hour for three consecutive days before dropping to 1.5 million during the following month. This was alarming and the sort of stats these intense solar winds were producing were considered by astrophysicists to be impossible. Clearly, something strange and quite extraordinary had taken place in our sector of the solar system and conventional physics was at a loss to explain it.

---

[337] Machado, Marcos E and Rust, David M., *Analysis of the August 7, 1972, White Light Flare by NASA*, Astrophysics Data System, 1974.

10. Tune In or Burn Out

Radio Outages

Solar storms of the type that hit the Earth in August 1972, invariably interfere with the electromagnetic field surrounding our planet. Depending on the degree to which the ions in our upper atmosphere become charged, the result can be experienced in a variety of ways. One of the more evident is a major disruption in regular radio waves for they are bounced off this layer as a way of extending their range and coverage. A month after the solar flare hit Earth, *Radio Communication*—the official monthly journal of the Radio Society of Great Britain (RSGB)—featured an article titled *A Natural Event*. Written by a contributor known only as R. A. Ham, it acknowledged the impact of the solar flare.

The RSGB had long since monitored electromagnetic field fluctuations around the planet. When they increase to the point of being disruptive—such as during times of intense sunspot activity—they are assessed for their impact upon the transmission and reception of radio signals; particularly on frequency bands designated for primary use by amateur radio enthusiasts. In his article, Ham commented on his monitoring of the build-up to the mass solar ejection over the previous month.

> "On 1 August 1972 thunder static was causing many unwanted spikes to be drawn on the pen recording chart during the midday solar observation made by the author at 95 and 136MHz. At 12:46BST both radio telescopes recorded an 8min burst from the sun which was strong enough to blot out the prevailing static. This burst served as a solar warning that big events were to follow.
>
> By first post on 2 August a postcard dated 1 August arrived from Robert Mackenzie, a BAA observer in Dover, which read: "Tremendous-sized spot group today. Be prepared for aurora, perhaps considerable aurora. spot chart follows."

> The solar observation the following day revealed that the prevailing noise storm was now very intense on both radio frequencies, indicated by the pens which were frequently at fsd. By evening the solar noise could be detected on both the 2 and 4m bands, using the normal VHF Yagis directed toward the setting sun. It was now obvious that this storm was reaching mammoth proportions.
>
> On Friday 4 August the solar noise was so strong that the meteor equipment (70-31MHz) which normally switches on at 09:00BST could not be used for three hours, and when the radio telescopes switched on at midday, both pens were almost 'fsd' for the whole two-hour period of the observation. "

Ham also described how later the same evening he had been setting up his radio rig in the recreation ground at Storrington, West Sussex, in preparation for an event the following day. Although the weather started out dark and foreboding the skies started to clear later so that by midnight the night sky was clearly visible. Ham gazed upwards and to his amazement saw an intense display of the Aurora Borealis, or Northern Lights, which he described as "a display of beauty which is rarely seen in the south of England".

Intense fields of electromagnetic energy in the upper atmosphere result in the most wondrous display of multi-coloured lights which weave and flow as they drift back and forth in the sky. Under normal circumstances they are visible only at the extremities of our planet. The fact that they were visible—even at the most northerly tip of Scotland for eleven consecutive nights during August 1972[338]—is a clear indication of the degree to which the electromagnetic field at the North Pole had become intensified. For the lights to be visible in the skies of Southern England was an unprecedented event.

The RSGB did not report on any specific impact the intense field of

---

[338] *Monthly Weather Report: Volume 89 No. 8*, The Meteorological Office, August 1972.

electromagnetism generated by the solar flare had on radio equipment, but one would assume that it was sizeable and became an issue for anyone relying upon shortwave communications.[339]

Due to the nature and power of the solar storm, very few people or organisations would have been prepared for its sheer magnitude or the negative impact it had upon technology, our planet, and particularly upon radio communications around the World: David Bowie may have been a notable exception. Could he have picked up on, or intuited, an impending solar event of this size? This is entirely possible for he appears to have encoded references to it within the lyrics to *Starman*.

In its first verse Bowie makes a cryptic reference to the scrambling of radio telecommunications by an external energy field.

"Didn't know what time it was.
The lights were low, oh, oh.
I leaned back on my radio, oh, oh.
Some cat was layin' down some rock 'n' roll lotta soul, he said.
Then the loud sound did seem to fade
Came back like a slow voice on a wave of phase.
That weren't no DJ.
That was hazy cosmic jive."

DEATH OF UFOLOGY?

Two years prior to the August 1972 solar storm, American author, and former journalist Howard Blum (1948-present day) obtained a M.A. degree from Stanford University. He subsequently entered journalism and worked for the *Village Voice* and the *New York Times* before being employed as contributing editor at *Vanity Fair*. In 1987, while trying to discover how involved the American government was in UFO research for his forthcoming book *Out There: Search for Extraterrestrial*

---

[339] The shortwave bands were, at that time, not only utilised by radio amateurs but they were also used extensively by shipping, aircraft, emergency services, satellites, state broadcasters and even by large-scale spy networks operated by all countries during the Cold War.

Intelligence,[340] Blum constantly encountered a wall of lies, secrecy, and disinformation. His initial research proved fruitless but he eventually managed to make contact with three National Security Agency (NSA) officials who maintained that they formed part of an ongoing, top-secret, UFO Working Group which had been established by the Defence Intelligence Agency. They included scientists from the CIA and generals from the Army and Air Forces. Once established, the US government summoned seventeen of America's intelligence specialists to a clandestine meeting in the Pentagon in an effort to determine whether humanity is, or is not, alone in the Universe.

In 1992, UFO researchers Randall Fitzgerald and Paul Mendoza maintained that the Group were connected to NSA listening posts which were under orders to flash-report to its headquarters at Fort Meade, Maryland, "...any signals or electronics intelligence that might have an extraterrestrial origin." They also maintained that Blum had uncovered evidence revealing that "contrary to all its public statements" the NSA had been secretly processing Worldwide reports of UFO activity. Blum asserted that this surveillance started in 1972.[341]

Exactly why this UFO monitoring programme was established in this particular year is unclear. However, it is worth noting that one of the effects of intense magnetisation of the Earth's upper atmosphere is the creation of plasma fireballs. In early August 1972, officials received many reports that featured sightings of multicoloured spheres flying through the skies of Canada and the United States—the exact same regions as those most impacted by the solar storm. In fact, during the second week of August 1972, America recorded one of its largest UFO flaps in history. Although categorised as UFOs, it is worth considering whether a number of these sightings were of the plasma spheres formed following the concentrated ionisation of the upper atmosphere. What is certain though is that the exponential number of UFO reports logged in late 1972 were of great concern to the US government and its security services.

---
[340] Blum, Howard, *Out There: The Government's Secret Quest for Extraterrestrials*, Simon & Schuster, 1990.
[341] Fitzgerald, Randall and Mendoza, Paul, *Cosmic Test Tube: Extraterrestrial Contact, Theories & Evidence*, Moon Lake Media; 1st Edition, 1998.

By way of clarifying the extent to which the number of UFO reports had grown exponentially from late 1972 through to early 1973, it is worth noting that in an article submitted by an unknown contributor to *Science News* titled *What Happened to UFOs?* was published on June 26, 1971. In it the author commented on the fact that there had been a sizeable decline in the number of reports of UFO sightings submitted to US authorities in the previous year. The contributor even quoted sources that suggested that numbers had fallen so low that, "we could be witnessing the end of interest in the phenomena".[342] This perhaps puts into perspective the enormous expansion of UFO activity that occurred in 1972...unless, of course, there was another reason for there being so many UFOs in the skies at that time!

CLOSE TO THE EDGE

In addition to the extraterrestrial Ziggy, another cosmic individual who appeared within our 3D reality in 1972 was the New Age teacher Drunvalo Melchizedek. Originally emerging from the womb on January 18, 1941, Drunvalo maintains that he subsequently took over the body of one Bernard Perona on April 10, 1972; thereby sealing what had been a relationship developed during the previous nine years.[343] Those who experience this extremely rare psycho-spiritual operation of soul-exchange are referred to in New Age parlance as 'walk-ins', 'aspect shifts', or 'overlays'. Such an event is said to occur when "...a higher consciousness level spirit "desperately" needs to incarnate into an adult body at a very specific moment."[344] It is a subject extensively covered by Evelyn Fuqua in her 1999 book *From Sirius to Earth: A Therapist Discovers a Soul Exchange*.

As a starseed with part-Sirian heritage, Drunvalo claims that Sirians had given him a spaceship with a crew of 350 members in which he travelled to Earth. Their flight path apparently took them to Sirius B via the core of Sirius A–a journey of just 90 seconds–prior to emerging

---

[342] www.sciencenews.org/archive/whatever-happened-ufos
[343] This complex re-assignment of Souls was facilitated by a contractual agreement between the two parties, for which Drunvalo states the other side was given "something very special" in return–though he does not say what it was.
[344] www.drunvalo.org/who-is-drunvalo-melchizedek

into our solar system through our Sun.

In the book, *Nothing in This Book Is True, But It's Exactly How Things Are*,[345] its author, Bob Frissell, includes material taken from a seminar presented by Drunvalo. In it, the purported Sirian emissary offered an extraordinary, metaphysical explanation for the August 1972 solar storm.

Drunvalo maintained that around 200 years ago extraterrestrials from the Sirius star system—a group he said had been actively overseeing the welfare of our planet for many hundreds of thousands of years—foresaw a major cosmic event which, if left unchecked, could completely decimate all life on planet Earth. The Sirians identified this as taking place at some point during the summer of 1972. Drunvalo explained to his audience that:

> '...they (the Sirians) knew that we had to be at the fourth dimensional level of awareness by then in order to survive. If we were at that level by 1972 there would be no problem, but if not, everything would be wiped out--the entire planet. And, as time passed, it more and more seemed as if we would not reach that consciousness level."

In a desperate attempt to save humanity and its life forms, a group of Sirians met to consider how this seemingly inevitable catastrophe could be avoided, and in a way that excluded human involvement. Their concern regarded the possible response by our species to Sirian engagement and the likelihood that they could end up being responsible for the complete destabilisation of human civilisation.

Drunvalo stated that the Sirians believed that the low vibratory state of our planet Earth[346] and most of its inhabitants, indicated that our

---

[345] Frissell, Bob, *Nothing in This Book Is True, But It's Exactly How Things Are*, Frog Ltd., 1995.
[346] All planets are said to have their own consciousness. In the 1970s English scientist James Lovecock (1919-2022–he died on his 103rd birthday) rose to prominence with a theory that our planet has its own consciousness. He called this Gaia after the Greek primordial deity of the same name. (See: Lovelock J., *Gaia: A New Look at Life on Earth*, Oxford University Press, 1979.) Lovecock was a keen

species was incapable of absorbing the high-energy vibrations hitting it during the impending cosmic event—a solar electromagnetic storm that would engulf the whole planet. Widespread political and social upheavals taking place throughout Western society during 1972[347] was evidence that not only had humanity failed to elevate itself to the necessary fourth-dimensional level of consciousness required to cope with the impending disaster but that governments across the globe would, in all probability, deem any extraterrestrial involvement in its affairs to be an act of supreme aggression.

The gravity of this situation is said to have presented cosmic intelligences with an immense dilemma. Either the Sirians and their allies could sit back and watch humanity fry or they could step-in and attempt to save it from certain extinction. Given their long-established policy of non-interference and non-engagement with humanity—as well as their traditional role as observers rather than leaders in our evolution—this was proving a difficult decision to have to make. According to Drunvalo, after extensive deliberation the Sirians came up with the idea of creating a:

> "...living vehicle that was fifty miles long, cigar-shaped, black, and seamless with both carbon and silicon life forms on it merged into one. The whole thing was a self-aware living unit. It had a transparent area on one end and was manned by about 300 to 350 men and women of the Sirian race from the third planet. They wore white uniforms with gold emblems.

---

environmentalist, but he was also critical of the emerging ethos within the radical ecology movement stating that "It just so happens that the green religion is now taking over from the Christian religion". (Source: https://en.wikipedia.org/wiki/James_Lovelock)

[347] The political and social unrest in the world at the time included the massacre of eleven Israel athletes by Arab gunman at the Munich Olympics, the arrest of five White House operatives for breaking into the offices of the Democratic National Committee, an event which signaled the start of the Watergate Scandal and resulted in the resignation of US president Richard Nixon. In Bowie's home nation, the British government had to declare a state of emergency following a national 47-day miners' strike.

> Dedicating as much time to this project as was necessary, they also made eight little flying saucer-type vehicles or ships that were to be unmanned; these were approximately twelve to twenty feet in length. The Sirians assembled this all together, worked out all its possibilities, then set it aside and waited."

As we saw earlier, the electromagnetic storm that accompanied the solar ejection did knock-out some of communication systems, but Drunvalo was unambiguous in his assessment of what could have been the outcome of the August 7 solar explosion had the ETs ignored our plight.

> "If the Sirians had not intervened, the explosion would have definitely killed us all. It would have killed everything on the planet right down to the microbial and algal levels."

The enormity and sheer audaciousness of the Sirian plan attracted the large-scale influx of other extraterrestrial groups into our Solar System. These 'rubbernecking' aliens arrived from distant outposts in our Universe—keen to witness the event and its possibly tragic outcome for themselves. Drunvalo explains:

> "At the time, 144,000 different races from the other dimensional levels came in here to assist. By mid-January 1972, about 80,000 of them had already arrived. They had a very intense discussion among themselves on the subject of the impending red pulse and about 79,900 of these cultures said, "There is no hope, there is no way, there is not a prayer of the humans surviving. Let's get out of here."

They went home because noninterference was their policy. The other hundred or so cultures--the Pleiadeans, the Aldebarans, the Arcturans and others led by the Sirians--decided to stay and help."

10. Tune In or Burn Out

In this last-ditch attempt to save our planet the Sirians are said to have dispatched ambassadors to Galactic Command—a multi-species, extraterrestrial government established to oversee and regulate major ET projects involving Earth—to request their permission to pursue their radical experiment. Given the seriousness of the situation this was granted.

> "...the Sirians immediately went to work and within thirty days had everything in place. They launched the large cigar-shaped object just outside the membrane of consciousness of the Earth, at 440,000 miles out, and they placed it one overtone higher, so it was invisible to us. They placed the eight small flying saucer-type ships on the apexes of the eight tetrahedral points-that is, the eight points of the star tetrahedron around the Earth. There is a star tetrahedron inscribed in the Earth. There is also a much bigger one, around 10,000 miles above the surface. The points are the chakra system of the planet. Again, these were set one dimensional overtone higher than the Earth."

With the necessary hardware in place, the Sirians are said to have fired a beam of laser light eight inches in diameter from their cigar-shaped craft positioned at the North Pole.

> "(This) hit the little flying saucer-type ship that was at that tetrahedral point. From there, the immense amount of information contained in the laser light was translated into three primary rays--red, blue, and green--that were beamed to the next three ships. These ships repeated this and sent the rays to the next three ships until the rays ended up at the South Pole. At the South Pole they were translated back into information and shot into the center of the Earth. From the center of the Earth, by refraction,

> the information came out in little, tiny beams of light by the billions, all over the whole planet. As these beams of light came out through the center of the Earth, they connected to all the humans and animals on the planet."

By implementing their complex scheme the Sirians hoped to protect our planet in a way that would leave the human race completely ignorant of their work at that time; for, as Drunvalo said in his presentation, "Our knowing would have completely changed the human equation." Not only were they trying to protect the delicate balance of the natural order of things but, almost as a side project, were also hoping to shift the destiny of humanity into a new, and improved phase of development.

> "They (the Sirians) also had to speed up our evolution so we could get to where we could handle a wall of flame.[348] They set a holographic field around the Earth; then they set up a holographic field around each person and animal. They then began to program events into these holographic fields."

The Sirians created their large holographic mirage behind which they worked to "...program events into our lives so that we would evolve as rapidly as possible." This appears to have worked for our planet clearly survived the Solar Storm of August 1972. In fact, according to Drunvalo, during the months that followed the event our planet and its lifeforms started to evolve in completely new and unexpected ways. He explained the reason behind this evolutionary shift by stating that "The Sirian intervention also bought time for the synthetic Christ-

---

[348] Although not specifically referenced by Drunvalo, it is entirely possible that the Sirians also initiated other, smaller projects which they implemented from January 1972 onwards, which were geared towards trying to raise the energetic vibrations of vast sectors of the populace in time for the August storm. Was one of them centred upon an attempt to raise the consciousness of individuals in and around the United Kingdom in particular, through popular culture? If so, then it places Bowie's *Starman* performance on *Top of the Pops* just one month prior to the mass solar ejection into a completely new context. It would certainly explain how, and why, Bowie was employed to heighten the psychospiritual resonance of millions of people through occult ritual and in accordance with extremely potent, cosmic timing.

10. Tune In or Burn Out

consciousness grid to be completed." Without this grid—which was completed on February 4, 1989—no one would have been able to make it through to the next level of consciousness which then started to unfold around 2012.

Consciousness Grid

When considered objectively, we are unlikely to ever know whether the impact of the destructive force of the solar flare of August 7, 1972, was lessened because of intervention by extraterrestrials from Sirius or not. When analysing Drunvalo's extraordinary claims it should be noted that not only are they scientifically unverifiable but that they also appear to contain elements found in the standard apocalyptic mythos of orthodox religion: including such concepts as 'Christ Consciousness', 'resurrection', and the sacred number 144,000 which plays an important role in the Biblical *Book of Revelation*. Even Drunvalo admits that his account of the event is a little light on detail but explains that it transpired "in ways we do not, and can not, understand". If the holographic experiment carried out by our cosmic overlords did occur then it could have created such a rift in the time-space continuum that from a third-dimension perspective it may well have not transpired in the way that Drunvalo describes it. In his defence, however, the writer does state that he:

> "...believes that all previous predictions regarding the future of the Earth are no longer valid. The Sirian experiment of 1972 changed everything. Nostradamus was very accurate in his predictions up until 1972, and since then his predictions have fallen way off."

What exactly was it that caused our Sun to eject such a massive wave of electromagnetic energy in the first place? A possible metaphysical explanation was offered by Ashayana Deane (1964-present day)—the founder of a spiritual process called "Keylontic Science". Deane claims to have had contact with extraterrestrials since childhood, that they trained her to become a speaker for the Guardian Alliance, and is now an emissary for the Sirian-Arcturian Council[349]—a position that credits her with an opportunity to offer a unique perspective to the Solar Storm event.

Deane maintains that in 1943, extraterrestrials from the Zeta Reticula star system presented the Americans with a form of technology that enabled their scientists to warp time and space in such a way that they could make objects disappear.[350] An example of its use involved the US Navy who conducted a remarkable experiment at Philadelphia, PA, on August 12, 1943, which observers say had the effect of rendering the battleship *U.S.S. Eldridge* completely invisible. The vessel was then seen briefly later that day. seemingly having miraculously teleported to Norfolk, Virginia, over 200 miles (320 km) away.[351]

What the Zetas rather conveniently failed to explain to the Americans at the time that a consequence of the experiment would be a major tearing in the etheric and/or electromagnetic field connecting our planet to the Sun. Their malicious intent, according to Deane's sources, was to utilise this distortion and invade our planet by infiltrating our airspace with their fourth-dimensional craft.

Once again, we only have Deane's word for this but in what may well prove to support the story, just seven years later, in 1950, Earth scientists began to notice an odd phenomenon taking place on our Sun. They discovered that it was periodically release spiralling streams of energy which flowed outwards and towards the Earth. This phenomenon was increased in strength and regularity between 1952 and 1968 and led to a concern among many astrophysicists that, should it continue to grow, it could lead to an explosion on the Sun of such magnitude that the resulting energy-field would knock our planet off its axis. They predicted that by 2012 all life on Earth would be rendered extinct.

---

[349] In 1996, The Guardians extraterrestrial group asked Deane to make their spiritual teachings more widely available and to bring into the public domain awareness of the science of 'vibrational mechanics'—an electromagnetic-pulse technology that is said to "accelerate the physical, mental, emotional and spiritual evolution of human beings." (Source: www.smashwords.com/profile/view/ashayana)

[350] Deane, Ashayana, *Voyagers: The Secrets of Amenti, Volume 2*, Wild Flower Press, 2002.

[351] Moore, William and Berlitz, Charles, *The Philadelphia Experiment: Project Invisibility*, Grosset & Dunlap Inc., 1979.

Deane also confirmed Drunvalo's account of the events of January 1972 when the consortium of the Guardian Races—which she said comprised members of the Sirius Council, Sirian-Arcturian Coalition for Interplanetary Defence, the Pleiadian Star League, as well as several other ET groups—made their intervention and protected the Earth from the impending catastrophe. In the end, the Council seems to have considered their experiment to have been so successful that the Sirians remained after the event; working to repair pockets of residual damage and continued upgrading the frequency of our planet. This work continued until 1980 when it was felt that the energy/consciousness of the Earth was high enough for humanity to cope with a further evolutionary leap—the 21-12-2012 event which had been predicted by the ancient Mayans.

Is there Life on Mars?

Not one but two seismic events took place on Monday, August 7, 1972. For decades scientists remembered it as the day the surface of our Sun erupted in spectacular fashion but it also proved to be a significant date in the weird and wacky world of conspiracy theories after NASA took a routine photograph of the planet Mars from the Mariner 9 space probe. It set the world of ufology alight.

Launched from Cape Canaveral Air Force Station, Florida, on May 30, 1971, Mariner 9 reached Mars on November 14 the same year and became the first spacecraft to orbit an exo-planet other than the Moon (which is technically a satellite). However, it was not until three months later that the probe was able to send back the first images of the surface of Mars. These revealed a barren and lifeless landscape.

NASA received the initial batch of low-grade photographs on February 8, 1972. They tried again six months later. On August 7, image #4205-78—taken while passing over a region on Mars known as Elysium Quadrangle (located 15 degrees north of the Martian equator)—featured a large outcrop of rocks which appeared to resemble regular shapes; two large and two small three-sided pyramids.[352]

---

[352] Picknett, Lynn and Prince, Clive, *Stargate Conspiracy: The Truth about Extraterrestrial Life and the Mysteries of Ancient Egypt*, Berkley Publishing Group,

The space agency published the image and it caught the attention of World-renowned astronomer Carl Sagan who, intrigued by the shape of the pyramidal structure, presented it to the Royal Institute, London, during his 1977 Christmas Lecture. Sagan later included the same photograph in his 1980 book *Cosmos* in which he stated:

> "The largest Mars Pyramids have a base width of 3 km and a height of 1 km, so they are much larger than the Pyramids of Sumer, Egypt and Mexico. With the ancient, eroded shape, they could be small hills, sandblasted for centuries, but they need to be viewed from nearby."[353]

A year prior to his lecture, Sagan was involved in the founding and management of another NASA mission to Mars. This included two orbiting and landing craft named Viking 1 and Viking 2. Viking 1 touched down on the surface of Mars at a northern location known as Chryse Planitia[354] on July 20, 1976, while the Viking 2 lander separated from its orbiter on September 3, 1976, and then landed at Utopia Planitia.[355]

This region—more commonly known as Cydonia—is a two kilometre (1.2 mile) long mesa believed by planetologists to have once been the location of ocean beds. A series of eighteen photographs of the area were taken by the orbiters and in one of them (photographed by Viking 1 on July 25, 1976) another anomalous rock formation could be seen. Closer examination of the image seemed to suggest that the Mars landscape had been deliberately sculptured into a large, human-looking, face. A second image—acquired following a further thirty-five orbits of the planet—was taken of the same area but from a different angle which revealed what seemed to be human eye sockets and a large mouth.

The "Face of Mars"—as it since become known—ignited a firestorm of controversy. Many of those who believed in the existence of

---

2001.
[353] Sagan, Carl, *Cosmos*, Random House, 1980.
[354] https://en.wikipedia.org/wiki/Viking_1
[355] https://en.wikipedia.org/wiki/Viking_2

10. Tune In or Burn Out

extraterrestrials considered it to be definitive proof that not only had Mars once been home to a race of advanced beings prior to some great catastrophe which laid it bare but that the almost Sphinx-like appearance of the Face[356] suggested that there had once been a connection between Cydonia and ancient Egypt. NASA scientists, on the other hand, were far less convinced and flatly refused to give any credit to the theory by releasing any sort of official statement. Their silence continued throughout the decades that followed but after increasing pressure from researchers they eventually agreed to re-photograph Cydonia with their Mars Global Surveyor probes in 1998 and 2001 and then again by the Mars Odyssey probe in 2002.

Many ufologists on the fringe of the topic hoped that a new generation of high-definition cameras would capture even finer details of the 'Face' and in so-doing finally resolve the mystery. Unfortunately, the opposite happened. The new images NASA released were indeed of much higher resolution than the originals and the additional details they showed revealed nothing more than an irregularly formed outcrop of rocky ground. NASA felt this vindicated their earlier stance regarding the veracity of the supposed 'Face'. They were now confident that their earlier photographs had not portrayed a human head and that what researchers thought was a carved human face was nothig more than an optical aberration.

Through their initial attempt to stifle any serious debate regarding the 1972 photograph of Cydonia the NASA publicity-machine ended up making a rod for their own back. Their updated collection of photographs came several decades too late to counter a growing narrative within ufology now that the Face of Mars had become an integral part of modern UFO lore. Myths related to the enigma of Cydonia had now become firmly established and was being promoted by researchers who included Richard Hoagland[357] and David Percy.[358]

[356] See: Smukler, H., *Dramatic Photos of Mars: The Home of the Gods, Ancient Astronauts*, January 1977 and Grossinger, Richard, *Planetary Mysteries: Megaliths, Glaciers, the Face on Mars and Aboriginal Dreamtime*, Berkeley: North Atlantic Books, 1986.
[357] Hoagland, Richard C., *The Monuments of Mars: A City on the Edge of Forever*, North Atlantic Books, 1992.
[358] Percy, David and Bennett, Mary, *Two-Thirds: A History of our Galaxy*, Aulis

220

Percy was convinced that several of the large rocks surrounding the Face had been deliberately positioned to form quite specific geometric alignments—occult relationships which he and others maintained provided additional proof that extraterrestrial life had once existed on Mars.

The Face of Mars was single-handedly responsible for a war of attrition between all parties. Those within the UFO community who had bought into the Face of Mars theory did not take kindly to NASA's efforts to squash a mystery which had now evolved to become an integral element in the newly-emergent 'ancient alien theory'. Neither did NASA's belated decision to rephotograph the Face deflect criticism regarding the space agency's apparent lack of transparency; which resulted in researchers such as Hoagland to accuse NASA of cover-ups and other nefariousness actions.[359]

From Mars to Giza

Whatever the NASA images proved or disproved, fascination in the idea of the existence of an ancient race of Martian extraterrestrials who may have once colonised the planet grew feverishly. A new generation of researchers took NASA's images and Hoagland's research and expanded upon many of the contentious theories surrounding the possible original function of Cydonia. For a while, one of the more popular theories regarding its pyramid-shaped outcrops was that their inherent mathematical ratios and angular relationships to one another revealed what was said to be the existence a 'stargate' linking the plateaus of Cydonia on Mars and Giza on Earth. It was said that such a portal—in addition to other forms of exotic technology—enabled ancient aliens to travel between these locations with ease. Some even maintained that the Cydonia region mirrored the ground-plan of the Neolithic site at Avebury in Wiltshire, England.[360]

In amongst this pseudo-archaeological melting-pot of ideas was a

---

Publishers, 1993.
[359] NASA has been implicated in a number of modern conspiracy theories: from the Moon Landing to the Flat Earth. See: Hoagland, Richard, Bara, Mike, Dark Mission: The Secret History of NASA, Feral House, 2007.
[360] www.aulis.com/mars.htm

10. TUNE IN OR BURN OUT

Above: Avebury Stone Circle, Wiltshire, England: constructed in 3rd-millennium BC (Copyright: Detmar Owen -Wikimedia - 70228378)

now established presumption that the Face of Mars is real and that it had been carved from what was initially a natural outcrop of rock in a deliberate attempt to reveal to humans the existence of its alien creators. Those early NASA photos did indeed appear to show a face peering skywards—as if it was staring back at Earth patiently awaiting the day that terrestrial astronomers would discover it and conclude that there is, as Bowie once put it, 'life on Mars'. As for the meaning of the Face itself, some researchers believed it to be a replication of the Sphinx. Others maintained it was a representation of the head of Jesus Christ but the most fascinating theory to emerge from the hotch-potch of ideas was the theory that the Face was actually a composite figure. It was discovered that by splitting the Face vertically into two equal parts and then mirroring each half on itself it revealed two distinctly different facades. The first revealed a man's facial features but the second, even more convincingly, appeared to represent the head of a lion.[361]

If this proved to be true then this analysis of the NASA photograph begs the obvious questions. Why would a dual-faceted edifice have been carved by an extraterrestrial race in such a way that it encodes the

---
[361] Other lion heads and feline faces have been 'discovered' in and around the Cydonia area of Mars. See http://jetpix.blogspot.com/2013/03/giant-lion-head-on-mars-in-cydonia.html

features of both a man and a lion? Might this suggest that ancient Martian inhabitants fashioned it in such a way that it referenced two, co-existing life forms? Did men and lions once cohabitate at some point in the distant past and, if so, then what was the nature of their relationship? Given our understanding of the lion as a man-eating predator then this theory appears somewhat unlikely.

However, what if none of these questions are valid and that there is another interpretation of this enigma? Is it possible that the composite image does not replicate two separate species—one human and one animal—but that the Face is representative of a single species—a hybrid-being comprised of part-man and part-lion?

8:8 - A Cosmic Gateway?

Whatever the truth regarding Cydonia, the publication of NASA's images exposed in glaring detail the wide chasm that has always existed between scientists and those engaged in paranormal research. Whether the revisionist cosmo-archaeologists were correct or not is, on one level, somewhat irrelevant. In a world that increasingly looks to the scientific establishment to confirm the existence of extraterrestrial life, the closed-debate they strove to initiate regarding the Face clearly added nothing to our understanding of the wider mystery of possible proof of the existence of extraterrestrials on Mars—regarding which several other related anomalies and pieces of circumstantial evidence can be found. Instead, NASA exposed itself as an intractable organisation which, despite being publicly funded, did not appear to be bothered for one moment about the breakdown in communication and trust between itself and the American taxpayer. The alternative theorists did not actually have to prove that the Face was real or otherwise as this is only part of the issue. More significant is the fact that, through their broader assessment of the Cydonia region, they exposed glaring inadequacies at the heart of the scientific community. Whether the pro-head lobby was barking up the wrong tree or not, they clearly demonstrated a more flexible and enquiring mindset compared to that of many employed by NASA.

10. Tune In or Burn Out

Those who are employed in the science and technology fields—particularly in the educational and academic sectors—tend to be predominantly skilled within a narrowly defined field of expertise. The result is that when they examine and analyse the machinations of the Universe using the technological tools at their disposal, they invariably filter out ancient ways of observing and interpreting stellar events. This is a major error on their part. NASA has been viewing space through its telescopes since its establishment in 1958 but cosmologists have tracked the motion and influence of the stars and planets for millennia—hence their ability to identify long-term cycles of stellar evolution, such as that of the Sun/Sirius binary relationship.

Scientists also tend to search for confirmatory data to prove their scientific hypotheses valid. On the other hand, alternative researchers seek to 'follow the evidence' wherever it might lead them; no matter how great the challenge to their belief systems or how dark the terrain becomes. The controversy that raged over the Face of Mars was a prime example of why it is often advantageous to evaluate our cosmos through a set of 'non-linear eyes'. Many of the conclusions that ufologists draw from their exploration of the unknown may prove to be incorrect in the short-term but the new avenues of inquiry they open-up are vital if mankind is to continue uncovering the true secrets of the Universe.

If a compromise can be found between the approaches taken by science and those working in the field of the paranormal then it may well be found in the world of astrology; for this is an ancient discipline which monitors planetary motion using the same data as science. Where it differs is in its subsequent analysis for astrologers apply methodologies that reference human motivation and personal consciousness. It is a soul-centric practice and not merely a cerebral exercise. Furthermore, by interpreting planetary events using proven insights that are thousands of years old, sacred knowledge which was compiled in a more enlightened era reveal a less mechanised and more holistic perspective of our cosmos.

Given that the solar storm of August 1972 can be described as a highly significant cosmic event it may be advantageous to re-evaluate it using astrological principles in combination with ancient astro-theological teachings. Drawing-up an astrological chart for 15:19 on August 7, 1972–the exact day and time of the solar explosion–it is interesting to note that our Sun had just reached a mid-point in its annual passage through the constellation of Leo, the Lion. This fixes it at its zenith in a zodiacal period over which astrology states it has dominance. At the time, the planet Mercury was also positioned at 15 degrees Leo while, on the same day, its close neighbour, our Moon, was positioned at the same degree as that occupied by Sirius.

In metaphysical terms this position (i.e., 15 degrees Leo) is highly significant for it is said to enable the Sun to operate as a 'stargate'–a portal through which extra- and ultra-terrestrial forces can freely enter our Solar System. This belief is also found within the teachings of the Sirius gnosis wherein contemporary occultists refer to the same degree in the solar year as '8:8' or the "Lion's Gate". It forms the point at which the energetic rays of Sirius are directed through to our planet via the Sun and Leo.[362]

Apocalyptic Signs

The Lion's Gate event of August 1972 was particularly significant. As we have seen, there was a common belief among many at that time that society, our planet, and civilisation were in imminent danger of falling apart. Whether it was Bowie and his five-year warning or Presley with his sense of the impending collapse of orthodox religion, there emerged an all-consuming belief throughout the 1970s that humanity had reached a crossroads in its evolution. As the soul/funk band The Temptations put it in their 1970 hit *Ball of Confusion (That's What the World is Today)*: "*So, round and around and around we go. Where the world's headed, nobody knows*". Few would have disagreed with them for, with the heightening of the Cold War, widespread social unrest, deep economic and political uncertainty, the World appeared to many to be running out of options.

---

[362] Many ET contactees who credit Sirians as the source of their messages, maintain that this date is specifically utilised by the star-people to beam light-based information through to mankind. It has the effect of drilling Solar/Siriun light-codes deep into the DNA of initiates.

10. Tune In or Burn Out

Whenever solutions to global problems seem non-existent it is inevitable that many of the World's citizens would turn to God as a possible source of salvation. While many millions of people were giving-up on organised religion this did not stem the growth of early Christian and medieval apocalyptic beliefs—particularly those which referenced the Holy Bible's *Book of Revelation*.[363] In it, its original author—a prophet known simply as "John",[364] describes a vision he had of an 'unveiling of heaven'. To many, his account is either the hallmark of a drug-induced hallucination or the product of an over-active imagination. Nevertheless, some of the text's darker elements reference esoteric numerology and cosmological themes—the most prevailing of which has been his reference to the Four Tetramorphs or, as they are more commonly known, the "Beasts of the Apocalypse".

The word Tetramorph is comprised of the Greek words 'tetra' (meaning 'four') and 'morph' (meaning 'shape'). The *Book of Revelation* describes them in the following way, "And the first beast was like a lion, and the second beast like a calf, and the third beast had a face as a man, and the fourth beast was like a flying eagle.[365]" This reference to the Tetramorphs is not limited to the Book of Revelation for Ezekiel in his Biblical text refers to the same four living creatures.

> "As for the likeness of their faces, they four had the face of a man, and the face of a lion, on the right side: and they four had the face of an ox on the left side; they four also had the face of an eagle."[366]

The Tetramorphs are not actually a Christian, Jewish, or even a Greek creation. They also appeared in Egyptian and Assyrian mythology but their widespread use can even be traced even earlier than that and to the Babylonians who used the same symbolic quaternary to reference the four signs of the zodiac. It was this use of the Tetramorphs that

---

[363] Despite its modern interpretation as a narrative that focuses on catastrophe and ruination, its title is actually derived from the first word of the Koine Greek text 'apokalypsis' meaning 'unveiling' or 'revelation'.
[364] Modern theologians believe the *Book of Revelation's* author was John of Patmos and that the text dates to the reign of the Roman emperor Domitian (AD 81-96).
[365] *The Book of Revelation*, Chapter.4, Verse 7.
[366] *Ezekiel*, Chapter 1, Verse 10.

10. Tune In or Burn Out

Left: A Christian rendition of the Tetramorphs - the combination of four disparate elements, or principles, in one unit.

established their cosmological representations of Taurus (bull), Leo (lion), Scorpio (eagle), and Aquarius (man). Accumulatively, these four zodiacal periods play an important role in esoteric astrology and are said to form a 'Fixed Cross'—the culmination of primary spiritual energies centralised within each midway point of their corresponding zodiacal period (i.e., the 15th and central point of each thirty-degree sign). Alice A. Bailey believed that within this relationship resides the deepest occult and arcane mystery and featured in her seminal works on esoteric astrology—as did A. E. Waite would included them in Arcana 10 and 21 of his tarot deck. Aleister Crowley also featured the Tetramorphs in an alternative version of Arcana 1 of his Thoth deck.[367]

A pessimistic evaluation of the Tetramorphs by Christian theologians of the *Book of Revelation* resulted in the Four Beasts being associated with the moral decline of civilisation and the destruction of humanity. The scenario the *Book of Revelation* portrays (i.e., war, disease, death, and decay) mirrors the sort of catastrophic, apocalyptic, post-nuclear environment that Bowie referenced in his song-writing. He described the chaotic aftermath of the apocalypse graphic detail in his song *Future Legend*—the opening track of his *Diamond Dogs* album.

> "And in the death. As the last few corpses lay rotting on the slimy thoroughfare. Fleas the size of rats sucked on rats the size of cats. And ten thousand peoploids split into small tribes."

In November 1973, Bowie was interviewed by the journalist William Burroughs for *Rolling Stone* magazine. At the time, he was planning a musical and television production based on the *Ziggy Stardust* story. When the topic of his alien emerged during the interview, Bowie shared his perceptions of the social decline that underpinned the pre-apocalyptic environment Ziggy found himself trapped in.

---

[367] It should be stated that neither occultist was the first to associate the Tetramorphs with the tarot for they also appeared in one of the earliest examples of the genre—in the Tarot of Marseille deck which dates back to c.1701–1715.

> "The time is five years to go before the end of the earth. It has been announced that the world will end because of lack of natural resources. Ziggy is in a position where all the kids have access to things that they thought they wanted. The older people have lost all touch with reality and the kids are left on their own to plunder anything. Ziggy was in a rock and roll band and the kids no longer want rock and roll. There's no electricity to play it."[368]

Bowie's imaginative evaluation of the world at war with itself and nature was prescient. He was correct in his prediction that our planet would be running out of natural resources and that the "kids" DO have "all the things they thought they wanted" (computers, video game consoles, mobile phones etc.). Its is evident that we live in a society where older people HAVE lost touch with reality through mind-numbing TV and prescription drugs and where the roving gangs of opportunistic thieves or looters Bowie described in *Diamond Dogs* has become a regular feature of the evening news. Worst of all, for a society that has previously relied upon popular music as a way of rebelling against authority, most of today's younger generation ARE no longer interested in such spontaneous, free-form music as rock and roll—preferring instead to digest automated, software-generated, auto-tuned drivel that passes for music and melody.

SCHOOL'S OUT!

In summing-up the apocalyptic, cosmological events of 1972, it is worth examining Drunvalo Melchizedek's assertion that Sirians were involved. While his story appears bizarre and fanciful, it is important to note that several of its key elements were subsequently confirmed by others in the New Age movement. In her 1995 book, *The Pleiadian Agenda: A New Cosmology for the Age of Light*, Barbara Hand Clow transcribed the words of "Satya" ('truth' in Sanskrit)—an extraterrestrial from the Pleiades about the 1972 solar event.

---

[368] Copetas, Craig, *Beat Godfather Meets Glitter Mainman: William Burroughs Interviews David Bowie*, Rolling Stone, February 2, 1974.

10. Tune In or Burn Out

> " Our library opened in your minds in 1992 as we recalibrated Earth with Sirius, the star that has been preparing you for this opening since August 1972. The electromagnetic field of Earth was so heightened in the summer of 1972 that many scientists reported later that they feared your planet might explode or undergo a polar shift...so your planet was very unstable in 1972.
>
> In August 1972, the Sirians generated a great stabilisation beam out of the stellar computer below the Great Pyramid at Giza, and directed it right into the Sun. This caused a green healing spiral to shoot out of the Sun, awakening solar initiates into remembering their Pleiadian origins."[369]

Sirian contactee William Gammill also referenced the event in his book *The Gathering*.

> "Two different star systems reforms an old alliance in 1972 to keep the polar axis of Earth from flipping due to a great explosion in the sun. As a result, it only flipped a little bit, and even that was hidden from us by the creation of a holographic protection field around the Earth intended not only to protect us, but to accelerate our own evolution to the point where we can protect ourselves. A lot of people changed their personalities at that time."[370]

As somebody who was in his teens during 1972, I categorically concur with Gammill. Something fundamental occurred during the month of August that year. I sensed it and, as the long school holidays ended that summer, nothing ever felt quite the same again!

---

[369] Clow, Barbara Hand, *The Pleiadian Agenda: A New Cosmology for the Age of Light*, Bear & Co., 1995.
[370] Gammill, William, *The Gathering: Meetings in Higher Space*, Hampton Roads Publishing Co., 2001.

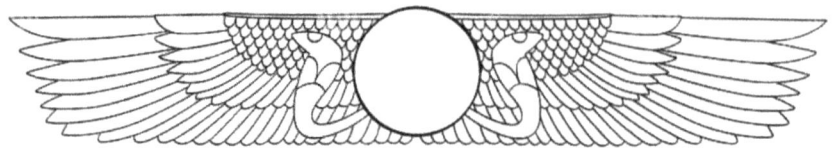

11. LAST DAYS OF THE PLAN?

> "The day came. The wrath descended. Sin, guilt, and retribution? The manic psychoses of those entities we referred to as states, institutions, systems - the powers, the thrones, the dominations - the things which perpetually merge with men and emerge from them? Our darkness, externalised and visible? However, you look upon these matters, the critical point was reached. The wrath descended."

Deus Irae by Philip K. Dick (1928-1982).

In 1845, Miles Goodyear—a mountain man—constructed a house and small trading post on the banks of the Weber river which flows from the Uinta Mountains in Northern Utah to the Great Salt Lake. Two years later, Brigham Young, second President of the Church of Jesus Christ of Latter-day Saints, happened to be passing through the area with a party of ministers in search of a suitable location for Smith's visionary city. The Mormons entered into a conservation with Goodyear who explained that he was keen to sell his property and move on. The explorers entered into negotiations with him for the purchase of his land and a price of $1,950 was agreed between the two parties on November 24, 1847.

Within a few months, the LDS had set about building their new settlement. By the end of 1850 more than a hundred Mormon families had moved into the area and a year later, on February 6, 1851, their settlement received a charter whereupon it was officially known as Ogden City. The conurbation expanded quickly and by 1856 was accommodating more than three thousand people. It seemed that after all the LDS's prior failings at finding a home it was finally able to establish the sanctuary of Joseph Smith's vision.

11. Last Days of The Plan?

On December 1, 1944, George Virl Osmond, Sr. (1917-2007) and Olive May Davis (1925-2004) were married at Ogden Church. Their first two children, Virl and Tom, had been born with a degenerative condition which left them partially deaf but the same affliction did not impact their subsequent offspring: Alan, Wayne, Merrill, Jay, Donny, Marie, and Jimmy.

George worked in real estate, insurance, and as a postmaster for the city of Ogden but he also loved to sing. He taught his sons barbershop harmonisation which they often performed in public. The ensemble caught the attention of American singer Andy Williams and he invited them to appear on his popular TV show. Between 1962 and 1971, the singers—now working under the stage name The Osmond Brothers—were regular guests. Once younger sibling Donny turned six years of age, he joined his brothers making them even more popular with TV audiences.

The experience of working on television turned the brothers into a highly proficient showbiz act. After seeing them perform live, record-producer Mike Curb signed them to MGM Records. They cut their first disc at Muscle Shoals Studio with R&B producer Rick Hall soon afterwards. Their Jackson 5-inspired song *One Bad Apple* was released as a single and it topped the US charts on February 13, 1971–where it remained for five weeks. With a growing sense of confidence in their own musical abilities, The Osmonds began to compose their own songs with the first of them appearing on their 1972 album *Crazy Horses*.

The Osmonds were known as as clean-shaven, momma- and poppa-loving kids but for all that they were not averse to making cutting-edge sociopolitical statements at times. This was most evident on the album's title track–a pulsating, hard-rocking number which was a damning indictment of what The Osmonds felt to be the massive environmental damage being brought about through widespread car ownership. Both the album and single were big hits and this led to the start of a universally successful recording and performing career.

Counting both group and solo recordings, members of the Osmond family charted thirteen hit-singles on the UK charts in 1973.[371] By the end of their career they had sold over 77 million records Worldwide.

Church Business

In 1972, the older members of the Osmond family had reached an age at which they were expected to leave home and carry out church missions for the LDS. However, because of their emerging Worldwide success it was felt that the group offered the organisation a more effective promotional platform by which to spread the Mormon message. Consequently, the brothers continued writing and touring. They returned to the studio to record their fifth studio album titled *The Plan*. Released on June 30, 1973, it was described by one music critic as "a Mormon concept album with progressive rock aspirations". From a lyrical perspective, the record did indeed feature LDS themes. Its title, for example, was derived from the Mormon text *The Plan of Salvation*[372] (also known as the *Plan of Happiness* or the *Plan of Redemption*)–a proposal said to have been devised by God to save, redeem, and exalt humankind via the atonement of Jesus Christ.

The Plan was a bold and brave experiment. However, it received a mixed reaction within the music press with many reviewers openly criticising the group for what they felt was a lack of musical direction and an over-focus on overtly religious themes. On the face of it, they had a point. With song titles such as *War in Heaven*, *Are You Up There?*, and *The Last Days*, the album's songs came over a little preachy–even to many hardcore Osmond fans. Sales were hit as a result although *The Plan* did attain gold certification (100,00 sales) in the UK where the group had become particularly popular. There, at least, was a country where the record's religious context went largely unnoticed. In the US it failed to even make the Top 50.

In retrospect, music critics were not wholly accurate in their critique of the album. While it was average musically, it was not the propagandist, evangelical recruitment device described by those who failed to understand or accommodate the Mormon message.

---
[371] https://en.wikipedia.org/wiki/The_Osmonds
[372] https://en.wikipedia.org/wiki/Plan_of_salvation_in_Mormonism

11. Last Days of The Plan?

Left: The super-slick, TV friendly, Osmond brothers dressed in their flamboyant stage-clothes in 1971.

Nevertheless, reviews of it left many with the strong impression that it was a product of a dangerous, cult-like, religious faction. Slightly less acerbic reviews gave the impression that that the Osmonds and their record represented the sort of happy-clappy, pseudo-Christian nonsense spouted by many of America's TV evangelists—preachers of the sort that Presley despised so much. In reality, *The Plan* was—from a lyrical perspective—a surprisingly dark record by a musical ensemble who enjoyed a strong reputation in the entertainment industry as a fun, clean-loving act.

It featured songs that contained a strong sense of self-examination and even self-recrimination. For example, *Are You Up There?* included the lyrics:

> "Why should I cherish living if there's no so called plan.
> Why, I would have no future if it were left to man".

The song *Traffic in My Mind* posed the question:

> "So, tell me who am I?
> Why am I here?
> Where in heaven's name am I going?"

and *Mirror, Mirror*—possibly the most introspective track on the album—included the words:

> "Mirror, mirror on the wall I don't like your life at all,
> How did we ever come to be,
> The kind of person that I see".

In the penultimate track on the album, *The Last Days*, the Osmonds expressed a similar evaluation of what they saw as a poisoned, dying and decaying civilisation to the one Bowie described on his album *Diamond Dogs*.

> *"People living lives of confusion.*
> *Billions caught up in revolution.*
> *Cities lost in their own pollution.*
> *Question, what is the Constitution.*
>
> *That's what they said, someday it would be.*
> *Now just look around if that's what we see.*
> *It's gotta be the last days.*
> *Gotta be the last days".*

With the inclusion of such dark and spiritually challenging themes, *The Plan* was a complete contradiction to the image the family portrayed in public, during concerts, and on the television. Given all these intensely contradictory impressions, it is perhaps not too surprising to find that the album failed to be the commercial success many in the LDS felt it deserved. Donny Osmond reflected upon the album's failure in his autobiography *Life Is Just What You Make It*.[373]

> "I think we miscalculated the public's response. First, we underestimated how much my teenybopper image had begun to candy coat the group. And second, we didn't factor in that the public may not have been ready for a serious album from us on any subject, much less one that spoke specifically (if you knew it) about the Latter-day Saints teachings.
>
> Today, even most people unfamiliar with our beliefs would recognise and probably understand if not agree with this conception of eternal spiritual life. The album doesn't go into explicit detail about the theological teachings of our Church. But if you knew what they were, you would hear the love songs, which

---
[373] Osmond, Donny, *Life Is Just What You Make It*, Orion, 2012.

like most pop love songs speak of stepping "toward eternity" and "goin' home," differently than someone who did not. Almost all of them- "*Goin' Home*," "*Mirror, Mirror*,' "*Darlin'*" could be easily read in both religious and nonreligious contexts. I regret that the promotion campaign left listeners no room to appreciate it as anything but a "religious" work, because I'm convinced that had *The Plan* been heard on its own terms, many things might have been different for all of us."

The Osmonds avoided making the same mistakes and for their next album, *Love Me for a Reason*–released the following year, the group employed professional songwriters. This time it charted in the US.

The Osmonds might well have been effective ambassadors for the Church of Latter-Day Saints but what exactly was the message they were bringing to the World through their music? It many ways, it almost seemed to be contradictory for, despite its outwardly Christian persona, *The Plan* clearly revealed a dark side to the religious teachings of the Church. We have already seen that Mormonism was founded on the magickal activities of Joseph Smith and his family so there is quite evidently an occult element within their religious teachings–but how far did this extend?

Kolob

In the summer of 1972, the Osmonds established a company called Kolob Records. They formed it as a way of overseeing their creative output as a group and to promote the projects of their individual members. Based in their hometown of Ogden, the record label–which had its own recording facilities called Kolob Studios–remained operational until 1978.

The word Kolob is important for it is a Mormon term. It appears in a sacred LDS text known as *The Book of Abraham*. This is a collection of writings taken from several Egyptian scrolls which were discovered during an archaeological expedition led by Italian antiquities excavator

Antonio Lebolo (Unknown-c.1830). The scrolls were taken to the United States and, on July 3, 1835, were purchased by members of the LDS who translated them into English. Their conclusion was that the scrolls featured the personal writings of Abraham[374] and that they were a record of his early life, including details of his travels to Canaan and Egypt along with accounts of his mystical visions regarding the cosmos and its creation. This was now seen by the LDS as a divinely-inspired scripture so they published it as part of the *Pearl of Great Price*–a selection of choice materials selected by the Mormon Church which cover many significant aspects of their faith and doctrine.[375]

The document includes the following reference to the term Kolob.

> "... and I saw the Stars that they were very great, and that one of them was nearest unto the throne of God; ...and the name of the great one is Kolob, because it is near unto me, for I am the Lord thy God. ... And the Lord said unto me ... that Kolob was after the manner of the Lord, according to its times and seasons in the revolutions thereof, that one revolution was a day unto the Lord, after his manner of reckoning, it being one thousand years according to the time appointed unto that whereon thou standest. This is the reckoning of the Lord's time, according to the reckoning of Kolob."[376]

Despite its purported relationship to a supreme deity[377], this is the only reference to Kolob found within sacred Mormon scripture– something which has led academics to presume that the word was either

---

[374] The original *Book of Abraham* papyri were believed to have been lost in the Great Chicago Fire of 1871. However, in 1966 several fragments of the papyri were discovered in the archives of the Metropolitan Museum of Art in New York and in the LDS church archives. They are now referred to as the Joseph Smith Papyri. (Source: https://en.wikipedia.org/wiki/Pearl_of_Great_Price_(Mormonism)

[375] https://en.wikipedia.org/wiki/Pearl_of_Great_Price_(Mormonism)

[376] *The Pearl of Great Price*, First Edition, The Book of Abraham, Published by F. D. Richards, 1851.

[377] Smith's interpretation of God's references to the Elohim (the grammatically plural noun for 'gods' or 'deities' in Biblical Hebrew) is that they that they originated from Kolob and visited Earth to mate with humans.

11. LAST DAYS OF THE PLAN?

a mistranslation by Smith or that it came about as a result of some other error creeping into his work. However, the word Kolob also appeared in the 1987 book *The Keys of Enoch* which was written by the founder and president of The Academy for Future Science, J.J. Hurtak. This strange publication purported to be a conduit for the channelled transmission of Enoch and revealed an idea that our local universe had a "triangular Light Core" which stretched ten million light years along with a "surrounding veil of twenty million light years". Hurtak/Enoch maintains that this zone surrounds a core, or central sun, which is Kolob.

An interpretation of the Kolob star/sun is also be found in LDS hymn No. 284 which was written by early Mormon elder William W. Phelps (1792-1872). Phelps purchased a copy of the *Book of Mormon* on April 9, 1830–just three days after the Church of Christ was established. On December 24, 1830, he and his wife met Joseph Smith in person and were convinced that he was a prophet.[378] Phelps became so embroiled in LDS doctrine that he printed the first edition of the *Book of Commandments* which went on to become a standard Mormon work. Phelps also wrote numerous hymns–some of which remain within in the current version of the Church of Jesus Christ of Latter-day Saints hymnal. Set to the music of a well-known folk tune known as *Dives and Lazarus*, the lyrics to Phelps's hymn *If You Could Hie to Kolob* states:

> *"If you could hie to Kolob In the twinkling of an eye,*
> *And then continue onward With that same speed to fly,*
> *Do you think that you could ever, Through all eternity,*
> *Find out the generation Where Gods began to be?"*[379]

The root meaning of the word Kolob has two possible interpretations. Egyptologist and Associate Professor of Ancient Scripture, Michael D. Rhodes (1946-present day)–in his publication titled *The Joseph Smith Hypocephalus...Twenty Years Later* suggests that the term 'Kolob' is derived from the common Semitic root 'QLB', meaning 'heart', 'center', or 'middle'.[380] A second, more convincing

---

[378] https://en.wikipedia.org/wiki/W._W._Phelps_(Mormon)
[379] https://en.wikisource.org/wiki/If_You_Could_Hie_to_Kolob
[380] Some have equated the Semetic root 'QLB' to that of 'QBL' which is often cited as

theory was proposed by LDS scholars John Laurence Gee and Stephen D. Ricks who, in *Historical Plausibility: The Historicity of the Book of Abraham as a Case Study*,[381] stated that:

> "The name Kolob (Abr. 3:3–4, 9, 16; 5:13) is perhaps the most famous name to come from the *Book of Abraham*. The transliteration system that Joseph Smith used for Hebrew used the letter k for two different Hebrew letters: k and q. Thus, the name Kolob fits well with two Semitic roots. Either it could be from *qlb (Arabic qalb, öheartö) or *klb (Akkadian kalbu, ödog,ö Ugaritic klb, ödog,ö Hebrew keleb, ödog,ö [e.g., Ex. 11:7], Syriac kelb, kalbŌ', ödog,ö Arabic kalb, ödog,ö Ethiopic kalb, ödogö). Both are used for stars or constellations, the former in Arabic for Regulus; the latter, in Akkadian, represents "the constellation Hercules," while in Syriac it represents the star Sirius; in Arabic it represents the constellation Canus Major, especially the main star Sirius. The root *qlb seems less likely because it is not attested until much later Arabic and not in earlier languages."

LDS leader and historian B. H. Roberts (1857-1933) also commented on Smith's references to Kolob. He interpreted them to mean that our Solar System—along with its central planet (the Sun) revolves around another, greater star called "Kae-e-vanrash" which itself revolves around a star called "Kli-flos-is-es" or "Hah-ko-kau-beam". These orbit Kolob, a stellar body which Roberts characterised as "the great centre of that part of the universe to which our planetary

---

the source of the word Qabalah, or Kabbalah. This may or may not be the case, but it is interesting to note that within the Tree of Life, 'QLB' refers to the central sphere of Tipareth, represented by our Sun, and the point around which the rest of the Tree radiates.

[381] Gee, John and Ricks, Stephen D., *Historical Plausibility: The Historicity of the Book of Abraham as a Case Study,* "in *Historicity and the Latter-day Saint Scriptures*, Religious Studies Center, Brigham Young University, 2001.

11. Last Days of The Plan?

system belongs".[382] This LDS reference clearly describes the binary system that underpins Sirius and its binary relationship with our Sun..

Chapter 7 of *The Book of Abraham* purports to be "*The Means By Which Abraham Was Taught Astronomy - The Abrahamic System of Astronomy - From The Earth to Kolob.*"[383] He maintained that his knowledge of the stars was derived from the following sources.

> 1. Through the records handed down to him from the antediluvian patriarchs.
>
> 2. By the use of the Urim and Thummim, which he received from the Lord in Ur of Chaldea.
>
> 3. By direct communication with the Almighty, who, face to face, and with His own voice, explained to him the laws that govern His countless creations.

This perspective of the machinations of the cosmos is widely different to orthodox astronomical theory. Abraham challenges established notions by stating that the system of astronomy revealed by God to him is, as Smith put it in his commentary, "...so vast, so grand, so comprehensive, that no uninspired man ever searched out its depths or ascended its heights." He also stated that:

> "I saw the stars that they were very great, and that one of them was nearest unto the throne of God; and there were many great ones that were near it; and the Lord said unto me, These are the governing ones: and the name of the great one is Kolob, because it is near unto me, for I am the Lord thy God; I have set this one to govern all those which belong to the same order of that upon which thou standest. And the Lord said unto me, by the Urim and Thummim, that Kolob was after the manner of the Lord, according to its times and seasons in the revolution thereof, that one

---
[382] https://en.wikipedia.org/wiki/Kolob#%22If_You_Could_Hie_to_Kolob
[383] https://www.sacred-texts.com/mor/tboa/chap07.htm

revolution was a day unto the Lord, after his manner of reckoning, it being one thousand years according to the time appointed unto that whereon thou standest. This is the reckoning of the Lord's time, according to the reckoning of Kolob."

Kolob is therefore a centre around which other planetary bodies revolve. As Smith stated:

> "...the Moon revolves around the Earth, and the earth with the other primary and secondary planets belonging to this solar system revolve around the sun, so has the sun a centre around which it, with all its earths and moons, revolves..."

He continues:

> "...while this grand centre has a governing planet also, a sun or world around which it, with its attendant systems of suns and worlds, revolves, and so on until we come to Kolob, the "nearest to the celestial or the residence of God," which is the grand centre which governs all the suns and systems of suns "which belong to the same order" as our earth and those that move with it."

Furthermore, *The Book of Abraham* reveals that:

> "I. Kolob is the greatest of all the stars because it is nearest to the celestial, or residence of God.
>
> II. It governs all the planets which belong to the same order as this earth.
>
> III It determines the rate of passage of "Lord's time".
>
> IV. Kolob signifies the first creation."

11. Last Days of The Plan?

Further revelations within *The Book of Abraham* state that "Oliblish stands next to Kolob." The term 'Oliblish' was used as one of the main symbols contained within the images of Smith's hypocephalus[384] (also known as the *Hypocephalus of Sheshonq*)[385] which formed a fragment of Joseph Smith's Papyri. This includes a diagrammatic representation of Kolob along with a figure with two jackals or dog (canine) heads facing away in opposite directions. The figure is carrying in its left hand the staff of Wepwawet.

Left: The dog-headed Egyptian God Anubis (Wepwawet) who is closely connected to the star Sirius: represented by Kolob. (Copyright: Mohamed Hassan)

In Egyptian mythology, Wepwawet meant 'opener of the ways' and he is often depicted as a wolf standing at the prow of a solar barque. Over time was also seen as one who opened the ways to the Duat (afterlife) for the spirits of the recently deceased. Wepwawet also became associated with the dog-headed deity Anubis.

In short, *The Joseph Smith Papers* state that the word "Kolob" is used to represent one of three central stars from which power emanates to govern all the other creations; including our Earth– which is referenced by the term 'Jah-oh-eh'. In addition, 'Enish-go-on-dosh' is said by the ancient Egyptians to be the Sun and that it borrows or receives its light from Kolob through the medium of 'Kae-e-vanrash'. Smith summarises the cosmological theories of Abraham by stating:

---

[384] https://en.wikipedia.org/wiki/Joseph_Smith_Hypocephalus
[385] "Hypocephali" are small disk-shaped objects, generally made of stuccoed linen or papyrus, bronze, gold, wood, or clay, which ancient Egyptians from the Late Period onwards placed under the heads of their dead. (Source: https://en.wikipedia.org/wiki/Joseph_Smith_Hypocephalus)

> "That this solar system is governed by Kae-e-vanrash, which is governed by Kli-flos-is-es or Hah-ko-kau-beam, which are governed by Kolob. Whether Oliblish belongs to the same order of systems as this earth, or simply holds the keys of power-pertaining to other planets, is not so apparent."

This triple-aspected body of power and influence, its relationship to the centre of our solar system, and the transference of light—as well as the imposition of time—are all concepts related to the ancient cosmological beliefs associated with Sirius. The fact that Smith—via Abraham—revealed them in the early part of the 19th-century is a notable achievement given that Sirius B was not discovered by astronomers until 1862.[386]

So, what, or where did Smith think Kolob was in the heavens? It seems that he mistakenly believed Kolob is Alcyone—a star located in the constellation of Taurus. He arrived at this conclusion by his belief that the word means 'centre' and that Abraham's teachings describe Kolob as playing "a central role". In this he is incorrect for he fails to take into consideration the fact that the ancient Egyptians—from whom he drew his source material—venerated Sirius above all other stars, established their own methodology of keeping time by its rising, and that their God, Anubis—the dog-headed God—is closely linked to the dog-star Sirius. The ancients also knew that the light of our Sun is ultimately drawn from the star Sirius and for that reason is known as the "Sun behind the Sun".

ANOTHER STAR WHO FELL TO EARTH?

To the average Mormon, these esoteric dynamics and principles mean very little. However, if Kolob/Sirius lies at the heart of the occult 'current' or 'ray' then there is every possibility that this star governs the LDS at an esoteric level. Is the same stream of energy that connects Freemasonry to an ancient Mystery School tradition also breathing its

---

[386] It is worth noting that Sir William G. Hamilton (1788-1856) of Dublin University had already been advancing the idea that our solar system had a centre around which the sun and all its attendant planets moved.

11. Last Days of The Plan?

life-force through and into Mormonism? This may well be the case and that it is worth tracing its exoteric expression which the average Church member would resonate to if not directly understand or appreciate.

Is the existence of a possible Siriun influence the reason why Elvis felt so drawn towards the teachings of the LDS? Did he intuitively recognise a natural resonance deep within his soul to its core principles; which, as we have just seen, resonates to the energetic radiance of the star Sirius? Is even possible that Elvis had an 'ancestral' Soul-link to Sirius and that, like Stockhausen, the star was the true spiritual home he was so desperate to find? If this is the case then Elvis could even be classified as an 'extra-terrestrial'—an alien visitor to our World: much like Ziggy.

An absurd idea? Well, maybe not for Elvis often commented on the fact that he felt himself to have been formed from 'starseed energy'. "I am not of this world." he once confided to Wanda June Hill—one of his' closest friends during the last fifteen years of his life. With his permission, Wanda recorded numerous telephone conversations that took place between them and in so-doing managed to capture Elvis at his most intimate and revelatory. On one occasion the super-star told her that:

> "I am a man, a human being now, but what is 'me' is not from here. I am from out there. ... You think I'm making this up, but it's true—you'll know that one day."[387]

The story of his involvement with extraterrestrials can be traced far back to his earliest memories. As a child he often heard voices when he was alone— usually when he was locked in a small closet as a form of punishment. On these occasions his 'visitors' played music to him, spoke about his home planet, and showed him visions of a man standing under stage lights dressed all in white. Elvis had no idea who this person was but then, many years later, he realised that the strangers had shown him an image of his own future as a show-business legend.

---

[387] Hill, Wanda June, *We Remember, Elvis*, Createspace, 2006.

Despite their shocking revelations, Wanda remained un-phased by Elvis's outspoken declarations. When walking out together at night he would often point out various stars to her and name each one. When she asked him how he knew so much about the cosmos, Elvis grinned, pointed to the stars, and said that he was "from up there". He also told her that the citizens of planet Earth would soon learn about beings who were living on planets located outside our solar system. He maintained that some of them had mastered the secrets to longevity and knew how to cure deadly diseases such as cancer.

As the relationship between the two strengthened, Elvis felt increasingly confident in opening up to Wanda. In one conversation, he spoke of "Cosmic Masters" who he said had made contact with him at a very early age and given him supernatural powers. These included the ability to move clouds in the sky, levitate objects through the power of his thoughts, and even heal the sick—a skill which many people have attested to having Elvis perform throughout his lifetime. As for his stellar home, the Masters told Elvis that he originated from a "blue planet far, far away at the foot of the Orion constellation which had many moons."

Could this have been Sirius? Although not recognised as part of Orion, the Dog Star is indeed located below, and just off from, the foot of the constellation...and is, from our perspective, blue in colour.

THE SIRIAN GENE

What exactly is the process that connects individuals to the energy and influence of Sirius and why is that so many successful musicians in particular appear to have been magnetised to the Siriun Ray? Do we not all fall under the same influence of the heavenly realm with equal measure or is it a case that some sort of hidden directive resides within, rather than external to, humanity and that it is this and not mere 'stardust' that determines why some individuals connect to the energies of the star more than others?

A possible explanation for why a Sirius-based ray only picks out certain individuals may be found in the pages of a 1984 book titled *Practical Egyptian Magick* by the English occultist Murry Hope. In it she makes an interesting observation.

> "Many reliable psychics and mystics firmly subscribe to the idea of a special gene, or personalised 'time capsule', programmed with the knowledge of the 'old ones' who came from the Sirius system centuries ago; this gene has been passed down from generation to generation to the present day. From this Sirian genetic strain a new school of magic The "new school of magic" to which Hope refers is equally clouded in mystery and intrigue. Unfortunately, she reveals little of its composition; other than to say that it is based around the application of power harnessed within our minds. has emerged."[388]

Did Elvis have this new strain of magick coursing through his veins? Like Bowie, he certainly attained astounding levels of professional success throughout his life and this may well be linked to his strong cosmic connection and the direct influence of his "Hidden Masters". In the course of one of his telephone conversations with Wanda he explained that, as a child, he had been approached by two 'men' awho showed themselves as "light forms". "One of them touched me and I felt light inside me—floating sort of." he said.

There are other important clues which indicate the possibility that Elvis was carrying the Sirian gene spoken about by Murry Hope. As we learnt earlier, the colour blue is closely associated with Sirius and later on in his life Elvis became convinced that it had a great spiritual significance. According to people around him, Elvis utilised blue light in healing and that whenever he performed healing prayers for people he would invoke the words "First we must think of the blue light." Elvis felt that this blue-light energy was the primary component in a strange 'force' that followed him through his life but he was not the only person to have experienced it. His father, Vernon Presley, also described seeing the same energy field on the night of his son's birth.

---
[388] Hope, Murry, *Practical Egyptian Magic*, Aquarian Press, 1984.

> "As I looked around, son, I noticed something strange. The whole area around the house was lit up with a blue light It seemed to surround the house. And just at that moment, the wind stopped blowing. It was so still you could hear a pin drop."

The colour blue was also evident in other areas of Elvis's life. When casually dressed he would often appear in blue clothes and several of his best-selling songs contained the word blue. These included titles such as *Blue Suede Shoes*, *Blue Moon of Kentucky*, and *Blue Christmas*. In addition, some of his biggest-grossing films also had the word blue in their title: examples being *G.I. Blues* and *Blue Hawaii*.

The light that followed Presley throughout his life may well have been an encapsulation of the energy of the powder-blue star Sirius but it was not only a contraction of a specific wavelength in the electromagnetic spectrum. It also acted as a guiding force and appeared to be imbued with the power to control his destiny and determine the trajectory his professional career went in. In this regard we must assume that the blue light both Elvis and his father experienced contained some inherent form of consciousness: but what was the nature of this intelligence?

From an astrological perspective, the energy of Sirius is understood to be an amalgamation of the dynamics of the grandiose expansion of the planet Jupiter and the fiery will-focused energy of Mars.[389] Whenever the star is prominent in a person's natal birth chart it is said to bestow honour, renown, wealth, ardour, faithfulness, devotion, passion, and resentment. It is also said that it imbues its natives with the opportunity to become prominent custodians, curators, and guardians. The author Eric Morse, in his book *The Living Stars*, maintained that it:

> "...marks immense creative talents in any field at all with 'only' the warning there may be more inner power than can be safely managed. Harshly aspected it can show a psychotic person truly a menace to

---

[389] In the Kabbalistic tradition, the path on the Tree of Life connecting the sphere of Mars (Geburah), and Jupiter (Chesed) is ruled by the major arcane card STRENGTH. This is ruled by the zodiac sign Leo.

11. Last Days of The Plan?

himself and the community, but in better condition, we have here the star of the truly Great figures in every field of human endeavour."[390]

In addition to the 'blue-light', there are a number of Sirian-related symbols which played a prominent role in Elvis's life. His stage wardrobe contained many stunningly designed, bejewelled caftans which are said to have been similar in style to those worn by the spiritual masters he adored. The jumpsuits he sported during his famous Las Vegas shows were heavily infused with ancient American Indian and Mayan glyphs but one of his favourite symbols was that of a phoenix and this often appeared in either red, blue, or black versions on his clothing.[391]

The prominent astronomical scientist Dr E. C. Krupp (1944-present day) links the phoenix with both the Sun and Sirius. In his book *In Search of Ancient Astronomies*, he stated that:

> "The Egyptians attached particular importance to a heron-like bird they called the "Bennu", and the Greeks identified the Bennu with the Phoenix. According to Herodotus, the red and gold Bennu was reported to return from Arabia to Heliopolis after five hundred years' absence, or, more curiously, according to others, after 1,461 years. In some versions of the legend the Bennu dies at Heliopolis, and from either its nest or its own burned remains a new Bennu arises to start the cycle of life anew."

The 1,461 years reference years acknowledges the Sothic Cycle—the time taken for the Egyptian solar calendar to coincide with Sirius—and this was represented by the phoenix.[392]

---

[390] Morse, Eric, *The Living Stars*, Amethyst Books, 1989.
[391] Betty luca Andreasson, a famous UEO abductee from Massachusetts, reported that the aliens she met on a spacecraft wore a surprisingly similar phoenix symbol on the sleeve of their uniforms. (Source: Fowler, Raymond E., The Andreasson Affair, Phase Two, Granite Publishing, 1994.)
[392] Krupp, E.C., *In Search of Ancient Astronomies*, Doubleday, 1978.

Another Sirian symbol Elvis felt a close resonance with was the 'ankh' glyph which the ancient Egyptians used to represent the concept of 'life'.[393] Handcrafted by Mike McGregor—a blacksmith and leather craftsman Elvis met in the 1960s—they were a regular feature on Elvis's stage regalia throughout the 1970s.

Whatever the true nature and purpose of the Siriun impulse is, it undoubtedly acts as a benevolent force in those who are closely connected to it.

Holding Out

In the world of American popular music, both Elvis Presley and the Osmonds ruled supreme in the years between 1970 and 1974. The close connection Elvis had with the group's mother, Olive Osmond, led to the formation of an even closer with her Mormon family. Elvis often shared his knowledge of the music business with them and offered advice on their stage presence and dress code. His contribution to their career undoubtedly aided in the stratospheric rise of the group. With their ultra-smooth, carefully honed stage act, and slick vocal harmonies, The Osmonds personified the clean-cut, God-fearing persona the Mormon Church was keen to present to the World. In many ways, the lyrical content of the Osmond's songs—whether they directly expressed LDS sentiments or not—were important elements in forging a favourable impression of their Christian aspirations. In his regard, the group was not only successful commercially but they also became a powerful recruiting agent. Most of their audience only become aware of the existence of the Church and its teachings through their appreciation of the Osmond's music. This formula proved so successful that, during the years in which they were at their most popular, the Osmonds were viewed by many as the externalised face of the LDS. They were, in many ways, a self-perpetuating promotion machine for when fierce critics of the brothers and their music voiced their opinion, they would invariably reference the family's religious associations which, once again, brought awareness of the LDS to larger numbers of people.

---

[393] The ankh references the flooding of the River Nile each year around the time of the rising of Sirius over the Egyptian horizon. It is also associated with Isis.

11. Last Days of The Plan?

As close as the Osmond family unit were, they were not averse to encouraging individual members to pursue their own musical projects. The dewy-eyed younger brother, Donny, grew up and soon emerged as a natural focal point to the group. A new generation of female adolescents were thirsty for a handsome pinup poster boy and so, with his fresh face, good looks and immaculate smile, Donny fitted their romanticised ideals.

Donny was not only highlighted during stage and TV performances but he also stepped forward to build a career as a solo performer. He released a handful of singles—initially to mixed reviews—but on September 20, 1971, the teenage heartthrob recorded his fourth solo single titled *Puppy Love* which was a cover version of a well-known Paul Anka song. After a delay of several months, the song was finally released on February 19, 1972. By April 1, 1972, it had climbed to number 3 on the Billboard Hot 100 singles chart. From there the song's popularity spread far and wide and became a best-selling record all over the World.

On the face of it, *Puppy Love* was a musical cliché. Donny's version of the song was so cringe-worthy that many found it strange that it became as successful as it did. In the UK—one of several countries where it achieved the highly-venerated number 1 position—the song was a massive hit, clogging up the radio airwaves for months on end.

If the song's success seemed inexplicable, then the huge sales figures it generated during this period was even more surprising given that it dominated a record chart full of more 'sophisticated' fare. This was a golden period in popular music and the charts reflected the fact.

During the month that *Puppy Love* was a hit in the UK, the singles chart contained a plethora of classic songs—many of which reflected a growing trend by songwriters to focus on outer-space and the cosmos in their lyrics. In the same week that *Puppy Love* reached number one in the UK; Elvis was riding high with *An American Trilogy*; Bowie's *Starman* was gaining traction; the Kinks had a hit with *Supersonic Rocketship*; space-rock legends Hawkwind were enjoying huge success with their only major hit *Silver Machine*; Elton John had his spaceman-inspired song *Rocket Man*; Mark Bolan/T. Rex had a major hit with

Metal Guru; and the Moody Blues found success with the philosophically-inspired song *Isn't Life Strange*?

Each of these artists were not only linked by the fact that they were enjoying immense commercial success all at the same time but that each one either had an interest in ufology or had reported their own ET/UFO encounter. Most remarkably, in 1966 the whole of the Moody Blues had an early-morning interaction with an alien-being who emerged from a downed UFO[394] they encountered while driving back to London from a gig in the northern town of Carlisle.

A Message in Time?

So, given that the UK singles charts of July 1972 most certainly indicated that the social zeitgeist was resonating with a cosmic or stellar vibration, the success of *Puppy Love* is even more inexplicable. Which leads one to wonder what was it that made it quite so popular. If *Puppy Love* did not become such a big record during July 1972 because of its artistic merit then what exactly was it that made it so successful all across the World?

It is perfectly possible that the throngs of young, adoring female fans bought it in sufficient numbers to make it a top seller but, as the Moody Blues might have put it, life is indeed somewhat strange. Could *Puppy Love* somehow have been 'promoted' to its elevated position as a result of the same occult forces that put the careers of Bowie and Presley on such exponential trajectories?

To answer this question it is worth comparing *Puppy Love* with events that were conspiring in the heavens above planet Earth throughout July and August 1972. This is a period of the year referred to by cultures both old and new as the "Dog Days" due to a common belief that Sirius initiates hot and sultry weather. Cosmically the Dog Days mark the energetic ray of Sirius as it pours through Leo and the Sun: its ruling planet.

Is it not extraordinarily coincidental that Donny Osmond's chart-

---

[394] https://forums.stevehoffman.tv/threads/moody-blues-ufo-encounter-article.738747

11. Last Days of The Plan?

topping song just happened to contain references to a young dog (Puppy) and a universal energy (Love) at a point when inhabitants of the Dog Star (i.e. Sirians) were said to have been hard at work constructing the solar defences required to safeguard our planet and all its lifeforms from apocalyptic catastrophe? Did the largely unfathomable popularity of this Worldwide hit-single occur because it was deliberately contrived as a composition and disproportionately elevated to its Worldwide success by paranormal forces (i.e. by the Sirians themselves)?

On the face of it—despite the extraordinary synchronicity of the two occurrences—many would suggest this is an unlikely proposition. Nevertheless, we cannot dismiss the possibility that *Puppy Love*'s place in musical history was an example of a deliberate intention by the Sirians to leave 'signposts' or 'breadcrumbs'—time-capsules embedded into the cultural history of western society—which would confirm their existence and activities during the summer of 1972: evidence which could be revealed later on when humanity was ready to accept the concept of extraterrestrial life.

Critics of this theory might suggest that this attempt to make a connection between *Puppy Love* and the Sirians is a mistake and that we are simply considering a pattern of coincidences where no real connection exists. Others might propose that the truth lies somewhere between these two opposing views and that the synchronicity is an unresolvable riddle—one best classified as an action contrived by a grand Cosmic Joker?[395] Let's dismiss both these rebuttals for a moment and consider that the reality behind the enigma of the success of *Puppy Love* is possibly even stranger than we can begin to suppose. Let's face it, when events connected to Sirius occur, things tend to get VERY weird!

A deeper study of *Puppy Love* and the circumstances surrounding it reveals several interesting connections.

---

[395] The term 'Cosmic Joker' is referenced use within paranormal research. It is used to describe the apparent influence of a higher intelligence acting within any one of a multitude variety of anomalous phenomena. Coined by the influential American researcher and archivist of mysterious events Charles Hoy Fort (1874-1932) Fort references the source behind them as "having a perverse and black-humoured sense of nature."

1. *Puppy Love* was recorded by Donny Osmond at music studios named after the Mormon term 'Kolob'—which, as we established earlier, directly references the star Sirius.

2. The corporate logo for the recording company that released *Puppy Love*—the same one that was set-up and controlled by the Osmond family—shows a hand of apparent friendship and support stretched out, holding, or supporting the Earth in the centre of its palm. Could this be an image redolent of the actions taken by Sirians in helping to save our planet?

As we have seen throughout this book, there are other methodologies at our disposal which, if applied, can reveal otherwise undetectable connections. Focussing upon the two primary musical compositions in this narrative and by applying occult principles to Donny Osmond's *Puppy Love* and David Bowie's *Starman* even more amazing 'coincidences' emerge.

1. What are the chances that the original songwriter of Puppy Love, namely Paul Anka—a highly successful musician and actor in his own right from the late 1950s up to the mid-2000s—would have a name with the Gematria value of '333'—the same as that of the word 'seirios' which the ancient Greeks gave to the star Sirius? The word 'seirios' is derived from the Latin 'dies caniculares' which means 'the puppy days'.

2. What are the chances that Annette Funicello (1942-2013)—the actress Anka dated and for whom he wrote Puppy Love—should have a name with the same Gematria value (644) as the term 'from Sirius'?

3. What are we to make of the fact that the Gematria value of the words 'Donny Osmond' is 798—the same value as the term 'blue rays' which is a direct reference to the intelligently sourced Siriun light that followed and

11. Last Days of The Plan?

fascinated his close-friend Elvis Presley throughout his life?

4. Why is it that the song which appeared on the reverse side of Donny Osmond's *Puppy Love*–an evangelical tune written by the sister's songwriting team Helen and Kay Lewis called *Let My People Go*–has the numerical value 812 which is the same value as the term 'Dog Star Sirius B'? Sirius B, rather than Sirius A will be found to become particularly significant later.[396]

5. With reference to single B-sides, the song that appeared on Bowie's 1972 single *Starman* was *Suffragette City*. The Gematria value of the term 'Suffragette City' is 1112 which is the same value as the term 'message from David'. This might be significant or may just be another example of wordplay witticism, an intentional pun from the dark Trickster-God of Humour.[397]

6. With further reference to the song *Starman*, we discovered earlier that its total length contained a Gematria value of some significance. Applying the same criteria to the official length of Donny Osmond's version of *Puppy Love*–which is 2 minutes and 45 seconds–we find that 245 is the value of the term 'Nine Gods'... and this is where things start to get very strange indeed!

---

[396] In addition, is there any connection to the fact that the term 'puppy' is suggestive of a canine that is younger than its parent? In this case it would appear to reference Sirius B–the lesser star known to orbit Sirius A.

[397] Just in case you think this is unlikely to be the case then it is worth mentioning that the same value, 1112, is identical to the phrase 'this isn't a joke'.

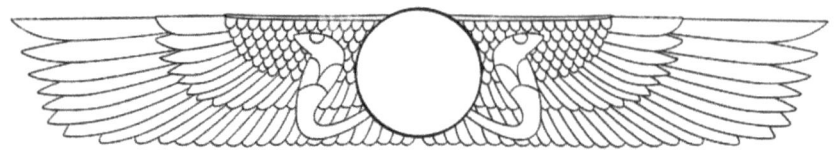

12. Return of the Nine

> "The Nine, who together make up One God, said that they come from Sirius and that they are heralding a time of great cleansing of the Earth, when the wicked shall be destroyed to make way for the good (very reminiscent of the Fundamentalist "rapture")"

The Mammoth Book of UFOs by Lynn Picknett and Clive Prince.

In August 1972, a young man from Israel called Uri Geller, walked onto the campus of the Stanford Research Center at Menlo Park, California. Geller was in America at the request of American physician and parapsychological researcher Andrija Puharich (1918-1995) who had brought him to the country for an assessment by the country's most prominent scientists and metaphysical researchers.

Puharich first heard of Geller two years earlier while chairing an international conference in New York in November 1970. Titled *Exploring the Energy Fields of Man,* the objective of the event was to consider the possible existence of an energy field which some scientists suspected to underpin certain types of psychic phenomena. At some point during the gathering one of its attendees happened to mention to Puharich that he had recently come across a young man in Israel who was gaining popularity by performing a range of remarkable psychokinetic feats.[398] This peaked his interest and decided to find out more for himself.

Geller had an interesting early history. Born in Tel Aviv (then part of

---
[398] Hermans, H G M, *Memories of a Maverick - Andrija Puharich*, Pi Publications, 1998.

12. RETURN OF THE NINE

the British Mandate of Palestine) and to an Austrian-Jewish mother and Hungarian-Jewish father, he first became aware that he had paranormal abilities at the age of seven when he discovered that he could make the hands of his watch move simply by focussing his mind. This led to him exploring and developing of a range of extrasensory powers; including the ability to correctly describe pictures drawn by his friends while he was blindfolded.

In addition to being a psychic, Geller was also a UFO contactee. At the tender age of three he was approached by the occupant of a huge bowl-shaped craft. The being emitted a blinding ray of light from his head which struck Geller so hard that he was knocked backwards and rendered unconscious. Around 1968, after sustaining another injury and being discharged from service in the Israeli Army's Paratroopers Brigade, Geller developed a stage act which he performed his paranormal skills in local theatres, public halls, auditoriums, military bases and universities in Israel. It was this that ultimately drew the attention of Puharich a couple of years later.

READING THE RING

Left: Andrija Puharich in 1959.

Puharich's deep fascination in extrasensory perception (ESP) first began in December 1951 when he was living in New York City. It was on February 16, 1952, that Dr. D. G. Vinod–a Hindu scholar and sage from Poona, India– performed a psychometric reading on Puharich's finger ring and, after holding it in his hand for a minute, spent the following hour describing Puharich's life to him in minute detail. The scientist was so astounded by the psychic's accuracy that he later described the consultation as one conducted with "utter precision–as though he were reading out of a book."[399]

---

[399] Puharich, Andrija, *Uri: A Journal of the Mystery of Uri Geller,* Anchor Press,

Puharich invited the doctor to his next parapsychological experiment session and on December 31, 1952, Vinod travelled from New York to his laboratory in Maine. The two men waisted no time. Vinod immediately sat down on a sofa and fell into a deep trance. Puharich detailed what happened next.

> "At exactly 9 P.M., a deep sonorous voice came out of Dr. Vinod's mouth, totally unlike his own high-pitched, soft voice, saying in perfect English without an accent.
>
> M. calling: "We are Nine Principles and Forces, personalities if working in complete mutual implication. We are forces, and the nature of our work is to accentuate the positive, the evolutional, and the teleological aspects of existence. By teleology I do not mean the teleology of human derivation in a multidimensional concept of existence. Teleology will be understood in terms of a different ontology. To be simple, we accentuate certain directions as will fulfil the destiny of creation. We propose to work with you in some essential respects with the relation of contradiction and contrariety. We shall negate and revise part of your work, by which I mean the work as presented by you. The point is that we want to begin altogether at a different dimension, though it is true that your work has itself led up to this.
>
> I deeply appreciate your dedicatedness (sic) to the great cause of peace which is a fulfilment of finitesimal (sic.) existences. Peace is not warlessness. Peace is the integral fruitage of personality. We have designed to utilize you and thus to fulfil you. Peace is a process and will be revealed only progressively. You have it in plenty, I mean the

1974.

patience which is so deeply needed in this magnificent adventure. But today, at the moment of our advent, the most eventful and spectacular phase of your work begins."[400]

The same group of extraterrestrials re-appeared in subsequent sessions and regular channellings with them continued until February 1953 when Puharich was called up to serve as a captain in the U. S. Army during the Korean War. While on leave, Puharich organised another session with nine attendees for June 27, 1953. At 12:15 A.M. Vinod re-entered a trance and one of The Nine, identifying himself as 'R', relayed to Puharich and his team what they described as "advanced spiritual and mystical information."

SPECTRA

On August 17, 1971, Puharich travelled to Tel Aviv in Israel to meet Geller who had been booked to perform a demonstration of his psychic skills at a magical show at a discotheque called the Zorba in Jaffa later that night.[401] Puharich turned up and watched in fascination as Geller opened his act with a demonstration of telepathy followed by a display of psychokinesis,[402]. He was so impressed by his skills that he met the young Israeli after the show and asked Geller if he would be prepared to have his psychic and psychokinetic powers analysed. Geller agreed and the experiments started in Tel-Aviv in November; but they did not go to plan. Rather than display his talents, fate intervened and Geller inadvertently made contact with an extraterrestrial intelligence which identified itself as "SPECTRA".

In a subsequent session held one month later, Geller was placed in a hypnotic state by Puharich and the same group of extraterrestrials appeared again. This time Geller felt that the voice of SPECTRA came not directly from the ETs themselves but via a highly advanced computer which he said was located on a UFO parked close to Earth.[403] The voice

[400] Ibid.
[401] Ibid.
[402] Psychokinesis is the ability to move objects purely through the application of mental willpower.
[403] In the mid-1970s, a number of scientists reported receiving 'communications'

258

explained that it was in actually an expression of same group of nine "principles or forces" Puharich had made contact with back in America. The group said that they had deliberately 'seeded' Geller with his psychic abilities when he was a child and maintained that they were behind Kenneth Arnold's famous 1947 sighting when the pilot observed nine "flying saucers".

Geller and the Nine's revelations had a deep impact on Puharich and in his personal journal, published in 1974, he wrote:

> "I believe that a prophet, an Uri Geller, if you wish, is specifically created to serve as an intermediary between a "divine" intelligence and man. The same idea would hold for living beings existing anywhere on any planet in the universe. I now fully believe that life exists anywhere and everywhere in the universe as divine intelligence dictates. I was prepared to believe that life exists in forms and states beyond the imagination of man to conceive."

Compass, Watches & Spoons

Puharich returned to the United States in April 1972. In August the same year, Uri travelled from Germany (where he had been performing stage-shows) to meet him in California. The series of examinations at the Stanford Research Institute (SRI) Geller underwent were supervised by scientist Russell Targ[404] and Harold Puthoff[405] who specialised in quantum physics. Despite having agreed to their investigations, Geller remained deeply apprehensive about the prospect of having his psychic skills assessed by unknown members of the scientific community. His concern was that if the results of their experiments confirmed that he was from a Sirian source maintaining it was a computer based on a nearby UFO. These claims are explored in depth in the second volume of *The Sirius Mythos* series.

[404] Russell Targ (1934-present day) is an American physicist, parapsychologist and author best known for his work on remote viewing. In 1978 he worked with Puthoff on the US Defence Intelligence Agency's Stargate Project which was established to test the possibility of using remote viewing in a military capacity.

[405] Harold E. Puthoff (1936-present day) is an American electrical engineer and parapsychologist. In the 2010s he co-founded the company To the Stars Academy with rock musician and UFO researcher Tom DeLonge.

an authentic psychic and not just a stage magician then this would destroy the aura of mystique he had built around himself and his stage act. His reticence proved to be well-founded for Geller subsequently received a great deal of push-back from newspapers, magazines, and particularly from the sceptical paranormal researcher James Randi (1928-2020) who regularly appeared on major US television shows denouncing Geller as a fraud.[406] In an effort to counteract the impact of this negative publicity, Geller toured the US and appeared at several leading universities and colleges where his paranormal demonstrations were popular with students.

Geller travelled to England in October 1973 where, following the broadcast of his spoon-bending routine on the BBC's *David Dimbleby Show*, he became an overnight sensation. He created such a stir all over the country that he found himself in high-demand from newspapers, television producers, and the media. This led to numerous appearances on a variety of prime-time television shows where he performed the same routine as the one that had gone down so well with American students.[407]

Geller's increasing popularity resulted in a strain in his working relationship with Puharich. The Israeli felt that he should prioritise his media work and this created a divergence in the two men's approach to psychic phenomena. During television appearances, Geller came over as a loveable, excitable, and mysterious individual—someone who often appeared to be as shocked by his psychic abilities as his audience. However, he was a shameless self-publicist and he felt that he had a duty to promote the mysteries of the paranormal to a wider audience. Puharich was not convinced by Geller's perspective on what he saw as a science rather than a medium of entertainment and wanted them to

---

[406] Randi, who was a stage magician himself, claimed that Geller had managed to "trick reputable scientists" with the type of sleight-of-hand routines that "are the kind that used to be on the back of cereal boxes when I was a kid". (Source: Anon, *How does Uri Geller do it?, The Skeptic Encyclopedia of Pseudoscience*. 2002.) For many years the two archenemies were rarely out of the courts: facing one libel and counter-libel case after another.

[407] TV shows were not only a showcase for Geller's talents but they also generated paranormal phenomena. Members of the audience often reported that they found spoons spontaneously bent in their kitchen cupboards at home. Others reported seeing watches and house clocks inexplicably run again after several years of inactivity.

Left: Uri Geller demonstrating his kinetic powers on The Tonight Show with Johnny Carson in 1973.

continue working towards a more academic appraisal of the Israeli's psychic skills. By late 1973, their relationship had broken down completely and they parted company leaving Geller free to develop his career into what very quickly became a major TV personality.[408]

Geller's trade-mark act was spoon-bending through what he ascertained were "powers of the mind". He later expanded on on this and included mind-reading and repairing faulty timepieces through mind power. When audiences tired of the same routines, Geller adapted his stage-persona and changed from performing regular paranormal/psychic acts to the promotion of such such New Age practices as positive-thinking and self-development.[409]

Decades later, Geller refined his media persona even further and strove to distance himself from his prior metaphysical activities. He even that he was, or ever had been, a traditional psychic and emphatically distanced himself from his prior associations with SPECTRA and The Nine.

Despite Geller's withdrawal from direct engagement with the extraterrestrials, lines of communication with The Nine continued and even strengthened following the involvement of Sir John Whitmore (1937-2017)[410] and Phyllis Schlemmer (1929-2103).[411] Together they

---

[408] Such was the level of public interest in the magician that he decided to settle in England permanently and moved to Reading, Berkshire.

[409] Interest in Uri Geller resurfaced in 2013 when a BBC documentary titled The Secret Life of Uri Gellar revealed that for three decades he had been working as an agent of Mossad—the Israeli Intelligence Community and the American Central Intelligence Agency (CIA). (Source: Uri Geller discusses his double life as a 'psychic spy' for Mossad and CIA, The Independent, September 9, 2015.)

[410] John Henry Douglas Whitmore had been a British racing-car driver. After retiring he studied transpersonal psychology and the principle of will and intent which he applied in competitive sports and business. It led him to write *Coaching for Performance* which was published in 23 different languages.

[411] Phyllis V. Schlemmer founded the Psychic Center of Florida in Orlando in 1969.

formed an organisation called Lab Nine.[412]

Lab Nine was active for only a short period and was disbanded in 1978 after a series of mysterious events that culminated in an arson attack on their headquarters on the Ossining estate: around the same time that Puharich was claiming he was being persecuted by the CIA which ultimately resulted in him fleeing to Mexico. He returned to America two years later but made no further effort to communicate with The Nine throughout the period leading up to his accidental death in 1995.

The group who emerged from the (literal) ashes of Lab Nine were joined by a new channeller—a Daytona cook known by the pseudonym Bobby Horne. They continued disseminating the spiritual wisdom of The Nine extraterrestrials but Home had to pull-out due to the psychological pressures of the intense work. Schlemmer was subsequently appointed as the authorised spokesperson for one member of The Nine who identified himself as 'Tom'.

MASS-LANDINGS

In earlier sessions held with The Nine, Puharich was told that his life mission was to use Geller's talents to alert the World to an imminent mass-landing of spaceships which would take place under their direct control. This path failed to unfold as Puharich was led to believe it would when Geller found Worldwide fame as an entertainer. Consequently the task of informing humanity of the existence of The Nine and their purported visit to Earth fell to the Lab Nine group.

In 1977, the topic of UFO mass-landings re-emerged in the book *Prelude to the Landing on Planet Earth*[413] written by British journalist Stuart Holroyd (1933-present day)[414]. Holroyd was commissioned by

---

She met Puharich in July 1974 and in a trance contacted The Nine.
[412] *Star Trek* creator Gene Roddenberry (1921-1991) wrote a screenplay based on his interactions with The Nine in 1974/75.
[413] The book was subsequently re-released as *Briefing for the Landing on Planet Earth* in 1979.
[414] Stuart Holroyd (1933-present day) is a Yorkshire-born, British writer, who published his first book, *Emergence from Chaos*, in 1957 at the age of twenty-three. Later in his career he authored books on Gnosticism, Tantra, and parapsychology.

Puharich to write *Briefings* specifically to publicise the group's dialogues with The Nine.[415] Under the auspices of Phyllis Schlemmer, the new group oversaw the publication of a follow-up book which was also written by Holroyd, titled *Nine: Briefing from Deep Space: The Controversial Record of a Unique 'Encounter' and a Message of Hope for All Mankind* in 1993. The book included a Preface by Schlemmer, a Foreword by Whitmore, and an Introduction by the famous writer Colin Wilson. It resurfaced again in 1996 when it was republished under the title *The Only Planet of Choice: Essential Briefings from Deep Space.*

The new communications from The Nine—those channelled by Phyllis Schlemmer while she was in a trance-like state,[416] referenced a wide range of esoteric subjects. Some were metaphysical and related to our place in the Universe: others were historical and revealed a pre-diluvian age when Atlantis was said to have been in existence. In addition, much was made of the ecological damage mankind has inflicted upon the planet; including the inevitable increase levels of carbon dioxide in the atmosphere (which The Nine said were due to the continual burning of fossil fuels), the depletion of the ozone zone, and the mass destruction of marine life resulting from over-fishing.

The Only Planet of Choice had a massive and universal impact: not only within the New Age movement but within the scientific community which has led to some paranormal researchers suggesting that it is perhaps one of the most important books on spirituality ever written.[417] Schlemmer was not the only conduit for The Nine. Other psychics were in contact with the group from the mid-1970s onwards. These included Jenny O'Connor from England who had been introduced by Sir John Whitmore to the Esalen Institute, California, where she regularly

---

[415] Holroyd, Stuart, *Prelude to the Landing on Planet Earth*, W. H. Allen, 1977. Just to clarify its timeline: it was later released in paperback as *Briefings for the Landing on Planet Earth*, Corgi, 1979, and then as a part of a revised edition *The Nine: Briefing from Deep Space: The Controversial Record of a Unique 'Encounter' and a Message of Hope for All Mankind*, Gateway Books, 2003. The initial title also resurfaced as *The Council of Nine: Briefing from Deep Space*, Old Kings Road Press, 2006.

[416] Schlemmer, Phyllis V., *Only Planet of Choice: Essential Briefings from Deep Space*, 2nd edition, Gateway Books, 1994.

[417] This is probably a gross over-statement but there is no doubt that many of the ecological problems that The Nine highlighted within its pages have become integral ideas within many of today's more radical social, ecological, and political movements.

channelled them. In 1976–after reading Puharich's biography of Geller titled Uri–former airline pilot Don Elkins and Carla Rueckert travelled to Ossining to meet Puharich and then accompanied him to Mexico during his flight from the CIA. Elkins had been a UFO investigator since the mid-1950s but in 1962 he turned his attention to extraterrestrials following his connection with Carla Rueckert. In 1970, they founded a group called L/L Research to study the contactee phenomena.

After their sojourn to Mexico, Rueckert started to channel and extraterrestrial who went by the name 'Ra' who identified himself as another member, or aspect, of The Nine.[418]

Some years later, former US Navy officer David P. Myers and London-based film producer David S. Percy rose to prominence in the UFO movement through their active research into the Cydonia area of Mars. Myers revealed what he said were key measurements and angular relationships between various rocks in the region and it was Percy who had made the connection between them and the Neolithic stone circle at Avebury. His somewhat contentious research appeared in the thoroughly unreadable 1993 book *Two-Thirds* which was co-authored with Mary Bennett and David Myers. In it, the trio described how a group of extraterrestrials from a distant planet called "Altea" had journeyed to our solar system 1.6 million years ago, colonised Mars, built the Cydonia complex, and then journeyed to Earth where they genetically modified the human species. The material for *Two-Thirds* is said to have been derived from telepathic communications received from The Nine.

And finally, The Nine also appeared in the work of social scientist and founder of The Academy for Future Science, James Hurtak, who, in 1977, had also published information on Kolob in his book titled *The Keys of Enoch*.

HISTORY OF THE ENNEAD

In the first session between The Nine and Schlemmer, Tom–the spokesperson for the ET group–revealed who he really was.

[418] Picknett, Lynn and Prince, Clive, *The Stargate Conspiracy*, Little, Brown & Company, 1999.

> "In truth I am Tehuti. Yes. I am also Hamarkos, I am also Herenkar, I am known as Thomas, and I am known as Atum."

Aum was said by ancient Egyptian historians to have headed The Great Ennead, or Nine Gods of Ancient Egypt. Other members included Atum, Shu, Tefnut, Geb, Nut, Osiris, Isis, Set, and Nepthys. Together they were said to represent all life and all wisdom– particularly those teachings related to magick and other streams of occult knowledge. These deities were said to have taken on a human form and to have ruled Egypt from their centre in Heliopolis for several centuries prior to the Greeks and Romans invading the country whereupon they are said to have withdrawn to the heavenly realm from which they had originated: namely Sirius. Their eventual return to planet Earth was expected and several modern psychics have predicted that this in imminent.

Speaking of his time on our planet, Tom maintained that he had incarnated as a representative of The Nine/Ennead but that they operated as a singular body, or collective, "separate and one at the same time".[419] Tom also maintained that the group were also well-known within the Hebraic tradition where they were referred to as the Elohim– the creator gods of mankind. When asked about the significance of them being composed of nine elements he replied:

> "Nine is complete. Everything is nine. In your world you have said seven so many times, when everything is truly nine. There are nine chakras, which are the nine principles and nine elements of what you call God. There are nine bands around this planet Earth. There are nine etheric bodies, and the purpose of growing your etheric bodies or going through your transformations and transitions is to attain the nine etheric bodies. Nine is a complete number, it is whole. When you go over a nine it cancels, it

---

[419] It is interesting to note that the word 'ennead' has a Gematria value of 95–the same as the word 'one' which suggests that at some level The Nine were indeed unified in a singular, collective sense.

becomes one, and a nine is complete. This does not change. But remember this: we ourselves are not God. All of you and all of us make God."

Regarding their appearance he said:

"We do not have a physical body. Although we may put on the mantle of a physical body when it is necessary. It would be difficult for us to describe to you exactly what we appear like. We appear in many forms, when that is necessary. And in your thought-process we may appear as a human, we may appear as an energy ball, we may appear as a very bright light. We have evolved beyond the point of needing a physical-type body, as many souls need. We are always here, but you do not always see us. When I say we, I do not mean me, but I mean all of us. We are often observing. There are particular times in your life when we do not observe, and that is when you are involved with your desires. We do not understand this, and it is none of our affair."

A belief in the existence of nine gods who watch over the Earth can not only be found in ancient Egypt and Rome but also in several other cultures. Notable examples are the Aztecs who worshipped nine gods they called 'The Lords of the Night'. Nine gods are also said to have survived the Ragnarok (destruction of the Earth) in the Norse tradition and in Buddhist legends, Emperor Ashoka consulted with a secret society called the "Nine Unknown Men" who were said to have possessed all knowledge contained within the Universe. The ancient Etruscans of Italy believed in nine gods who influenced the fate of mankind and in Greek mythology Zeus led a council of nine gods.

A central belief runs throughout all the cultures who worshipped an ennead. In each case they are reported to have been closely involved in the evolution of the human race. They do, however, have an apocalyptic tendency for ancient legends state that they occasionally "have to clean things up", "wipe the slate clean" prior to reseeding life on this planet with an entirely new form of human being.[420]

And finally, The Nine, were referenced in an inscription at the ancient Mayan site Tortuguero, in the Mexican state of Tabasco. Erected around 669 A.D., it references the infamous date of December 21, 2012–which many in the New Age movement believed denoted the end for humanity, or at the very least the unfolding of a New World. This inscription states that:

> "At the next creation (i.e., 2012) the Bolon Yokte Ku, or Nine Support Gods, will return."

Many millions of people all over the World are awaiting this seismic event with bated breath but maybe they are missing the fact that they are already here and have been manipulating our reality for a very long time.

I just hope they do not force a record as bad as Donny Osmond's *Puppy Love* into the World consciousness ever again!

---

[420] The same beliefs are found in New Age spirituality which often refers to the impending emergence of a New Earth, hybrid-humans, and 5D consciousness.

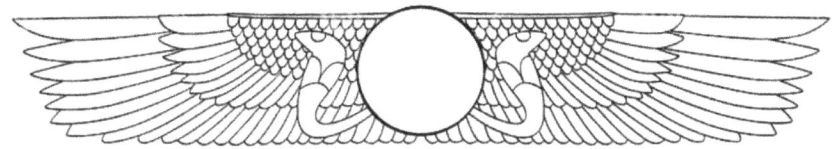

13. Touched by Sirian Hands

> "I never did believe in aliens. But since then, every day of my life, every time I see something moving in the sky, or blinking in the sky, I'm outside looking up for it."
>
> **Johnny Sands. American musician and actor.**

The imminent arrival of UFOs, a mass-landing, and the systematic takeover of mankind by extraterrestrials has been a prevalent theme within ufology ever since the early to mid-1950s—a time when when aliens from the planets Saturn, Venus and Mars assured contactees they would soon make themselves visible to governments throughout the World.

The "I'll believe in aliens when I see them landing on the White House lawn" meme subsequently become embedded into our culture as a result but only as a direct result of the lies and obfuscations that so often characterised verbal exchanges between contactees and otherworldly entities. Most UFO researchers are now starting to realise that the whole debate over whether extraterrestrials will ever demonstrate their existence to humanity is actually a red-herring; there is ample evidence to show that they are already here, working surreptitiously and with covert intent.

The Raëlians are one UFO cult that has never given up on the dream of making a traditional form of contact with "visitors from outer space" and have even built a Worldwide organisation based around the idea that the 'Elohim' are due to return shortly. Their patience seems limitless for they have been waiting ever since December 1973 when the group's leader, a French sports-car journalist and test driver by the name of

Claude Vorilhon, or Raël, (1946-present day) met with an extraterrestrial called "Yahweh".

More recently, the promise of imminent mass-landing by extraterrestrials in their craft emerged in 2013 when American spiritual teacher and film-distributor Tom T. Moore—who channels an extraterrestrial called "Antura" from a planet close to Sirius B, published his book *First Contact* in 2013. Moore's initial contact with Antara started on July 5, 2008 (the same, fateful date which underpins so many Sirius-related events). Following their initial meeting, Moore's ET contact presented him with a succession of insights into life, our Universe, and the future development of humanity. With reference to the alien agenda, the Sirian stated that the European Union would be releasing a cache of files related to the UFO phenomena in the summer of 2013 and that this would be followed by a mass-landing by Pleiadeans in 40-50ft. (12m-15m) wide spaceships sometime in 2015. Moore's contact also stated that the Sirians would subsequently appear to humanity in 2017.[421] None of these events transpired.[422]

Despite the long history of aliens who have promised to bless humanity with their presence, the event has not, and will not, ever occur—at least, not in the form that people are expecting. Some ETs (including the Pleiadeans and the Sirians) might think it would be a good idea to make some sort of grand entrance in order to impress governments and the human race but the briefest consideration of this idea reveals major flaws within it. In fact, the idea of a mass self-unveiling by extraterrestrials is probably en par with the equally pointless drive by some ufologists towards trying to force the US government to officially disclose the ET presence.

While the World waits with baited breathe for either, or both, of these events to take place, thousands—maybe millions—of individuals from every corner of this planet continue to have their lives turned completely upside down either as a result of trauma instigated by

---

[421] Moore. Tom T., *First Contact: Conversations with an ET*, Light Technology Publishing, 2013.
[422] None of those who predicted and promoted these dramatic events felt it necessary to explain why they never took place. Equally concerning is the fact that the public never held them to account for their provably false claims`.

13. Touched by Sirian Hands

meeting an extraterrestrial in the 'flesh' or following the sighting of a UFO. If the central intention behind the instigation of a mass-landing is to bring awareness of the existence of alien life to the majority of this planet's citizenry then they need not waste their time—it has already occurred!

How, where, and when did aliens penetrate mass-culture? The story of involvement between extraterrestrials and World governments—particularly the American government—has been documented by many hundreds of books on the subject. However, no definitive proof has ever been provided to confirm whether alien bodies are stored at Wright-Patterson Air Force Base or that UFOs are housed at Area 51. If this avenue of research fails to come up with concrete proof of the existence of extraterrestrials then it is necessary to look for evidence of their existence in other areas: places you would might least expect to find them!

Regarding ET involvement in the arts, one could argue that ET groups have infiltrated Hollywood and the film industry and that an alien connection to the TV series *Star Trek* (through the series founder Gene Roddenbury) is fairly certain. In addition, extraterrestrials may well have exercised an influence over the book publishing industry by encouraging the writing and publication of works that promote their agenda. These are areas of our cultural mass-media that have clearly been influenced, if not infiltrated by, the debate surrounding extraterrestrial life. In the previous chapter, I revealed how a 'fingerprint' of some sort of cosmic intelligence permeated early-1970s pop music. It is now time to consider whether, back in the 1960s and 1970s, ETs were used rock musicians as their conduit for contact.

Brothers from Muswell Hill

One of the most renown musicians who admit to having had first-hand experiences with the Sirian ET group is Dave Davies; guitarist with the British rock group The Kinks. As a band, The Kinks are rated as highly as many other classic British rock acts from the 1960s; including Led Zeppelin, The Who, Rolling Stones and The Beatles.

Formed in 1963 by brothers Ray and Dave Davies from Muswell Hill in London, the Kinks drew inspiration from a wide range of musical genres; including early rhythm and blues, rock and roll, music-hall, folk, and American country music. Despite the infusion of so many disparate musical influences, they are thought of as a quintessentially British band—one whose songs lyrics often featured a whimsical and light-hearted commentary on English suburban life.

The brothers musical careers began at the William Grimshaw Secondary Modern School where they formed the Ray Davies Quartet. Their debut gig at a school dance was well received and this encouraged the group to perform at local pubs and bars. In late 1962, Ray Davies left home to study at Hornsey College of Art where he pursued a variety of interests; including film, sketching, theatre, and music (mostly jazz and the blues).[423] Ray pursued his musical interests outside college by playing live; from which a number of opportunities led them to change their name to The Ramrods and to auditioned for a number of record labels. In early 1964, their manager secured them a contract with Pye Records and they recorded under the name The Kinks.

Their first single for the label was a cover of Little Richard's *Long Tall Sally*. This was released in February 1964 but received scant interest from the wider world. Their second single, *You Still Want Me*, also failed to sell in any numbers which this led to their record label becoming frustrated and impatient with the lack of return on their investment in the group. They threatened to cancel their contract with the Kinks should their third single prove to be a commercial flop. Fortunately it bucked the trend and this time Davies' song, *You Really Got Me*, hit the mark. It immediately launched the band's career by becoming an international hit: first by topping the UK singles charts and then by reaching the top 10 in the United States.[424]

Over the following decade the Kinks released a string of albums full of catchy melodies and classy lyrics. Their top-selling records, *Face to Face* (1966), *Something Else* (1967), *The Village Green Preservation Society* (1968), *Arthur* (1969), *Lola Versus Powerman* (1970), and

---
[423] Kitts, Thomas M., *Ray Davies: Not Like Everybody Else*, Routledge, 2008.
[424] https://en.wikipedia.org/wiki/The_Kinks_discography

Muswell Hillbillies (1971) placed the band in the forefront of the British music scene. However, the hits dried-up and an inevitable decline in the public interest followed. The band did enjoy a revival of interest in the late 1970s and early 1980s with their albums *Sleepwalker* (1977), *Misfits* (1978), *Low Budget* (1979), *Give the People What They Want* (1981), and *State of Confusion* (1983).

The Kinks' musical legacy is impressive. It lasted for over three decades and between 1964 and 1996 they released 24 studio and 4 live albums, had three UK number-one singles, and 18 Top 40 singles in the 1960s with further Top 40 hits in the 1970s and 1980s.[425]

Deep Darkness: Into the Light

Despite his somewhat rebellious nature and chequered early life, Dave Davies is a deeply spiritual person. This became evident when, in February 2010, he released an autobiographical documentary titled *Dave Davies Kronikles: Mystical Journey*. A mixture of film footage, interview segments, and archival material—including vintage home movies of The Kinks on tour—*Kronikles* offers an insight into his deep interest in Eastern philosophies, spiritualism, astrology, meditation and psychic phenomena. In the film he explained that:

> "It's something that I've touched on in interviews over the years, but I've never really had a chance to talk about at length. Music is extremely important to me, of course, but it's not the only thing. And I think that introducing people to the spiritual side gives some perspective to the music I've done. For years, it was very difficult to talk about these things, Davies adds. In the Kinks, we'd be having a few beers after a gig and I'd be reading a book on spiritualism or astrology[426], and someone would pick it up and

---

[425] Bowie was a fan of the Kinks—both musically and personally. He included a cover of their song *Where Have All the Good Times Gone?* on his album *Pin Ups* which was released in October 1973. The album featured his interpretations of songs that he often saw played live by their original artists at the Marquee Club, London, between 1964 and 1967.

[426] Dave Davies began studying astrology intensively soon after the birth of his first

they'd be horrified. With every step I'd take towards seeking out my spiritual life, I'd have to deal with family and friends thinking I'd gone a bit mad."

The musician also spoke openly about the intense feelings of loneliness and social isolation that both he and other free-thinkers invariably suffer from when trying to follow a path of self-illumination—an unfortunate consequence of following one own "True Will" and something touched upon earlier in connection with Bowie and Presley. As Davies explained:

"When I was very young and first became interested in these subjects," he recalls, "they were kept very hidden and very quiet. At the time, there were only a few people you could talk to about these things, and the information wasn't readily at hand. So, if you wanted to investigate this stuff, you really had to dig."

Dave's spiritual path took a strange twist once evening in August 1972 during a Kinks 40-date tour of the United States. Despite the tour's success he stayed in his New York hotel room all evening; overwhelmed with a deep sense of paranoia that left him feeling suicidal. His desperate feelings of loneliness and isolation suddenly intensified when, for no apparent reason, he felt a wave of black energy surround him. He described the experience as one in which he felt he was being "...devoured by a dark psychic swamp that was dragging (him) into its secret world in all its subtle and insidious power."

Davies was, quite naturally, terrified by this inexplicable intrusion into his personal space and given the emotional state he was already in he felt sure that this nebulous black force might take him down into a psychosis from which he might never return. Fortunately, an ex-girlfriend—who happened to be a psychiatric nurse—appeared and she managed to pull the musician out of his despair. Nevertheless, the

child in the autumn of 1967 and was able to cast horoscopes himself. (Source: Falk, Geoffrey D., *Rock and Holy Rollers: The Spiritual Beliefs of Chart-Topping Rock Stars in their Lives and Lyrics*, privately published, 2006.

13. Touched by Sirian Hands

experience left him completely transformed. He was quite sure that some sort of divine intervention had played a pivotal role in his rescue—as he later explained.

> "I know that I have been helped many times in my life, sometimes quite inexplicably.... I no longer believed in coincidence and from that day forward I started to believe in God."[427]

Dave consequently gave up drugs, turned vegetarian, and, much like his friend David Bowie, started to read books on the Jewish Kabbalah.

Left: Kinks guitarist Dave Davies in 1971.

In 1974—around the same time as the release of the Kink's two-part vaudevillian rock opera *Preservation*—Dave began studying occultism under the auspices of a trance medium in North London who claimed to be able to channel spiritual insights from "an ancient Egyptian child king." She proved instrumental in driving Dave's fascination in the world of psychism to the degree that, in an interview for his *Mystical Journey* documentary, he admitted to having once been close to leaving the music industry at the time in order to pursue his interest in psychic healing and mediumship.

In 1980, Dave released his first solo album, *AFL1-3603*. His subsequent records—both with the Kinks and as solo projects—included songs in which he specifically referenced the many dark and unexplored aspects to human consciousness. These included lyrics relating to astral projection (*Sleepwalker*), visualisation as an effective way to create reality (*Imagination's Real*), finding personal enlightenment

---

[427] Ibid.

(*Glamour*), and human communication via thought[428] (*Telepathy*).[429]

ONE FAMILY

Dave's esoteric interests extended beyond spirituality for he became equally fascinated in UFOs and believed in the existence of extraterrestrial life. In an interview with *Vulture* magazine, the musician revealed how he first became involved in the subject.[430]

> "I've had several experiences seeing UFOs. It was really interesting. I saw them in north Devon in England - lights and zigzags in the skies. Then when I started to dig deeper into my experience, I understood I was also getting communications - psychic impressions - from aliens."

He then described an event that changed the course of his life and strengthened his belief in otherworldly beings. It occurred in early 1982 when the Kinks were on a month-long tour of North America. On January 13–immediately prior to a sound-check for a show in Richmond, Virginia–Dave was relaxing alone in his hotel room when he suddenly felt a similar crushing force as the one that had incapacitated him in August 1972.[431] A pressure, which he described as being like an

---

[428] In a 2017 Dave was asked "What does Ray think about your interest in spiritualism and UFOs?"–to which he replied "He gives me a hard time about everything. The funny thing is that Ray is a very psychic person. It runs in our family. My mom had so much wisdom. Sometimes I'm just waking up from sleeping and I can swear I hear Ray's thinking – his ideas and songs. He's very sensitive. When he and I used to walk into the studio, we'd never really have to communicate verbally. I actually found it difficult when I started playing with other musicians because they wouldn't know what I was thinking. I'd be feeling, Why don't they just know what to do? [Laughs.] Life is strange and just gets stranger." (Source: Marchese, David, *The Kinks' Dave Davies on His Best Riff and UFO experiences*, Vulture, March 27, 2017.

[429] Falk, Geoffrey D., *Rock and Holy Rollers: The Spiritual Beliefs of Chart-Topping Rock Stars in their Lives and Lyrics*, privately published, 2006.

[430] David Marchese, *The Kinks' Dave Davies on His Best Riff and UFO experiences*, Vulture, March 27th, 2017.

[431] This event, took place on August 23–a date which appears on a regular basis in connection with the UFO myth. (John Lennon had his New York UFO experience exactly two years later on August 23, 1974). In another synchronous connection, The Kinks performed at the Wollman Skating Rink in New York the same night of Dave's 'black cloud' experience. They opened the gig with their hit song *Top of the Pops*.

13. Touched by Sirian Hands

"invisible metal band", tightened around his skull. This was accompanied by the sound of five different internal voices, each of which seemed to be coming from above his head. He explains:

> "I had felt strange all morning, distant, detached (sic.), as if observing my surroundings from afar... As I began sorting through my things the most astonishing thing happened. It was around 1.30 p.m. I looked up, startled by a sudden pressure in and around my head. It felt as if an invisible metal band or something had suddenly attached itself to my forehead and was pressing in on me. After a few moments it subsided, giving way to the strangest sensation that my whole head was expanding. Then it started again. It was as if some kind of psychic switch had somehow been turned on inside my head. Momentarily dazed, I tried to collect myself.
>
> All of a sudden, I began hearing these strange voices talking to me, in clear and unmistakable tones. Their voices were authoritative but warm and strangely comforting, which lessened my initial alarm. This was unlike anything I had experienced before. They felt as if they were a little distance above my head; that's how I perceived it at the time. For all I knew they could have been operating from thousands of miles away. I couldn't see them, but I could hear them and, more importantly, I could feel them and smell them.
>
> There were five distinct intelligences and each one gave off his or its own particular odor. It felt as if they were all male, but it is possible they may not all have been. The smells were very stimulating and deep, extremely pleasant and uplifting, and after a while I was able to distinguish one entity from another by its

smell. Smells that I cannot begin to describe, like exotic flowers, jasmine, but deeper, magnolia, but so full it was as if you could taste them, touch them.. .These intelligences communicated by pure energy and, most interestingly of all, by smell and sound.

They used the vibration of 'scent' or smell as a vehicle to convey various types of energy, of information. In between thought as we know it there is other information that is not readily assimilated by the conscious mind, but more through feeling. They were gently gaining control over my consciousness, but without actually tampering with my own ideas or thoughts.

The intelligences took complete control of my being. They showed me a hidden side of life, a view of a world within a world. My lower abdomen became numb and although I was able to walk around normally, I seemed to lack sensation there. They told me that I was not to have sex, the reason being that part of what was happening to me was due to the fact that they were manipulating latent forces in my body. In other words, they were transmuting sexual energy on to a higher vibrational level, enhancing consciousness.

The intelligences did not tell me who they were, but two of them said they had always been my spirit guides, and two others were entities that were not of this Earth but were involved in missions here as watchers and nurturers of our race."[432]

Later that evening Dave had another profound mystical experience while performing on-stage with the Kinks.

---

[432] Davies, Dave, *Kink: An Autobiography*, Hachette Books, 1997.

13. Touched by Sirian Hands

"I could see in the surrounding ethers mischievous demon-like creatures impinging themselves on the auric bodies of the unsuspecting crowd, impressing them with negative images and thoughts. Confronted by this bad energy, the intelligences poured a brilliant beam of white light through my forehead and out to the crowd. The results were startling. The same people suddenly looked more pleasant."

After the gig, Dave had experienced an almost Vince Taylor-like moment in which he "...became acutely aware of the presence of Jesus" and was shown "...unknown aspects of the savior (sic.) and his teachings" in a vision. It was a profound mystical experience and most of the songs Dave wrote for his self-produced 1983 album *Chosen People*,[433] were inspired by his spiritual experience on that fateful day.

The album also references another UFO/ET contact event he had. In the song *True Story* he wrote:

"As I walked home the other night,
I looked up to the sky.
It hit me like a light in the head.
He showed me of the world.
In a different way.
Oh, I'll never be the same.

By 1986, Dave was deeply involved in the study of UFOs. He purchased a camper van and spent the summer UFO spotting in North Wales. He saw so many unidentified craft that he submitted reports of his sightings to the UK Ministry of Defence. He received no reply.

In 2017, he released *Open Road*–an album he co-wrote with his son Russ. In promotional interviews for it he also spoke candidly about his UFO experiences and specifically about his connection to the Sirians.

---

[433] The lyrics for the album's title track, *Chosen People*, were based on the life story of the Lakota Indian medicine man, Black Elk.

"I'm sure there are many people in the world who can explain it better than I can. You have an experience with a UFO, and you keep those feelings, and then it gets into your subconscious and super-conscious. When I investigated what those feelings could be, when I got really into ufology, I could've sworn I was having connections with the Dog Star, with Sirius. Sirius has very deep connections with Earth."[434]

STEVE BOUCHER AND HARMONY GROVE

Dave Davies is one example of a musician who had a psychic interaction with Sirians. There are, however, other musicians who are equally convinced that they had a close-up, physical exchange with beings from the same star.

One of the most fascinating accounts of Sirian contact is told by Steve Boucher (1953-present day) who, back in the early 1970s, was a member of a rock band from Ontario called Harmony Grove. On October 17, 1971– following a gig at the American Hotel in Niagara-on-the-Lake–the group were invited to provide the musical entertainment at a party in Vineland to which they enthusiastically agreed. Once the party was over the musicians started their journey home. At some point during the early hours the driver of the van they were traveling in encountered a large obstacle stationary in the road ahead. He applied his brakes and brought the vehicle to a halt. Peering out through the windows, the musicians were astonished to find that the object was in fact a large, brightly-lit, saucer-shaped craft, –an object Boucher later described as "...greyish in colour, with portholes and a dome on the top of it."

Recalling the event in greater detail sometime afterwards he added:

"It had lights panning back and forth all over the place... blue lights coming out of the bottom of it that

---

[434] David Marchese, *The Kinks' Dave Davies on His Best Riff and UFO experiences*, Vulture, March 27, 2017.

> scanned the road like searchlights. There are little red lights around the perimeter. I could hear all these sounds coming out of it, sounds like a street sweeper makes, or like pneumatic air pressure being released, things like that. It looked hot like it had been traveling fast. There was heat around it."

The group of youngsters panicked and the driver attempted to turn the van around but the vehicle's controls failed to respond. Unable to flee the scene they were forced to watch with open mouths as four alien beings emerged from the craft, walked towards them, surrounded the vehicle, and then attempted to enter it. One of them succeeded in forcing the driver's door open which alarmed its occupants even more. They looked around them for anything that they could use to defend themselves with but each one instantly became frozen in their seats. They were as immovable as their vehicle.

It is at this point that the band's memory of the incident proved hazy and each musician found it difficult to recall exactly what had happened next but in 1982, after coming across a copy of the classic ET contact book *Missing Time*, Steve Boucher wrote to its author Budd Hopkins (1931-2011) and shared his 1971 extraterrestrial encounter with him. Hopkins wrote back and invited Boucher to take part in a course of hypnotic regression which he felt might help the musician access subconscious memories related to the incident.[435] Boucher agreed and in his first session the musician was able to provide a clearer account of that night–starting with his interaction with the first alien.

> "I'm trying to get a look at his face. His eyes are very dark... seems to have a ridge above his eyes where an eyebrow should be, but there isn't one. His head is very large. I'm seeing the eyes a little different now. His mouth kind of droops down at the sides; it is just a small mouth, like a slit, and it drops down a little at

---

[435] A report into the incident titled *Canadian Rock-Band Abducted?* by the Canadian UFO Research Network (CUFORN) appeared in *Flying Saucer Review*, Volume 29, Number. 3 in 1984.

the sides."[436]

Boucher then recalled that the aliens had coerced the band into leaving the confines of their vehicle and had then made them walk back towards their craft.

> "I can see the shape of the ship a lot more clearly now. It's silvery, metallic... looks like aluminium and the door is open. There's a wall inside of the door, and the steps go around into it... metallic steps. They were corrugated looking. And there's a little overhang. They take us up these steps, it is dark, and there's a passageway. The walls look black and dark. Then it kind of curves around to the left, and inside the ship, it's lit."

At this point, Boucher was forced to undergo a medical examination by the aliens.

> "I remember some big machine like a dentist's machine there over top of me... a big metallic machine with an arm on it. Sort of a thing pointing down that looked like a drill or a big spike or something. They had this big machine there that had all kinds of arms on it with different devices, and the aliens were examining me with parts of this thing, checking me over. They had little bags with samples that they had taken from me, hair, and things."

Eventually, the aliens allowed Boucher to leave and exit the craft.

> "The leader was standing there by the door. He started to tell me things that touched me, things about myself, and my life. It was like he knew me. There was some affinity between him and I. It was almost like he was a family member. I felt very close

---
[436] Boucher, Steve, *Beyond the Extraterrestrial Firewall: An Experiencers Point of View*, independently published, 2020.

> to him. Just this feeling alone made me feel sad. It was like love. The kind of love you feel for a best friend or someone you care for. I think this is where I started crying. I wasn't crying loud, but it just brought tears to my eyes. He told me he would see me again, that there was lots of work yet to be done, and that I had been a very good subject."

During their extended conversation–which included a demonstration by Boucher of how he played his bass recorder–the alien turned the conversation towards a more personal theme.

> "He said that he was going to give me a purpose, that I would be a great help to my friends and people around me. There were things that he said that made me feel good. He left me with a feeling of usefulness that I'd helped them and that he was grateful. I was so emotionally tied up in what he was saying. It was hitting me deeply. He decided to break the tension by asking me if there was something that I had, that I wanted to show him. I didn't want the tension to be broken. I was still thinking about what he had said."

Despite the mind-challenging experience of his ET contact, Steve Boucher continued working in the music industry and became a seasoned musician, singer, songwriter, and multi-instrumentalist; playing with a variety folk, jazz and rock bands. However, he never forgot his meeting with the aliens and in 2016 decided that it was time to go public; to share his recollections of extraterrestrial contact and to explain how "they" had forever changed his life by formulating his strong spiritual beliefs.[437]

In 202, he published, *Beyond the Extraterrestrial Firewall: an Experiencer's Point of View*–his recollection of the 1971 ET incident. In it he describes how it "... led him on an explorative journey into religion, Gnosticism, reincarnation, interdimensional portals, quantum

---

[437] https://experiencer.ca/books/

mechanics, the simulated holographic universe hypothesis, multidimensional realities, mysticism, spirituality and eventually consciousness."[438]

Many of these esoteric topics appeared in the lyrics of his song *The Land of the Midnight Sun*.

> *"They say we're nearing a polar change.*
> *The sea floor's rising and the rivers reversing.*
> *UFOs appearing in the skies*
>
> *Some warning men with their angelic cries*
> *They were there and saw it happen before.*
> *Now they're warning us what we're in for*
> *Better get out before it's too late.*
>
> *Lest we suffer this horrible fate*
> *When the ground starts crackin' and the sea starts splashin'*
> *And the rivers pour over and the voice in the sky says.*
> *We are entering the land of the midnight sun.*
> *Into the land of the midnight sun..."*

Boucher's lyric "*The Land of the Midnight Sun*" specifically relates to the star Sirius as a source from which black (i.e. 'invisible'), light is ejected. His lyrical reference "*We are entering the land...*", (i.e., increasingly falling under the influence of its Ray) references a belief within astronomy that the star (system) is hurtling towards the Earth on its return to our Solar System.

When summing up his life, ET experiences, and general spiritual philosophy, Boucher stated about humanity's possible cosmic future:

> "That time is now. The message that was given to me is currently unfolding. There is an event soon to take place, which will change our reality forever. It is

---
[438] Boucher, Steve and Cameron, Grant, *Beyond the Extraterrestrial Firewall: an Experiencer's Point of View*, Independently published, 2020.

spoken of in many ancient writings from cultures all over the world. We might call it the 'ascension.' The bible calls it the 'harvest.' Christians call it the 'rapture.' I won't get into the details of what this event entails at this time, but for now, let me say that when this event occurs, the veil over our conscious minds will be lifted and the illusion of separation that we now experience, will diminish, and we will experience our harmonious oneness with all of creation."[439]

JOHNNY SANDS AND THE EXPLODING SPHERE

Steve Boucher and Harmony Grove's contact with extraterrestrials in 1971 is not an isolated case and is similar to one experienced a few years later by country and western singer Johnny Sands.

In an interview with Brent Raynes in June 2009[440], Sands–a registered Native American from Cherokee, North Carolina–explained that he had 35 years of experience in the music business as a singer/songwriter[441] and had been employed as a professional stuntman on such hit US TV series as The Wild, Wild West and High Chaparral.[442]

In the same interview, Sands revealed details of an other-worldly event that happened to him late in the evening of January 29, 1976. The musician had just completed a show in Nevada and was driving from Pahrump to his home in Las Vegas in preparation for an appearance at the Sierra Hotel. This was a promotional tour for his latest album and he was part way through a string of media appearances, live performances, and newspaper interviews. Driving down Blue Diamond Road–20 miles from Las Vegas city center– he lost his bearings. Stopping the car to check his map, Sands decided to turn around and take a different route.

[439] Ibid.
[440] Raynes, Brent, An Interview With Johnny Sands - Singer, Songwriter, Stuntman, Native American, and an Alien and MIB Eyewitness! Alternate Perceptions Magazine, Issue #138, July 2009.
[441] Sands performed on NBC's Today Show and Grand Ole Opry and worked with Charlie Daniels, Razzy Bailey, Merle Haggard, and Conway Twitty.
[442] Sands worked on a variety of popular He worked with Elvis Presley in two of his motion pictures: Charro and Roustabout.

As he did so, something in the sky caught his eye—a 60ft. (18m.) long, cigar-shaped object at an altitude of around 1,000ft. (304m.). He presumed it was a plane coming into land at a local airport but changed his mind when he saw it was "rusty orange" in colour and had a "large, round ring" around its girth. He also noticed windows, or portholes, and a series of flashing red and white lights positioned along each side.

At this point his car which inexplicably malfunctioned. Thinking it must be running out of fuel he freewheeled over to the side of the road, got out, opened the cover to the gas tank, and shook the side of the vehicle to see if he could detect liquid inside. Satisfied that a lack of fuel was not the reason for the car's sudden stalling he raised its hood intending to inspect the engine for possible signs of mechanical failure. As he did so, he happened to look skyward again and saw that the object had changed position and was now hovering directly above him. To his utter amazement, it then emitted a powerful beam of light which hit the ground around three or four hundred feet in front of him. From within it emerged two humanoid figures who walked slowly towards him. Sands panicked, who attempted to run but found he was unable to move: completely trapped in a suspended state. The strange figures drew closer and Sands was able to make out their physical features. He described them as: "...around 5' 7"/5' 8" tall, muscular in build, and with a pale complexion....they had no hair, eyebrows, or ears, sported very wide noses and appeared to have mouths that were devoid of teeth." Strangest of all, he saw growths extending out from the sides of their necks which he described as "fish-gills". These were in constant state of motion: as if pulsating or breathing. Sands said their bodies were covered in black, all-encompassing overalls with no visible seams. Later on, when one of the humanoids brushed up against his arm he felt the "rough, heavy-duty sandpaper" texture of the creature's fabric.[443]

The leading visitor either walked, or floated, up to Sands and began a conversation with him. He spoke not from his mouth but from a white belt wrapped around his waist. A second belt, similar in colour and size to the first, stretched from his right shoulder down to the left-hand side

---

[443] Lowth, Marcus, *The Bizarre and Intriguing Johnny Sands Humanoid Encounter Case*, UFO Insight, 2019.

13. Touched by Sirian Hands

of his waist. Several silver objects hung from it and these emitted a sound similar to "an old-fashioned telephone engaged in a long-distance call."

Sands—who was visibly shaking but otherwise still unable to move—spluttered out the first thought that came to mind. "Where did you come from?" he asked. The stranger said nothing but responded by pointing a finger up into the sky. There was a brief pause and then the alien asked the frightened musician what he was doing there. "I'm doing a record. I'm a country music singer." he explained. His inquisitor appeared to understand this but before Sands could speak again the strange creature reached behind himself and withdrew a silver-coloured ball. This was initially the size of a grapefruit but as he held it out in his outstretched hand the sphere expanded until it was the size of a basketball. He let go of it. The sphere hovered and then started to rotate. The alien placed his fingers lightly over the top of it and a series of small firecrackers went off around them. The voice from the belt spoke again.

> "You see, nuclear explosions are causing a problem in the solar system. These things that you're setting off on this earth are causing troubles not only for you but for us and we cannot have this kind of thing to continue because it is going to upset the balance of everything that we intend for the future."

Sands, not knowing nor understanding a great deal about nuclear tests, was confused by this and felt threatened by the stranger's brusque tone. "But are you bringing harm to us?" he asked. The response was curt and cryptic. "Harm comes from evil." Sands quickly changed the subject. "How old are you?" he asked. Once again, the stranger's response was odd. "We are before the beginning of what you know as time." Sands struggled to comprehend the meaning behind this statement but asked "Why did you pick me? I'm a music guy. I don't know anything about science. I don't know anything about this." The alien replied, "You will know, in time, the reason we picked you." Sands then remembered that there were numerous US Bases in the locality. "Are you military?" he asked, to which the stranger answered "We are not military, but your leaders know about us. They know us and know all about us." and then added "Don't say anything about this meeting. We know where you are and will see you again!" With that parting remark there was a flash of light and both the aliens and their craft disappeared. Sands jumped back into his car, locked the doors, and turned the key to start the engine. It fired up without any trouble. In Sands' own words, he then "...peeled out for Las Vegas, like the devil was after me!"[444]

OFFICIAL INDIFFERENCE

Johnny Sands was so shaken by his contact with the aliens that he started to question his sanity. He became so concerned that he checked in at a local hospital later that same night. Tests were performed but they came back negative. Despite the craziness of his account, he was diagnosed as completely sane. This comforted the musician but he felt that officialdom needed to know about his experience and should be warned of any danger the aliens might pose to the local community. He approached the Las Vegas Police Department but found them either unwilling, or unable, to help him. They advised him to contact the Office of Special Investigations at the nearby Nellis Air Force Base which he did but they were equally unhelpful: stating that they no longer investigated UFOs. He was told to contact the Aerial Phenomenon Research Organization (APRO) in Tucson. He took their advice and found an organisation that was at last prepared to take his account seriously.

At APRO he was introduced John Romero who asked Sands permission to carry an independent assessment; including polygraph and voice-analysis tests. The musician agreed and a consultation was arranged with Dr Leo Sprinkle—a psychologist and a specialist in hypnotic regression.

By this time, the story of Sands' strange encounter had reached the public—mainly because of a front-page article that appeared in the Las Vegas Sun newspaper. Sands had not bargained for the immense level of public interest in his story and found it a major distraction as it effectively brought his promotional tour to a premature end. It seemed that everyone wanted to talk to him about his contact experience rather

---

[444] Andrews, Arlan Keith, *Country singer claims: I Saw Creatures from Another World*, UFO Update, Winter 1980, No. 5.

13. Touched by Sirian Hands

Above: Country and Western musician Johnny Sands holds up a book featuring an artist's interpretation of the amphibian being from Sirius he met in 1976.

than his music; which surprised him for, as he often pointed out in subsequent radio and TV interviews, there had been numerous reports of UFO sightings on the same night from locations throughout New Mexico, Arizona, and Nevada. All of them appeared to describe an object similar in appearance to the one he encountered.

The Men in Black

The first examination of Sands was a lie detector test run by Dr R. L. Nolan. Nolan was highly respected in his field of work and had nearly three decades of experience working with the FBI which made him difficult to deceive. He grilled Sands thoroughly, asking him question after question about the smallest details of his encounter; all of which the musician passed with 100% accuracy. Then voice analyst Dr Leo Sprinkle tested Sands for flaws in the way he had given his account but, once again, he passed. The only question mark that surfaced from Sand's examination was a suspicion that the musician had mentally suppressed a great deal of his experience and that additional details remained trapped within his subconscious mind.[445]

Meanwhile, John Remara wanted to create a pictorial reconstruction of the aliens Sands had conversed with so they took him into a room at the Sierra Hotel where the illustrator started to sketch out the basics facial features of the aliens according to Sands description of them. A few moments in he paused and a puzzled look came over his face. "I'm confused." said Remara. "They've got a nose, but they have gills. Why do you think they have those?" Sands replied, "I really don't know." It was at very moment that two unknown men, dressed in black, entered the room. Sands felt that they had been listening in on the two men's conversation.

> "One of the men, in an awkward lean, leaned over, almost like a robot, in front of my face, and he said, "That's because of where they're from.", he said. You see, there's a planet in the solar system of a star called Sirius and that planet is an aquatic type planet, which is half the time under water and half of it is on land, and because of the heat from Sirius and the sun, it's eight and a half light years from here, and he said that they would be part time under the water so that they could resist the heat. The rest of the time they'd be on land where they'd breathe through the nose. They're kind of like a frog."

The strangers made the two men feel uneasy but, despite not knowing who they were or what their authority was for making such a statement, they accepted it. Fortunately, the strangers did not remain in the room for long. One of them patted Sands on the shoulder in the same way he recalled the alien doing during their encounter. "We've got to go now, but we will see you again real soon." he said. Sands and Remara immediately prepared to leave but a hotel security guard entered and

---

[445] When Sands explained to his examiners that the aliens had warned him not to tell anyone about their meeting they concluded that some of his deeply-concealed recollections about the incident might relate to the US government. Even under hypnotic regression his subconscious mind appeared to refuse to reveal what these secrets might be.

asked them to follow him at which point the day's event took an even stranger turn. Sands explains:

> "Now look, we're talking about the Sahara Hotel. The halls would normally be jam packed, but for some reason there was nobody in any of the hallways. Nobody except us. These two men walked down the hallway with security right behind them. He was less than 15 feet behind them. They went out two double doors and before the doors could close, he grabbed the door and was pushing it open. When he went out, I saw him lean forward, look both ways, look across the street, he turned around and walked back. He was as pale as the alien I was just showing you on the picture.

He said, "You won't believe this. Them people vanished in mid-air. There's no car, there's nobody on the streets." That's a broad street out there, and he said, "Let's look at this hallway. There's nobody here. Why?" He said, "They've gone."

Sands associate, John Worth, joined them and was so concerned by the threatening actions of the men-in-black that he recommended taking avoiding action.

> "So we drove every alley, every alley, every alley all the way through Vegas out to his place and drove me into his parking lot and the minute that we stepped out of the car a long black Cadillac limousine drove down to the edge of the road, they rolled down two windows, a front one and a back one, and two men looked out the windows at us. It was those men that were in the casino. They looked at us, and then they turned their heads straight ahead, rolled the windows up and drove off. John said, "How could they have found us?" He was beginning to really wonder."

Long Gone

The next day, Sands received a phone call at John's house which he found strange as he had informed nobody of his whereabouts. The male caller said that he was from Dave Dunn's Filming Production Company based in Hollywood, California. He had just heard about Sand's contact with the Sirians and wanted to make a film documentary about the event. Sands was intrigued and arranged to meet him the following day.

> "When I knocked on the door this Dave Dunn (or who said he was Dave Dunn) answered the door. He was dressed in a black/greyish turtleneck shirt, black pants, and as I came in the door, I noticed that there were two more men. One standing in the back bedroom door looking out, not saying nothing, and one leaning against the bar. The house was completely furnished with looked like New England furniture. Heavy duty big time stuff, beautiful fireplace, a mirror with hand painted murals on the glass.
>
> I sat down in the chair like I'm sitting here, and we began to talk a little bit. He asked me about my experience and where it was at. The others were looking at him but not saying anything, and he said, "We need to write a song about this," and I said, "Well, I'm not really into a song right now." He said, "Well we need to write this about the aliens all pale white and about the headlights." He said, "You write this for me because I want to meet you tomorrow." I said, "Well I ain't never wrote a song quite that fast." He said, "Well with my help you can." He gave me some lay outs and he said, "You go home and work on it and we'll see you tomorrow."

Sands completed the song overnight and the next day he and Worth returned to the apartment only to discover upon their arrival that the Dave Dunn Filming Production Company had completely and inexplicably vacated their office. This unsettled the two men but they decided to investigate further and tracked down the building's

13. Touched by Sirian Hands

maintenance man for information pertaining his tenant. He was puzzled by Sand's questions and assured them that he had never heard of Dave Dunn which left Sands and Worth equally confused. They talked him into letting them into the apartment but once inside found it completely empty—devoid of all the heavy furniture they had noted it contained on their first visit. Given the size of the task in hand, Sands felt it would have been impossible for them to have completely emptied the premises during the few hours since they were last there.

> "We knocked on doors after doors after doors in that apartment complex. "Did you hear anything? Did you see anything?" Nobody had seen anything. They never seen these men. I said, "Did you ever see that black Cadillac?" One person said, "I thought that I might have seen it at one time." But they disappeared. Now John Worth run an investigation, APRO run an investigation, trying to locate these people. They don't exist. They didn't exist then, and they don't exist today."

Many years later, Sands shared his impressions of the experience:

> "But I just see these to be very intelligent, supernatural human beings. I don't know if they're from heaven. I don't know if they're from hell. But I believe they're powerful. I don't believe that they're here to do destruction to us. I believe they're here to find out our directions and I don't know where we're headed but if you're a Bible believer we're headed for destruction, and I think they're well-prepared and with knowledge to see and be aware and be prepared for the times of what is to come.
>
> I may be wrong. I'm not a genius, but I do know this. It was told to me that it was eight and a half light years to Sirius. In the time that they told me the telescope to see Sirius had just recently been invented. They

> didn't know what Sirius was. Yet Africa, and even before the Egyptians, talked about the star Sirius and they said that life-like aliens came from Sirius, and they rotated down in a thing like an ark and whirled down to the earth. There were thoughts that there were Gods that come from the Sirius to earth, far beyond what we even knew what the star was, they knew. They knew more about our solar system than we know today actually. How did they know that? It had to be because there were creations above us and more life with knowledge than we could ever imagine that we've got."

Sands eventually recorded the song he wrote for 'Dave Dunn' under the title *Blue Diamond Encounter* for his 2017 album *Trump That* and gave his analysis of it in a 2014 interview with Timothy Green Beckley

> "Yes, I wrote the song 33 years ago and didn't put it out 33 years ago. I'm 64 now and looking for more, so yes, I think I stood the statute of limitations with them, I think I was a good host to them, I hope that they come back and see me once again. I think I've been a gentleman with them, and I'd like to be that gentleman again. I'd like to answer any and all of their questions and see them on a first-hand basis. But the song told the story of my life, they helped me write it, and so I do have it."[446]

Despite the personal challenges, Sands remained grateful for his experience and the spiritual insights it led to. He remained in awe of the two humanoids he met on the road that night.

> "These people I seen were intelligent people. You could see wisdom in their face. You could see that strength in them. I mean, from an Indian

---

[446] *Men In Black and Alien Encounters With Country Singer Johnny Sands*, www.youtube.com/watch?v=Ls89j80aZc0

Reservation, we know power, we know strength, and we know what the feeling of a spiritual feeling is all about, and I could feel that spiritual, that strength, that realism far beyond what most people can understand. I knew that I was talking to somebody who not only just knew what they were talking about but knew far beyond what I could ever be talking about. I felt like a little pea on in a great big shell."

Here Sands states that he recognised a sense of "wisdom in the face" of his alien visitor. He does not say that he he felt the ET had 'highly-intelligent features' but that they were similar to those of someone who has attained deeper metaphysical rather than scientific insight into the nature of reality.

The question now has to be: what exactly is the nature of that "wisdom" and how might it connect with our understanding of the role that the Sirius Mythos plays in occultism?

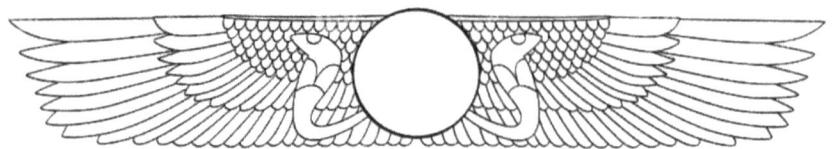

14. Lore of the Sacred Lion

> "It is my opinion that all these personalities are purely manifestations of the energies of the stellar logoi (the guiding intelligences) of the Siriun system, one of which carries a leonine aspect and the other a highly evolved homonid accent."

Ancient Egypt: The Sirius Connection, Murry Hope (1929-2012).

In 1939, archeologists located in Baden Wurtenburg, Germany discovered a remarkable statuette in the inner chamber of a cave. The 31cm. tall artifact was believed to have been sculpted from mammoth ivory around 40,000 years ago.

This was no ordinary sculpture. It depicted a human figure, with a slender body, standing erect (perhaps on tiptoes), legs apart, and with its arms hanging down its sides. However, its shoulders, hips and thighs were those of a cat and its head had been delicately carved into that of a lion. Labelled 'The Lion-Man', this statuette was classed by experts as the "oldest known representation of a being that does not exist in physical form but symbolises ideas about the supernatural."[447]

The archeologist's assumption that the figure had originally been carved to depict an ethereal rather than physical entity is rather a broad assumption to make for there is no evidence to suggest that this was the ancient sculptor's intention. Whether the figurine was meant to be viewed as literal or symbolic is not that important at this point. What is more significant is that the statuette is one of the earliest representations of a man-lion hybrid.

---
[447] Cook, Jill, *The Lion Man: An Ice Age masterpiece*, www.britishmuseum.org, 2017.

Why such a creature should even be considered a concept in southern Germany is strange enough but what is even more remarkable is that lion-headed Gods can be found within the religious beliefs of many cultures. It is in ancient Egypt that we discover a whole pantheon of lion-headed deities; including Maahes (the son of Ra), the feline goddesses Bastet (Bast), and Sekhmet. Each of these were portrayed in Egyptian art as a leonine form but demonstrating the ability to stand erect on two legs as if a humanoid. Another prominent deity from the old world was the seventh and eighth century protector of the god Vishnu who was known as Narasimha—a man-lion which historians believe to have originated from either Afghanistan or northern Pakistan.

Clearly there was once a widespread tradition of hybrid humanoid-feline species throughout the World and the fact that they were worshipped tells us something about the high regard humans had for these creatures.[448]

Murry Hope and the Paschats

Someone who studied the world of lion-headed beings in depth was the English occultist, writer, psychic, healer, and astrologer, Jacqueline Murry Hope. Her fascinating life-story is worth recounting in detail.

Murry, as she came to be known, was born on September 17, 1929, to Violet and Beresford Hope. Beresford died of throat cancer soon after her birth and immediately following her father's funeral her mother walked out of the family home; abandoning Murry to the care of her house-staff. It was the family nanny and cook-housekeeper, Rhoda Adams, or Berrie, who took responsibility for the young child and her sister. She looked after them in her own home in Blackheath, London—a property that Murry described as a "shrine to Victoriana" for it featured interior decor and antiquities from that period.

The girls were cared for with what she described as a "practical and grounded approach to life"—something which Murry felt imbued her with a strong sense of individuality and personal inner-strength

---
[448] These cross-hybrid lion/human beings are a reminder that some researchers regard the Face of Cydonia to have been deliberately carved in such a way that it represents a similar man-lion cross-over species.

throughout her formative years. They remained with Berrie for the following six years and during this period Murry had a variety of paranormal experiences; including strange and lucid dreams which made her feel that she was partially living in a parallel universe—one she was able to fully access while asleep. These were disorientating experiences for the young child who clearly had no idea what was taking place in and around her. In retrospect, Murry saw that she was developing latent psychic powers but they did leave her feeling increasingly distant from many around her. At times she felt that she was not even a child at heart but was living her life as an adult.[449]

At the age of seven, Murry's mother Violet visited the house and demanded the immediate return of her youngest daughter. Murry's sister had already been officially adopted by the nanny so it was agreed that she should live with her mother and new stepfather in a rather cramped apartment in a different part of London instead. The move was not a success. Murry contracted the highly contagious disease Diphtheria shortly afterwards and, afraid of catching it himself, her stepfather decided he did not want Murry in the house so her mother returned Murry to her former nanny before having another change of mind two years later when, once again, she demanded the re-return of her eight-year-old daughter. Nanny consented to her request and Murry was taken to live with the couple in a new property in Southall, London. It was while under their supervision that Murry suffered from further neglect which led to a court order forcing her to live under the care of the Sisters of Nazareth in their Catholic orphanage.

Life in the convent was hard. The older children were obligated to undertake their own washing and laundry while younger members were set to polishing the wooden floors. The nuns constantly meted-out harsh punishment for even the smallest transgression of their strict Catholic code and violence from them towards the children in their care became a normal part of daily life.

World War Two broke-out in in September 1939 and, fearing

---

[449] This is a common experience for 'old-Souls'—individuals who incarnate with strongly developed spiritual instincts. Murry did not even like other children, often feeling them to be cruel, unfeeling, and noisy.

intense bombing by the German Luftwaffe, the British government evacuated children from London and were taken to rural destinations for their safety. Murry was sent to the town of Devizes in Somerset and from there was moved to Heaton Park in Manchester where she remained until March 1944, prior returning to London and her former life with Berrie.

Murry had now become a young woman and in December 1948 she joined the WAAFs, or Women's Auxiliary Air Force which required her to attend a training centre at RAF Wilmslow in Cheshire. Now that she was beginning to find her feet in a more adult environment she took this opportunity to discover more about the strange, other-worldly events that had occurred to her during throughout her early life. She joined a local public library from which she borrowed numerous books on palmistry, numerology, astrology, and other related occult subjects.

Fate intervened once again and, following another debilitating period of illness, Murry had to prematurely end her service career. This forced her to return to civilian life in London where she found employment at the Officers Association of the British Legion. It was at this point in her life that Murry also expanded upon her love of music and joined a Roman Catholic Church in St. Albans simply so that she could pursue her passion for music and singing.

Hello-Archanophus

In 1951, at the age of twenty-two, Murry married her long-time boyfriend, Tony Neate. Soon afterwards they formed an agency providing singers, dancers, and dancing troupes to clients. They also hosted concerts at the Civic Hall, Croydon, which husband Tony produced and at which Murry sang. In addition to his business acumen, Murry felt Tony was also psychic. In 1955, with her encouragement, he joined the Marlybone Spiritualist Association (MSA) in Belgrave Square, London.

Despite her own interest in the subject, Murry did not join him at first but continued to pursue her love of the theatre by joining a West End production as a professional singer. Meanwhile, Tony's spiritual interests deepened as a result of his involvement in the MSA. He even organised seances and held demonstrations of his psychic skills which included psychometry and automatic-writing. Sadly Murry's involvement in the theatre came to an abrupt halt after a serious illness struck her down again. This resulted in her having more time to spend with Tony so she decided to join him at MSA meetings. These included in-depth group discussions on a chosen esoteric subject during which Murry demonstrated her understanding of the metaphysical knowledge she had gleaned reading the many library books borrowed during her time in Cheshire. A MSA member recommended that she broaden her range of spiritual interests even further by researching mythology, religion, ancient cultures, and Freudian/Jungian psychology.

It was during one of these evening psychic sessions that a discarnate entity appeared in the flat and spoke directly through Tony. It introduced itself as 'Hello-Archanophus' (HA); a term which translates to mean 'Chief High Priest of the Sun'. HA revealed to the group that he had once reigned in Atlantis when it was at its height as an advanced culture and centre of occult learning. This resonated with Murry for she had long-since held a deep fascinated for the fabled mystical realm.

HA reappeared at subsequent meetings and began instructing the group in how to make a deeper connection with Atlantis—a place Murry described as the "Old Country". Interest in the subject became so great that HA suggested that the group founded a formal society called "The Atlanteans". Members were in full agreement and it was founded on April 11, 1957.

The Atlanteans

News of the occult work being carried out by this new occult society spread quickly outside the group and attracted an increasing number of new members who were keen on joining in on the adventure. Society membership became so large that they were forced to relocate to the headquarters of the Vegetarian Society located on Earls Court Road, London. Around this time, HA suggested that Murry might want to write a book which focused upon recollections of time spent in Atlantis during

14. Lore of the Sacred Lion

her earlier incarnation. She took his advice and *Daughter of Atlantis* was published—although Murry was not pleased with the results and subsequently disowned it.[450]

The Atlanteans continued to go from strength to strength. They had grown so large that they established regional groups throughout the United Kingdom; including Bromley, Bristol, Cheltenham, Croydon, and Brighton. The society attracted a few celebrities; including actors, actresses and as others who were working in the film and theatrical industries.

Despite this success, things were not going well domestically. Outside of her metaphysical interests, Murry had resumed her stage career and in 1959 landed an audition at the Royal School of Music from which she obtained a scholarship for a course starting in February 1960. This was good news for Murry but for over a year she had felt that her twelve-year relationship with Tony was starting to crumble and that he had been looking for a way out of the marriage for some time. Circumstances brought it to a rapid end and Tony remarried soon afterwards.

Even though their marriage had folded, Murry and Tony continued working together on expanding The Atlanteans society. The group was now poised to become a major esoteric force in the UK and as a result were attracting attention from other leaders in the same field. One of those was George King (1919-1997). King was well known in ufology as the founder of the Aetherius Society in the mid-1950s. This UFO-cult emerged following a contact he had with extraterrestrial intelligence he came to know as the "Cosmic Masters"[451]—a group of advanced beings he said would help humanity solve its Earthly problems and aid its advancement into a New Age.[452]

---

[450] The book was later amended and updated prior to being republished under the title *The Ancient Wisdom of Atlantis* by The Aquarian Press in 1991.
[451] The voice King heard in 1954 supposedly told him to "Prepare yourself! You are to become the voice of Interplanetary Parliament."
[452] The Aetherius Society is best known for its use of a spiritual energy battery which the group believe to be capable of holding a powerful charge of ethereal, or Vril-like energy for an indefinite period of time. (Source: https://en.wikipedia.org/wiki/Aetherius_Society)

Left: Dr. George King: founder of the Aetherius Society and the channel for over 600 Cosmic Transmissions.

Hearing about the growing success of The Atlanteans, King approached Murry with a proposal to unite their two associations. Exactly what common ground he felt united his UFO-cult and an Atlantian occult society in open to conjecture for, at the time, the theological beliefs of the Aetherius Society were based around Theosophy, ufology, yoga, and a potpourri of similar theological concepts extracted from various world religions—most notably from Hinduism, Buddhism, and Christianity.

Either way Murry was less than impressed with the terms of King's proposal; which included his insistence that he would act as the head of any joint venture. She declined his offer.

CALIFORNIAN PSYCHOBABBLE

Murry met Michael Thorburn during Christmas 1964 and they married the following spring: for reasons that are unclear given that Murry described him in her memoirs as a "...man of few words and a brooding character." He had even darker secrets for, unknown to her at the time, Michael was an epileptic which made the task of creating an income to sustain them such a challenge that, with rapidly depleting savings, Murry was obliged to sell many of her most valued possessions.

To help with the challenges presented by the expanding network of Atlantean societies Tony took over more of its duties and felt that the society should move its base headquarters to the quiet, Regency town of Cheltenham in Gloucestershire, where they had already established an offshoot. Murry agreed and she and Michael sold their London flat and moved into a bungalow in Charlton Kings on the outskirts of the picturesque town. They were later joined by several other members of the Atlanteans society and, with the natural environment of the surrounding Cotswold Hills and the world-famous healing Spa waters of Cheltenham, Michael's health improved notably. The move out of the of grime and chaos of London was clearly beneficial to him for he found employment with the education department of the local authority in the nearby city of Gloucester.

Although their lives were improving at a personal level. Murry was concerned by the actions of the local Atlantean group and felt that her position as its founding leader was increasingly being undermined. On one occasion, during an intimate meal at a local restaurant, she and Michael overheard other members of the group discussing plans to break-away and establish their own commune. They agreed between themselves that they would keep their plans secret and not invite either Michael or Murry to join them. Murry was deeply hurt by their actions– so much so that she and Michael planned to sell their home in Charlton Kings and move to Brighton on the south coast of England. They amended their plans and returned to London instead where, as a temporary measure, they moved into the ground floor of a large property owned by popular radio and television presenter, *Sunday Times* journalist, author, and Atlantean member, Nerys Dee.

The schism within the Cheltenham lodge brought to a head more than just an awareness of a fracturing membership of the society of which Murry was head. She became disillusioned with the spiritual direction that the Atlanteans were now taking: feeling they were moving away from core principles and embracing what she described as "Californian psychobabble". The society appeared to be increasingly drawn towards a preoccupation with the 'self' rather than with remaining focussed on developing and strengthening a personal relationship with the ancient stellar tradition which, if we believe historians and researchers, formed the foundation for the original Atlantean Mystery Schools. Murry's response to what she saw as the Americanisation of spirituality was to focus upon strengthening her own occult interests and this resulted in her writing for the monthly UK publication *Prediction Magazine*.[453] The resulting exposure of herself as a writer led to a groundswell of support

---

[453] *Prediction Magazine* is the UK's oldest esoteric and astrological magazine having been established in 1936.

and she found herself in demand from the magazine's readers to lecture and hold spiritual workshops.[454]

Murry was changing as a person and so was her personal life. In the summer of 1978 she and Michael divorced following her discovery that he had been having and affair with a younger woman. While legal proceedings were taking place, Murry received a letter from Robert; an older man from Canada whom she had never met but who presented her with a marriage proposal. They agreed to meet in New York and to test their compatibility by travelling together for a few months. This went well and Murry agreed to marriage but in November 1978, as she was preparing to settle with her latest husband in Vancouver, she received news that one of the cats she had left behind in the UK was seriously ill. She packed her bags and returned to the UK in February 1979: knowing in her heart that she was unlikely ever to return to Canada. Robert joined her soon afterwards and Murry returned to Cheltenham where the newly-weds purchased a flat in the centre of town.

Robert did not take to living in England and was keen to return to his homeland. Their short marriage dissolved and once again, Murry found herself embroiled in divorce proceedings. Keen to remain in the flat she settled into the local community by joining several local music groups, teaching music, and then by joining the Cheltenham Opera Company where she met Jed Collard whom she subsequently married.

The End of Life

Sometime during the early years of her marriage to Jed, the Atlanteans changed their spiritual direction again and rebranded themselves as the Pegasus Trust. Despite their earlier rejection, they asked Murry aid them in making a transition over to the "Greek Ray". She agreed and composed a short, closing ceremony intended to mark the transfer from the Atlantean current.

Murry settled herself in preparation for the ritual but to her surprise

---

[454] Murry moved from occasional contributor to having a regular column at Prediction Magazine where she wrote under the name Athènes Williams. Williams was a family name. She also made occasional TV appearances on shows such as the *Derek Nimmo Show* and *Arrows of Time* with Dr Lyle Watson.

Hello-Archanophus made an unexpected appearance part-way through her oration. He addressed Murry directly and stated that she should continue to "...ground the Atlantean Ray into the Earth" as "Gaia required it to continue her own spiritual transformation." Evidently he was not overly impressed with The Atlanteans rejection of the Egyptian Ray that he espoused.

This was clearly a significant development but Murry appears to have put his request on the back-burner. In 1985, she and Jed purchased a former farmhouse in Devon requiring extensive renovation to bring it back to a liveable condition; which took all their money, time, and energy. Soured the experience of transforming the property, they very quickly sold-up and moved to the seaside town of Bognor Regis on England's south-coast where Murry's professional career took-off. In 1998 she embarked upon work-related trips to Australia and–having apparently made her peace with "psychobabble"–to California where she founded the Institute for the Study and Development of Transpersonal Sensitivity.

Jed's failure in business added to the pressure and forced them to sell their house and to move into rented accommodation. The strain of fulfilling her professional obligations resulted in yet another fracture within Murry's marriage. They divorced soon afterwards leaving Jed to return to the United States in May 1991 leaving Murry to relocate to Chichester where she hoped to establish a happier and more secure lifestyle. This failed to materialise. In January 1993–with increasingly depleted funds and a lack of a solid income–she fell on hard times once again. As if to compound her troubles, her landlord evicted her and she had to move into a local authority owned apartment.[455] This environment proved equally challenging for she was constantly harassed by local youths and her mental health deteriorated by this and other forms of anti-social behaviour taking place around her. By May 1993 she

---

[455] Around this time Murry had a couple of psychic experiences that do not fit into her Atlantean Ray work, and which are more commonly related directly with Sirius and Thelema. In the first she experienced what she described as a negative interaction with Aleister Crowley on the astral plane. On another occasion she met an entity who said to her "My name is John, but you can call me Horus - I have been waiting for you to come." (Source: Hope, Murry, *The Changeling*, The College of Psychic Studies, 1999.)

Left: Ancient Egypt: The Sirius Connection (1990 edition): Murry Hope's seminal work on the importance of Sirius to the ancient Egyptian culture.

Murry Hope

had had enough and moved into a converted stable on a small estate. This was also a temporary measure as it was condemned leading her to return to cramped Council accommodation.

A slight respite from her continuing woes came in 1995 when she was approached by her publisher, Element Books, with a request to redraft and expand a former title she had written for them in the 1980s. Murry agreed and this was published under the title *The Sirius Connection*. With royalties derived from its sales, she was able to clear her debts and purchase a small car which she used to travel around the country giving lectures and workshops. Murry, who was now of an advanced age, found the work tiring and went into retirement. Murry died on October 25, 2012, in Emsworth, West Sussex, aged 83. Her remains were cremated at Chichester Crematorium[456] on November 12, bringing to an end a remarkable life and highly productive incarnation.

THE LION PEOPLE

However, the story of Murry Hope's life does not end there. In 1980 she turned fifty years of age.[457] It proved to be a sobering experience and it brought her to the realisation that she should take stock of her life. This necessitated a complete reassessment of the occult impulses that had flowed through her ever since her early, unsettling psychic experiences she had as a young child. Her hectic (and often chaotic) life had made her too pre-occupied to evaluate them properly but she now sensed that this was a point in her life when she might search for a clearer

---

[456] Jacqueline Murry Hope: Obituary, Chichester Observer, Ref. 1-4432534)
[457] The same number of years it takes Sirius B to orbit Sirius A.

understanding strange, past-life memories which had emerged from the depths of her consciousness on so many occasions.

Murry took the plunge and, with the hope that with a little guidance the significance of her mysterious inner-life world might become revealed, she signed-up for a course of therapy with a hypnotherapist in Cheltenham. Murry was looking for some sense of closure regarding a long-term secret she had deliberately avoided sharing with anyone else.

In one session she confessed to her therapist that she had been having regular interaction with a small group of highly-intelligent 'creatures' she could only describe as "part-human and part-lion" in nature. She explained they had taken a central role in her life and had remained loyal to her for as long as she could remember; from her time as a young child when she experienced the acute sense of loss resulting from constant abandonment and neglect by her mother, through the endless succession of illnesses, losses of career opportunities, and broken relationships. Despite her life being an endless succession of personal struggle and intense hardship she always knew that she was being aided and supported by these leonine creatures who, during her darkest hours, would appear and instil within her a deep sense of calm, love, and peace.

During her first session of hypnosis, Murry was regressed to a stage where she was able to release trapped subconscious memories. She described observing herself many thousands of years ago, travelling at speed in a spacecraft which had developed a serious malfunction. Along with an eight-member crew she found herself in a life-and-death situation whereby they were struggling to make the journey back home.

The hypnotherapist asked for further details and Murry explained that both herself and her crew were leonine creatures and that the home planet they were attempting to return to was in the Sirius star system. She added that she knew her companions as the "Lion People". "What do they look like?" asked her therapist. Murry thought for a moment and replied.

"We are very tall, and very, very strong. Although we

> now walk upright, we are not unlike your lions, in that we have manes, and within the races on our planet there are several colours of skin and mane."[458]

This validation of her inner-world connection to the lion-headed entities was a pivotal experience in Murry's life. She continued her course of therapy and this led to an even deeper understanding of the lion species of which she had once been a member.

"Who are they?" asked her therapist during a subsequent session. Murry explained that they were "...beings from another time-zone which does not exist concurrently with our own, and which could loosely be described as representing our future." [459]

At a later date Murry revised her name for her feline-like companions and changed it from "Lion People" to "Paschats" which she formed from an amalgam of the Egyptian goddess Pasht—the ancient Egyptian lioness goddess of war—and 'chat' which is the French word for 'cat'.

In her autobiography titled *The Changeling* Murry describes the impact that the first Paschat session had on her.

> "From that moment on, these elusive doors of time were finally opened, and I was able to recall in some detail the life I had been privileged to enjoy among these gentle giants. As memories came streaming back, so a strong telepathic contact was forged with two of them in particular, Ka-ini and Mi-Kiki."

Murry strengthened the bond with these two leonine creatures and through them was able to access even more memories of her time spent living on a planet they described as orbiting Sirius A. Transcripts of communications between herself and her lion friends—recorded between 1980 and 1987—subsequently appeared in her books *The Lion People: Intercosmic Messages from the Future* (1989)[460] and *The*

---
[458] Hope, Murry, *The Changeling*, The College of Psychic Studies, 1999.
[459] Hope, Murry, *The Lion People: Intercosmic Messages from the Future*, Thoth Publications, 1988.
[460] Ibid.

14. Lore of the Sacred Lion

Paschats and the Crystal People (1992).[461] These weave a detailed history of the Paschats and their close neighbours the Crystal People who were said to have lived on a decaying planet called "Ishna". They also include advanced information on the structure of Paschat society, the different tribes to which they belong, and some of their general metaphysical teachings.

A ROYAL ROLE

Murry Hope's detailed description of her close association with the Paschats from Sirius is more significant than many in the world of ufology realise. Her first-hand account of them—albeit that it was given under hypnosis—may well offer an important insights into accounts of lion-headed deities seen by ancient cultures all over the world.

Were these creatures 'real' in the sense that they could be interacted with directly? Could the Neolithic Lion-Man statuette found in southern Germany have been someone's representation of this type of cross-breed extraterrestrial? Murry was insistent that the Paschats were/are very real creatures—albeit that they originate from a higher dimension reality and have an ability to hold 3D form.

For decades Murry's interaction with the lion-headed beings has been ignored with very few UFO researchers taking her claims seriously. Despite this, her books describing them and the form of society they have created, sold well and have even been republished in recent times. Nevertheless, many researchers have tended to classify her claims along with other rather spurious assertions made by some contactees and that these creatures are no more than an aspect of the imagination. Murry must have wonder that herself at times but confirmation that they do exist independently of herself emerged a few days after her initial session with the Cheltonian hypnotist.

One afternoon a group of friends paid Murry a visit. They might have expected it to have been an everyday social call but they were shocked to find that a tall, lion-like entity could clearly be seen standing directly behind Murry. Whether she had informed them earlier of her experience

---
[461] Hope. Murry, The Paschats and the Crystal People, Thoth Publications, 1992.

Left: The cover of Murry Hope's autobiography The Changeling (1990) in which she identifies herself as half-human and half-leonine.

with the Paschats is unknown but unlikely. Further confirmation of the presence of the lion-like humanoid came in the form of the visitors description of the creature which they said emitted a high-frequency energy they equated with the human qualities of deep love and intense compassion. This was exactly the same vibration that Murry had always sensed them carrying whenever they visited her to give her comfort as a psychologically wounded child.

Further circumstantial evidence that the lion-headed beings are real and not merely a figment of Murry Hope's and her friends imagination emerged shortly after the publication of her first book on the Paschats. It was read by an elderly American lady who claimed to have a doctorate in psychology. In a letter to Murry she explained that, back in the 1940s, she and a doctor used to practise meditating together. During one of their sessions they received insights into former lives they had both spent somewhere in the Sirius star system: she as a plant-like entity[462] and he as a lion-headed being.[463]

This is possibly one of the earliest records in our modern era of any individual claiming to have leonine, stellar lineage but in recent decades an increasing number of individuals have claimed to have had direct contact with the lion-headed extraterrestrials. These include James Gilliand, Simon Parkes, Carolyn Evers, Peter Slattery, Denise Le Fay,

[462] The *Ra Material* is a series of transcripts taken from tape recordings made by a small group of independent researchers during an experiment to communicate with extraterrestrial beings. In 1981 they contact made with an alien intelligence who identified itself as Ra, described by Don Elkins, one of the contactees, as a "sixth-density social memory complex". During the course of their communications Ra referred to tree-like entities who were said to originate from Sirius.
[463] Hope, Murry, The Changeling, The College of Psychic Studies, 1999.

14. Lore of the Sacred Lion

and Lyssa Royale.

Trying to piece together a clear understanding these somewhat enigmatic and shy creatures is not easy but the general consensus appears to be that the Sirian Paschats play an important role in determining the evolution of humanity, that they fight to rebalance injustices, and are deeply protective of their own kind. There is no real evidence that they are spiritual beings in any mystical sense but they do promote a form of sacredness that fails to fit into accepted New Age philosophy. In fact, there is some evidence that suggests they are more closely aligned to a deeply magickical or occult tradition.

Someone who has come to understand this better than most is Robert Masters (1927-present day)—a director at The Foundation for Mind Research. Masters has worked with the ancient Egyptian, lion-headed deity Sekhmet for decades. In the introduction to his book *The Goddess Sekhmet* he sums-up his impression of the goddess.

> "In opening yourself to Sekhmet, you open yourself to direct experience of what for thousands of years have been called the awful and numinous powers of the Divine and the Magical. You may eventually be led to fulfillments greater than any you have yet imagined. You may be seized by Sekhmet, and then unspeakable horrors as well as indescribable delights are among the possibilities."[464]

Sekhmet, Bastet, the Paschats, and lion-headed beings in general do express a unique and quite specific occult dynamic. Their 'current' or 'ray' has been recognised by historians and theologian for centuries: even if these creatures have not. It is now time to explore the sacred elements of their world realm and reveal some of their esoteric secrets.

---

[464] Masters, Robert, *The Goddess Sekhmet, Psychospiritual Exercises of the Fifth Way*, Llewellyn Publications, 1991.

Above: Wall relief of the lion-headed goddess Sekhmet at the Temple of Kom Ombo. Sekhmet is said to "breathe fire, and the hot winds of the desert were likened to her breath".

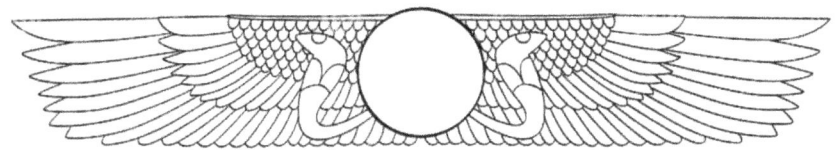

15. Pathway To the Star

> "Many, many years ago you came to Earth in service to humankind, as a being of pure light and truth. A Sirian light-being. The form that you took was the shape and guise of a White Lion. You were a White Lioness, and you were accompanied by your twin flame, who was a great White Lion. You were beats of truth and you carried the knowledge with you. And the place where you roamed is that place of which you know speak as Timbavati."
>
> **Mystery of the White Lions, Linda Tucker.**

On November 10, 1991, Linda Tucker—a high-flyer in international marketing and fashion—came face-to-face with her own, seemingly inevitable demise. Accompanied by her husband and six tourists, Linda was out in the Timbavati game reserve, late at night, trapped inside their broken-down Land Rover. Worse still, the group discovered that they were surrounded by a pride of lions who were slowly closing in on them. Base camp was located only a few kilometers away but with no radio with which to summon help, a dark, foreboding sense of fear fell came over the group when they realised that leaving the protection of their vehicle would mean near-certain death as the lions picked them off one by one.

In the stillness of the night they could now hear the slow, creeping advance of the hungry animals as they approached in preparation of making a kill. Hysteria overwhelmed members of the group and their piercing screams did little to calm the others. Now in a state of primal terror they resigned themselves to their fate. It was surely just a matter of time before the first lion struck and took its prey.

Just as their situation appeared to be its bleakest, out of the darkness of the Bushveld emerged a native African woman; dressed in tribal costume and carrying a baby on her back. Hearing the group's cries for help across the reserve, the African hurried to investigate. She strode fearlessly up to the encircling lions and her presence immediately had a calming effect on the animals. The snarling and growling heard earlier subsided, the animals slowly retreated, and the night fell silent once more. The stranger approached the group and spoke a few words in Tsonga to their driver. He immediately climbed out of his vehicle and started the trek back to base camp where he commandeered a second vehicle with which to rescue his stricken passengers.

This death-defying event left Linda a radically changed person. She returned to her former, highly pressurised job in the business world, but was unable to get the memories of that fateful night out of her mind. The corporate life she had been living became increasingly meaningless—to the extent that within three years she had become so depressed that she felt suicidal. In her book, *Saving the White Lions*, Linda describes the way that she felt at the time.

> "My disillusionment mounted day after day, every day, intensifying the emptiness I felt under the facade I showed to the outside world. When it came to my profession, I no longer enjoyed the thrill of leading trends, playing with people's minds, manipulating them into buying products they didn't need or really want. And personally, in my own everyday existence, I could no longer endure the hollow sense of barely living, all the while consuming—eating, buying, spending, utilising, wasting—and giving nothing back."[465]

Linda knew that she had to give up her city-life, house, career, even her marriage, prior to returning to Africa in search of the heroic woman who had saved the lives of her and her associates that night.

---
[465] Tucker, Linda, *Saving the White Lions: One Woman's Battle for Africa's Most Sacred Animal*, North Atlantic Books, 2013.

15. Pathway to the Star

Lion Queen of Timbavati

Maria Khosa was a beautiful woman. Aged somewhere between sixty and seventy years she had managed to retain a powerful and attractive physique. She was also a uniquely spiritual individual—someone who was blessed with shamanic insight which she said had been "gifted to her" after a cobra spat into her eyes causing one of them to change to a murky blue colour.

As a 'sangoma'—a medicine woman—Maria was deeply connected to an ancient lineage of shamans initiated into what were known as "sacred lion teachings". She regarded every member of the species as if they were a beloved member of her own family and this led her to becoming known as the "Lion Queen of Timbavati". Members of the indigenous population would travel on foot in great numbers over long distances to meet her—either to obtain shamanic healing or to glean insights into her profound spiritual knowledge.

Once Linda quit her job and put her personal affairs in order, she returned to the Timbavati—intent upon locating Maria whom she found "...living in conditions that were humble to the point of poverty." Despite offering so much to her community Maria did not seek any financial reward for her healing work. Her only source of income was from employment as a house cleaner and her accommodation had few facilities. At night she slept on a grass mat on the floor of her mud hut.

As the friendship between the two women developed they often talked about the night Maria rescued Linda and her group from the lions. Linda was still confused as to how the woman had been able to intervene and protect them from the animals with such ease and a demonstrable lack of fear. Maria explained that on the night in question she had approached the lions, entered into telepathic communication with them, and asked them to withdraw from the stricken group. Linda found this incredible and was fascinated to learn more about the shamanic lineage Maria espoused.

The same animals that had threatened Linda that night formed an essential part of the tradition that Maria had been born into. She explained to Linda that she held a deep-seated, spiritual reverence for all lions but felt that the most sacred of all were the White Lions—a rare variant of the species which African spiritual tradition maintains once represented the "Soul of Africa"—that was until they were hunted and poached into near extinction.

The White Lions are a variant of the leonine family. They are not albinos but a genetic rarity of 'panthera leo' which occur naturally.[466] According to African oral records, their existence in the Timbavati region had been known for over 400 years[467] but by 1991 there were none left roaming freely in the bushveld plains. Their decimation proved to be a tragedy on so many levels but according to Linda the loss of the White Lions in the wild carried a profound message for the rest of humanity.

> "Maria taught me to appreciate that there is an ancient contract with nature, which humankind has broken—to our detriment. Every contract involves a give and take—yet we humans expect that nature is simply here for the taking. We have raped, pillaged, exploited and destroyed virtually all the world's natural riches—and what have we given back? Where is our side of this contract?"[468]

Not only was the loss of these majestic creatures an ecological tragedy but it also lessened any opportunity to understand and appreciate the sacred tradition associated with them. As a lion shaman, Maria represented a unique spiritual impulse—a specific line of sacred teaching that was interwoven with the myth and legends surrounding these rare and elusive creatures. Even the region they once reigned in—the Timbavati—was said to exhibit magickal properties for, as Maria explained, the word Timbavati (Tsimba-vaati) means "the place where

---

[466] The earliest sighting of a White Lion in the wild by a European was Joyce Little in 1938. The earliest photographic record of the animals can be dated back to the 1970s.

[467] Cruickshank, K. M. and Robinson, T. J., Inheritance of the white coat colour phenotype in African lions (Panthera leo), 1997.

[468] Tucker, Linda, *White Lions: Reintroduction to Their Natural and Spiritual Homelands*, USDA Forest Service Proceedings RMRS-P-49. 2007.

something angelic came down to Earth from the heavens."[469]

Linda worked alongside Maria for several years and used the opportunity to learn as much as she could about the tribal wisdom connected to the lions. She absorbed their teachings so deeply that—in a similar way to that recounted by Murry Hope—she began to receive psychic messages from lion-beings in her dreams. One of Linda's recurring nightmares—which she had experienced ever since childhood—featured a huge male lion sporting a golden mane who she could see while in an astral state: staring down at her while she slept. Time and again she sensed his powerful presence so vividly that she was filled with deep-rooted terror and was jerked out of sleep screaming wildly. Linda shared details of these nightly experiences with Maria who explained that the lion in her dreams was her ancestral guardian and spiritual guide who also happened to live in physical form as a pride ruler within the Timbavati region.

As a nocturnal guide, Maria explained to Linda that her guardian lion was also attempting to relay to her messages that originated from her stellar-family, "...whom she sometimes referred to as the Lion People. She told me to record it all, because these messages might one day change the world."

Linda now recognised that her true calling in life was unfolding before her. She realised that not only did she have to share Maria's profound sacred lion wisdom with the rest of the World but that she had to make every effort to conserve what remained of White Lion teachings and to dedicate her resources towards the protection of the few animals that remained in captivity.[470]

---

[469] "Furthermore, 'tsimba' means 'lion' and 'vati' means 'to come down' so Timbavati could be translated as "place where the angelic lions came down" or "place where the starlions came down." (Source: Tucker, Linda, *Saving the White Lions: One Woman's Battle for Africa's Most Sacred Animal*, North Atlantic Books, 2013.)

[470] To ensure the survival of this legendary animal, Linda Tucker founded the Global White Lion Protection Trust with the intention of returning White Lions to their natural habitat via the White Lion Protection Plan™ which also works to ensure the protection of the cultural heritage of the Sepedi and Tsonga peoples who honour the White Lions as a sacred heritage. In 2012 she founded the White Lion Leadership™ Academy which is attended by local community leaders and students from around the globe.

Sacred Lion Teachings

In 1996 Linda's research into brought her into contact with the African lion-shaman, Vusamazulu 'Credo' Mutwa (1921-2020)—a native African who at the time was living in the foothills of the Magaliesberg Mountains. Credo was a 'sanusi'—the highest rank among the African medicine people. In later years he became the spokesperson for the indigenous African (Zulu) people and wrote several books about African mythology, traditional Zulu folklore, extraterrestrial encounters; as well as other biographical accounts detailing his own supernatural experiences. Credo both liked and came to trust Linda to the degree that he felt prepared to share his sacred knowledge of the White Lion tradition with her.

Credo was of the same opinion as Maria regarding the sacredness of these animals. He too believed that they held a secret that could save humanity during the upcoming period of planetary crisis—a period he described as "...a time during which a great celestial master-plan would unfold bringing severe consequences for our planet and all life upon it." Linda enjoyed her intimate conversations with Credo and always had a plethora of questions to ask him about the African lion-lore tradition. "How is Sirius connected with the great lion mystery, Credo?" she once asked him. The wise old African replied:

> "Our people believe that the Great Earth Mother came from the Sirius star system. The Sirius symbol was used in the ground plan of Great Zimbabwe." was his reply, and then, rather enigmatically added, "Sirius is the "eye" of the sky lion".

Linda not only studied under Credo and Maria but she also deepened her understanding of the sacred lion tradition with frequent visits to several major South African education centres in search of any information they might have on the subject. When not involved in academic pursuits she made strident efforts to get to the heart of her nightly visions and travelled into the outback in an attempt to track down the physical manifestation of her lion spirit-guide whom she now knew

15. PATHWAY TO THE STAR

as "Ingwavuma" (trans. Roar of the Creator). Eventually Linda made contact with her guardian lion but shortly afterwards, on August 22, 2000, he was killed—shot by a wealthy American trophy hunter who paid $25,000 for the privilege of ending his life. Linda describes the grief and immeasurable sense of loss she felt upon hearing of the death of Ingwavuma in her book *Saving the White Lions*. It is an account that is both palpable and heart-rending but in looking for a positive outcome from the tragic murder of such a beautiful animal a remarkable synchronicity emerged.

> "With a burning, aching, weeping heart at Ingwavuma's senseless murder, I submerged my sorrows in astrology books and sacred texts, trying to etch out meaning for my loss. It was then that I discovered the timing of this tragic event was profoundly poignant. The particular day of his death—that day only, and at that very time—the setting sun was in perfect alignment with Regulus, the heartstar of the Leo constellation. I knew from my studies of Ancient Egypt that the moment when the sun passes through Regulus is the pinnacle of cosmic events. In old Africa, as in Ancient Egypt, this moment symbolizes the birth, or death, of a Lion King or kingdom on Earth. The ancient mysteries of Egypt also indicate that this cosmic occurrence is the moment when the Pharaoh, or Lion King, becomes immortal and returns to the stars."[471]

From her death-defying encounter with a pride of hungry lions through to a deep understanding and appreciation of Africa's lion-lore lineage, Linda underwent an astounding psychospiritual transformation. The challenge she now faced was how she might best get the message contained within the lion tradition out to the rest of the World. She had a wealth of experience in marketing and promotion as a result of the time spent in the corporate world. She applied this in an

[471] Tucker, Linda, *Mystery of the White Lions: Children of the Sun God*, Hay House, 2010.

318

attempt to bring awareness of the precarious state of the few remaining White Lions in captivity but, in the end, it was the unnecessary death of her Sirian spirit guide, Ingwavuma that caught the attention of the international media..

From an occult perspective it is worth noting that, although drawn from a completely different spiritual tradition, the Jewish Gematria reveals a hidden side to this story. The numerical value of Linda's guide, Ingwavuma, is 1888. It is the same value as the term 'Shot heard around the World'. The bullet that put an end to Linda's Guardian Lion failed to garner much attention outside of the African states but it was sufficient to fuel interest in an even more significant event that took place on July 2, 2015, when a second 'Shot heard around the World' rang out and ignited universal anger. On this date another African lion, called Cecil (named after the famous South African Prime Minister Cecil Rhodes (1853-1902)) died in what many saw as a senseless and barbaric killing by a bow and arrow wielded by an American dentist called Walter Palmer. News of the event very quickly reverberated around the world.[472] Representatives of national governments, conservation societies, and animal rights groups were incensed and outraged by the hunter's actions and this resulted in a wide-scale condemnation of hunting practices in Africa. Fortunately, it led to major changes of policy in many associated institutions in the hope of avoiding a similar scenario.[473]

BETWEEN THE PAWS

So, from the Face of Mars to the Sphinx, the Paschats to the lion-shamen, and the lion deities of ancient Egypt to the tribal African healers of the Timbavati, the path that leads into the inner mysteries of the Sirius Mythos has been guarded by sacred leonines for millennia. In fact, wherever a lion appears within sacred texts and ancient teachings a mystery emerges that is as profound as it is deep. Sometimes you do not even have to go out looking for it: threads of its influence reach-out in an attempt to engage with those who hold within their hearts a genuine love

---

[472] https://en.wikipedia.org/wiki/Killing_of_Cecil_the_lion
[473] For more information about Linda Tucker's Global White Lion Protection Trust visit www.whitelions.org

15. Pathway to the Star

for these creatures. A good example of this occurred involving George Hunt Williamson.

Williamson (1926-1986)–aka Michael d' Obrenovic–was closely associated with George Adamski (1891-1965)–the grandfather of modern ufology. In 1954 Williamson published his first book titled *The Saucers Speak*[474] in which he described ouija-board sessions he held from 1952 onwards. He maintained that he had been able to make contact with several types of extraterrestrials using this method and that they originated from a variety of locations within our Solar System. He shared some of the information he gleaned from conversing with these ETs a lecture he gave in Detroit, Michigan, on June 21, 1954,

> "These saucers are coming from many different places in the universe. The only thing that men on earth can accept is a physical phenomena such as a saucer or mechanical device and even then some people in the world are laughing at flying saucers. Incidentally, we were told that these ships operate in a resonating electromagnetic magnetic field. They say we have not yet discovered the fourth grade primary force of the universe, which is what they are using. It is the same force that makes a space ship out of our own planet. ALL celestial bodies operate in a resonating electromagnetic magnetic field. The small craft have counter rotating wheels. They say that this power is to be ours also and that earth will in time be taken into the interplanetary brotherhood.
>
> They claim that at the present time there are fifty-one solar systems in the confederation and that they have over three and one-half million space craft surrounding our planet at the present time."

Williamson then mentioned in his presentation how the ETs he was in contact with appeared to have a religious aspect to them–which seems

---
[474] Other books by Williamson includes; *Other Tongues, Other Flesh* (1957), *Secret Places of the Lion* (1958), *UFOs Confidential* (1958), *Road in the Sky* (1959), and *Secret of the Andes* (1961).

strange given that religion is essentially a philosophical construct developed by the human race. He said:

> "I want to make it very clear that I am not representing any church or any particular group and my opinions are not important; I can only repeat what was said by the space people. They say life is eternal and that Christ is in charge of the planet earth. The saucer people are the "hosts" that were prophesied about as coming to earth proceeding the Second Coming of Christ. They say it is true that Christ will return and that there will be a judgment day. There will also be earthquakes, etc. We are in the transitional stage or in the beginning of a new dimension or new density right now. As the change is coming slowly we do not notice it too much. Many people say we are going from Pisces to Aquarius. These space people are here merely to help us, and to usher us into this new dimension -- usher us into this New Age."

GHW AND THE SACRED PLACE OF THE LION

In their biography titled *The Incredible Life of George Hunt Williamson,* its authors Michel Zirger and Maurizio Martinelli give an account of how, during a visit to Venice, Williamson happened to be walking across St. Mark's Square when he encountered a tall, majestic granite column—a grand basilica erected next to the Doge's Palace. Looking up, he caught sight of a stone-carved replication of a winged-lion which was supporting a copy of the Gospel associated with the saint.[475] As he focused in on it he felt giddy and started to lose consciousness. It was then that he spontaneously experienced a vivid vision in which he found himself deep inside the Great Pyramid of Giza. He 'saw' himself in a high gallery within the pyramid along which he

---

[475] The Lion of Saint Mark is used in Christianity to represent Mark the Evangelist. He is usually represented in the form of a winged lion. It also references the Leo/Lion element of the Tetramorphs.

'walked' until the vision brought him to the granite sarcophagus located within the King's Chamber. Looking around him, Williamson found he was not alone and that a small group of poorly-defined figures wearing black masks were standing nearby. Williamson had the strong impression that they had been waiting for him to appear in an astral state; ready for him to take part in a group initiation. It was then that Williamson heard them intone a mantra over and over again.

> "You shall go wherever the lion guards the entrances...! You shall go wherever the lion defends the entrances...! And you shall reveal to the world the secrets that lie hidden between the paws of the lion!...the secrets...the secrets..."[476]

The phrase "secrets that lie hidden between the paws of the lion!" references the Edgar Cayce (1877-1945) readings in which he maintained that there was a sealed library concealed deep beneath the Sphinx he called the Hall of Records. He maintained it was originally established by Atlanteans at a time when they wanted to conceal their knowledge regarding many esoteric subjects. Cayce stated that the entrance to the library was accessible via a hidden door which could be found between the paws of the Sphinx but that its exact position would only reveal itself at a time when mankind was ready to receive the revelations contained within the ancient records.[477]

Clearly something within the environment of St. Mark's Square had initiated inner-plane forces which invited Williamson to become an initiate into ancient knowledge connected to the Sacred Lion—a Siriun-related, occult impulse that seemingly transcends time, regional, theological, and ethnic constraints.[478]

---

[476] Zirger, Michel and Martinelli, Maurizio, *The Incredible Life of George Hunt Williamson*, Verdechiaro, 2017.
[477] Bunker, John and Pressler, Karen, *Our Research into Cayce's "Hall of Records"*, www.edgarcayce.org/12362
[478] Williamson also claimed that a secret society on Earth had been in contact with Sirius for thousands of years and that the emblem of this secret society is the Eye of Horus or 'All-seeing Eye'. American conspiracy researcher Jim Keith (1949-1999) arrived at a similar conclusion.

The Chronotopology of Charles Musès

Williamson had spontaneously tripped over what might be referred to as the 'Way of the Sacred Lion'—an occult path which leads to revelation regarding the sacred teachings of the ancient leonine-beings. This living, breathing, intensely sacred tradition, often singles out potential initiates whom it feels genuinely resonates to its unique energetic footprint. It forms part of an ancient spiritual heritage—one that is an essential aspect to the religious teachings of ancient Egypt.

One occultist who traced it back to this era and subsequently revealed some of its esoteric secrets was Charles Muses. Musès[479] was born in Jersey City on April 28, 1919. His father abandoned the family while he was young leaving his mother, a schoolteacher, to support them. Her success in bringing up Charles on her own is evidenced by his remarkable intellect, impressive academic attainments, and ability to master over twenty different languages. In 1938, Charles studied for a B.Sc. at the City University, New York; majoring in mathematics and chemistry. In 1947 he took an M.A. degree in philosophy at Columbia University, New York and then, in 1951, he received a Ph.D. from the same university for his thesis on Symbolic Logic.[480]

Charles Musès was a contentious character. In 1967, he developed a mathematical concept he called "Musean Hypernumbers" and described it as containing "hypercomplex number algebras such as complex numbers and split-complex numbers as primitive types." His system did not find favour among other mathematicians with most academics considering it to be without merit. Musès, on the other hand, insisted that his system had profound applications when applied to human consciousness, religion, and metaphysics. As he put it:

> "The contemplation and use of hypernumber forms

---

[479] Musès wrote under various pseudonyms including Musès, Musaios, Kyril Demys, Arthur Fontaine, Kenneth Demarest and Carl von Balmadis.

[480] During the same period Musès wrote, and later published, dissertations on the philosophy of the German seer Jacob Böhme and the philosopher Schopenhauer. So intrigued was he by Böhme that he established The Jacob Böhme Society of America and became editor of its quarterly journal. (Source: https://en.wikipedia.org/wiki/George_Hunt_Williamson)

and properties will prove and already has proved both by self-experience and teaching to be a most efficacious and irreplaceable method of evolving into conscious access the powers and capabilities of our superconscious selves. And that way man's future lies."[481]

Musès also proposed an astrological method which he called "Chronotopology"–a process by which he could measure the qualitative multidimensional structure of time. He described it in the following way.

> "The word astronomia, even the word mathematicus, meant someone who studied the stars, and in Kepler's sense they calculated the positions to know the qualities of time. But that's an independent hypothesis. The hypothesis of chronotopology is whether you have pointers of any kind – ionospheric disturbances, planetary orbits, or whatnot – independently of those pointers, time itself has a flux, has a wave motion, the object being to surf on time."

Falcon Wing Ranch

Musès also had a deep fascination in metaphysics and other strands of esoteric philosophy. In 1952, his fiancé, Charlotte Howell, purchased 640 acres of land in Indian Hills where the couple-built Falcon Wing Ranch—a spiritual learning center based around the concept of an Egyptian mystery school.[482] Its main building was carefully designed and constructed to measurements which replicated ancient sacred geometry. Each room was purposefully constructed with walls made from 8″ (20cm.) cement block reinforced with steel. These were said to resonate to different harmonics and could be applied in a variety of

---

[481] Musès, Charles, *Hypernumber*, Annals of the New York Academy of Sciences No. 138, 1967.
[482] While the ranch was being built, Charlotte established a non-fiction publishing house called The Falcon's Wing Press dealing in rare scholarly books. She and Charles married in April 1961 but passed away May 27, 1977, in Mexico City.

Unit	Symbol	Definition	Power Orbit formed by u^k
u_0	$z\ (\equiv 0)$	$z\ u_n = 0$ $\quad 0 \le n \le 7$	origin
u_1	$r\ (\equiv 1)$	$(+/-r)^{2n} = +r\ \ (+/-r)^{2n+1} = +/-\ r$	Point pair +1 und -1
u_2	$i\ (\equiv \sqrt{-1})$	$(+/-i)^2 = -r\ \ (+/-i)^4 = 1$	unit circle in the i,r-plane
u_3	$\mathcal{E}\ (\equiv \sqrt{+1})$	$(+/-\mathcal{E})^2 = +r\ \ \mathcal{E} \ne +/-1$	a circle (in a 4-D-space) with radius $2^{-0.5}$
u_4	w	$(+/-w)^6 = 1\ \ (+/-w)^2 = -1 + w$	A pair of mutually orthogonal ellipses given in Cartesian form $x^2 +/- xy + y^2 = 1$
u_5	p, q	$p^3 = q \quad q^3 = p \quad p^2 = q^2 = 0$	Curve whose polar form is given by $:a = [\cos(b)-\sin(b)]^2[\cos(b)+\sin(b)]$
u_6	Ω	$\Omega^k = \Omega \quad \Omega^{+/-\text{unendlich}} = 0$	a double, normalized Cornu spira
u_7	m	$m^k = m\ \ (\sqrt{(2m)})^2 = 0$ $(\sqrt{(2)})^2\ m^2 = 2m$ $(\sqrt{(3m)})^2 = -1$ $(\sqrt{(3)})^2\ m^2 = 3m$	A set of normalized ovals of Cassini
u_8	v	$v\ u_n = u_n{}^*$ $\quad 0 \le n \le 7$ where $u_n{}^*$ is the anti-form of u_n	A circle. The circumference undulates with fractional dimensional waves

Above: Museum Hypernumbers. secrets of the universe?
esoteric roles.

> The ranch comprised six bedrooms with three fully fitted libraries and a kitchen with an eating area big enough to accommodate many visiting students. Its crowning feature was a two-story master-suite with what he called an "Ascension Room" which featured a rounded ceiling and a cathedral-like window offering a nightly view of Denver city lights.

The center developed into an important spiritual hub within which Musès instructed his students in several esoteric sciences. These included astrology, numerology, and Egyptology. It was the study of the ancient Egyptian culture and history that fascinated Musès the most and this led him to several archaeological trips to the country—one of which landed him in trouble with Egyptian authorities when they accused him of trying to smuggle ancient artefacts out of their country.

Esoteric Beliefs

Musès' esoteric beliefs also courted controversy. He believed that

15. Pathway to the Star

humans are trapped in an alien and hostile world—a prison from which, under normal circumstances, the Soul is unable to escape. However, according to Musès, metaphysical keys exist which are capable of opening specific portals. By passing through them it is possible for an individual to escape its endless cycle of incarceration. He maintained that these protocols were known to the ancient Egyptians and that he was able to trace them as far back as the time of Seti: the second pharaoh of the Nineteenth Dynasty (c.1290BCE-1279BCE).

The portals that these codes opened were said by Musès to have enabled Egyptians to ascend in consciousness and become reborn in a completely new form on a higher plane. That ethereal realm was said to be the star Sirius. Musès was so convinced by his discoveries that he pledged to re-establish the long-lost connection to the star and "to be the first person in 3,000 years to make the journey back to it."

The bridge connecting the two realms was identified by Musès as "The Lion Path"—an ancient ceremonial and transformative process that was practiced by members of the Egyptian royal families and other high-ranking associates. It also purportedly symbolised the transmutation from the form exemplified by the Egypt's primary deity Osiris into a state that espoused the form, energy and dynamic qualities of the god Horus. Musès described the qualities of his process of transmigration in the following way:

> "To follow the Lion Path, one simply has to meditate in the correct way at specific times, tuning into astrological forces (using a completed re-invented astrology that includes two as yet undiscovered planets in our solar system, as well as Sirius A and B). The final force, the object of the Lion Path, is Sirius."[483]

Musès, now using the pen-name Musaios, included a timetable for the various processes a student had to take in his book *The Lion Path:*

---
[483] Picknett, Lynn and Prince, Clive, *The Stargate Conspiracy: The Truth about Extraterrestrial Life and the Mysteries of Ancient Egypt*, Berkley Publishing Group, 2001.

You Can Take It With You. This also contained a breakdown of the metaphysical principles underlying the transformation process.

> "The teaching was quite specific. The "Osiris" or inert pupal stage was the seat of divine transformative powers and became the numinous Egg or "golden lotus hud" – another Egyptian image that long antedates the Sanskrit hiranyagarbha or golden womb of the god-to- be. Out of the Egg or "Eye" will emerge the regenerated Osiris or Horus, brought forth by the womb-power of the Divine Mother, Isis- Neith-Nut, whose star was the brightest in our heavens, the glorious Sirius (Sothis). Compare the ancient cult of Venus (Aphrodite)-Urania and note the play between the German Ei "egg", the English Eye "eye" and German Auge ("eye")."[484]

Musès believed that a series of specific planetary configurations occurred during the 1980s and 1990s which offered humanity a rare window of opportunity by which to integrate Lion Path teachings. As an aid to his students wanting access to this information, his publishing house produced a range of support materials, workbooks, and spoken audio cassettes which he made available via mail-order. He also established teaching schedules at his Falcon Wing Ranch for any student requiring closer supervision during their own transition to Sirius.

The Lion Path sessions[485] Musès conducted started in the mid-1980s and continued until 1998 when the relevant planetary powers were said to have "metamorphosed and transformed into their pleromic (Divine) form". This was said to take place immediately prior to a climax, or <u>culmination, of</u> the planetary powers sometime between January and

---

[484] Musaios, *The Lion Path: You Can Take It With You,* House of Horus, First published 1985.

[485] Musès stated that "The set of foundational sessions of the Lion Path consists of some eight months (243 days, to be exact, which turns out to be exactly one rotation of the planet Venus on its axis). This should not be surprising as Venus is the lowest level of Sothis, which rules the entire Path." (Source: Musaios, *Grail Most Ancient: Advanced Guide for the Lion Path*, House of Horus, 1993.)

15. PATHWAY TO THE STAR

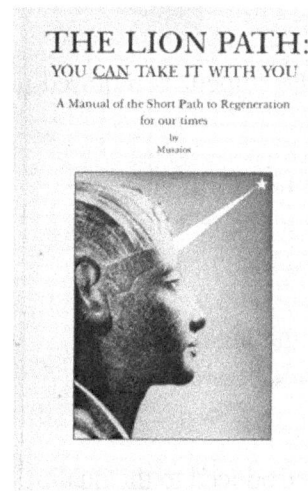

Left: Cover of The Lion Path by Musaios (Charles Muses) showing an initiates Third Eye connection to the star Sirius.

August 1999.

According to Musès this concluded the first phase of the Lion Path. A second phase was then initiated via "Cycles of Initiation" (based around the four ancient Celtic festivals; Samhain, Imbolc, Beltane. and Lughnasadh) and these were activated by specific lunar phases. It was only under these specific circumstances that a student would have the opportunity to make a connection with the Sirius star system.

Musès system, like his mathematical theory, seemed overly complicated to his students but he addressed this in his publication *The Eternal Door*[486] Musès in which he tried to encapsulate its complexities.

> "The decade 1984 -1994 covers a very short but very intense span of years for both humanity and the earth ~ a crucial interval of great spiritual decisions that will affect all the future thereafter of our unique planet and the life it bears on it. It was during that key period that the Lion Path was re-found and transmitted, and in which its first two "rainbows" of possible cycles were offered, plus the added bonus of a 28th Cycle, all starting before the periastron or syzygy of Sirius and Horus ("Sirius B") that occurs in April 1994. The question is now, how to continue the Lion Path thereafter? For the special dispensation of the synchrony of Pluto's Perihelion and the Sothic Periastron is a very rare event, even though a new surge of spiritual power was then

---
[486] Musaios, *The Eternal Door*, House of Horus, 1991.

released."

During the Lion Path transition process the student is required to focus upon the companion star to Sirius first.

> "For Sirius-B has the power to burst forth into supernova energy and brightness." and then, "Once at Sirius-B, the transition to Sirius-A, the great star of Sothis Herself, is almost immediate, and we find ourselves in her presence at the midnight hour following the previous midnight session of Horus."[487]

In his *Session 27*, students of Musès were introduced to the qualities of "Sothis Herself".

> "Personal harmony and love expands and becomes universal, but without losing the ability to love on a personal level. Lion Path candidates too have to remain in the presence of the Goddess, nourished by her in the following Pre-Pleromic Sessions, which further uplift the basic 7 imago powers into a form through which the Pleromic Powers can be ultimately evoked."[488]

In another of one of his House of Horus publications, titled The Eternal Door (1991), Musès revealed the nature of the energy underpinning the Lion Path. He states that it "...both begins in and is constantly, intimately and necessarily nourished by transcendent love – which is also and literally the flow of nourishment that permits the higher, non-molecular, and enduring body to grow." Musès considered the principle of love to be central to the process undertaken by his students.

> "The lack of that nurture would simply halt higher

---
[487] Musaios, *Grail Most Ancient: Advanced Guide for the Lion Path*, House of Horus, 1993.
[488] Ibid.

> development. Indeed, if we have not, before even beginning the Lion Path, developed sufficient love and insight to desire a world far beyond the sorrows and ills of the one in which we are presently ~ rooted in a savage ecology of 'who-eats-whom' — we are not ready for the Path, but are instead confined in our current stage of development, or lack of it."[489]

Charles Musès died on August 26, 2000. The place of his death and location of his burial is a mystery—which is a pity for we will never know whether he actually realised his ambition to escape the prison he maintained humanity is trapped within and complete his journey to Sirius

OUT OF AFRICA

Time and again it has become evident that Egypt—and specifically Africa as a whole—has, from a historical perspective, resonated closely to a number of aspects within the Sirius Mythos. From the Ennead of Heliopolis through to the sacred teachings of the White Lions, the hidden cultural and societal construct of the whole region clearly retains elements of a long-lost spiritual tradition which was so vast and endemic that it permeated the culture of Ancient Greece, through the veneration of Isis, and early Christianity via the esoteric principles within the Tetramorphs.

However hidden it might appear to be, this strand of esoteric wisdom emerged from within a small, little known area of East Africa in an astounding way. Its impact forever changed the direction of ufology and is perhaps the most convincing evidence that the human race has been in contact with visitors from outer space.

---

[489] Musaios, *The Eternal Door*, House of Horus, 1991.

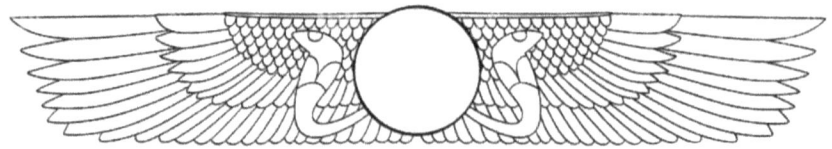

16. FROM WATERY DEPTHS

"After everything I've been through, the last thing I'm going to apologize for is my paranoia."

Richard Finney, DEMON DAYS - Angel of Light.

O ur story returns at this point to Uri Geller's mentor, Andrija Puharich who, in 1954, was re-drafted into the US Army in preparation for America's involvement in the Korean War. While Puharich was away, the work of his Round Table Foundation[490] was continued by his associate Arthur Middleton Young (1905-1995). Young was an American inventor, cosmologist, philosopher, astrologer, and author; but he was better known as the designer of Bell's Model 30 helicopter and the inventor of a stabiliser-bar used on several early Bell helicopter designs.[491]

Young had a deep fascination with the workings of the human mind and he developed a philosophical process which sought to integrate human thought and science. In 1972, he established the Institute for the Study of Consciousness in Berkeley, San Francisco later that year collaborated with Dr. Charles Musès on a publication titled *Consciousness and Reality: The Human Pivot Point*.[492]

---

[490] Picknett and Prince reported that there was another trustee at the Foundation; Alice Bouverie, who was working with a young Dutch psychic called Harry Stone. On June 16, 1954, she tested his psychometric powers by handing him a gold pendant that had belonged to Queen Tiye—the mother of Akhenaten. Stone went into a deep trance, uttered words in a strange language, and then drew a series of hieroglyphs. He also spoke about entering an underground hall where he came across a statue of a dog-headed man which came to life. (Source: Picknett, Lynn and Prince, Clive, *The Stargate Conspiracy*, Little, Brown & Company, 1999.)
[491] https://en.wikipedia.org/wiki/Arthur_M._Young
[492] Musès, Charles, and Young, Arthur M. (editors), *Consciousness and Reality: The Human Pivot Point*, Outerbridge and Lazard, 1972.

16. From Watery Depths

Although Young was a scientist at heart, he was deeply entrenched in the newly emerging Californian spirituality movement. As far back as the early 1940s he had pursued what we might refer to today as 'New Age' philosophies and practices. In his personal diaries he described his continuing attempt to perfect Hatha Yoga, referenced Zen Buddhism, and wrote about using Jungian dream analysis techniques.[493] In addition to these fringe topics, Young also had a deep interest in ufology—he was present at their very first appearance of The Nine at the Round Table Foundation in 1952/1953. American clinical psychologist Jerry Mishlove (1946-present day) spoke about Young's passionate interest in the subject.

> "He actively sought out... the most extreme literature in the UFO field. He wanted to read accounts from contactees and from aliens of the science and cosmology of extraterrestrial civilisations. He hoped that he might be able to expand and refine his theories based on this information. I know of no one more informed than Arthur of this very exotic area."[494]

The eminent scientist and UFO researcher Jacques Vallée (1939-present day) maintains that Young even lectured in the San Francisco area on the existence of underground alien bases which he said were located throughout the United States.[495]

THIRST FOR KNOWLEDGE

In 1965, Robert K. G. Temple (1945-present day) started studying at the University of Pennsylvania. He was assigned Arthur Young as his tutor.[496] One day, Temple found him engrossed in a book titled *African Skies*. Young explained that the book included a chapter about the

---
[493] Young, Arthur Morris, *The Bell Notes: A Journey from Physics to Metaphysics*, Delacorte Press/Seymour Lawrence, 1976.
[494] www.arthuryoung.com
[495] Vallée, Jacques, *Revelations: Alien Contact and Human Deception*, Ballentine Books, 1999.
[496] In 1966, at the age of twenty-one, Temple acted as the secretary for Young's Foundation for the Study of Consciousness.

Dogon tribe of Mali who maintained that they had a relationship to the Sirius star system: particularly with Sirius B. Temple showed a passing interest in this but thought little more about it until 1966 when, after moving back to London, he recalled the conversation his discussion with Young and decided he wanted to find out more. He wrote to his mentor and asked him whether he had any additional insights into this enigmatic group of tribesmen.

Young had commissioned a translation of a publication by the French anthropologists Marcel Griaule (1898-1956) and Germaine Dieterlen (1903-1999) titled *Le renard pâle* (trans. *The Pale Fox*). The source of this document is rather intriguing for according to Picknett and Prince, Young obtained it from Harry Smith (1929-1991) who was a high-ranking member of the O.T.O.[497] and an initiate of Aleister Crowley's magickal order Argentium Astrum (A.A.). Further details of the connection between Sirius, the A.A., and the O.T.O. will feature in a subsequent volume in this series but for the moment it is worth noting Picknett and Prince's commentary on Crowley's secret Argentium Astrum society.

> "The A. A. emphasised the importance of Sirius - the order was obliquely named after it - and believed in non-human intelligences, which, in postwar California, came to be seen as extraterrestrials."[498]

OGOTEMMELI AND THE NUMMO

Young sent Temple his copy of the *The Pale Fox* and Temple read it with great interest. It told the story of how, in October 1946, a blind elder of the Dogon tribe called Ogotemmeli taught Marcel Griaule the meaning behind the basic sacred symbols employed by the Dogon

---

[497] Ordo Templi Orientis (trans. Order of the Temple of the East or Order of Oriental Templars) is an occult initiatory organisation founded by German-speaking occultists Carl Kellner, Heinrich Klein, Franz Hartmann, and Theodor Reuss at the beginning of the 20th century. The society was modeled upon European Freemasonry but later changed to being more focused upon Crowley's religion of Thelema.
[498] Picknett, Lynn and Prince, Clive, *The Stargate Conspiracy: The Truth about Extraterrestrial Life and the Mysteries of Ancient Egypt*, Berkley Publishing Group, 2001.

16. From Watery Depths

religion. Prior to their exchange, Griaule had been living with the Dogon people for fifteen years: building up trust with the solitary and insular, cave-dwelling tribe. Its leader was now prepared to share Dogon spiritual and religious teachings—sacred insights that Ogotemmeli said were passed down to tribal leaders from one generation to the next. It was essentially an oral tradition comprised of thousands of signs which had taken him more than twenty years to learn. He told Griaule[499] that they revealed:

> "...their own systems of astronomy and calendrical measurements, methods of calculation and extensive anatomical and physiological knowledge, as well as a systematic pharmacopoeia".

The astronomical information that the tribe had regarding Sirius—which they called 'sigi tolo' (trans. Star of the Sigui)—was quite specific. They stated that Sirius does not stand alone but has two companion stars, 'po tolo' (trans. 'Digitaria star'), and 'emme ya tolo', (trans. 'Sorghum star').[500] Being that neither of these bodies are visible to the naked eye it is extraordinary that, back in the 1930s when Ogotemmeli shared his tribe's astrological knowledge with the Frenchman, science had not discovered Sirius C (its gravitational impact upon its neighbours was only detected in 1995). At the same time the existence of Sirius B was still only a concept in astrophysics; although Alvan Clark (1832-1897) claimed to have momentarily glimpsed it with his high-powered telescope in 1862. The Dogon also knew that the orbital period of Sirius B around Sirius A is 50 years and that its path is elliptical—something that did not emerge in the West until several decades after Ogotemmeli's revelations.

How on Earth could a 'primitive' tribe such as the Dogon have obtained such an extensive repository of knowledge regarding the Sirius

---

[499] Griaule, Marcel, *Conversations with Ogotemmêli: an Introduction To Dogon Religious Ideas*, 1965. (Originally published as DIEU D'EAU (Trans. *The Water God*) in 1948.

[500] Digitaria and Sorghum are part of a species of African cultivated grasses used to make porridge, bread and beer. Their seeds are tiny, and the Dogon used this as an indication of the relative size of Sirius B and Sirius C to Sirius A.

star system given the tribe's geographical remoteness and lack of any connection to western science? Griaule was equally intrigued by this to this and asked Ogotemmeli how the Dogon had originally come by this information. The tribal leader's response is astonishing. He explained that it had been taught to his ancestors by a group of "amphibious beings" they called the 'Nommo'—a word in Dogon that means 'to drink'.[501] He also maintained that these 'extraterrestrials' originated from the Sirius star system, landed nearby in a spaceship, met the Dogon, and passed onto them an extensive library of knowledge on a range of advanced astronomical subjects.

THE TRUE SIRIUS MYSTERY?

While he waited for a response from Young regarding his request for more information about the Dogon tribe, Temple paid frequent visits to the library of The Anthropological Society in London to discover what they might know. His efforts proved fruitful and he unearthed a document, also written in French, which he was unable to understand but he did recognise the word 'Sirius' in its text. This intrigued Temple so much that he obtained a copy from the library and commissioned a French scholar to translate it for him.

Arthur Young's response to Temple arrived soon afterwards and within his letter he enclosed a photostat copy of the relevant section of *African Skies* which he had shown to his young student years earlier. Using his mounting library of research material, Temple was able to publish a series of articles which, by his own account, were "universally ignored or criticised". Nevertheless, following encouragement from the science fiction novelist Arthur C. Clarke, Temple decided to ignore the rejections and in 1967 pressed ahead with a book about the Dogon and their assertion that they had been educated in astronomy by amphibious ET beings.[502] Once completed, Temple approached a publisher from whom he received an advance of £250. However, and to his intense

---
[501] The Nommo are said to have had green skinned covered in green hair, were humath the Dogon during the day but returned to rest in a "reservoir of water" they had created, during the night.
[502] The Dogon called the amphibious beings "The Monitors", which is similar to the phrase "The Guardians"—the name given to the Sirians who contacted Chris Bedisloe.

16. From Watery Depths

Left: The cover of the 1999 reprint of Robert K. Temple's The Sirius Mystery.

frustration, they sat on his manuscript for a further three years. It eventually went into print as *The Sirius Mystery: Was Earth visited by Intelligent beings from a planet in the system of the star of Sirius?* in 1976.

This time Temple's research was met more favourably. The book attracted rave reviews from all major UK newspapers and similar favourable appraisals by a broader range of publications such as *Nature Magazine*. It was also well-received by the Professor of Astronomy in Canada and received an endorsement from the President of the Royal Astronomical Society.

Title alone, *The Sirius Mystery* was an intriguing publication—one that captured the imaginations of public and academics alike. It became an international best-seller and has been translated into 44 different languages. In its introduction Temple shared his belief that:

> "...the information which the Dogon possess is really more than five thousand years old and was possessed by the ancient Egyptians in the pre-dynastic times before 3200 B.C., from which people I show that the Dogon are partially descended culturally, and probably physically as well."[503]

As for the amphibious beings who visited the Dogon, Temple's research revealed numerous ancient texts describing similar amphibious entities who were often categorised as 'fish-gods'. In the Sumerian and Babylonian tradition, they were referred to as 'Oannes'[504] and were

---
[503] Temple, Robert K. G., *The Sirius Mystery*: Was Earth visited by Intelligent beings from a planet in the system of the star of Sirius? St. Martin's Press, 1976.
[504] Other names for them were 'Musari' and 'Annedoti'.

Left: Carved stone images of Oannes (Adapa and Uan) who were Mesopotamian fish-gods said to have been sent by Ea to guide humanity.

portrayed as human in form but with the body of a fish. In each example of their appearance, Temple found that these ancient sources credit then with seeding humanity with advanced technical and scientific knowledge—just as they had to the Dogon.

Fierce debate surrounding the mystery of the Dogon and their knowledge of Sirius continued in the decades following the publication of Temple's research. In most cases the critique of Marcel Griaule's and Germaine Dieterlen original research has suggested that the astronomical and mathematic knowledge the Dogon acquired could have originated from other Western sources. This would seem extremely unlikely but what critics of the Dogon/ET theory fail to recognise is that the Dogon were/are not the only African tribe to venerate Sirius or to claim contact with the amphibious aliens. The Zulu nation in particular has been openly aware of their existence for a very long time.[505]

In his book *Hidden History: The Reptilian Agenda*, the renowned Zulu historian Credo Mutwa (who worked with Linda Tucker on her research into the sacred lion tradition) referred to the amphibious gods from Sirius in the following way:

> "In Africa these mysterious gods are known by various names, in West Africa, in the land of the Bumbara people these amphibian or reptilian sky gods are known as Zishwezi. The word zishwezi means either the swimmers or the divers or the

---

[505] Sutherland, Mary, *Dogons Could Hold the Answer to the Mysteries of Our Past*, www.burlingtonnews.net/dogons.html

gliders. It was said that these sky gods could dive from above the clouds down to the top of a mountain whenever they felt like it, they could also take deep dives into the bottom of the ocean and from there fetch magical objects and then bring them to the shore, placing them at the feet of the astonished black people.

In West Africa again, these creatures are called the Asa, which means the mighty ones of magic. It is from this word asa, a word that speaks great magical power that comes the name Asanti, which means a king, but literally means, 'the child of asaand' as you know Asanti gave birth to the word, Ashanti."

CHARLIE HICKSON AND THE AMPHIBIAN BEINGS

Part-fish, part-human: amphibious extraterrestrials were not only a feature of African tribal lore. They have also been encountered in modern America and featured in a contact case from 1973 when Charles Hickson and Calvin Parker—while fishing at a lake in Pascagoula, Mississippi—became caught up in a paranormal event of terrifying proportions.

Sometime between 9:30 p.m. and 10:00 p.m. on Thursday October 1, 1973, the two anglers were close to packing up their equipment and leaving. It had been a fruitless, frustrating day for them as the fish in the lake had been refusing to take their bait. Rather than return home with nothing to show for a day spent fishing they decided to remain where they were for a little while longer. As they cast their lines into the water for one last time their attention was suddenly drawn towards an odd, football shaped craft which they saw flying across the surface of the lake roughly 60-70ft. (18-21m.) away. They later estimated it to be around 30 feet (9m.) wide, had a small dome-like structure on top, a pair of windows in its body, and featured a pulsating blue light. It exhibited no sound that might suggest that it was powered by a combustion engine but made a sort of "zipping sound" as it moved.

The two men remained motionless—transfixed by the sight of the strange craft. To their utter amazement, the object came closer, stopped, and the end of it opened up to reveal a bright light shining from inside. Three beings then emerged and floated a short distance off the ground over to where the two men stood. As they approached, Charlie was able to get a clear look at them and later described the group as "having heads that came down to their shoulders (i.e., no necks) with something resembling a nose and a narrow slit for mouths". He also noted that they had "short, ear-like appendages sticking out of each side of their heads. Their arms were like those of a human but were overtly long in proportion to their bodies". Charlie also noticed that on the ends of their arms were hands which were webbed to the extent that they were almost like mitten-glove like in form. The rest of their bodies were wrinkled and greyish in colour with feet that Charlie could only describe as "being similar to those of an elephant".

The aliens approached the men and two of them grabbed Charles firmly by his left arm and was now in pain and unable to move. The other entity caught hold of Calvin and, with both men now completely incapacitated, the creatures led them back towards the craft which they entered and were immediately bathed in bright light. Charles recalled[506] how the two men stood still for a moment, trying to adjust their eyes to the intense glare.

> "Then I saw it: something that resembled a big eye seemed to come out directly from the wall. I tried to close my eyes but couldn't. For one instant I thought I felt pain in my left arm again. "What the hell have they done to me? I can't move." The "eye" came closer and stopped about six inches from my face. The end focused on me was a different colour or type of material than the rest of it. I tried again to close my eyes, but some force kept them open. The eye lingered there for a while then started to move down my body and returned to move over my entire body.

[506] Hickson, Charles, Mendez, William, *UFO Contact at Pascagula,* Wendelle C. Stevens, 1983.

16. FROM WATERY DEPTHS

No pain, no sensation. I remember trying to wiggle my toes, no way! "Why in hell don't they just stop me from breathing and let my life end here?"

The 'eye' finally completed its scan and then moved back into the wall from which it had emerged. The end of the craft opened once again, the aliens took hold of the men once again, marched them back to their fishing spot and returned to their craft which emitted a flash of bright, blue light before leaving the ground, rising vertically at speed, and disappearing completely from view.

Years later Charlie was able to recall further details regarding the incident while under hypnosis. He recollected a sort of buzzing sound coming from at least one of the aliens and that the two extensions he saw sticking out from the sides of his head appeared to move: retracting back and forth into the side of his skull in a regular motion. This description of the aliens facial features contains several similarities to the report given by Johnny Sands when he described his encounter with similar-looking creatures three years later in 1976. On this occasion Sands also noted that the aliens he met had moving protuberances on each side of their heads through which he felt they were breathing. He too noted that his aliens also had rough skin and that they appeared to float rather than walk. As we noted earlier, on that occasion the strange men dressed in black who appeared before Sands in the hotel room specifically identified these creatures as originating from Sirius; which causes us to conclude that the three beings who abducted the fishermen came from the same location as those that Sands met.

In the collection of channelled messages that comprise *The RA Material*, RA was asked about Charles Hickson's and Calvin Parker's experience on their fishing-trip in 1973–an event that later became known in ufology as "The Pascagoula Incident".

> **Questioner**: What density were the entities who picked up Charlie Hixson (sic.) from?
>
> **Ra**: I am Ra. The entities in whom you show such

interest are third-density beings of a fairly advanced order. We should express the understanding to you that these entities would not have used the mind/body/spirit complex, Charlie, except for the resolve of this entity before incarnation to be of service.

Questioner: What was the home or origin of the entities who picked up Charlie?

Ra: I am Ra. These entities are of the Sirius galaxy."[507]

SIRIAN TYPES

So far, we have identified three specific types of Sirian aliens who have appeared in physical form on this planet: the highly- advanced 'blue beings, the 'amphibious types', and the 'lion-heads'. Human interaction with any of these entities can be is a traumatic experience for it completely deconstructs the core beliefs of the experiencer. Accounts given by seemingly sane individuals following their reported encounter with them tend to be so divorced from what we accept as normality that most people's response is to immediately dismiss them as pure fantasy. In addition, those clandestine forces who have a vested interest in keeping a lid on extraterrestrial disclosure find it tempting to discredit individuals who, with no small amount of bravery, have shared their remarkable stories. These normal, ever-day people have nothing to gain and everything to lose by so doing.

Discrediting an individual who has specific knowledge or understanding regarding the true nature of the subject of extraterrestrials is one thing, but the outright vilification of them once the knowledge they share becomes available to a wider audience is another. This is an unfortunate aspect of the Sirian Mythos and a topic I will engage with more fully in subsequent volumes in this series of books. However, at this point it is worth revealing some nefarious activity connected with Robert Temple and the publication of his *The*

---

[507] Elkins, Donald, Rueckert, Carla, McCarty, James, *The RA Material: Book One*, Whitford Press, 1984.

16. FROM WATERY DEPTHS

Sirius Mystery book in 1976.

Firstly—and by way of forming a background to this story—it is worth sharing the experiences of the American writer and occultist Robert Anton Wilson (1932-2007) who documented his own experiences with the star Sirius in his *Cosmic Trigger* trilogy (published in 1977, 1991, and 1995 respectively); as well as in his *Illuminatus* books which first appeared in 1975). Wilson maintained that undisclosed Masonic contacts within the United States and Europe told him that the secret of their 33rd-Degree—the highest known rank in Freemasonry—was an admission that the Craft were in contact with intelligent beings from Sirius—something they had been trying to keep secret for a very long time.

If this is true then it is perhaps not too surprising to find that researchers investigating the Sirius Mythos from a position outside the remit of such secret societies as Freemasonry invariably leave themselves open to suppression, persecution, and even threats from clandestine forces who would want to keep their knowledge of the star secret. This is certainly what happened to Robert Temple. In 1999, a second edition of *The Sirius Mystery* was published which included an extended introduction by its author. In this revised version, Temple revealed some of the immense challenges he faced soon after the book's initial publication in 1976.

Speaking at The Origins Conference, London, in November 2014, Temple explained how in 1977 he had come under personal attack from groups of connected individuals he believed was being orchestrated by the CIA. His suspicions were later confirmed following inside information he received from various individuals; including the science-fiction writer Arthur C. Clarke. A policeman who was engaged to Temple's next-door neighbour advised him that he had been approached by MI5—the UK's internal intelligence service—to do a full-scale report on him—which he did and gave him a good reference.

The plot against Temple grew significantly darker when Brigadier Bidwell, a retired soldier and military historian, told Temple he had been asked by MI6—the UK's foreign intelligence service—to do a report on

342

both Temple and his book. The personal attacks upon Temple's integrity continued for several years with the CIA actively advising people not to associate with the academic so as to discredit him as an individual and to disparage his Dogon/Sirius research as a whole.

Reading about Temple's tribulations leaves one wondering what exactly was contained in the pages of *The Sirius Mystery* that rattled so many people in positions of authority. Were there some great secrets encoded within the book that not even Temple was aware of at the time of its publication? This is the only conclusion one can make and is borne out by Temple himself for, in the introduction to the 1999 revised edition, he stated that following the book's initial publication he was contacted by an elderly relative who happened to be a 33rd-degree Freemason.[508] He informed Temple that "his book was more correct than he could possibly have imagined and that there was much that he wanted to tell him." He explained to Temple that as a result of the strict ethic code of Freemasonry he was unable to provide him with further information: unless he became a 33rd-degree Mason.

The fact that certain high-ranking Freemasons might be interested in Temple and his work is really no great surprise for, as we saw earlier, Alice A. Bailey maintained that a direct link exists between Freemasonry on this planet and a similar Masonic structure located on Sirius. In 1922, she wrote:

> "One great fact to be borne in mind is that the initiations of the planet or of the solar system are but the preparatory initiations of admission into the greater Lodge on Sirius. The first four initiations of the solar system prior to the first cosmic initiation. The fifth initiation corresponds to the first cosmic initiation. that of "entered apprentice" of the Lodge Sirius. The sixth initiation is analogous to the second degree in Masonry, whilst the seventh initiation

---

[508] In an open letter published by Robert Bauval titled *A Note about Freemasonry* and dated December 29, 2001, Robert Temple revealed a family connection to Freemasonry. He signed it *"Robert Temple, Master Mason."* (Source: https://grahamhancock.com/phorum/read.php?1,70997,71018)

makes the Adept a Master Mason of the Brotherhood of Sirius. A Master, therefore, is one who had taken the seventh planetary initiation, the fifth solar initiation, and the first Sirian or cosmic initiation."[509]

Maybe there is something after all to Robert Anton Wilson's suggestion that Freemasonry is connected to Sirius and Sirians for, as the eminent Masonic historian William Hutchinson (1732-1814) wrote when explaining the importance of Sirius to Freemasonry:

"It is the first and most exalted object that demands our attention in the Lodge."[510]

THE GREAT MASK

In 1972, French filmmaker and anthropologist Jean Rouch (1917-2004), travelled to Mali to film a documentary featuring Amadingue Dolo (the late 'Chief of the Masks') and Diangouno Dolo (late chief of 'Sangha') during the Dogon's closing ritual of what they called "The Great Mask" ceremony which took place at Songo. The Dogon explained to him that this face mask is made once every 60 years—a time when the Sigui ritual comes around and starts seven years of celebration. 1972 was this festival's penultimate year.

Laird Scranton is an expert on Dogon mythology. He has published several titles on Dogon tribal customs; including *The Science of the Dogon* (2006), Sacred Symbols of the Dogon (2007), *Cosmological Origins of Myth and Symbol: from the Dogon and Ancient Egypt* (2010). He disputes their contention that the Sigui Festival is marked every 60 years.

"Publicly, the Dogon state that their sigui is based on a sixty-year cycle, but in actual practice it is observed every fifty years. This difference between word and

---

[509] Bailey, Alice A., Initiation: Human and Solar, Lucifer Publishing Co., 1922.
[510] Hutchinson, William, *The Spirit of Masonry, in Moral and Elucidatory Lectures*, London, 1775.

action is attributed to deliberate obfuscation on the part of the Dogon priests, as a way of disguising an important calculation of their religion."[511]

Another Dogon researcher, Shannon Dorey—whose publications about the esoteric traditions of the Dogon include *The Rose: Dogon Star Knowledge* (2016), *Day of the Fish* (2012), *The Nummo* (2019), and *The Master (Mistress) of Speech* (2018)—maintains that Dogon religious beliefs can be directly related to Masonic principles. She states:

> "The result of the Philalethan Congress held in Paris from 1785 to 1787 tends to support my research connecting the Dogon religion with the Masonic Society. "This meeting called upon eminent Freemasons from all lands and all rites to convene 'to discuss and clarify the most essential points of the doctrine, the origin, and the historical affiliation of the true Masonic science.'" These individuals brought their diverse opinions with them and the "resulting understanding generally agreed upon was that Freemasonry was the 'original religion'." According to those who met at the Congress, this religion was handed down from various sources including individuals such as King Arthur, the Gnostics, the Templars, Pythagoras, Plato, the Rosicrucians and Hermes Trismegistus, just to mention a few. All of these individuals have been discussed in my books and articles. My research indicates that this early religion, which was known across Europe at one time, evolved from the Dogon religion, which was the purest form of this religion."[512]

---

[511] Scranton, Laird, *The Science of the Dogon: Decoding the African Mystery Tradition*, Inner Traditions, 2006.
[512] Dorey, Shannon, *Day of the Fish*, EEL Publishing, 2012 and 2022.

16. FROM WATERY DEPTHS

Above: Members of the Dogon tribe celebrating during their mask festival.

According to Dogon myth, death does not exist but that men are metamorphosed into serpents. The Great Mask festival represents the first ancestor who transited in the form of a serpent with its elongated form acting as a receptacle for an ancestor's soul. Each festival requires a new mask. This is sculpted and used to replace the previous one which is kept for posterity. In 1930, Marcel Griaule counted nine Great Masks in the village of Ibi which suggests that the beginnings of the Sigui cult in this village can be traced back as far as the 14th-century, or to around 540 years earlier.

To mark this important occasion the dignitaries of the Society of the Masks teach a small group of young men the secrets of their tribe. They are also expected to be present during the mask carving and to learn Sigi So—the secret language of the Sigui.[513] Following their initiation they replace the previous generation of Olubaru initiates.

The actual Sigui Festival begins when Sirius is first seen by the village; rising above the horizon and between two local mountain peaks.

---
[513] The Great Mask, www.dogon-lobi.ch

Prior to the day of the ceremony, the young men go into seclusion for three months during which they are only allowed to converse with one another in a secret language. This practice is said to be a recognition of the original visitation some 3,000 years ago by the amphibious beings from Sirius.

Rouch's documentary[514] of the ceremony never received a full public viewing and remained unseen until 2017 when an event called *"Stockhausen & The Dogon People: Transmission to Sirius B"*—which was organised through the Joshua Tree National Parkeast of San Bernardino and Los Angeles—projected the 16mm., 50-minute film onto Cap Rock. Stockhausen's music was a highly suitable choice to accompany its showing for, on several occasions, the composer stated that his personal preference was for his Sirius suite to be performed in a planetarium: preferably under a nocturnal sky. His wish was fulfilled, albeit posthumously, when the holding of this event which was attended by a small gathering of like-minded artists, curators, scientists and poets.

PISTIS SOPHIA

In a final exposition of some related to the events of 1972, and the ancient 'star-gods of Sirius', the Ennead (or The Nine), the Cosmic Masters and their ilk, it is worth adding one additional thread that, in a sense, highlights a fundamental key to the Sirius mythos.

The ancient Gnostic text *Pistis Sophia* was discovered in 1773 and was believed to have been written sometime around the 3rd- and 4th- centuries A.D. Theologians credit it with being one the most important work of Christian wisdom ever discovered. The exact meaning of the expression 'Pístis Sophía' is unclear but some English translations suggest that it means 'The Wisdom of Faith'.

In Gnosticism, the term 'Sophia' is feminine and is used to refer to the 'Spirit of Wisdom'. She is also called 'The All', 'The Maternal Being', 'The Queen', and 'Lady Wisdom'— terms which mirror those used to describe the Egyptian goddess Isis. In fact, many early scholars—

[514] Sigui *1972: The Loincloths of Lamé*, CNRS, Systèmes de pensée en Afrique Noire, 1972.

16. FROM WATERY DEPTHS

including the Greek philosopher Plutarch (46 A.D.-119 A.D.)—have asserted that Sophia and Isis are one and the same.

Pístis Sophía is said to be the esoteric teachings of the transfigured Jesus and that they were recorded following an address he gave to a group of assembled disciples; including, his mother, Mary Magdalene, and Martha, following his resurrection. The Gnostics believed that Christ spent eleven years teaching his disciples lower-grade versions of the esoteric mysteries into which he had been initiated. It is said that he was now able to reveal higher-grade mysteries to them—ideas related to cosmological theory along with other metaphysical insights: including instruction on how a Soul can reach the highest of the divine realms.

In chapter 93 of *Pistis Sophia*—a number central to the tenets of Crowley and the law of Thelema[515]—the following veiled statement appears which references both the Eye in the Triangle motif and the return of the Ennead: the Nine Gods of Sirius.

> "And that mystery knoweth why the three gates of the treasury of the light have arisen and why the nine guards have arisen."

This verse has a Gematria value of 9552. The total running time of Stockhausen's epic Sirius Suite is exactly 95 minutes and 52 seconds!

---

[515] Using the Greek technique of 'isopsephy'—a similar numerological system to the Jewish Gematria—the letters of words 'thelema' (meaning 'will') and 'agape' (meaning 'love') each add up to the value 93. Thelemites will often just use the term "93" as shorthand for Crowley's occult maxim "Love is the Law, Love Under Will."

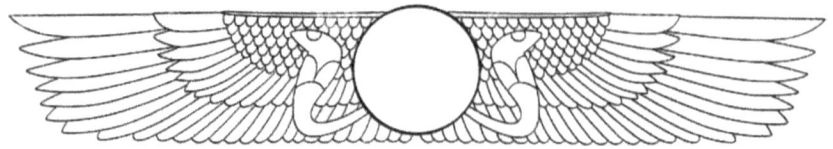

Postscript: It's All in the Egg

"I am discounting reports of UFOs. Why would they appear only to cranks and weirdos?"

Stephen Hawking (English theoretical physicist 1942-2018).

The web of etheric energy surrounding this planet—through which the 'Universal Mind' expresses itself—is becoming denser. As a result, we are not only seeing UFOs in our skies but also other types of strange phenomenon as cosmic forces encroach into our 3D reality. Energy from the trinary Sirius star system is also having a direct impact on this plane of etheric energy through its electromagnetic effect upon our Sun. This process is cyclic. It rises and falls over millennia and we are currently entering an upswing.

During the same phase of a previous cycle this etheric field became so dense that it was relatively easy for extra- and ultra-dimensional entities to enter and remain in our 3D reality. Whenever this band of etheric energy recedes, it is difficult for these advanced intelligences to maintain a 3D form: so they withdraw or fade into the background. In our current time-frame, the Gods are sitting tight: waiting for the time when they can re-manifest on this planet. The current, near-apocalyptic, collapse of societies throughout the World is a preparation for what will be a new era—a time when humanity truly discovers both its innate psychospiritual powers and stellar heritage.

This cosmic unfolding forces us to evaluate the UFO enigma; not from a material perspective but from a psychospiritual one. Trying to unravel the mystery of UFOs from our current scientific perspective is pointless but it still remains as the dominant paradigm simply because we have no other point of reference to draw upon. Ufologists will eventually be forced to interpret the phenomena with reference to the wisdom of arcane, mystical philosophies and ancient occult teachings. These may appear strange and incongruous to the modern eye but we cannot ignore the fact that metaphysics and the occult were—prior to the emergence of the scientific renaissance in the 15th-century—prevailing and established scientific modalities in their own right. It may seem strange to connect the UFO phenomena to such fringe topics as astrology, secret societies, secret masters, Atlantean Mystery Schools,[516] numerology, and magick, but this will change as we reintegrate old knowledge into paradigms deemed relevant to the modern UFO community.

THE SIRIUN INFLUENCE

The wave of energy that constantly pulsates from the heart of Isis (Sirius A) ebbs and flows to a specific cycles (determined by Sirius B). It reached a temporary crescendo during the 1960s and 1970s—a time when many rock musicians responded to its rhythm and were actively engaged in this process of occult revelation. Their time has since passed and many of them have either retired or passed away. However, their music has become immortalised in ways that ensures its survival for future generations of occult explorers who will come to recognise and appreciate the important role they played in humanity's 'Grand Unveiling' of gnostic, esoteric, and stellar wisdom.

If Bowie, Lennon, Dylan, McCartney, and Richards were tapping into the astral void and extracting inspiration for their art from their experiences then what of today's musicians? Are they giving expression to a heightened stratum of consciousness: one more relevant to their era? Sadly, I fear this not to be the case and that the unchecked rise of materialism we were warned about by extraterrestrials has closed avenues of creative exploration that were once fully open to so many contemporary artisans.

---

[516] For a fuller examination of mystery schools and their relevance to modern esoteric knowledge see Ambrose, Kala, *9 Life Altering Lessons: Secrets of the Mystery Schools Unveiled*, Reality Press, 2007.

One musician who is bucking this trend is Puscifer (James Keenan Maynard, 1964-present day)—a solo artist and the lead singer of the American rock band Tool. Maynard was born into what could be classed as the 'Indigo Era'. He even references the phenomenon in his song *Indigo Children* which he included on his 2022 album *V is for Versatile*.

> "*E.M.P. from the mother and son*
> *Tore the digital down.*
> *Dawned are the age of the innocent ones.*
> *The indigo children.*"

Although Puscifer has not specifically attributed these lyrics to the 1972 event it is interesting to note that his reference to "EMP" (Electro-Magnetic Pulse) mirrors the energetic explosion that proceeded the August 1972 solar storm.[517] His lyrical reference to "*mother and son*" reflects the Christian pairing of Mother Mary and Christ as a child. While there is no reason at all to suspect that Puscifer had this connection in mind when writing the lyrics to *Indigo Children* it is worth noting that the archetypal mother/child relationship employed in Christianity was taken from the relationship between the Egyptian goddess Isis and her son Horus. In the chorus to the same composition Puscifer sings:

> "*Sirius, Venus and the Lunar Child.*
> *Giggle and the flames grow Higher.*
> *Dance in a circle around a Central Fire.*
> *When the Indigo Children come.*
> *An analog time piece skywide synced to the ticker inside.*
> *No more need for the old empire...*
> *When the Indigo Children come*"

Puscifer's occult leanings were also revealed on the cover art of his 2020 album *Existential Reckoning* which features a collage of images symbolising several current UFO/ET themes; those such as alien

---

[517] Another interpretation of this might be that Puscifer is intuitively picking up on another, possibly imminent, EMP event in the future and in the same way Bowie did back in 1972.

abduction and ET medical examinations. These are infused with other esoteric elements; including, chakras, sacred geometry, alchemy, and angels. The album-cover even contained a reference to Elvis Presley!

When Puscifer sings "*No more need for the old empire*" he is standing in a direct alignment with the forces of change, destruction, and renewal that is currently taking place right across the globe. Like all growing pains, this is not an easy process for humanity to go through. The extraterrestrials know this and are offering help, support and guidance as this unfolding takes place.

NEW SPECIES FOR OLD

Sirians are often categorised by ET experiencers as 'guardians' rather than as 'shepherds' or 'herders' (i.e. guiding rather than steering their protégés). If this is correct, then it may explain why they appeared so reticent towards revealing their existence to the inhabitants of this planet; preferring instead to work behind the scenes aiding humanity without its direct knowledge and consent.

This theory does run counter to the established UFO narrative though. Ever since the first wave of extraterrestrial interaction with humans began in the 1950s, contactees have maintained time and again that our star-visitors have no intention of directly interceding in the affairs of humanity. This is demonstrably not true. What they really mean to say was ETs had no desire to become embroiled in the 'politics' of the human race: in the way in which we conduct our daily affairs. There is ample evidence to suggest that they do, and have, worked tirelessly to keep the evolution of our species moving forward and quite possibly in accordance with some undisclosed but pre-defined destiny.[518]

This may explain why it was that the Sirians wanted to help humanity during the solar storm of August 1972 and yet were not willing to let us know they were doing so. Shortly after the solar-storm struck, an unprecedented number of UFO reports were submitted to the authorities by the public. This exponential rise increased from 1973 up

---

[518] This is work they cannot do alone for it also requires the support of those humans who are accepting of the idea of extraterrestrial life and who want to be part of the 'grand project'.

until the point when the energy of our planet was dramatically raised in 1989.[519] As I mentioned earlier, many of these reports could have been of plasma balls but it is equally possible that UFOs were hard at work at that time clearing our atmosphere of the radioactivity that had been released by the nuclear bomb tests carried out between the 1960s and 1980s[520].

In addition to helping clean up our atmosphere there are other ways in which Sirians might be at work trying to repair the ongoing decimation of our natural world. One contactee who wished to remain anonymous, shared his account of having visited Sirian scientific laboratories while in an astral state. He discovered that they were developing many new species of plants and animals being developed in preparation for their introduction on Earth where they would replace older species which are currently dying out because of the dramatic raising of planetary vibration.

Prior to 1972 the Sirians may well have preferred to carry out this sort of work in secret. However, they may also have been aware that a time would come when proof of their existence and involvement in the affairs of this planet would be recognised by mankind. This is not 'hard disclosure'—an acknowledgement of the existence of ETs by governments—but 'soft disclosure'—a subtler and more effective way of slowly acclimatising the public to accept the reality of UFOs.

If Sirians were directly involved in the events of 1972 then it would indeed have made sense for them to have created signposts, time-capsules, or other forms of historical evidence that identifies their work. These hidden codes could well be infused into music, art and cinema—for these are all permanent records of timelines—whereby the written word and formal historical record-keeping are invariably modified or

---

[519] An indication of the progress that humanity was making at this time could be indicated by the collapse of Soviet Russia, the fall of the Berlin Wall, and even the success of the *Intermediate-Range Nuclear Forces Treaty* signed by US President Ronald Reagan (1911–2004) and Soviet General Secretary Mikhail Gorbachev (1932-2002) in 1987.

[520] Circumstantial evidence suggests that they are also at work trying to reduce the damage done to our ecosystems through centuries spent burning hydrocarbons. If this is true, then maybe we have less to fear about the long-term health of our planet than many fear-mongers eco-warriors suggest.

falsified to hide uncomfortable facts.

Has rock and pop music been areas in which Sirians deliberately deposited evidence of their existence? Maybe. What is clear is that rock music has been used for decades as a tool by which to initiate changes within society—whether we believe that the Sirians deliberately planned it that way or not. The music of the Hippy Generation promoted a principle of Universal Love and this initiated, among many other things, the end of the Vietnam War and the curtailment of military activity by the Americans throughout that region of the world. Early 1970s Heavy Metal music was responsible for a very important cleansing process, or cathartic release, of dark energies trapped deep within a troubled society. Even Punk Rock, for all its anarchic simplicities, had an important role to play in clearing out the old order and in initiating new, more creative art forms within the world of popular music, publishing, art and fashion.

Dark Well of Creative Inspiration

When you peer behind the veil that separates human consciousness from the reality of the UFO enigma you discover wondrous miracles and unimaginable nightmares in equal measure. Humans instinctively recognise this but invariably avoid facing-up to anything that appears to threaten their fixed belief system.

As an example of this occurred in 2019 when Jill Hughes, author of *Spirit of Prophecy* and a candidate for the UK's Brexit Party, claimed she was thwarted from standing as a potential Member of Parliament by the organisation she was a member of. She maintained that they threw her out after they discovered social media comments she made in 2017. What did she say that was terrible and directly challenged the authority of the Brexit Party? She simply posted the following comment: "I have just come to truly realise that my purpose is to raise consciousness here on earth - I originated from Sirius."[521] Party bigwigs clearly categorised her as a nut-job—which is a little ironic given the extremely low moral and intellectual calibre of most members of the English parliament!

---

[521] Bartlett, Nicola, *Brexit Party candidate who believes she comes from the star Sirius stands down*, Daily Mirror, November 4, 2019.

New Paradigms

How can our current state of stasis within ufology be reversed? I believe that in order to understand the essential message contained within the UFO phenomenon we have to rediscover mythic and symbolic elements in every area of our culture. Fortunately, a handful of researchers have already established the path before us. Mythologist Joseph Campbell (1904-1987), the renown scientist/folklorist Jacques Vallée (1939-present day), and psychologist Carl Gustav Jung are just a few of those forward-thinkers whose ground-breaking work in their chosen field lights the way.

The common thread that links each of them is the recognition of the existence of such non-verbalised languages as those used in art, magick, mythology and music. At the heart of each of these is symbolism—ideagrams which seek to encapsulate advanced metaphysical concepts in a way that is conveyable across boundaries of time, language and culture. The Canadian author, mystic and Freemason, Manly Palmer Hall (1901-1990) wrote extensively about occult symbolism—most notably in his seminal work, *The Secret Teachings of All Ages* (1928). Hall believed that:

> "When the human race learns to read the language of symbolism, a great veil will fall from the eyes of man. They shall then know truth and, more than that, they shall realize that from the beginning truth has been in the world unrecognized."[522]

How is symbolism connected with ufology? There have been many accounts given by contactees and abductees who, during their interaction with extraterrestrials, have not only witnessed advanced technology in use but have also spotted a variety of both recognisable and unknown mystical symbols on display. These are often found imprinted onto the side of the craft, shown on display screens in their control centres, and have even appeared on clothing worn by extraterrestrials. The example of the phoenix[523] was given earlier is one

[522] Hall, Manly P., *The Secret Teachings of All Ages*, Crocker & Co., 1928.
[523] The myth of the phoenix tells of a great bird (Greek: phoenix, Egyptian, bennu).

example but there have been many others such as the ancient Egyptian symbol the ankh[524] and, more commonly, the infamous Masonic 'Eye in the Triangle' motif which is best known for its appearance on the US Dollar bill but which, for some reason, has also appeared as insignia on overalls worn by aliens.[525]

Perhaps the strangest case of the appearance of mystical symbolism in a UFO case is that of the Kecksburg Bell incident in December 1965 when a large, acorn-shaped craft was observed crash-landing in woods in Pennsylvania, United States.[526] Several witnesses who viewed the craft at close quarters reported that it displayed a sequence of Viking runes etched along its perimeter.

An even more striking example of how magick and occultism interpenetrates the UFO enigma can be found in the Enochian language which Elizabethan magickian John Dee (1527-1608) and his scrying partner Edward Kelly (1555-1597) received from 'angels' in England on March 26, 1583.

Dee and Kelly demonstrated that magick—and specifically Enochian magick—can open up a connection to, and dialogue with, higher dimensional entities. At least two occultists have tested this theory. Firstly, the well-known American ceremonial magickian Benjamin Rowe (1952-2002)—publisher of numerous articles on the Kabbalah and the magical system found within the Enochian language—asserted that by

---

that returns to Heliopolis—the abode of The Nine—every Sothic cycle (i.e., 1461 years). There it is consumed in fire before rising from its own ashes to begin a new cycle. The bennu is said to have landed and perched on top of the benben, a sacred conical or pyramidal-shaped stone located in the temple at Heliopolis. Holburg reports that "In Egyptian creation mythology the benben was the first hillock of dry land to emerge from the primeval waters. This association is evident in the hieroglyphic symbol for Sirius." (Source: Holberg, Jay B., *Sirius Brightest Diamond in the Night Sky*, Springer Praxis Books Popular Astronomy, 2007.)

[524] The Egyptian ankh is associated with the goddess Isis. (Source: Morris, Peter J., *The Power of the Ankh*, Kinsett Publishing, 2012.)

[525] "It should be noted that Eye in the Triangle emblems have been seen on some UFOs and the uniforms of their occupants, that Men in Black sometimes wear the same emblem and speak of themselves as being members of the "Nation of the Third Eye". (Source: Keith, Jim, *Saucers of the Illuminati*, Adventures Unlimited Press, 1999. Also see Mack, John E., Passport to the Cosmos, White Crow Books, 2010.)

[526] Some witnesses to the Roswell crash also reported seeing strange hieroglyphic writing etched into the metal framework of the downed craft.

using Enochian magick in a ritual setting extraterrestrial entities could be summoned to appear.[527] Secondly, in *Ritual Magic, Mind Control and the UFO Phenomenon*[528], Adam Gorightly revealed that during the 1950s and 1960s, George Hunt Williamson "summoned forth certain denizens purportedly from Sirius and that he conversed with them in the same 'Enochian' or 'Angelic' language divulged to John Dee and later expounded upon by Aleister Crowley."

COSMIC HATCHING?

In an interesting parallel to the modern UFO mystery, two years prior to John Dee making his connection with an Enochian angel the magickian had a close encounter with an ethereal being while praying in the chapel of his Mortlake home.

One night, Dee was disturbed by a sharp rapping sound coming from behind his curtained windows. Drawing them aside he found himself face-to-face with a shining being who appeared to be floating some twelve feet off the ground. The entity gestured to Dee to open the window and when he did it handed him a smoky quartz egg roughly the size of a baby's head. Dee took it and the figure immediately vanished.[529]

In 1918, Aleister Crowley performed an occult ritual which has come to be known as 'The Alamantrah Working'. The result of his evocations was the appearance of an extraterrestrial known as 'LAM' who explained that his function was to forge a link between the star systems of Sirius and Andromeda. In his diary entry for Monday, January 14, 1918, Crowley recorded how Alamantrah informed him that "It's all in the egg." When questioned further by the magickian about the egg reference and its significance the alien replied, 'Thou art to go this Way.' Crowley surmised that this referenced LAM, the entity he evoked and which he later illustrated with an egg-shaped cranium.

In November 1974, Uri Geller and John Lennon met up in a New York City restaurant. During the course of their meal the topic of

---
[527] Rowe, Benjamin, *The Lotus of the Temple: Contacting Extraterrestrial Influences with the Enochian Temple*, 1993.
[528] www.conspiracyarchive.com/UFOs/UFO_Ritual_Magic.htm).
[529] www.sangraal.com/library/SS3.html

conversation turned to a discussion of the subject of extraterrestrials. It was then that Lennon shared with Geller his account of an extraordinary event which had taken place six months earlier.

Left: Contactee Uri Geller with the golden egg given to him by John Lennon.

He described how he had awoken in the middle of the night and found himself face-to-face with four, insect-like creatures.[530] Some sort of interaction followed which the musician was unable to recall but before they left, one of his visitors handed Lennon a golden egg-shaped object. Prior to his death, he gave it to Geller who has retained it to this day.[531]

The symbol of the egg also features in Dogon creation myth where the early story of the universe featured a struggle between creator God Amma and Ogo: one of her creations. Their tribal tradition states that: "In the beginning, Amma, alone, was in the shape of an egg: the four collar bones were fused, dividing the egg into air, earth, fire, and water, establishing also the four cardinal directions."[532]

The symbol of the "Cosmic Egg" is an ancient symbol—one that Helena Blavatsky maintained, "...was incorporated as a sacred sign in the cosmogony of every people on the Earth and was revered both on account of its form and its inner mystery." Blavatsky stated that the egg was sacred to Isis and is symbolic of our cosmos; or, as Aiwass put it to Crowley in *The Book of the Law*, as "Infinite Stars, Infinite Space" within which lies the potential of all things.

---
[530] A species of ETs is called the "Mantids" due to them looking like a praying mantis.
[531] www.urigeller.com/alien-visitations-what-john-lennon-told-uri-geller-before-his-death/
[532] Scheub, Harold, *A Dictionary of African Mythology*, Oxford University Press, 2002.

Above: Model of the "Kecksburg Bell" created for the American television series Unsolved Mysteries.

Above: Aleister Crowley's drawing of LAM - the extraterrestrial he invoked through a magickal ritual in 1918.

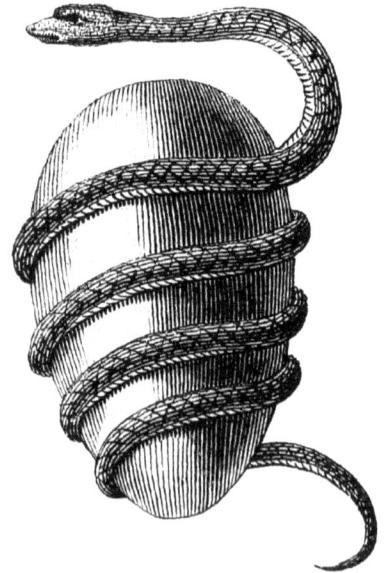

Above: Jacob Bryant's rendition of the Cosmic Egg. ((1774).

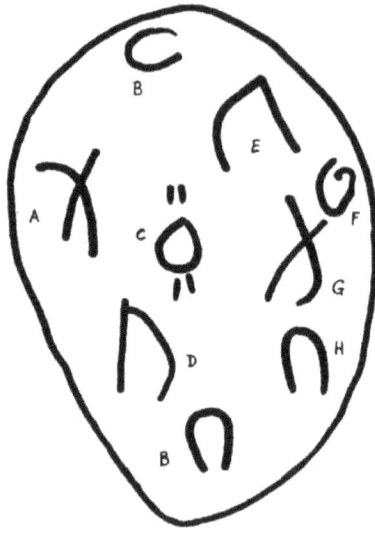

Above: A drawing of the Dogon tribe's primary deity 'Amma' in the symbolic form of an egg.

Postscript: It's All in the Egg

The egg-like face of LAM which Crowley painted and featured n his Dead Souls Exhibition held in Greenwich Village, New York, in 1919[533] has also been associated with the alien image featured on the cover of Whitley Strieber's (1947-present day) 1987 book *Communion* which was said by the author to be a representation of the alien he encountered.[534] In his follow-up book, *Transformation* (1988), Strieber observed an interesting bridge between the modern extraterrestrial hypothesis and the ancient mystical tradition. He describes how he came to associate the sound of loud bangs or knocks in the roof of his cabin with the manifestation of aliens beings.

> "The knocks were so exactly spaced that they sounded like they were being produced by a machine. Both cats were riveted with terror. They stared at the wall. The knocks went on, nine of them in three groups of three, followed by a tenth lighter double-knock that communicated an impression of finality. They were not like the vague tappings associated with spiritualism. These were hard and strong and totally real, and their spacing, in three groups of three followed by the lighter double-knock, was precise and regular."[535]

Three by Three

A similar sequence of three-by-three knocks heard by Whitley Strieber also features in Masonic initiation and ritual. It was a pattern the classical composer and Freemason Wolfgang Amadeus Mozart (1756-1791) employed when he encoded Masonic symbolism into his opera *The Magic Flute*. His composition features three ladies, three trials, three spirits, and three doors.[536] The same three-by-three pattern—creating the number nine in total—also appears in the Masonic legend of Hiram Abiff who was employed to oversee the construction of

---

[533] https://en.wikipedia.org/wiki/Aleister_Crowley
[534] The cover of Communion popularised the modern portrayal of extraterrestrials.
[535] Strieber, Whitley, *Transformation*, Beech Tree Books, 1989.
[536] https://medium.com/the-collector/the-hidden-symbolism-behind-mozarts-the-magic-flute-baffb21e0731

Solomon's Temple.

This pivotal Masonic myth describes how while worshipping the Grand Architect of the Universe in the Holy of Holies, Hiram was approached by three strangers who demanded that he gave them the Master's Word—that is to say, the secret name of God. Hiram refused their request, was attacked, and killed by his assailants.[537] Solomon, finding his architect dead, appoints Nine Masters to track down his killers. Some researchers have associated these nine individuals with Puharich's Nine Gods of Heliopolis. This may or may not be correct but there is no doubt that numbers play an important role in conveying spiritual truths. On page 130 of *Transformation* Strieber writes:

> "The moment the knocks ended I had glanced at the clock on the videotape recorder. It read 11:35. The cat remained in hiding for nearly twenty-two hours after hearing the sound. To me, the knocks were an absolutely clear indication that something entirely and physically real was present and that it was taking an interest in me."

One wonders why Strieber felt compelled to look at the time and then to record it. Was there something significant about it which offers a deeper understanding of the aliens themselves? This might be the case for in Gematria the value 1135 refers to the phrase 'Queen of Heaven'— the term commonly used to describe Isis.

Musical Respect

As Mozart indicated, there is a close connection between music and mathematical theory. Sound is frequency which can be measured and harmony is often used to open up spiritual and mystical channels. Modern rock music, like ufology, has an interesting cultural history. The earliest form of rock and roll effectively emerged in 1956 with artists such as Little Richard, Bill Haley and Elvis Presley. In the same year

---

[537] Legend states he was struck in three places; the forehead, throat and heart; thus, referencing the three centres referred to by Alice Bailey as we saw in an earlier chapter.

these artists were creating societal mayhem, extraterrestrial contactee Howard Menger (1922-2009) met two mysterious men. One of them claimed to originate from Venus and the other from Saturn. Menger asserted that they instilled within him a musical talent he had not formally possessed. The extraterrestrials told him that:

> "From this time on you will be able to play a piano whenever you are moved to do so, and not only this tune, but any melody you wish." They also explained to him that anyone who heard his renditions "would get a feeling, or reach an awareness, which would act as a mental assist to release something from the subconscious. People hearing the theme would react in their conscious state with increased understanding and brotherly love toward one another."

The following year Menger released an album of ET-inspired music titled *Authentic Music from Another Planet*. Its cover featured one of his own black and white Polaroid photos (it was tinted blue for effect) which carried the caption "Actual photograph of interplanetary spacecraft."

A Holistic Perspective

If we are to take anything of value by weaving together the seismic events of 1972 then it has to be that at the very heart of the UFO mystery the lines separating music, magick, universal and human consciousness blur until, if you dig deep enough, it becomes nearly impossible to differentiate between any or all of them. Gematria, the science that links numbers and mystical concepts, can appear to help clarify the mystery from a 3D perspective but is it, and the Jewish Kabbalah that oversees it, a legitimate tool by which to assess the UFO phenomena? I have applied Gematria several times throughout this book and in a way that reveals what I feel to be an occulted dynamic to many of the events highlighted in this story. Although they reveal some extraordinary synchronicities one might wonder whether Gematria is as significant to the extraterrestrials themselves.

An answer to this question might be found in the case of clinical psychologist Lois Wetzel who uses art as a form of therapy. In 1998, she was contacted by 12th-dimensional, blue-coloured, star-beings from Sirius B.[538] They asked her to work with them in developing a new healing system they believed would aid humanity during a forth-coming social and planetary transition. The Sirians explained that this was a new form of energy medicine—one which offered those individuals who were attempting to raise their spiritual vibration during such a challenging period—an easier and safer way of doing so. The technique they proposed is called 'EDINA'—an acronym for "Energy Dynamics for the Integration of Natural Attributes". During their initial contact, the star-beings revealed details regarding their identity. Lois explains:

> "I reached over with the other hand and wrote down the name: "The Ankenash." They then told me their name was derived from three letters of the Kabbalah, and that if I looked at a book about those letters, I would know from exactly which letters their name was derived. The name is not exactly those three letters strung together verbatim; it is derived from the three letters.
>
> Extremely curious as to what I would find, I went to a bookstore that day and found a few books on the Kabbalah, a subject which I had never been even mildly curious about before. I had never to the best of my memory even cracked open a book on this subject, even though I am an avid reader. As I flipped through the names and meanings of the letters, I easily found the three that I was sure were the right ones. Ayin, Kalph and Aleph. The book I consulted at the time had the meanings as Eye, Palm of Hand,

---

[538] When Lois was first contacted by the ETs she had not even heard of Sirius but had a primary response to it. "While pronouncing those words, something deep stirred within me, and I had an immense longing, a homesickness that was by far the deepest well of homesickness I had ever known possible. I knew in an instant that I was from Sirius, and that I wanted desperately to go home." (Source: Wetzel, Lois, Edina: Energy Medicine from the Stars! Hot Pink Lotus Press, 2013.)

Conclusion: It's All in the Egg

and Flame, Diagnosis or Final Resolution. At least, that was what caught my eye first. I now know that those three letters have a vast multiplicity of meanings."[539]

There is no indication in any of Lois Wetzel's publications that she ever applied Gematria to the phrase 'Ankenash' but if she had, then she might have been surprised to discover that its value is 195—the same as the term 'ETs'.

Whenever numerical and symbolic interpretation is applied to the UFO mystery, it becomes evident that it contains a significant psychospiritual component. How this is evaluated is, in many regards, determined by the spiritual, religious or philosophical values of the researcher. Although this is not a popular notion in current UFO circles, it should be noted that as far back as 1959—a time when UFOs were deemed to be pure nuts-and-bolts flying-machines—Swiss psychologist, Carl Jung challenged this prevailing belief. In *Flying Saucers: A Modern Myth of Things Seen in the Sky*, Jung posited the theory that UFOs are psychic projections of the observer which partially explains why some UFO eyewitnesses were able to intuitively sense what their 'light in the sky' was going to do next.

Looking Ahead

If the UFO mystery is worthy of our time and effort then its research has to be founded on new analytical methodologies. As of yet, mankind has learnt very little of value regarding the UFO enigma from our established scientific community and so the future of ufology (if it has one at all in its current state) must reference the past and re-integrate the ancient ways once employed by our predecessors. When magickally-attuned musicians such as Bowie, Davies, Presley, Stockhausen—as well as others too numerous to mention—offer a unique perspective on either the UFO phenomena or our sacred mysteries then it is surely incumbent upon us to consider their message carefully. They may be working within a commercialised medium but this does not preclude them from

---
[539] Wetzel, Lois, Edina: Energy Medicine from the Stars! Hot Pink Lotus Press, 2013.

giving expression to an otherwise uncommunicable message from cosmic intelligences and advanced civilisations. Music is an extremely important way for us to conceptualise the UFO phenomena for, as we saw in the contact reports submitted by Boucher and Menger, the extraterrestrials they encountered expressed their appreciation for any musician that was attempting to communicate their message to mankind via songs, lyrics, or musical composition. Perhaps we should follow their lead and pay those musicians who are brave enough to challenge the world of ufology the same respect for it could just be that they are taking on the form and function of the ancient Gods—returning to help guide humanity away from the self-induced death spiral it is currently on.

We all have a part to play in this process of unfoldment and Bowie's 'Homo Superior' archetype does indeed reside within every one of us. Bringing this into realisation is a challenge but it is worth reflecting upon the exhortations of many creatives, contactees, musicians and magickians who insist that, in order to express our potential as both individuals and as a species, we have to re-engage with the cosmos and reinvigorate our relationship with it. As Jung put it, we must re-energise what he called the "Cosmic Man".[540] Humanity's authentic cosmo-spiritual essence has remained unrealised for far too long but it is beginning to re-emerge for, as Bob Dylan once said "The times they are a-changing". The psychospiritual apocalypse that was foretold by himself, Presley and Bowie, is upon us and is fracturing society in exactly the way they predicted. The 'End Times' spoken of by so many is ostensibly a spiritual Armageddon—one in which the competing forces of darkness and light seek to dominate human consciousness. Navigating this chaos does not require us to become righteous or pious but to integrate ancient cosmological myths and primal archetypal patterns as delineated by the stars.

We are not, however, alone in making this challenging journey. The message of the ultraterrestrials—whether you classify them as gods, goddesses, angels or Masters—is that by understanding the mythic and magickal essence of our Cosmos we can find the solution to many of our planetary problems and thereby take our next evolutionary step as a

---
[540] https://en.wikipedia.org/wiki/Cosmic_Man

peace-loving, intelligent, and caring species.

If I interpret the signs correctly, then this is the essential reason why we should consider the profoundly sacred message inherent within ufology and extraterrestrial contact. For the first time in over two-thousand years, it is not one that is being preached AT us from a pulpit but is being sung INTO our Souls through art, musical harmony and unconditional love.

Recommended Reading

Adams, W. Marshall, *The Book of the Master of the Hidden Places*, The Search Publishing Company, London, 1933.

Adapa, Kwame, *The Guardians*, Akandia Books, 2020.

Alford, Alan F., *Gods of the New Millennium: Scientific Proof of Flesh & Blood Gods*, Hodder & Stoughton, 2000.

Anka, Daryl, *Bashar: Blueprint for Change: A Message from Our Future*, New Solutions, 1990.

Bailey, Alice A., *Esoteric Astrology*, Lucis Press, 1951.

Bailey, Alice A., *Externalization of the Hierarchy*, Lucis Press, 1957.

Beckley, Timothy Green, *The Authentic Book of Ultra-Terrestrial Contacts*, Global Communications, 2012.

Bauval, Robert, *The Egypt Code*, Disinformation Books, 2008.

Brosch, Noah, *Sirius Matters*, Springer, 2011.

Budge, E A Wallis, *Egyptian Magic*, Dover Publications Inc., 1985.

Cameron, Grant, *Tuned-In: The Paranormal World of Music*, CreateSpace, 2017.

Cody, Darla, *Sirius: The Ascended Masters*, CreateSpace, 2015.

Cori, Patricia, *Atlantis Rising*, North Atlantic Books, 2008.

Cori, Patricia, *No More Secrets, No More Lies*, North Atlantic Books

Cori, Patricia, *The Sirian Revelations: Galactic Prophecies for the Ascending Human Collective*, North Atlantic Books, 2017.

Cruttenden, Walter, *Lost Star of Myth and Time*, St. Lynn's Press, 2005.

Dorey, Shannon, *Day of the Fish*, Elemental Expressions Ltd., 2012.

Dorey, Shannon, *The Master of Speech*, EEL Publishing, 2017

Dorey, Shannon, *The Nummo*, EEL Publishing, 2019.

Elkins, Rueckert and McCarty, *The Law of One: Book One*, Schiffer Publishing Ltd., 1989.

Essen, Virginia and Nidle, Sheldon, *You Are Becoming a Galactic Human*, Spiritual Education Endeavours, 1994.

Fortune, Dion, *Cosmic Doctrine*, Rider & Company, 1949.

Fortune, Dion, *Psychic Self-Defence*, Rider & Company, 1933.

Frissell, Bob, *Nothing in This Book Is Not True, But It's Exactly How Things Are*, Frog Ltd., 1994.

Fuqua, Evelyn, *From Sirius to Earth*, Oughten House Publications, 1999.

Gammill, William, *The Gathering*, Hampton Roads Publishing Co., 2001.

Godwin, Joscelyn, *Atlantis and the Cycles of Time: Prophecies, Traditions, and Occult Revelations*, Inner Traditions, 2014.

Gordon, J. S., *Esoteric Egypt: The Sacred Science of the Land of Khem*, Bear & Company, 2015.

Grant, Kenneth, *The Magical Revival*, Muller, 1972.

Hancock, Graham and Bauval, Robert. *The Master Game*, Disinformation Co., 2011.

Holberg, Jay B., *Sirius: Brightest Diamond in the Night Sky*, Springer, 2007

Hope, Murry, *Practical Egyptian Magic*, Aquarian Press, 1984. .

Hope, Murry, *The Lion People: Intercosmic Messages from the Future*, 1989 (republished by Thoth Publications, 2006).

Hope, Murry, *Ancient Egypt: The Sirius Connection*, Element Books, 1991.

Hope, Murry, *The Paschats and the Crystal People*, Thoth Publications, 1992.

Hope, Murry, *The Changeling: The Autobiography of Murry Hope*, Light Publishing, The College of Psychic Studies, 1999.

Jackson, Leslie, *Isis: The Eternal Goddess of Egypt and Rome*, Avalonia, 2021.

Jackson, Leslie, *Thoth: The History of the Ancient Egyptian God of Wisdom*, Avalonia, 2013.

Johnson, Brad and Viscardi, Jefferson, *Insights with Adronis from Sirius*, Outskirts Press, 2010.

K, The Akan, *Other Africans and the Sirius Star System*, Akandia Books, 2020.

Keenan, Roger, *The Voice of At-Hlan: Channelled Information from Atlantis to Sirius*, Rotographic Publications, 1996.

Logan, Ray, *The Sirius Papers*, Overlord Communications, Year undocumented.

Luckman, Michael, *Alien Rock: The Rock n' Roll Extraterrestrial Connection*, Gallery Books, 2005.

Moore, Tom T., *First Contact*, Light Technology Publications, 2013.

Munroe, Wendy, *Journey into the New Millennium: Transmissions from Sirius*, Triad Publishers Pty. Ltd., 1998.

Nidle, Sheldon, *Your First Contact*, Blue Lodge Press, 2000.

Ovason, David, *The Secret Zodiacs of Washington*, Century, 1999.

Paxton, Anne, *Opening the Door to the Worlds*, Basidian Publishers, 2009.

Picknett, Lynn and Prince, Clive, *The Stargate Conspiracy: The Truth About Extraterrestrial Life and the Mysteries of Ancient Egypt*, Berkley Books, 2014.

Reedijk, Lenie, *Sirius, the Star of the Maltese Temples*, MaletBooks,

2018.

Robbins, Dianne, *Messages from the Hollow Earth*, CreateSpace, 2017.

Rose, Lynn E., *Sun, Moon, and Sothis. A study of calendars and calendar reforms in ancient Egypt*, Kronos Press, 1999.

Schwaller de Lubitz, R. A., *Symbol and the Symbolic: Ancient Egypt, Science and the Evolution of Consciousness*, Inner Traditions International, 1981.

Scranton, Laird, *Sacred Symbols of the Dogon: The Key to Advanced Science in the Ancient Egyptian Hieroglyphs*, Inner Traditions, 2007.

Scranton, Laird, *The Cosmological Origins of Myth and Symbol*, Rochester, Inner Traditions, 2010.

Scranton, Laird, *The Science of the Dogon*, Inner Traditions, 2006.

Swagger, E A., *The Newgrange Sirius Mystery- Linking Passage Grave Cosmology with Dogon Symbology*, Claygate-Grosvenor House Publishing Ltd, 2012.

Temple, Robert K., *The Sirius Mystery*, St. Martins Press, 1976.

Tucker, Linda, *Mystery of the White Lions: Children of the Sun God*, Carlsbad, Hay House, 2010.

Tucker, Linda, *Saving the White Lions: One Woman's Battle for Africa's Most Sacred Animal*, North Atlantic Books, 2013.

West, John A., *Serpent in the Sky: The High Wisdom of Ancient Egypt*, Quest Books, 1993.

Wetzel, Louis, *EDINA: Energy Medicine from the Stars!*, Hot Pink Lotus Pod, 2012.

Williamson, George H., *Other Tongues - Other Flesh*, Amherst Press, 1953.

Williamson, George H., *Road in the Sky*, London: Futura, 1975.

INDEX

A

Abraham 237, 240
Adams, Rhoda 296
Africa viii, vii, 79, 124, 293, 313, 315, 318–319, 330, 337–338, 371
Agartha 49, 53. See also: Hollow Earth
Ageless Wisdom 67
Aiwass 118, 156–157, 170, 358
Akhenaten 331
album
    3:47 EST (album) 88
    2112 101
    Abbey Road 110
    AFL1-3603 274
    Agents of Fortune 104, 111
    Aladdin Sane 19, 37, 75, 185, 187, 189
    Authentic Music from Another Planet 362
    Blackstar 166, 169
    Bustin' Out 189
    Chosen People 278
    Crazy Horses 232
    Curse of the Hidden Mirror 109
    Dark Side of the Moon 110
    Diamond Dogs 14, 18–19, 75, 167, 228–229, 235
    Eve 111
    Existential Reckoning 351
    Eye in the Sky 111, 113
    Heathen 168
    Hunky Dory 38, 47–48, 72, 188

I Hear a New World 129, 136
I Robot 110
Infidels 55
Journey to the Centre of the Earth 54
Link, The 102
Love is the Law 142
Love Me for a Reason 236
Man Who Sold the World, The 37, 47, 155, 167, 171, 188
Mars to Sirius 102
Mighty Grahame Bond 142
Nun Permanently 189
Open Road 278
Permanent Waves 100
Pin Ups 69, 189
Plan, The 233, 235–236
Play Don't Worry 69
Pyramid 111
Reality 168
Rise and Fall of Ziggy Stardust and the Spiders from Mars, The 18, 25–26, 28, 188
Secret Treaties 106
Sgt. Pepper's Lonely Hearts Club Band 100, 146
Slaughter on 10th Avenue 189
Spanish Train and Other Stories 86
Starpeace 92
Station to Station 172
Symbol Remains, The 109
Tales of Mystery and Imagination 110
Terra Incognita 102
Test for Echo 101
The Next Day 168
Tonight 37
Trump 293
Turn of a Friendly Card, The 111

Two Heads Are Better Than One 143
V is for Versatile 351
Voyage of the Acolyte 114
Walls and Bridges 56, 58
White Light/White Heat 69
Your Arsenal 189

Alcyone 243

Alexandria v, 63, 99

all-seeing eye 53, 110, 112–113, 135, 201, 322

America 2, 12, 27, 33, 43, 55, 142, 191–192, 196, 198, 202–203, 209, 255, 259, 262, 275, 323, 338

Amma 358

amphibious beings 109, 111, 193, 288, 333, 336–338, 341, 347

Ancient Egypt vii, 59–60, 62, 109, 114, 118, 143, 154, 157, 163, 197, 218, 220, 242–243, 249, 265–266, 274, 295–296, 307, 310, 318–319, 323, 325–326, 336, 344, 356, 369–371

Andromeda 111, 169, 357

Ankenash 363–364

ankh 105, 249, 356

apocalypse 201, 204, 226, 228, 365

Apollo Missions 3, 7–9, 14

Area 51 270

Argentium Astrum 333

Ascended Masters 67, 78, 111, 147, 169, 368

astral light 42, 44–45, 52

astrology vii–viii, 43, 59–60, 64, 80, 87, 96, 101–102, 116, 156, 177, 179–180, 194, 199, 224–226, 228, 247, 272, 296, 302, 318, 324–326, 331, 334, 350, 368

Atlantis 52, 63, 263, 299–300, 368–370

AUM 73–74, 150–151, 265

Avebury Stone Circle 222, 264
Aztecs 266

B

Balthazar 105–106
band
    Alan Parsons Project 110
    Alexis Korner's Blues Incorporated 142
    Bauhaus 35
    Beatles 13, 54, 56, 90, 100, 110, 133, 146, 270
    Blink-182 86
    Blue Men. 130
    Blue Öyster Cult 104, 106, 111
    Boards of Canada 166
    Can 100
    Cream 142
    Crestas, The 188
    Death Grips 166
    Deep Purple 133
    Duran Duran 35
    Echo and the Bunnymen 35
    Foo Fighters 79
    Genesis 114
    Gojira 102–103
    Goudie Charles Quintet 142
    Graham Bond Organisation 142
    Graham Bond Quartet 142
    Harmony Grove 279
    Herman's Hermits 52, 113
    Honeycombs, The 124
    Hype, The 188
    Ian Gillan Band 133
    King Bees 55
    Kinks 250, 270–275, 277, 279

    Klaatu 88
    Leather Nun 189
    Led Zeppelin 119, 144
    Mariners, The 188
    Moody Blues 251
    Mott the Hoople 189
    Osmonds, The 191, 232–236, 249–250, 253
    Outlaws, The 132–133, 138
    Pink Floyd 100, 110
    Pure Prairie League 189
    Radiohead 86
    Ramrods, The 271
    Rats, The 188
    Ray Davies Quartet 271
    Rich Kids 189
    Ritchie Blackmores Rainbow 133
    Rolling Stones 15, 54, 270
    Rush 100–101
    Slaughter & The Dogs 189
    Soft White Underbelly 104
    Spiders from Mars, The 18, 25–26, 28, 149, 187–188
    Strawbs, The 188
    T. Rex 85
    Tangerine Dream 100
    Temptations, The 225
    Tool 86, 351
    Tornados, The 124, 141
    U2 35
    Velvet Underground 69
    Wildhearts, The 189
    Yes 54, 188
Baphomet 43–45, 167
Barnbrook, Jonathan 168–169
Bastet 296, 310
BBC 14–17, 29, 55, 59, 64, 87–88, 126, 128, 160, 162,

169, 188, 261
bennu (bird) 248, 355–356
binary star system 60, 161
Black Sun 52, 61
Blue Lodge 81, 200
Book of Abraham 236–237, 241–242
Book of Commandments 238
Book of Mormon (book) 191, 194–196, 198–199, 238
Book of Mosiah 195
Book of Revelation 216, 226, 228
Book of the Law 118, 152, 156–157, 159, 169
Book of Thoth (tarot) 116, 152, 154
Bowie, Angie 33–34, 149–150
Bradley, Ed 55
Buddhism 40, 43, 301, 332
Bush, George W. vii

C

Cancer (zodiac) 59, 64, 102
Canis Major 60, 63, 159
Caspar 105
Catholic Church 42, 112, 298
chakras 69, 71–72, 74, 176, 214, 265, 352
    head center 70–71
    heart center 71–72
    throat center 69–72, 296, 361
    triangle of force 71–72, 75
Cheltenham 300–303, 306
Christ 20–21, 23, 37, 80, 82, 86, 88, 176, 181, 190, 196–198, 201, 215–216, 222, 231, 233, 238, 321, 348, 351
Christianity 11, 23, 46, 63, 73, 83, 86–87, 95, 99, 105,

145, 147, 175–176, 179, 183, 187, 190–192, 198, 201, 212, 226, 228, 234, 249, 280, 284, 301, 321, 347, 351
Church of Scientology 187, 199
City of Zion 196–197
composer
    Beethoven, Ludwig van 39
    Brahms, Johannes 91
    Mozart, Wolfgang Amadeus 39, 360
    Puccini, Giacomo 92
    Stockhausen, Karlheinz 93, 129, 244, 347–348, 364
    Strauss, Richard Georg 91
    Wagner, Richard 91
composition
    Das Rheingold 91
    Madama Butterfly 91
    Magic Flute, The 360
    Star-Sound 95
    Sternklang 95
contactee
    Adapa, Kwame 83, 368
    Anka, Daryl 101, 368
    Arnold, Kennet 1
    Bennett, Mary 220, 264
    Bledsoe, Chris 83–84, 111, 333
    Carroll, Lee 50
    Cori, Patricia 84, 368
    Deane, Ashayana 216
    Elkins, Donald 264, 341
    Evers, Carolyn 309
    Gammill, William 230
    Geller, Uri 255–256, 259–262, 264, 331, 357
    Gilliand, James 309
    Hickson, Charles 338–340
    Hoglund, Richard 51

Hughes, Jill 354
King, George 300
Le Fay, Denise 309
Logan, Ray 51, 370
Melchizedek, Drunvalo 210
Menger, Howard 362, 365
Moore, Tom T 269, 370
Mutwa, Credo 317, 337
Parker, Calvin 338, 340
Parkes, Simon 309
Raël 269
Richard Hoglund 51
Royale, Lyssa 310
Rueckert, Carla 264, 341
Schlemmer, Phyllis 261–264
Slattery, Peter 309
Stone, Harry 331
Strieber, Whitley 360–361
Wetzel, Lois 363–364
Wilson, Robert Anton 342, 344
Cosmic Masters 300, 347
Crystal People, The 308
Cydonia 219–223, 264, 296
Cygnus 73–74

D

Dee, Nerys 302
Desdenova 106–107
Digitaria 334
Djwhal Khul (DK) 67–68, 78–79
dog days 101
dog star vii, 60, 95, 107, 164, 245, 252, 254, 279
Dogon vii, 111–112, 170, 333–337, 343–347, 358–359,

E

Earth 3, 5–6, 9, 18, 20, 25, 30, 34, 36–37, 41, 49, 51–54, 65, 80–83, 89, 96–97, 99, 108, 154, 163, 171, 174, 178–179, 197, 206, 210–211, 214–218, 221–222, 230, 237, 240–242, 245, 251, 253, 255, 258, 262–267, 277, 279, 283, 286, 293, 300, 304, 312, 316–318, 320–322, 328, 335–336, 353, 358, 369, 371

EDINA 363

Elohim 268

England 19, 27, 31, 43, 65, 67, 115, 154, 182, 191, 207, 221–222, 260–261, 263, 275, 291, 302–303, 356

Ennead 264–266, 330, 347. See also: Nine, The

Esoteric Order of Dagon 108–109

European Union 269

extraterrestrials vi, ix, 5–10, 13, 18–19, 24–25, 30–33, 37, 51, 74, 77–78, 80, 82–85, 91, 93, 103, 106, 130, 136, 149, 163, 200–202, 208–214, 216–218, 220–223, 229, 244, 252, 258, 261–262, 264, 268–270, 275, 280–284, 300, 308–309, 317, 320, 326, 332–333, 335, 338, 341, 350, 352, 355, 357–360, 362, 365–366, 370

Eye in the Triangle 58, 71, 348, 356. See also: all-seeing eye

Eye of Horus 113, 322. See also: all-seeing eye

F

Face of Mars 222, 224, 296

Festinger, Leon 201–202
film
    1972: The Loincloths of Lamé (film) 347
    2001: A Space Odyssey 50, 176
    Blue Hawaii 247
    E.T. 36
    G.I. Blues 247
    Labyrinth 203
    Man Who Fell to Earth, The 36, 41
    Truman Show, The 159–160
France 43, 59
Freemasonry 39, 43, 53, 65, 71, 74, 81–82, 115, 170, 174, 187, 200–201, 243, 333, 342–345
Freemasons 63, 65, 109, 153, 170–171, 177, 197, 343, 345, 355, 360
Freud, Sigmund 113, 299

G

Geller, Larry 175, 177, 180, 183
Gematria 111, 128, 159, 162–165, 171, 253–254, 265, 319, 333, 348, 361–362, 364
Germany 93–94, 259, 295–296, 308
Gloucester (England) 122–123, 302
Gloucestershire 120, 123, 125, 301
Gnostics 262, 345, 347–348
God v, 21, 23, 46, 61, 77–78, 80, 83, 91–92, 175, 186, 192, 195, 197–200, 202, 226, 233, 237–238, 240–241, 243, 249, 255, 265–266, 274, 361
Great Old Ones 108
Great Provider, The 60–62, 114
Great Pyramid vii, 65, 118, 176, 230, 321
Great White Lodge 53, 81

Guardians, The 83–84, 111, 202, 333

H

Harris, Marguerite Frieda 116, 139, 156
heliacal rising vii, 62
Heliopolis 248, 265, 330, 356, 361
Hello-Archanophus (HA) 298–299, 304
Hermetic Order of the Golden Dawn, The 43, 87, 115, 147
Hermeticism 116
Hidden Masters 67, 246
Hierarchy, The 59, 78, 80–82, 158, 192, 368
Hill, Wanda June 244–246
Hinduism 43, 69, 301
Hiram Abiff 360–361
Hitler, Adolf vii, 47
Hollow Earth 49, 54, 371. See also: Agartha
Holy Bible 163–164, 176, 183, 193, 284, 292
Homo Superior 47, 50, 199, 365
Horus 112–113, 118, 170, 304, 322, 326–330, 351

I

Iceland 24
Illuminati 53, 135, 356
Imaginos 104, 106–108
India 67, 256
Indigo Children 50, 351
Ingwavuma 318–319
Inner Earth 53–54. See also: Agartha
Isis 62, 99, 114, 163, 170, 175, 249, 265, 327, 330, 347–348, 350–351, 356, 358, 361, 370

Islam 43, 63
Israel 212, 255–256, 258

J

Jesus Christ 21–22, 35, 105, 176, 190, 196, 198, 200, 222, 231, 233, 238, 278, 348
Jung, Carl Gustav iv, 32, 39, 180, 299, 332, 355, 364
Jupiter 8, 247

K

Kabbalah 40, 42–43, 116, 145, 147, 154–155, 162, 176, 193–194, 239, 247, 274, 356, 362–363
Kecksburg Bell 359
Knights Templar 37, 39, 345
Kolob 186, 236–243, 253, 264
Kolob Records 236

L

LAM 111, 169, 357, 359
Lazarus (Stage Show) 167, 171
LDS (Latter-Day Saints) 190, 196–199, 201, 231, 233, 235, 237–240, 249
Leo 11, 225, 247, 251, 287–288, 315, 318, 321
Lion Path, The 92, 326–330
Lion-Man, The 295
Lion's Gate 225
Lodge on Sirius 343
London 14, 18, 24, 26, 32–33, 40–41, 43, 54–55, 74, 79, 91, 110, 113, 115, 142–143, 147, 171, 182,

188–189, 219, 251, 264, 271–272, 274, 296–299, 302, 333, 335, 342, 344, 368, 371
Lucifer 44, 344

M

Macia, Tony 33
Madame Keech 202
Magi 86, 105, 158
Malta vii
Mariner 9 218
Mars 5, 218–224, 247, 264, 268, 319
Mary Magdalene 348
Master Mason 200, 343
Masters, The 59, 67, 78, 81–82, 111, 147–148, 169, 181, 203, 245–246, 248, 300, 347, 350, 361, 365, 368
Melchior 105
Mercury 35, 153–154, 156, 189, 225
Mesmerism 44
Midnight Sun 61, 106, 166, 283
Monitors, The 111, 333
Moon 3, 9, 14, 30, 35, 100–102, 110, 179, 200, 209, 218, 221, 225, 241, 247, 371
Moroni 111, 169, 192–195, 198, 203
musician
    Anka, Paul 250
    Baker, Ginger 142
    Blackmore, Ritchie 133, 138
    Bolan, Marc 85
    Bond, Graham 142, 144, 149
    Bouchard, Albert 106
    Boucher, Steve 83, 279–284, 365
    Boulder, Trevor 156, 187–188

INDEX

Bowie, David 14, 24, 31, 33–34, 37, 39–40, 47, 55, 57, 75–76, 85, 148–149, 155, 160, 163–166, 168, 171, 176, 185–186, 188–189, 208, 229, 253, 274, 364–365
Brel, Jacques 183
Brown, Pete 143
Bruce, Jack 142
Burt, Heinz 141
California, Randy 94
Cambridge, John 188
Cassidy, David 189
Cave, Nick 93
Clapton, Eric 142
Cochran, Eddie 23
Collins, Phil 114
Corea, Chick 187
Daltrey, Roger 189
Danks, Ralph 22–23
Davies, Dave 270, 364
de Burgh, Chris 86–88, 90, 105
Dio, Ronnie James 133
Duplantier, Joe 102, 104
Duplantier, Mario 102, 104
Dylan, Bob (Robert Zimmerman) 55–56, 90, 189, 350, 365
Eddy, Duane 187
Foley, Ellen 189
Gahan, Dave 35
Gallagher, Noel 35
Garcia, Jerry 94
Garson, Mike 187
Gillespie, Dana 189
Goddard, Geoff 127, 130
Hackett, Steve 114
Hendrix, Jimi 54, 94

Holly, Buddy 130–132, 135, 142
Hollywood, Kenny 129
Hunter, Ian 189
Jagger, Mick 85
Jarre, Jean-Michel 100
John, Elton 189
Kingston, Bob 128
Lamar, Kendrick 166
Layton, Johnny 127
Lee, Geddy 100
Lennon, John 32, 54, 56–58, 85, 90, 92, 178, 275, 350, 357–358
Lifeson, Alex 100
Marr, Johnny 35
Martin, George 120
Maynard, James Keenan 351. See also: musician, Puscifer
McCartney, Paul 54
McGuinn, Roger 189
Meek, Joe 120, 136
Mellencamp, John 189
Mercury, Freddie 189
Morrissey 35, 189
Newley, Anthony 183
Noone, Peter 52, 113
Ono, Yoko 56, 92
Osmond, Donny 232, 235, 250–251, 253–254, 267
Page, Jimmy 119
Parsons, Alan 113
Pastorius, Jaco 94
Pearlman, Samuel 'Sandy' 104, 106
Peart, Neil 100
Presley, Elvis 17, 175–178, 186, 190, 249, 254, 284, 352, 361, 364–365
Presley, Elvis Aaron 175
Puscifer 351. See also: musician, Maynard, James Keenan

Reed, Lou 69, 189
Richards, Keith 54
Ronson, Mick 17–19, 30–31, 36, 38, 55, 69, 149, 156, 159, 187–191
Rutherford, Mike 114
Sands, Johnny 20, 268, 284–293, 340
Seger, Bob 93
Siouxsie 35
Smith, Robert 35
Spector, Phil 120
Taylor, Vince 20–24, 119, 181, 278
Underwood, George 55
Vaughan, Stevie Ray 94
Visconti, Tony 168, 188
Voice, The 188
Wakeman, Rick 54, 187–188
Williams, Andy 232
Williams, Marlene 123
Williams, Robbie 93
Wilson, Brian 120
Woloschuk, John 88
Woodmansey, Woody 156, 187–188
Woolfson, Eric Norman 113
mystery schools 52, 59, 62–63, 66, 70, 147, 158, 177, 302, 350

N

NASA 3, 5–9, 30, 124, 205, 218–224
National Socialism 47
New Age x, 45, 48, 77, 102, 163, 183–184, 210, 261, 263, 267, 300, 310, 321, 332
New Jerusalem 196
New York 2, 11, 41, 43, 56–57, 84, 104, 115, 150, 152,

155, 165, 171, 182, 185, 191–192, 195, 208, 237, 255–257, 273, 275, 303, 323–324, 357, 360
Newent 120–123, 126, 140
Newgrange vii, 371
Nine, The 254–255, 257–259, 261–267, 347–348, 356, 361. See also: Ennead
Nommo 335
novelists
    Burroughs, William S. 25
    Lovecraft, H.P. 53, 106–108, 110
    Orwell, George 19, 42
    Poe, Edgar Allan 110
    Stapledon, Olaf 47
    Tolkien, J.R. 32, 90
    Verne, Jules 54
    Wheatley, Dennis 44, 117, 135
Nuit 118, 170

O

Oannes 109, 336–337
occultist
    Agrippa, Cornelius 199
    Bailey, Alice A. 67, 70–73, 75, 77, 80, 82, 170–171, 343–344, 368
    Barrett, Francis 199
    Blavatsky, H.P. 43, 53, 74, 82, 358
    Bulwer-Lytton, Edward 52–53
    Coleman-Smith, Pamela 115–116
    Colin Wilson 42, 263
    Crowley, Aleister 116–118, 134–135, 139, 142, 144, 146, 153, 155–156, 159, 162, 186, 199, 333, 357
    Dee, John 356–357

Éliphas Lévi 186
Farrant, David 133–134
Fortune, Dion 147, 150, 369
Grant, Kenneth 111, 169, 185, 369
Hall, Manly Palmer 355
Hope, Murry 158, 245–246, 295–309, 316, 369–370
Hubbard, L. Ron 199, 202
Kelly, Edward 356
Lévi, Éliphas 42, 45, 116, 145, 154, 172
Lorber, Jakob 95, 97
Masters, Robert 310
Mathers, Samuel Liddell MacGregor 116
Mesmer, Franz Anton 44
Musès, Charles 323–331
Neate, Tony 298–301
Olcott, Henry Steel 43
Pike, Albert 170
Reuss, Theodor 333
Rowe, Benjamin 356
Samuel Liddell MacGregor Mathers 43
Smith, Joseph 196, 199–201, 203, 236
Steiner, Rudolf 53
Vinod, D. G. 256–258
Waite, Arthur Edward 43–44, 114–115, 117, 146, 152, 154, 170, 176, 228
Whitmore, John 261, 263
William Wynn Westcott 43
Williamson, George Hunt 59, 203, 316, 320–323, 357, 371
Wilson, Colin 42, 263, 342
Yeats, William Butler 87–88
Ogotemmeli 333–335
Order of the Golden Dawn 67, 115–116, 157, 162
organisations
    Aetherius Society 300

Albert Einstein Spacearium 98
Artists Against Racism 101
Association of Sananda 203
Atlanteans, The 299–301, 304
Brooklyn Museum (New York) 41
Brotherhood of the Seven Rays 203
Center for UFO Studies 6
Church of Christ 238
CIA (Central Intelligence Agency) 9, 209, 261–262, 264, 342–343
Dublin Hermetic Order 87
Esalen Institute 263
Foundation for Mind Research 310
Foundation for the Study of Consciousness 332
Fraternity of the Inner Light 147
FREE Foundation 10
Greenpeace 104
Institute of Noetic Sciences 9
International Flying Saucer Bureau 88
L/L Research 264
Lab Nine 262
Lucis Trust 68, 171
National Academy of Sciences 4
Philalethan Congress 345
RAF Wilmslow 298
Royal Astronomical Society 5
Royal College of Music 54
Royal Institute 219
Royal School of Music 300
Saint Raphael Catholic Church 112
Sea Shepherd Conservation Society 104
Space Environment Services Center 205
Stanford Research Institute 9
Study and Development of Transpersonal Sensitivity 304
Swedish Broadcasting Corporation 98

Theosophical Glossary, The 63
　　　Theosophical Society, The 43, 67, 74, 181
　　　UFO Research Associates 4
　　　UFO Research Network 280
　　　University of Pennsylvania 332
　　　University of Utah 5
　　　Victoria & Albert Museum 41
　　　WAAFs (Women's Auxiliary Air Force) 298
Orion vii, 60, 245
Osiris 99, 265, 326–327
OTO (Ordo Templi Orientis) 333
Overlords, The 50–51

P

Pang, May 57
Paris 21, 23, 43, 345
Parker, Ed 190
Pascagoula Incident, The 340
Paschats 307–309
Path of Sirius 68
Perennial Philosophy 67
periodicals
　　　Circus 28
　　　Cream 19
　　　Flying Saucer Review 280
　　　Louisville Courier Journal, The 5
　　　Melody Maker 48
　　　Musician 73, 151
　　　National Enquirer 10–11
　　　Nature Magazine 336
　　　New York Times 2, 208
　　　Prediction Magazine 302–303
　　　Psychic News 127

Rolling Stone 35, 37, 102, 151
Santa Ana Register, The 5
Science News 205
Sunday Times 41, 302
Top Pop Scene 75
UFO Research Newsletter 5, 11
Village Voice 208
Vulture 275
Washington Post, The 5
Young Woman's Journal, The 200

Phelps, William W. 238

philosopher
- Hermes Trismegistus 345
- Kant, Immanuel ii
- Nietzsche, Friedrich 40, 45–47, 50, 145, 186, 199
- Plato 63, 345
- Plutarch 347
- Rand, Ayn 101

Pineal Gland 53, 71, 74

Pink, Patrick 140–141

Pístis Sophía 347–348

Pleiadeans 213, 269

Pleiades 229

Project Blue Book 6

Project Snowbird 9

R

Ra 296

Raëlians, The 268

Ragnarok 266

Rameses the Great 136

researcher
- Bauval, Robert 343, 368–369

Dorey, Shannon 345, 368–369
  Holroyd, Stuart 262–263
  Koening, Peter 33
  Myers, David 264
  Nancy Ann Tappe 48
  Percy, David 220–221, 264
  Rhodes, Michael D. 238
  Robert, B. H. 239
  Temple, Robert 332, 336, 342
Rider-Waite (Tarot) 115–116, 148, 153
Rosicrucians 52, 63, 115, 177, 345
Roswell 2, 4, 66, 356

S

Sanskrit 69, 167, 229, 327
Saturn 68, 161, 179–180, 184–185, 268, 362
scientists
  Clarke, Alvan 60
  Clarke, Arthur C. 1, 50–51, 335, 342
  Dieterlen, Germaine 333, 337
  Griaule, Marcel 333–334, 337, 346
  Hoyle, Fred 5
  Jürgenson, Friedrich 126
  Kepler, Johannes vi
  Montagu, Ashley 6
  Oparin, Alexander 5
  Parsons, Jack 199
  Puharich, Andrija 255–260, 262–264, 331, 361
  Puthoff, Harold 259
  Randi, James 260
  Raudive, Friedrich 127
  Sagan, Carl 5–6, 8, 219
  Salisbury, Frank 11

　　　　Swann, Ingo 9
　　　　Targ, Russell 259
　　　　Tesla, Nikola vi, 66, 162
　　　　Vallée, Jacques 7, 332, 355
　　　　Von Braun, Wernher 6
　　　　Young, Arthur 332, 335
　　Scientology 187, 199, 202
　　Secret Chiefs 67
　　Seekers, The 202–203
　　Sekhmet 296, 310
　　Shambhala 53, 67
　　Shenton, Violet 140–141
　　Sigi So 346
　　Sigui 334, 344, 346–347
　　Sirian High Council 84
　　Sirians ix–x, 51, 65, 70, 84, 93, 98, 103, 111, 210–218, 225, 229–230, 245–246, 249, 252–253, 259, 268–270, 278–279, 291, 310, 312, 333, 341, 344, 347, 350, 352–354, 357, 363, 368
　　Sirius vi–xi, 47, 50–52, 59–66, 68–69, 80–81, 83, 92–93, 95–103, 105–109, 111–114, 143, 152, 156–157, 159–161, 163–165, 169–170, 174–175, 199, 201, 210–211, 216, 218, 224–225, 230, 239–240, 243–249, 251–255, 259, 265, 269, 279, 283, 288–289, 292–293, 304–309, 317, 319, 322, 326–330, 333–337, 340–344, 346–349, 351, 356–357, 363
　　　　Sirius B 60, 83, 93, 96, 102–103, 210, 224, 243, 247, 254, 269, 305, 328, 333–334, 347, 356, 363
　　　　Sirius C 61, 103, 334
　　　　Sirius Mythos, The viii–xi, 68, 110, 114, 259, 347
　　Societas Rosicruciana in Anglia 115
　　song

(Don't Fear) The Reaper 104
#9 Dream 54, 56
2112 101
Ace of Wands 114
Aliens Exist 86
All the Young Dudes 189
Are You Up There? 233–234
Arizona 93
Ashes to Ashes 28
Astronomy 106
Bad Penny Blues 123
Ball of Confusion 225
Blue Christmas 247
Blue Diamond Encounter 293
Blue Moon of Kentucky 247
Blue Suede Shoes 247
Calling Occupants of Interplanetary Craft 88–89
Changes 54, 171, 187
Cygnet Committee 73
E.T.I. (Extra Terrestrial Intelligence) 105
Eye in the Sky 111
Fame 85
Fill Your Heart 72
Five Years 28
Flying Whales 102
Future Legend 228
Glamour 275
Global Warming 103
Hands of the Priestess 114
Hermit, The 114
Heroes 171
Hound Dog 17, 182
I Am the One You Warned Me Of 107
I Hear a New World 130
I Wonder 93

If You Could Hie to Kolob 238
Imagination's Real 274
Its Alright Ma (I'm Only Bleeding) 56
Jean Genie 19, 37
Johnny Remember Me 127–128
King Sized Nick Cave Blues 93
Land of the Midnight Sun, The 283
Last Days, The 233
Laughing Gnome, The 37
Lazarus 75, 171, 174
Life on Mars? 54, 188
Lovers, The 114
Loving the Alien 37
Magic Star 128
Memory of a Free Festival 34
Mind Games 58
Mirror, Mirror 234
Oh! You Pretty Things 47–48, 50, 52, 54, 113, 164–165, 179, 181, 187
Old Gods Return, The 109
One Bad Apple 232
Puppy Love 250–252
Purple Haze 54
Quicksand 47, 145–146, 157
Rock n' Roll Suicide 28
Rosetta Stoned 86
Satisfaction 54
Secret, The 113
Shadow of the Hierophant 114
Sirius 111
Sky Men 137
Sleepwalker 274
Song for Bob Dylan 55
Sorcerer's Apprentice, The 113
Space Oddity 14, 19, 35, 37, 187

INDEX

Spaceman Came Travelling, A 86
Star of Sirius 114
Starman 18–19, 25, 29–32, 34–36, 38, 60, 64, 86, 149, 155–157, 162–165, 185, 208, 215, 250, 253–254
Subterranean Homesick Alien 86
Suffragette City 29, 254
Supermen, The 47, 53, 181
Telepathy 275
Telstar 124–125
Top of the Pops 275
Tower Struck Down, A 114
Traffic in My Mind 234
Tribute To Buddy Holly 131
True Story 278
Walk With Me My Angel 137
War in Heaven 233
We Real Cool 93
Yesterday 54
You Really Got Me 271
Sons of God 77–78, 80
Sophia 170, 347–348
Sorghum 334
Sothic Cycle 62, 248, 328, 356
Sothis 60–61, 63, 327, 329, 371
soul ix, 19, 31, 70–71, 91–92, 148, 163, 174, 208, 210, 224–225, 244, 266, 297, 315, 326, 346, 348, 360, 366
SPECTRA 258, 261
spiritual sun 61, 106, 165
St. John 105
Star of Bethlehem 86–87
Sumeria vii, 109
Sun vi–vii, 52, 59–61, 64, 68, 95, 98, 106, 109, 156–

157, 159–160, 163, 166, 177, 204–207, 211, 216–218, 224–225, 230, 239–243, 248, 251, 283, 289, 299, 318, 349, 371
Sun behind the Sun 61, 243

T

Tame, David 92
tarot 43–44, 105, 114–116, 120, 139, 148, 152–156, 163, 172, 228
Tetramorphs 226, 228, 321, 330
Thelema 111, 118, 142, 146, 304, 333, 348
Theosophy 87, 170, 202, 301
third eye 53, 71, 75–76, 328, 356
Thorburn, Michael 301
Thoth 62, 116, 153–155, 163, 228, 370
Thummim 193, 240
Tibet 53, 67, 72
Top of the Pops (TV) 14–17, 26, 29, 31, 35–36, 38, 59–60, 64, 155–157, 160, 164, 204, 215
Tree of Life 172, 174, 239, 247
Trismegistus 345
Tucker, Linda 312–313, 315–316, 318, 337, 371
Typhonian OTO 109

U

UAP (Unidentified Aerial Phenomenon) 3
Übermensch 45–47, 172, 199
ufologist
    Beckley, Timothy Green 293
    Cameron, Grant 20, 26, 83–84, 149, 151, 368

Good, Timothy 51
Hopkins, Budd 175
Hynek, J. Allen 6, 11
Luckman, Michael C. 84, 370
Mitchell, Edgar 9–10
von Däniken, Erich 86–87, 194
United States 6, 9, 33, 41, 48, 56, 60, 67, 84, 94, 100, 104, 111, 202–203, 209, 237, 259, 271, 273, 304, 332, 342, 356. See also: America
Urim 193, 240
US Dollar bill 71, 356

V

Venus 268, 327, 351, 362
Vietnam War 12, 56, 354
Viking Missions 219
Vril 52–54, 88, 300
Vril-Ya 52–54

W

Wald, George 6
Walker, Johnny 29
Ward, Brian 157–158
Washington, D.C 2
White Brotherhood 181
white lions 312–313, 315–318, 330, 371
Will 45–46, 52, 111, 142, 179–180, 333
Woodward, Geoff 123
World Contact Day 89–90
World War Two 79–80, 104, 297
Wright-Patterson Air Force Base 270

Y

Yahweh 269

Z

Zarathustra 45–46, 176
Zeta Reticula 217
Zulu 317, 337

www.ingramcontent.com/pod-product-compliance
Lightning Source LLC
Chambersburg PA
CBHW071646160426
43195CB00012B/1371